HIDDEN®
Wyoming

"Provides much of the travel information needed to discover the famous sights and hidden locales of the state."
—*San Antonio Express-News*

"Offers ideas for outdoor adventures such as camping in the Cloud Peak Wilderness Area, hiking the Pahaska-Sunlight Trail or skiing Jackson Hole's steep terrain."
—*Denver Post*

HIDDEN®

Wyoming

John Gottberg

SECOND EDITION

Ulysses Press®
BERKELEY, CALIFORNIA

Published by:
ULYSSES PRESS
P.O. Box 3440
Berkeley, CA 94703-3440

ISSN 1524-1270
ISBN 1-56975-175-7

Printed in Canada by Transcontinental Printing

10 9 8 7 6 5 4 3

EDITORIAL DIRECTOR: Leslie Henriques
MANAGING EDITOR: Claire Chun
COPY EDITORS: Lily Chou, Steven Schwartz
EDITORIAL ASSOCIATES: Jen Anderson, Marguerite Clipper,
    Aaron Newey, Natasha Lay
TYPESETTER: David Wells
CARTOGRAPHY: XNR Productions; Yellowstone
    National Park map by Stellar Cartography
COVER DESIGN: Leslie Henriques
INDEXER: Sayre Van Young
COVER PHOTOGRAPHY:
    FRONT: Larry Ulrich (Rocky Mountain elk,
    Yellowstone National Park)
    CIRCLE: Jan Butchofsky (teepee)
    BACK: Dave Houser (Oxbow Bend, Snake River)
ILLUSTRATOR: Doug McCarthy

Distributed in the United States by Publishers Group West, in Canada by Raincoast Books, and in Great Britain and Europe by World Leisure Marketing

For my son, Erik,
who has stalked elk in the hot springs of Yellowstone,
chased calves through the Cody rodeo arena
and clambered across fallen rocks beneath Devils Tower,
all in the name of research.

Acknowledgments

I wish to thank the Wyoming Division of Tourism, especially Kristi Leavitt and Carol Johansen, and chambers of commerce and visitors bureaus across the state for their assistance with this project. In particular, thanks go to Shelly Simonton, Karen Connelly, Kimberly Martin, Jesse O'Connor, Ponteir Sackrey, Doug Lindauer, Steve and Lisa Price, Carol Waller, Claudia Wade and Stephanie Jukes-Amer.

Ulysses Press would like to thank the following readers who took the time to write in with suggestions that were incorporated into this new edition of *Hidden Wyoming*: Alison Young from Hillsborough, North Carolina, and Charles Young from Kimberton, Pennsylvania.

What's Hidden?

At different points throughout this book, you'll find special listings marked with a hidden symbol:

◄ *HIDDEN*

This means that you have come upon a place off the beaten tourist track, a spot that will carry you a step closer to the local people and natural environment of Wyoming.

The goal of this guide is to lead you beyond the realm of everyday tourist facilities. While we include traditional sightseeing listings and popular attractions, we also offer alternative sights and adventure activities. Instead of filling this guide with reviews of standard hotels and chain restaurants, we concentrate on one-of-a-kind places and locally owned establishments.

Our authors seek out locales that are popular with residents but usually overlooked by visitors. Some are more hidden than others (and are marked accordingly), but all the listings in this book are intended to help you discover the true nature of Wyoming and put you on the path of adventure.

Write to us!

If in your travels you discover a spot that captures the spirit of Wyoming, or if you live in the region and have a favorite place to share, or if you just feel like expressing your views, write to us and we'll pass your note along to the author.

We can't guarantee that the author will add your personal find to the next edition, but if the writer does use the suggestion, we'll acknowledge you in the credits and send you a free copy of the new edition.

ULYSSES PRESS
3286 Adeline Street, Suite 1
Berkeley, CA 94703
E-mail: readermail@ulyssespress.com

Contents

Maps

OUTDOOR ADVENTURE SYMBOLS

The following symbols accompany national, state and regional park listings, as well as beach descriptions throughout the text.

Camping		Waterskiing	
Hiking		Windsurfing	
Biking		Canoeing or Kayaking	
Horseback Riding		Boating	
Downhill Skiing		Boat Ramps	
Cross-country Skiing		Fishing	
Swimming			

ONE

Exploring Wyoming

Yellowstone's Old Faithful geyser spouts explosively over its volcanic landscape as hundreds of onlookers cheer its eruption from the flanks of a huge and venerable log lodge. Vestiges of Oregon Trail wagon ruts still cut the sagebrush on the outskirts of Old West towns that may have changed little since pioneers founded them well over a century ago. A rodeo rider whoops and shouts as he digs his bootheels into the haunches of a gyrating one-ton bull and holds on for his life. Cowhands saddle their horses to round up cattle beneath the dramatic crags of the Teton Range. Pronghorn antelope graze a seemingly endless prairie.

All of these are indelible images of Wyoming, perhaps the most visited yet least known state in the Rocky Mountains. With fewer than a half-million residents, its land area is nearly half again as large as the six New England states combined; only Alaska has fewer citizens per square mile. Wyoming is a place of high mountains and broad plains, rich in animals and natural resources, with few towns, fewer cities and a lot of wide-open space in between.

Ask the man on the street to name a place in Wyoming, and 49 out of 50 times he will tab Yellowstone National Park. This wonderland in the state's northwest corner was the world's first national park, although its almost unimaginable natural features—geysers and hot springs, canyons and waterfalls—led most Americans to consider it a myth until little more than a century ago.

Unfortunately, most tourists see little more of Wyoming than Yellowstone, its wild sister to the south, Grand Teton National Park, and one or both of Yellowstone's Wyoming gateway cities, Jackson and Cody. They miss out on the "big towns" of the southeast: Cheyenne, the state capital, Laramie, a bustling university town, and Casper, a commercial and mining hub. They may slide over from South Dakota's Black Hills for a peek at the fluted columns of Devils Tower National Monument, but they don't take in the splendor of the Big Horn and Wind River mountain ranges, nor the geological drama of the Bighorn Canyon and Flaming Gorge national recreation areas.

There is much to see in Wyoming, from American Indian spiritual sites to restored pioneer forts to bustling modern shopping strips. And there is also much to do, if you're an outdoor-recreation sort. Fishing and hunting are almost religions, and the unarmed will find plenty of opportunities for hiking and horseback riding, skiing and bicycling, boating and whitewater rafting. This is a state for all seasons.

Hidden Wyoming is designed to help you take full advantage of your vacation. It covers popular, "must-see" places, offering advice on how best to enjoy them; it also tells you about many off-the-beaten-path spots, the kind you might find by talking with folks at the local café. It describes the state's history, its natural areas and its residents, both human and animal. It suggests places to eat, to stay, to play, to camp. Taking into account varying interests, budgets and tastes, it provides the information you need whether your vacation style involves backpacking, golf, museum browsing, shopping or all of the above.

After providing introductory information, this book starts its statewide tour in Wyoming's northwestern corner with Yellowstone National Park (covered in Chapter Two), and adjacent Jackson Hole and Grand Teton National Park (Chapter Three). Yellowstone, integral to any visitor experience in Wyoming, preserves thermal and geological wonders and remarkable wildlife. To the south of the park, the abrupt and craggy Teton Range towers over the Old West–style ranching hub of Jackson and the surrounding Jackson Hole, a vast valley well known to 19th-century mountain men.

Chapter Four focuses on the Big Horn Basin east and southeast of Yellowstone. This region centers on rodeo-crazy Cody, a tried-and-true capital of cowboy culture—named for the irrepressible "Buffalo Bill" (1847–1917)—that is home to Wyoming's finest museum. Other features of the sector include Bighorn Canyon National Recreation Area, the mystical Medicine Wheel National Historic Landmark, and Hot Springs State Park at Thermopolis.

Chapter Five covers the Wind River region. The state's highest and wildest mountain range and its only Indian reservation both carry the Wind River name. Riverton and Lander are the main towns here—the former a farming center surrounded by native lands, the latter a haven for environmentalists and outdoor recreational guides. An outstanding nearby attraction is South Pass City, a restored ghost town located near the highest point on the Oregon Trail (7550 feet).

Chapter Six features southwestern Wyoming, a desolate neighborhood notable as the site of Flaming Gorge National Recreation Area, Fossil Butte National Monument and Fort Bridger

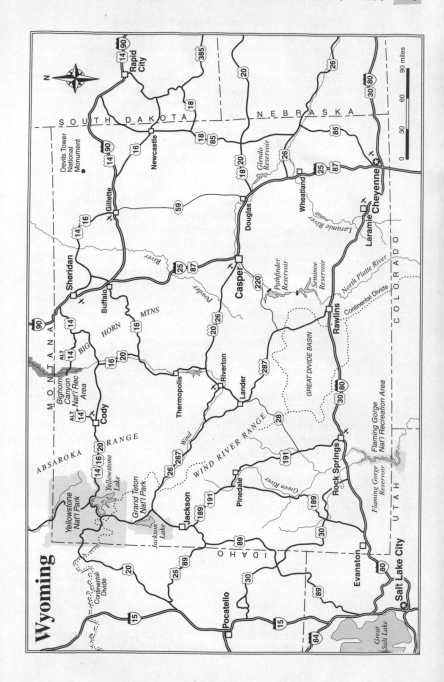

Historic Site. Extraction—of oil, gas and soda ash—supports the regional hubs of Rock Springs and Green River, while little Kemmerer as notable as the town where J.C. Penney opened his first department store in 1902.

Chapters Seven and Eight zoom in on Wyoming's population belt, such as it is. Cheyenne, the state capital of 50,000 residents, is well known as the late-July home of Cheyenne Frontier Days, the world's largest professional rodeo. Laramie is a college town whose style is dominated by the 10,000 students of the University of Wyoming, the state's only four-year institution. North of these two towns, the North Platte River flows easterly from the Continental Divide, through Casper, a thriving city of similar size to Cheyenne whose economy is built on oil and gas, and past Fort Laramie National Historic Site, where Park Service personnel re-enact frontier life in period costume.

Chapter Nine canvasses northeastern Wyoming, from the lofty Big Horns to the gentler Black Hills. Sheridan is perhaps Wyoming's most authentic "cowboy town," its Main Street—still living with memories of 19th-century range wars—having preserved more 100-year-old buildings than any other in the state. Gillette, the region's largest population center, is a modern boom town thriving on coal, oil and uranium mining. Devils Tower crowns the state's upper right-hand corner; chosen by President Theodore Roosevelt as the first national monument, it has more recently become known to millions worldwide as a popular UFO destination in *Close Encounters of the Third Kind*.

What you choose to see and do is up to you. One of the joys of exploring Wyoming is its isolation, and along with that, its decided lack of traffic congestion. Some visitors may use that freedom to scoot quickly from attraction to attraction, while others relax and watch mile after mile of mountain and prairie go by.

▼▼▼▼▼▼▼▼▼▼▼▼▼▼▼
The Story of Wyoming

GEOLOGY

Wyoming was once a vast and shallow inland sea; its bedrock dates back two and a half billion years and more. It was "only" about 100 million years ago, with the formation of the Rocky Mountains, that it began to take on an appearance recognizable today.

The modern Rockies consist mainly of granite, an igneous rock made up of quartz, feldspar and granite, along with traces and veins of metals such as gold, silver, lead and zinc. As molten elements, these minerals blended deep within the earth and welled upward, to the great sea plain and marshy wetlands on the surface.

Very slowly two tectonic plates that make up most of the North American continent—the Canadian Shield and the Pacific Plate—drifted inexorably toward one another, floating on the molten rock that still bubbled far under the earth's surface. In a slow collision, the plates crushed against each other and started to buckle and fold, pushing the granite layer upward. The collision of tectonic plates and the uplifting of the granite rock continues even now, though the process is so slow that the mountains have only gained a few inches in height during the time humankind has walked the earth.

> Three of the nation's largest river systems—the Missouri, the Colorado and the Columbia—have their major headwater tributaries in Wyoming's Rockies.

Dinosaurs, which were abundant in the area when the formation of the Rockies began, would have experienced the buckling phenomenon as occasional earthquakes. Perhaps not coincidentally, the granite mass cracked through the sandstone surface about the time of the great beasts' extinction, 60 million years ago.

As the north–south block of mountains tilted upward, the softer sedimentary rocks at the surface slid eastward, their waters draining ahead of them. Today's Big Horn, Green River and Powder River basins are among their legacies. On these often treeless plains, water and wind have been the principal geological forces.

The Rocky Mountains as we see them today, however, were shaped by glaciers. A series of ice ages, the last of which ended only 10,000 years ago—a mere eyeblink in geological time—covered the high country in accumulations of snow and ice. These glaciers slowly flowed down the mountainsides, in frozen rivers that gouged deep valleys (called moraines), creating steep mountain faces and establishing the courses for the turbulent rivers that would slice canyons hundreds of feet deep.

The lofty mountains (the Teton, Wind River and Big Horn ranges all exceed 13,000 feet) attract storm clouds like magnets, making for rainfall and snowfall many times greater than in the semi-arid prairies with which they are interspersed. Runoff from the melting snowpack in spring and the thunderstorms of summer gives birth to Wyoming's rivers. Chief among them are the North Platte, which flows east (through Nebraska) to the Missouri; the Big Horn (née Wind), which flows north to the Missouri (in Montana), and the Green, which flows south to the Colorado (in Utah).

The rivers give significance to the Continental Divide, the dotted line on maps that meanders through the wilderness connecting the highest mountain passes. All precipitation that falls east of the Continental Divide, flows eventually to the Atlantic Ocean via the Gulf of Mexico. West of the Divide, it flows to the Pacific. In Wyoming, only four highways cross the Divide. The three northerly crossings of the continent's backbone—one of them in Yellowstone Park, the other two on either side of the Wind River

Range—climb high over forested mountain passes. The antithetical southerly route, an interstate freeway, transits the Great Divide Basin, an arid flat through which no rivers flow and which, ironically, though on the very roof of North America, is one of the few places in Wyoming from which not a single mountain is visible.

Volcanism has had a profound effect on parts of Wyoming. The earth remains especially restless in and around Yellowstone Park, which encompasses a giant ancient caldera. Geysers, fumaroles and boiling mud appear here in greater concentration than anywhere else on earth, and the area weathers more earthquakes than anywhere in the lower 48 states outside of California. Hot springs in disparate parts of Wyoming are reminders that volcanism remains a force.

HISTORY   **NATIVE PEOPLE** American Indians touched Wyoming lightly and with reverence. The people of the mountains—principally Shoshones—lived as nomads, huddling around fires in bison-leather tents through thousands of long, brutal winters along the foothills, waiting to follow the spring snowmelt into hidden canyons and ancient forests of the high country. Their numbers were never large (the total native population of Wyoming probably never exceeded 15,000), and they rarely came into conflict with other mountain tribes, such as the Utes to the south or the Flatheads to the north. In fact, they rarely encountered one another except on purpose, in intertribal powwows held at traditional times and places for purposes of trade, social contests, spiritual ceremonies and political diplomacy.

Where warfare did occur, it was mainly against or among the Plains Indians tribes east of the mountains. The Arapaho and Crow, Cheyenne and Dakota (Sioux) would send hunting parties into the rich high-country valleys of the mountain people. Before the arrival of the whites, intertribal battles bore little resemblance to the bloodbaths that would come later. War parties were generally small and had no firearms, steel or horses. The limited supply of arrows a warrior could carry did not last long in battle, and it was better to save them for hunting, if possible, since each handmade arrow represented many hours of work.

At least two non–American Indian influences—horses and guns—began to change the tribes' way of life long before the first white man set foot in what is now Wyoming at the beginning of the 19th century. Horses had first come into Indian hands in northern New Mexico in 1680, via the Spanish. By the 1750s, virtually every tribe in the Rockies and Great Plains had bought, captured or stolen enough horses to breed its own herd. Many horses were driven off or escaped; these spawned the herds of mustangs that even today inhabit remote areas of Wyoming. Horses let the American Indians travel much farther and faster, bringing more frequent contact—friendly or hostile—between tribes.

Guns spread more slowly. In the British and French settlements along America's eastern coast, armies of both colonial powers gave rifles to tribes that helped fight the Seven Years' War (1756–63). Guns meant power to conquer other tribes. Fur traders on what was then the American frontier found that the self-defense needs of the tribes made guns extremely valuable as items of exchange; they also empowered the tribes to hunt more efficiently and trade larger quantities of valuable furs for more guns. As a tribe got guns by trading with whites from the east, it often turned them against rival tribes to the west to expand its hunting territory. In this way, firearms often made their way westward in advance of the first white explorers.

EXPLORERS AND MOUNTAIN MEN   At the time of the first incursion into Wyoming by white men, the region was part of the vast Louisiana Purchase, acquired from Spain by France in 1800 and sold to the United States for $15 million in 1803. Some 150 wilderness-bound French trappers and traders penetrated the Rockies shortly thereafter, ignorant of the fact that the territory was now American. Not that it mattered much: Virtually all of these frontiersmen took native wives and never returned to civilization.

The historic Lewis and Clark expedition of 1804–1806 bypassed Wyoming in favor of Montana, but one of the party's members became the first white man known to have explored the future state. John Colter left Lewis and Clark in 1806 to seek his fortune as a trapper and trader on the new frontier. He returned to St. Louis four years later with stories of boiling springs and smoke spewing from the earth: Colter was the first non-native to see the strange landscape that would become Yellowstone National Park. Although most people dismissed his tales as the product of an imagination gone mad in the wilderness, no one ignored the fact that he had brought back a fortune in beaver pelts.

In 1811, less than a year after Colter's return from the wilderness, John Jacob Astor's American Fur Company sent its first expedition into the Rockies. As large international fur-trading companies established trading posts along the eastern edge of the Rockies, hundreds of freelance adventurers set off to probe deeper into the mountains in search of pelts. These "mountain men," as they were called—men like Jim Bridger, Jedediah Smith, David Jackson, Jeremiah "Liver Eatin'" Johnston and Thomas "Broken Hand" Fitzpatrick—explored virtually every valley in the Rockies during the next 30 years, bringing back more than half a million beaver pelts each year. In order to kill animals in such phenomenal numbers, the mountain men not only set their own traps but also traded gunpowder and bullets to the Indians for furs. By the

1840s, beavers had become nearly extinct in Wyoming and elsewhere in the Rockies. The last of the old-time trappers either became guides for army expeditions and pioneer wagon trains or established their own trading posts, where they continued to sell firearms and ammunition to the tribes—a practice that soon would become controversial, then illegal.

WAGON TRAINS AND RAILROADS The first wagon train crossed the Continental Divide in 1842. It comprised 100 frontier families, traveling in Conestoga wagons with a herd of cattle, bound for Oregon. The route they established came to be known as the Oregon Trail. It crossed the future Wyoming, following the North Platte and Sweetwater rivers to South Pass, at 7550 feet the highest point on the Oregon Trail, then proceeding west across the Green River to the valley of the Bear River and the future Idaho. This same path would be used by virtually all pioneers en route to the western territories for the next 27 years. A series of forts sprang up at several days' intervals along the trail to provide the immigrants with supplies, information and a breath of security before continuing their arduous journey. In Wyoming, the most important of these were Fort Laramie (1834) and Fort Bridger (1843). The forts were key points in the original Overland Trail route of the Pony Express, established in 1860, and the first national telegraph route, created the following year. Fort Laramie, on the banks of the North Platte, is now administered as a historic site by the National Park Service; Bridger, in what is now Wyoming's southwestern corner, has been elaborately restored by the state. In various other places throughout Wyoming you'll find wagon-wheel ruts and such natural landmarks (with inscriptions of passage) as Register Cliffs and Independence Rock.

The first woman to hold U.S. public office was Esther Hobart Morris, Wyoming's justice of the peace in 1870; the first elected to office was Mrs. Cort F. Meyer, superintendent of public instruction in 1894.

Wyoming's earliest towns were established with the advent of the transcontinental railroad in the late 1860s. Although Casper dates from the institution of a ferry across the North Platte in 1847, other population centers—Cheyenne, Laramie, Rawlins, Rock Springs and Evanston among them—owe their origins either to the Pony Express or the Union Pacific. With these centers of settlement in place, the Territory of Wyoming was created in 1868.

Ranching followed quickly on the heels of the railroad. The boundless grasslands of eastern Wyoming, left empty by white and Indian hunters' mass depletion of native bison herds, were ideal for grazing livestock. The first herds of longhorn cattle were being driven overland from Texas as early as 1866, but it was the new transportation network that really made this industry economically feasible. Beginning in the 1870s, vast ranches that measured in the millions of acres were established east of the Big Horn and Laramie ranges under absentee ownership—often British. These ranches thrived, employing thousands of cowboys and earning their owners bigger profits, in many cases, than mining would ever yield. On some of these ranches, cattle numbered in the millions . . . on paper, at least. The unfenced rangeland was so big that actually counting the cattle, let alone rounding them up and branding them, was impossible.

The demand for more land for railroads and ranches inevitably led to conflict between the settlers and the native Indians, who fought to protect their traditional hunting grounds. The Sioux in particular won a few battles—beginning with the Grattan Massacre near Fort Laramie in 1854 and continuing through the Bozeman Trail Indian wars of the late 1860s (near Sheridan) and the Battle of the Little Bighorn ("Custer's Last Stand"), just north of the border in Montana in 1876—but, inevitably, they lost the war. Most Sioux were resettled on reservations in Montana and South Dakota; the sole Indian reservation in Wyoming, the Wind River reservation near Riverton, is home to Shoshone and Arapaho tribe members.

OLD WEST TO NEW WEST   Statehood was granted Wyoming in 1890, even though its territorial population of 63,000 was less than that normally required for admission to the Union. But the frontier already had begun to change more rapidly than anyone could have predicted. In the brutal winter of 1887, a single blizzard heaped snow higher than the cattle's heads and was followed by weeks of record cold temperatures. When the spring thaw came, few cattle could be found alive: Most had frozen and/or starved. Some ranch owners lost 90 percent of their herds and went bankrupt, leaving the former ranches unsupervised.

Newcomers rushed in to seize pieces of the abandoned lands. Many started their own ranches on a more modest scale. Others, however, raised sheep, which foraged so thoroughly that they ruined the rangeland for cattle. Still others, known as "grangers," started dry-land farms; they were universally hated by both types of ranchers because they fenced open rangeland and built roads. Legal title to lands that had been part of bankrupt ranches was vague at best, so violent clashes, known as "range wars," erupted between cowboys, sheepmen and grangers. The 1892 Johnson County War, near the town of Buffalo, was the most notorious of these. The lawlessness was made worse when some cowboys from the early ranches turned to crime after losing their jobs, forming outlaw bands that lived by armed robbery. Rampant lawlessness continued into the early years of the 20th century. Eventually, when landholders had occupied their ranches and farms long enough to file for legal title under the law of adverse possession, the violence faded.

The tourism industry was launched on Yellowstone's shoulders after the thermal wonderland was designated the world's first national park in 1872. Initially, visitors entered the park at Mammoth Hot Springs via a spur rail line from Livingston, Montana. By the 1920s, however—with the rapid evolution of the automobile and the development of America's highway system—many tourists were driving into the park via the Wyoming gateway towns of Jackson and Cody.

Cody was founded in 1895 by William F. "Buffalo Bill" Cody (1846–1917), whose life, perhaps more than that of any other single person, bound together the eras of the Old and New West. Cody's courage and élan as a Pony Express rider (from age 13), army scout, Indian fighter and buffalo hunter—he was credited with shooting more than 4000 bison in eight months while employed by Union Pacific—led to his transformation by paperback novelists into a folk hero. His resultant fame brought out his latent abilities as a showman: The West subdued, Cody made it his mission to conquer audiences with his Wild West Show. For three decades he toured the major cities of the East Coast and Europe with a fanciful tribute to the American West.

Among other things, the romantic image Cody conveyed led to the development of the dude ranch industry, which catered to "city slickers" wanting a taste of the West. The world's first guest facility was the Eatons' Ranch, which opened in 1904 on 7000 acres just west of Sheridan. Today there are hundreds of other ranches throughout the American and Canadian West.

Gold, silver and copper were never major players in the settlement of Wyoming, as they had been in the surrounding states of Colorado, Montana, Idaho and South Dakota. But fossil fuels attained paramount importance. Coal mining, for instance, began in 1867 at Newcastle, on the edge of the Black Hills, and it remains strong today: The 16 open-pit mines in Campbell County,

STATE OF THE "BUFFALO BELLES"

Surprisingly to some, "Buffalo Bill" Cody was an outspoken advocate of women's rights. "If a woman can do the same work that a man can do and do it just as well, she should have the same pay," Cody said. His friend Annie Oakley may have helped to convince him, but Cody was certainly in the right state: Wyoming was the first to grant equal voting rights to women (written into territorial laws in 1869, its state constitution in 1890), and was the first state to elect a woman governor (Nellie Tayloe Ross in 1924).

surrounding Gillette, produce more coal than either Kentucky or West Virginia states.

The first oil well was tapped near Casper in 1889, and by 1915 a full-scale oil boom was underway, spurred by the military demands of the First World War. This particular boom was doomed by the political ignominy of the Harding administration's Teapot Dome scandal of the 1920s: In a Supreme Court case, Secretary of the Interior Albert Fall was jailed for secretly leasing a lucrative government oil field north of Casper to his friend, oilman Harry Sinclair, without taking competitive bids. The world petroleum market has fluctuated dramatically ever since, but crude has remained in the forefront of the Wyoming economy.

At the end of the 20th century, coal and oil remain Wyoming's most important natural resources, although natural gas, uranium and trona (soda ash) also are of key importance. Tourism and ranching continue to be the other primary industries, although there are important grain farming and logging economies as well.

Altitude and precipitation are the primary factors affecting plant life in Wyoming. Because Wyoming doesn't have the same western mountains/eastern plains topography as Colorado and Montana —on this high plateau, the two are largely interspersed—weather patterns are harder to classify.

FLORA

Climatically, nearly all of the state is semi-desert; true sagebrush deserts (with as little as 5 inches annual rain and snowfall) exist in the Great Divide and Big Horn basins. Except in river valleys that draw their water from the mountains, feeding cottonwoods (the state tree) and a variety of shrubs, natural prairie grasses are so sparse that it takes from 25 to 40 acres to graze a single cow, making irrigation essential. The high, cool mountains get most of Wyoming's rain and snow, with up to 40 inches a year in the upper elevations.

The foothills may be even drier than the prairies, since they are steep enough that whatever rain may fall quickly spills away like water off a duck's back. The foothills are just high enough, however, that cooler temperatures let snow melt more slowly, seeping into the top layer of earth to sustain scrub trees like juniper and numerous flowering shrubs.

Mountain forests change with elevation, forming three distinct bands. On the lower slopes, especially those in the eastern part of the state, ponderosa pine stand 50 feet tall and more. Spirelike Douglas fir and Engelmann spruce dominate the higher reaches of the western mountains. Between the two bands of evergreen forest, shimmering stands of aspen trees cover the eastern mountainsides and paint them bright yellow in September. On the wetter western slopes, lodgepole pine forests are more frequently found in this transitional zone. Both the aspen and lodgepole pine are what forestry experts call opportunistic species: Stands grow wherever clearings appear in the evergreen woods, because of forest fires, clearcutting or pine beetle infestations. Gradually, over a span of centuries, the taller evergreens will crowd out old aspen and lodgepole stands as new stands appear elsewhere. The distinctive aspen is a delicate tree that cannot tolerate extremes of high or low altitude.

The upper boundary of the deep-green conifer forests is known as timberline, the elevation above which nighttime temperatures drop below freezing year-round and trees cannot grow. Timberline ranges between 8500 and 9000 feet in Wyoming. Above timberline lies the alpine tundra, a delicate world of short grasses and other green plants rooted in permafrost where tiny flowers appear for brief periods each summer.

At the highest elevations, above 12,000 feet, summer freezing prevents even the small plants of the tundra from growing. Clinging to the granite cliffs and boulders grows lichen, a symbiotic combination of two plants that survive in partnership: A type of moss forms a leathery shell that protects an alga, which in turn provides nutrients by photosynthesis to feed the moss. This ingenious arrangement maybe the ultimate tribute to life's amazing capacity for adapting to even the harshest environments.

FAUNA

An abundance of wildlife is one of Wyoming's greatest attractions. You are most likely to get a good look at large animals in Yellowstone National Park, where long-standing prohibitions against hunting have helped them lose their fear of humans. The wildlife populations are about the same in national forests and wilderness areas, but sightings are much less common because animals generally keep their distance from roads, trails and any human scent.

The high plains are a favorite habitat of jackrabbits and prairie dogs, coyotes and pronghorn antelope, as well as prairie birds such as hawks, grouse and pheasants. Coyote populations are on the increase just about everywhere in the west. Scientists have discovered that as the number of coyotes in an area declines, the number of coyote pups born in a litter increases to compensate; so although states have paid hundreds of thousands of dollars annually for nearly a century to eliminate these wild canines because ranchers believe they pose a threat to livestock, there are now more coyotes than ever. They are commonly seen not only in open grasslands, but also on the outskirts of urban areas. Intelligent and curious, coyotes can often be spotted observing humans from a distance. They are not dangerous to humans, though they sometimes attack small pets.

Pronghorn antelope, once hunted nearly to extinction and until recently listed as a threatened species under the federal Endangered Species Act, have multiplied to the point that they are now a common sight on the northeastern plains. Two-thirds of the world's population of pronghorn, in fact, live in the grasslands to the north and east of Casper. Although these tan-black-and-white deerlike creatures with short legs and large heads are commonly called antelope, they are not related to the true antelope of Africa and Asia; in fact, they are not related to any other living species. Pronghorns were so heavily hunted in the late 1800s that by 1903 there were fewer than 5000 left in the world. Along with bison, they were one of the first animals to be legally protected, but today, they number more than a half-million.

American bison, more often called buffalo although they are unrelated to Asian buffalo, once roamed throughout the Great Plains and Rocky Mountains. Today they are only found on buffalo ranches (a growing industry here) and in a few protected areas including Yellowstone and Grand Teton national parks. One of the world's largest private bison herds, 3500 strong, resides on the 55,000-acre Durham Buffalo Ranch south of Gillette.

There are also rattlesnakes in the lower mountains and high plains. The good news is that they rarely venture into the higher mountains. Snakes and other reptiles are cold blooded and cannot function in low temperatures, so they are hardly ever found at elevations above 7000 feet. When hiking at lower elevations, walk loudly and never put your hand or foot where you can't see it.

Deer, mountain lions and bobcats inhabit the lower mountain ranges, foothills and plateaus. While white-tailed deer and especially mule deer may be spotted anywhere in the mountains, they prefer areas where they can browse on undergrowth. Mountain lions hunt deer and prefer areas with high rocks, where they can spot both dangers and prey a long ways away. Since mountain lions, also known as cougars, are nocturnal and reclusive, it's a stroke of luck to glimpse one darting across the road in your headlights at night. Wild horses also graze some remote areas on the west side of the Rockies, including the Great Divide Basin's Red Desert and Bighorn Canyon on Wyoming's northern border with Montana.

In Rocky Mountain forests and meadows, common small mammals include squirrels, chipmunks, raccoons, porcupines and skunks. Large animals include elk and black bears. Since elk prefer high mountain meadows in the warm months, they are usually seen (outside national parks) by serious hikers who venture deep into the wilderness. Sightings are more common in winter, when they descend to lower elevations where grass is easier to reach under the snow. In some areas, usually marked by signs and sometimes observation areas, herds of elk can often be spotted from the road in winter. The world's largest concentration of elk

Text continued on page 16.

The Bison: An American Saga

The bison is Wyoming's state mammal; an outline of this largest land mammal in the Western Hemisphere graces the state flag. Yet it is nearly impossible to imagine the scene in Wyoming's vast grasslands at the time when bison were at their peak as a species.

Somewhere between 60 and 75 million *Bison bison* (better known as American buffalo) roamed North America from Alaska to Florida, from New York to California, in the 16th and 17th centuries when Europeans first arrived on the continent. They were most prevalent in the Rocky Mountains and Great Plains, where immense herds of as many as four million animals migrated hundreds of miles between their summer and winter ranges. The Lewis and Clark expedition of 1804–06 reported that buffalo "darkened the whole plains," and Oregon Trail travelers told of herds that stretched from horizon to horizon and could drink a river nearly dry.

That was probably no tall tale. The bison is a massive beast—a mature male can stand 6½ feet at the shoulder and weigh more than a ton—made even more imposing by its prominent shoulder hump, the curved horns on its huge head, and the coarse, dark-brown hair that may hang from its chin like a beard. Though it is strictly herbivorous, this grazing animal can be dangerous. Despite its size, the bison is surprisingly fleet and agile, and its unpredictable temperament leaves one guessing as to its intentions at any particular moment.

The economy of the Plains Indians was based upon the availability of bison. They used every part of the animal: the meat for food, of course, but also the pelts (for clothing and shelter), the horns (for weapons and tools), the hooves (for utensils), the hair (for jewelry) and the rawhide (for drums) were employed. Other body parts were boiled down for use as glue, and the ubiquitous buffalo dung made fine fuel on the treeless prairies.

Before they inherited horses from early Spanish visitors to the American Southwest, American Indians hunted bison by means of *pishkun*. For thousands of years, herds of the great beasts were driven up embankments that ended in cliffs, from which the beasts plunged to their deaths. Horses enabled the Sioux, Cheyenne and other tribes to swoop swiftly upon the bison herds and take the numbers they needed with bows and arrows, spears and knives. When fur traders passed on rifles in exchange for beaver hides, the taking of bison became that much simpler.

Bigger changes began in the 1840s with the first waves of westward migration on the Oregon Trail. Then the death knell for the native way of life struck in the late 1860s and early 1870s. First, with beavers having been hunted nearly to extinction and Argentine cattle having been decimated by disease, there was a sudden major world demand for buffalo robes and hides. Second, the transcontinental railways began constructing several lines across the Great Plains, and there was no more ready source of high-protein food than the bison. William F. "Buffalo Bill" Cody alone killed more than 4200 bison as meat for the laborers.

And once the trains were on the tracks, a new "sport" emerged: Blood-thirsty rail passengers were challenged to shoot the great beasts from special excursion trains, often leaving them to rot on the plains. Between 1872 and 1875, more than three million buffalo hides were brought to railroad shipping stations, and the Indians themselves contributed another 400,000. Whereas the native peoples traditionally had used all parts of the animal, now it was only the hides, cured hams and tongues that were saved.

The wanton slaughter continued unabated until 1894, by which time naturalist Ernest Thompson Seton estimated that only 800 bison survived in all of North America. That meant a single bison lived for every 75,000 that had roamed the prairies just a few generations before. Federal legislation initially protected buffalo in only in Yellowstone National Park; other preserves were later added, including Montana's National Bison Range in 1908. At the time President Theodore Roosevelt established the latter, perhaps 20 American bison still lived in the wild.

Clearly, the picture was dismal. Yet in the 20th century, the bison has made a remarkable comeback. From near-extinction, the American buffalo has rebounded to an estimated population approaching 100,000 in the United States alone. (There are many more in Canada.)

Today you can see bison in many locations throughout Wyoming. About 2000 live in Yellowstone Park, competing with elk for food, frequenting warm areas in winter and climbing to higher alpine grasslands in summer. The Durham Buffalo Ranch, 30 miles south of Gillette in northeastern Wyoming, claims 3500 head—one of the largest private herds in the country. Smaller populations of bison live in Grand Teton National Park, in Hot Springs State Park, near Thermopolis, and in various private herds around the state.

is in Yellowstone National Park, mainly in the Mammoth Hot Springs area. Moose are also found in Wyoming, especially in the streams and marshes of Yellowstone. The best time to look is around dawn or dusk, but these herbivores are hard to spot because of their ability to blend in with forest surroundings.

Black bears are elusive but more common than most hikers realize. In times of drought, when food becomes scarce, it's not unusual for a bear to raid trash cans along the fringes of civilization. Black bears rarely attack people, but they are unpredictable and can be dangerous because of their size; they typically weigh 250 to 350 pounds. Most injuries involving bears happen because campers store their food inside tents with them at night. When camping in the forest, it's a better idea to leave all food inside a closed vehicle or suspended from a tree limb. Grizzly bears, larger and more aggressive cousins of black bears, live in the backcountry of Yellowstone and Grand Teton national parks and adjacent wilderness areas, but are extinct in most other parts of Wyoming. They are listed as a threatened species by the federal government. Attacks on campers and hikers by the 600- to-1000-pound bears are rare but not unknown.

Attacks by grizzly bears on campers and hikers are rare but not unknown.

Wolves were virtually extinct in this region until 1995, when in a highly controversial move the first gray (timber) wolves were reintroduced to wilderness backcountry in Yellowstone Park, Montana and Idaho. Initial reports are that the several-dozen canine relatives are flourishing—much to the outrage of area ranchers, whose forebears paid bounty hunters for their slaughter.

Beavers once inhabited virtually every stream in Wyoming and neighboring states. Trapped by the millions for their pelts in the early 19th century, the largest of North American rodents once stood on the brink of extinction. In more recent times, they have too often been considered pests because their habit of damming streams (to create ponds surrounding their dome-shaped stick-and-mud lodges) floods the most desirable areas of mountain valleys. Landowners persisted for many years in poisoning the beavers, or dynamiting their dams and putting up low electric fences to keep them away. Now a protected species, beavers seem to be making a slow comeback. It's not unusual to discover beaver ponds on backcountry streams, and if you watch a pond near sunset, you may get a look at the animals themselves.

Near timberline, Rocky Mountain bighorn sheep are common and easy to spot in alpine meadows. Herds of ewes are protected by a single ram, while other males lead a solitary existence elsewhere until mating season. Then the high crags echo with the crash of horns as young rams challenge their elders for dominance over the female herd. Mountain goats—shaggy, snow-white and solitary—may also be seen in some high mountain areas. The smaller animals most often seen above timberline are golden marmots, large, chubby rodents nicknamed whistlepigs because they communicate with shrill whistles. Smaller rodents called pikas colonize high-altitude rockpiles, where swarms of hundreds of them are sometimes seen.

Wyoming is not a state you can truly explore in a single two-week trip . . . especially if you devote half that time to Yellowstone and Grand Teton national parks, as you

▼▼▼▼▼▼▼▼▼

Where to Go

must. Any attempt to visit all the areas described in this book in a single vacation is doomed from the outset. If you try to "see it all," you may find yourself so focused on covering large distances that you sacrifice quiet moments to appreciate the natural beauty you came for.

Deciding what to see and where to go is a tough choice. The good news is, no matter how many times you visit, there will always be more places to discover the next time you come.

The obvious first stop is **Yellowstone National Park**, the world's first national park (it was established in 1872) and undoubtedly its most famous. A remarkable 2.2-million-acre wonderland of more than 10,000 geysers, hot springs and boiling mud caldrons, plus impressive canyons, waterfalls and high-elevation lakes, Yellowstone sits on the crest of an ancient volcanic crater. It has perhaps the Rocky Mountains' most varied and accessible wildlife, from elk and moose to bison and grizzly bears.

Immediately south of Yellowstone are **Jackson Hole and the Tetons**. Jackson Hole, a vast valley well known to 19th-century trappers and mountain men, focuses around the bustling year-round tourist town of Jackson. Not only is Jackson a center for outdoor recreation enthusiasts, including summer mountaineers and winter skiers; with its charming Old West facade, it is a shoppers' paradise. Adjacent Grand Teton National Park preserves some of North America's most spectacular mountain scenery and some of its most memorable fishing, rafting and backpacking.

To the east of Yellowstone lies the **Big Horn Basin**, an arid plateau flanked by the Absaroka Mountains to the west, the Big Horn Range to the east and the Owl Creek Mountains to the south. The Big Horn River runs through the heart of the depression, irrigating fields of barley and sugar beets and culminating in the dramatic Bighorn Canyon National Recreation Area on the Montana border. The most important town is rodeo-crazy Cody, a capital of cowboy culture that includes Wyoming's finest museum, the Buffalo Bill Historical Center. But you won't want to miss other highlights, including the thermal waters of Hot Springs State Park at Thermopolis and Medicine Wheel National Historic Landmark, an ancient and sacred American Indian monument reminiscent of England's Stonehenge.

West central Wyoming is **Wind River Country,** where the Wind River transits the Wind River Indian Reservation on the northeastern flank of the Wind River Mountains. These fertile lands were a reward to Shoshone Chief Washakie for his cooperation with the U.S. government; Arapahoes were later settled on the reservation as well, and the grave of famed guide Sacajawea is located here. Riverton and Lander, the main towns of the district, attract recreation lovers; the National Outdoor Leadership School is located in Lander. The region's most important attraction is South Pass City, a carefully restored ghost town near the apex of the Oregon Trail. Wyoming's high point, 13,804-foot Gannett Peak, is surrounded by the seven largest glaciers in the lower 48 states.

Warm "chinook" winds have been known to raise winter temperatures by 40°F in under ten minutes.

Southwestern Wyoming is for the most part open semi-desert, with a fringe of mountains along the Utah–Idaho border. But it is rich in history. Fur trappers rendezvoused here with Indian tribes as early as 1834. Fort Bridger was an important Oregon Trail oasis beginning in 1843. The Pony Express and Overland stages ran through this corridor in the early 1860s. John Wesley Powell launched his exploration of the Green and Colorado rivers from here in 1869 and named Flaming Gorge, now a national recreation area. Even J.C. Penney got in on the act, establishing his first store in 1902 in tiny Kemmerer, otherwise notable as the gateway to Fossil Butte National Monument. The regional hub is Rock Springs, a mining and refining center.

The most "civilized" part of the state is **Southeastern Wyoming;** here you'll find the state capital of Cheyenne and the university town of Laramie. At the western edge of the Great Plains just ten miles north of the Colorado border, Cheyenne is quiet as capital cities go, except for one week in late July when it hosts Cheyenne Frontier Days, the world's largest professional rodeo. In Laramie are the University of Wyoming, the only four-year institution in the state (founded in 1886), and Wyoming Territorial Prison and Old West Park, an outstanding living-history park in a restored prison. Within and beyond the Medicine Bow Range, west of Laramie, you'll find the delightful resort towns of Centennial and Saratoga.

The valley of the **North Platte River,** the state's largest, dominates east central Wyoming as it flows from the Continental Divide through a series of reservoirs before entering Nebraska and eventually joining the Missouri River near Omaha. Casper, the bustling commercial center whose economy is pegged to oil, gas, coal and uranium, is the regional hub. The Oregon Trail followed the North Platte for much of its course; reminders are Fort Laramie National Historic Site, which preserves a frontier post originally built in 1834, and Independence Rock, a massive boulder on which more than 5000 19th-century travelers carved their names. Pronghorn antelope now dance across the slopes of Teapot Dome, whose name became synonymous with government corruption in the 1920s.

Extending from the crest of the Big Horn Mountains to the Black Hills of South Dakota, **Northeastern Wyoming** may offer the most varied topography of any corner of the state. The Big Horns drop dramatically to the Powder River Basin, witness to bloody Indian wars in the 1860s and range wars in the 1890s. Sheridan remains a decidedly cowboy town with its turn-of-the-century downtown and a world-renowned ranch store, King's Saddlery and Ropes. Gillette, surrounded by Thunder Basin National Grassland, is Wyoming's fastest-growing city and the West's most important coal-mining center. Less than an hour's drive east rises the monolith of Devils Tower National Monument, a unique volcanic plug that attracts rock climbers and UFO enthusiasts from around the world.

▼▼▼▼▼▼▼▼▼▼

When to Go

SEASONS

Wyoming's climate is characterized by extremes. Summers are generally hot and dry; winters are the most severe of any of the lower 48 states. Even in the warmer months, thunder and hailstorms will interrupt a pleasant day's outing; even in the frigid season, chinook winds can raise temperatures to a frightening thaw level in just a couple of hours.

The spring thaw is not an especially appealing time to visit Wyoming. Cold winds, occasional avalanches, brown vegetation and plenty of mud are a few of the reasons why many people in the tourist business shut down their shops and motels in April and take their own vacations to more southerly climes.

Colorful wildflowers usher in the traditional summer tourist season, which runs from Memorial Day to Labor Day. This period is characterized by cool nights, mild days and sudden, brief afternoon rainstorms. In most parts of the Wyoming Rockies, it's a good idea to start outdoor activities early and carry ponchos or waterproof tarps on all-day hikes, since rain is almost inevitable. Clouds typically build in the early afternoon and then burst into thunder, lightning and sometimes hail . . . especially in the Laramie Mountains west of Cheyenne, where the concentration of such storms reaches 60 per year.

In a common, peculiar phenomenon, wind currents called "waves" can carry precipitation for long distances from clouds hidden behind the mountains, causing "sun showers." Old-timers say that if it rains while the sun is shining, it will rain again tomorrow. This adage almost always holds true; but then, if it doesn't rain in the sunshine, it's still likely to rain tomorrow. The good news is that summer rains rarely last more than an hour, and skies generally clear well before sunset.

Above timberline, temperatures may fall below freezing at night all summer and typically reach only 40° to 50° at midday. It is not unusual for the highest Big Horn passes and the byways of Yellowstone National Park to be closed by blizzards even in August, sometimes stranding motorists for an hour or two before snowplows clear the road.

Early fall—around mid-September—is one of the most delightful times to visit Wyoming, as the turning of the aspens paints the mountainsides in yellow with splashes of orange and red, brilliant against a deep green background of evergreen forests. Mountain highways tend to be crowded with carloads of leaf-gawkers on weekends but not on weekdays, while hiking and biking traffic on forest trails is much lighter than during the summer. The weather is generally dry and cool in early fall, making it a great time to take a long wilderness hike or mountain-bike excursion. The first light snowfall can be expected in the high country toward the end of September; the first heavy snow typically comes around Halloween. November is hunting season—a good time to stay out of the mountains unless you're armed and dangerous.

The winter season runs from Thanksgiving through March, the period in which all ski areas expect a reliable snow base. If you're planning ahead for a major ski vacation, you'll want to schedule it between those dates. Skiing may continue well into April, however, until spring temperatures rise enough to erode that base. Uncrowded ski trails, discount lift tickets and lots of sunshine make the late season a favorite time for many local ski enthusiasts.

Wyoming's only destination ski resorts are in the Tetons near Jackson, although there are smaller day areas near Afton, Laramie, Casper, Sheridan, Buffalo and Cody. In all parts of the state, cross-country skiing and snowmobiling are popular throughout the winter. These sports are heavily undertaken in Yellowstone National Park, where the glaciers and silica terraces take on a magical appearance when blanketed by snow.

CALENDAR OF EVENTS

Festivals and rodeos are a big part of life in Wyoming, especially after the snows have melted and the summer sun warms the state. There's something for everyone here: Music and art celebrations, reenactments of historical events, cultural observances, harvest fetes and much more, including a plethora of old-fashioned county fairs in July and August. Cowboy culture is preeminent in the Cowboy State: You'll even find a bucking bronco on vehicle license plates. Rodeos and roundups, horseshoes and ballad recitals, chili cook-offs and American Indian powwows dot the calendar. Below is a sampling of some of the leading events. Check with local chambers of commerce (listed in the regional chapters of this book) to see what will be going on when you are in the area.

Southeastern Wyoming   Top professional cowboys and cowgirls
from Wyoming and Colorado compete in the **Mountain States
Circuit Finals Rodeo** in Cheyenne. Saratoga's annual **Ice Fishing
Derby** is one of the top such derbies in the United States.

Jackson Hole and the Tetons   The three-day **Cowboy Ski Challenge** features novelty ski races and rodeo events, cowboy poetry
readings, a Dutch-oven cook-off, a barn dance and a concert.
Big Horn Basin   Cody hosts the **Buffalo Bill Birthday Ball** on
Presidents Day: Cody's actual birthday was February 26.
Wind River Country   The **Wyoming State Winter Fair** at Lander
includes a horse show, livestock exhibits, dog weight-pulling contests and dances. The **Wild West Winter Carnival** featuring ice
sculptures, ice bowling, ice golf and a snowmobile rodeo, takes
place partly in Riverton and partly in Boysen State Park.
Southeastern Wyoming   Saratoga's **Snowsation Winter Carnival**
includes cross-country skiing, skating, snowmobiling and the **Don
E. Erickson Memorial Cutter Races**, in which two-horse teams
race down a straightaway.
North Platte Valley   Casper's cold-weather events include the
Casper College Jazz Festival early in the month and the **Cowboy
State Games Winter Festival**, including skiing and skating, over
Presidents Day weekend.
Northeastern Wyoming   Newcastle's **Winter Festival** provides a
weekend of sports competition, Western dancing and horse-drawn
sleigh rides.

Jackson Hole and the Tetons   The annual **Celebrity Ski Extra-
vaganza** in Jackson includes ski races, a stage show and a Wild
West night to benefit charities. Grand Targhee resort hosts its annual **Nordic Fest** and telemark ski race at the beginning of the
month. Its **Spring Snow Carnival** includes ski and snowboarding
races and other events.
Southwestern Wyoming   Wyoming claims to be the birthplace
of cutter racing, a high-country winter sport in which two-horse
teams pull a wheeled, lightweight chariot down a snow-covered,
quarter-mile straightaway. The **Cutter Racing State Finals** are held
in Afton, main town of the Star Valley, where the event is said to
have been born.
Southeastern Wyoming   The **Laramie County Community College Rodeo** in Cheyenne features some of the best collegiate rodeo
around. In Laramie, a **American Indian Powwow** brings traditional culture to the University of Wyoming campus.

Jackson Hole and the Tetons   April Fools' weekend brings the
World Championship Snowmobile Hill Climb to Jackson's Snow
King Mountain. Meanwhile, competitors in Teton Village's **Pole-**

Pedal-Paddle ski down Rendezvous Peak, bicycle to the Snake River and kayak or canoe to the finish line.

Big Horn Basin   Thermopolis hosts the **National Cutting Horse Association Finals** this month: Cowboys demonstrate how well they've trained their horses to cut calves from a herd. **Cowboy Songs and Range Ballads** are featured in Cody at the Buffalo Bill Historical Center.

Southeastern Wyoming   Rawlins hosts the **Carbon County Gathering of Cowboy Poets.**

North Platte Valley   The **High Plains Oldtime Country Music Show & Contest** in Douglas features nonstop guitars, fiddles and banjos.

MAY

Jackson Hole and the Tetons   The **Elk Antler Auction** in Jackson raises money for Scouts and the National Elk Refuge. **Old West Days** greet the summer season with a Memorial Day parade and rodeo, street dances, stagecoach rides and a country music concert. A more rustic **Mountain Man Rendezvous** is held at Teton Village the same weekend.

Wind River Country   Dozens of musicians take part in the **State Championship Oldtime Fiddle Contest** in Shoshoni over Memorial Day weekend.

Southwestern Wyoming   Rock Springs hosts the **Cowboy Poetry Music Festival.**

North Platte Valley   Cowgirls rush to Torrington from area ranches for the **Margaret Hume Memorial Barrel Race.**

JUNE

Yellowstone National Park   The **Upper Yellowstone Roundup** offers a rodeo, parade and community dance in Gardiner, at the park's north entrance.

Jackson Hole and the Tetons   **Mountain Days** in Alpine include the likes of a gum-spitting contest, a buffalo chip throw, a beard-growing competition and a country music jamboree.

Big Horn Basin   The family-oriented **Cody Nite Rodeo** begins this month and runs nightly through August. Late in the month, about 300 American Indian dancers and drummers from throughout the Rockies and Canada participate in traditional costume at the **Plains Indian Powwow** at the Buffalo Bill Historical Center; onlookers are invited to take part. Lovell celebrates **Mustang Days** with a rodeo, melodrama, street barbecue, fireworks and other activities. The **Days of '49 Rodeo**, with attendant parades and dances, kicks off Greybull's summer rodeo season.

Wind River Country   The annual **Popo Agie Rendezvous** in Lander is a reinvention of such mountain men's challenges as tomahawk- and knife-throwing, black-powder shooting and pack racing. Fort Washakie is the site of the **Indian Days Powwow and All Indian Rodeo.**

Southwestern Wyoming   Green River's **Flaming Gorge Days** are the trona mining community's major annual event. **Aviation Days** in Afton honors small aircraft, including ultralite craft and hot-air balloons; twin-engine planes have long been manufactured in the Star Valley.

Southeastern Wyoming   The highlight of Encampment's **Wood-choppers Jamboree & Rodeo** on Fathers' Day weekend is a series of contests for the Rocky Mountain Champion Lumberjack title. **Medicine Bow Days** in, of course, Medicine Bow feature horse races, a parade, dance, barbecue and staged hanging.

North Platte Valley   The **Cowboy State Games** in Casper are an Olympics for Wyoming residents; they include track, basketball, swimming and other team and individual sports. Casper also hosts the **Fort Caspar Mountain Man Rendezvous & Primitive Skills Contest** this month.

Northeastern Wyoming   The 19th century comes back for **Bozeman Trail Days**, a living-history program held at Fort Kearny and various locations in Sheridan, Story and Buffalo. Buffalo also hosts the **Wyoming High School Championship Rodeo** and the **Big Horn Mountain Horse Show.**

Jackson Hole and the Tetons   The eight-week **Grand Teton Music Festival** at Teton Village is in full force, with regular concerts by the likes of the Moscow String Quartet and members of the New York Philharmonic Orchestra. Jackson is busy with its **Teton County Fair** and **Arts on the Hill Summer Dance Festival.** Grand Targhee's **Rockin' the Tetons Festival** features live rock bands, a street breakfast and chairlift rides for summer sightseers.

Big Horn Basin   The biggest rodeo of the year in Cody, self-proclaimed "rodeo capital of the world," is the **Cody Stampede;** festivities include four rodeo sessions, two parades, country-and-Western dances, art shows and Fourth of July fireworks. On subsequent weekends, Cody sees the annual **Winchester Gun Show** and the **Yellowstone Jazz Festival**, which attracts world-renowned musicians. A highlight of the **Park County Fair** at Powell is pig mud wrestling; there's also a parade, demolition derby, children's parade and agricultural exhibits. **Pioneer Days** commemorate the Mormon heritage of the town of Cowley. The **Fourth of July Celebration** in Ten Sleep includes a working cowboys' rodeo.

Wind River Country   An old-time **Fourth of July** celebration is held at South Pass City. The four-day **International Climber's Festival** in Lander includes demonstrations and seminars, a mountain-bike race, feasting, dancing and a trade fair. The **Green River Rendezvous** near Pinedale is one of the oldest gatherings of would-be mountain men in North America; launched in 1936, it encourages modern trappers to compete in such events as storytelling and black-powder shooting. Riverton's ten-day **1838 Rendezvous** is a re-creation of a fur trappers' gathering, and includes period costumes, skill events and craft sales. **Traditional Sun Dances** are held on the Wind River Indian Reservation for three days. **Chuckwagon Days** in Big Piney include a rodeo, parade and fireworks. **Southwestern Wyoming** The three-day **Red Desert Roundup** kicks off the eight-day **Sweetwater County Fair** in Rock Springs. At the end of the month, Kemmerer celebrates its **Turn of the Century Days** with a parade, street dance and three-day carnival. **Southeastern Wyoming** **Cheyenne Frontier Days,** the world's largest outdoor rodeo, held annually since 1896, features free pancake breakfasts, chuckwagon races, carnival rides, Old West gunfights, American Indian dancers, parades and country music concerts. Ten days long, it attracts more than 1000 contestants and 300,000 visitors. Rawlins celebrates **Rawlins Renegade Roundup Days** with a barbecue, dance and fireworks display. **Jubilee Days** in Laramie include a professional rodeo, Wild West parade and carnival.

North Platte Valley Casper hosts the **Central Wyoming Fair & Night Rodeo** over five days late in the month, often extending into August; it includes world champion cowboys and top-name country singers. Other July events in Casper include the **Beartrap Music Festival** and the **Platte Bridge Encampment,** the latter a mountain men's rendezvous. The **Governor's Cup Regatta** on Lake Alcova, 30 miles south of Casper, is Wyoming's largest boating event. The **Sheepherders' Fair & Mutton Cook-off** at the village of Powder River, 35 miles west of Casper, includes sheepdog trials and sheep roping. Since 1947, the townsfolk of Lusk have presented **"The Legend of Rawhide,"** an outdoor play based on an 1849 pioneer-Indian incident.

Northeastern Wyoming Sheridan's biggest annual festival is **Sheridan WYO Days,** including a parade and one of the oldest rodeos in the United States. The world's largest rodeo, with nearly 1400 American and Canadian youth competing, is the **National High School Finals Rodeo** in Gillette at the end of the month.

AUGUST **Yellowstone National Park** The **Yellowstone Rod Run** at West Yellowstone is a spirited gathering of hot-rod car and truck owners. The nearby **Burnt Hole Rendezvous** is a week-long re-creation of a pre-1840 mountain men's camp.

Jackson Hole and the Tetons Grand Targhee's **Bluegrass Festival** features three days of music, arts and crafts. Hardcore runners enter the **Rendezvous Mountain Running Race** up a 7.2-mile course from Teton Village to the 10,450-foot summit of Rendezvous Peak.

Big Horn Basin The colorful **Gift of the Waters Pageant** in Thermopolis honors Chief Washakie and the U.S. government for their foresight in protecting the healing waters of Thermopolis

Hot Springs in 1896. The town of Basin hosts the **Big Horn County Fair**, parade and demolition derby.

Wind River Country Dubois hosts the **Whiskey Mountain Buckskinners Rendezvous**, while modern Western culture is celebrated at the **Fremont County Fair** in Riverton.

Southwestern Wyoming The **Great Wyoming Polka & Heritage Festival** is an annual event in Rock Springs.

Southeastern Wyoming Part of the River Festival, the **Official State Microbrewery Competition** brings custom brewers and beer drinkers to Saratoga. The **Old West Summerfest** is a part of Rawlins' **Carbon County Fair and Rodeo**.

North Platte Valley The ten-day **Wyoming State Fair** in Douglas features livestock shows, arts and crafts, a carnival, big-name country music concerts and a three-day rodeo. The town of Lingle, near Fort Laramie, hosts its annual **Harvest Fest**. The **Goshen County Fair** in Torrington, **Platte County Fair** in Wheatland and **Niobrara County Fair** in Lusk are rostrums for crop and livestock displays by local farming families.

Northeastern Wyoming Gillette hosts the **Campbell County Fair** in the middle of the month, including horse races, roping events and a parade. Buffalo is the site of the **Johnson County Fair and Rodeo**, whose events are limited to county residents only. The youth of Weston County compete in calf roping, pole bending, goat tying and other junior rodeo events during the **Weston County Fair** in Newcastle. Sundance is the site of the **Crook County Fair**.

Yellowstone National Park **Buffalo Days** in Gardiner includes a parade, street dance and buffalo-meat barbecue. **SEPTEMBER**

Jackson Hole and the Tetons The **Jackson Hole One Fly** is an invitation-only competition that attracts fly-fishermen to the Snake River from around the world. The **Jackson Hole Fall Arts Festival**, with most events in Jackson, extends through the middle of September.

Big Horn Basin Since 1912, Meeteetse's **Labor Day Celebration** has put it on the map with a huge parade, rodeo, street games and dances, craft shows and concerts, outhouse races and a Lions Club barbecue. The **Buffalo Bill Art Show** brings culture to Cody near the end of the month.

Wind River Country The **One Shot Antelope Hunt** attracts three-person teams of big-game hunters from around the world to Lander: Hunters are permitted only a single cartridge in pursuit of Wyoming's swiftest animal.

Southwestern Wyoming The **Fort Bridger Rendezvous**, the state's largest gathering of latterday mountain men, is held on Labor Day weekend at Fort Bridger State Historic Site. Participants dress in buckskin, live in tepees, cook over open fires and mug for tourists. **Cowboy Days,** held the same weekend, is the year's biggest festival in Evanston; it is the traditional end to the Wyoming rodeo season. The **Rock Springs Hispanic Festival** includes arts and crafts, food and games, and celebrates Basque culture.

Southeastern Wyoming   The **Copper Days Festival** in the old copper-mining town of Encampment incorporates a popular tractor pull competition.

North Platte Valley   **Septemberfest** in Torrington is a favorite among German-style beer drinkers.

Northeastern Wyoming   Sheridan's **Big Horn Mountain Polka Days** draws thousands of folk-dancing enthusiasts over Labor Day.

OCTOBER   **Big Horn Basin**   **Sheepmen's Holiday** in Powell includes sheep dog trials, a lamb barbecue and cook-off, an awards banquet and dance.

Wind River Country   The **Cowboy Poetry Roundup** in Riverton brings balladeers and storytellers to the edge of Shoshone country for two full days of storytelling and Western music.

Southwestern Wyoming   Rock Springs observes **Oktoberfest** with beer gardens and live entertainment.

Southeastern Wyoming   Rawlins holds its popular **LeClare Square Dance Festival**, while Pine Bluffs calls out the goblins with an annual **Halloween Carnival**. Laramie hosts the **Western Square Dance Festival**.

Northeastern Wyoming   The coal miners of Gillette celebrate **Oktoberfest** with a variety of musical performances and carnival activities . . . plus, of course, beer drinking well into the night.

NOVEMBER   **Southeastern Wyoming**   Cheyenne's **Christmas Parade** is held during Thanksgiving weekend.

North Platte Valley   The annual **Christmas Parade** in Casper follows Thanksgiving as well.

DECEMBER   **Jackson Hole and the Tetons**   **National Elk Refuge Sleigh Rides** begin in December and extend into March. Jackson Hole and Grand Targhee ski resorts sponsor **Torch Light Parades** on Christmas Day and New Year's Eve.

▼▼▼▼▼▼▼▼▼▼

Before You Go

VISITORS CENTERS

For free visitor information packages, including the annual *Wyoming Vacation Guide, Wyoming Vacation Directory*, state highway map and current details on special events, accommodations and camping, contact the **Wyoming Division of Tourism.** ~ Route 25 at College Drive, Cheyenne, WY 82002; 307-777-7777, 800-225-5996, fax 307-777-6904; www.

wyomingtourism.org. In addition, most towns have a chamber of commerce or visitor information center. Tourist information centers are usually not open on weekends.

The adage that you should take along twice as much money and half as much stuff as you think you'll need is sound advice as far as it goes. In the more remote reaches of Wyoming, though, stores selling something more substantial than beef jerky and country-and-western cassettes are few and far between.

Westerners in general, and Wyomingites in particular, are casual in their dress and expect the same of visitors. Leave your suit and tie at home. Even in summer, you should pack a couple of long-sleeve flannel shirts, jeans and your cowboy boots for evening or ranch wear, but most of the time, you'll be happy in shorts and a T-shirt. In spring and fall, layers of clothing are your best bet, since the weather can change dramatically from day to day and region to region. Winters are downright cold, so pack your warmest clothing for this time of year!

Other essentials to pack or buy along the way include a good sunscreen and high-quality sunglasses. Cool temperatures often lull newcomers into forgetting that thin high-altitude air filters out far less of the sun's ultraviolet rays; above timberline, exposed skin will sunburn faster than it would on a Hawaiian beach. If you are planning to camp in the mountains during the summer months, you'll be glad you brought mosquito repellent. Umbrellas are an oddity: A Wyomingite keeps chilly afternoon rain from running down the back of his or her neck by wearing a cowboy hat.

For outdoor activities, tough-soled hiking boots are more comfortable than running shoes on rocky terrain. Even RV travelers and those who prefer to spend most nights in motels may want to take along a backpacking tent and sleeping bag in case the urge to stay out under star-spangled western skies becomes irresistible. A canteen, first-aid kid, flashlight and other routine camping gear are also likely to come in handy. Both cross-country and downhill ski rentals are available in resort areas during the winter, though serious skiers may find that the quality and condition of rental skis leave something to be desired. In the summer, mountain bikes may be rented as well. Other outdoor recreation equipment—canoes, fishing tackle, golf clubs and gold pans—generally cannot be rented, so you'll want to bring the right gear for your special sporting passion.

A camera, of course, is essential for capturing your travel experience; of equal importance is a good pair of binoculars, with which you can explore distant landscapes from scenic overlooks and bring wildlife up close. And don't, for heaven's sake, forget your copy of *Hidden Wyoming*

LODGING   Accommodations in Wyoming run the gamut from tiny one-room cabins to luxury resorts that blend traditional alpine-lodge ambience with contemporary elegance. Bed and breakfasts can be found in most of the larger or more tourist-oriented towns you'll visit, even in such off-the-beaten-path places as Dubois and Encampment. They come in all types, sizes and price ranges. Typical of the genre are lovingly restored Victorian-era mansions comfortably furnished with period decor; these usually have fewer than a half-dozen rooms.

The abundance of motels in towns along all major highway routes presents a range of choices, from name-brand motor inns to traditional ma-and-pa establishments that have endured for the half-century since motels became a part of American culture. While rather ordinary motels in the vicinity of major tourist destinations can be pricey, lodging in small towns away from major resorts and interstate routes can offer friendliness, quiet and comfort at ridiculously low rates.

At the other end of the price spectrum, high-season (midsummer and midwinter) rates in the Jackson area can be very costly. To save money, consider staying in more affordable lodging as much as an hour away and commuting to the ski slopes during the day, or plan your vacation during "shoulder seasons" just before or after the peak seasons. Even though the summer is a lively time in many ski towns, accommodations are in surplus and room rates often drop to less than half the winter rates.

In some Wyoming towns, you'll find lavishly restored historic hotels that date back to the mining-boom days of the late 19th century. Many combine affordable rates with plenty of antique decor and authentic personality. Both Yellowstone and Grand Teton national parks have lodges that offer distinctive accommodations at mid-range rates; Yellowstone's Old Faithful Inn ranks high among the Rockies' most memorable historic inns. National

WHERE CITY SLICKERS GATHER

Guest ranches are located throughout the state. Horseback riding is the common theme. Some offer luxury lodging and a full range of activities that can include fishing, boating and swimming. Others operate as working ranches, providing lodging in comfortably rustic cabins and offering the opportunity to participate in roundups, cattle drives and other ranching activities. Guest ranches tend to be comparatively expensive but include all meals and use of recreational facilities. Most guest ranches have minimum-stay requirements ranging from three days to a week.

park lodges are highly sought after, however, so travelers must make reservations several months in advance.

Whatever your preference and budget, you can probably find something to suit your taste with the help of this book. Remember, rooms can be scarce and prices may rise during peak season: summer in most of the state, winter as well in Jackson. Travelers planning to visit a place in peak season should either make advance bookings or arrive early in the day, before the No Vacancy signs start lighting up.

Lodging prices listed in this book are high-season rates. If you're looking for off-season bargains, it's good to inquire. *Budget* lodgings generally run less than $50 per night for two people and are satisfactory and clean but modest. *Moderate* motels and hotels range from $50 to $90; what they have to offer in the way of luxury will depend on where they are located, but they generally offer larger rooms and more attractive surroundings than budget lodgings. At *deluxe*-priced accommodations, you can expect to spend between $90 and $130 for a homey bed and breakfast or a double in a hotel or resort. In hotels of this price you'll generally find spacious rooms, a fashionable lobby, a restaurant and often a bar or nightclub. *Ultra-deluxe* facilities, priced above $130, are the finest in the state, offering all the amenities of a deluxe hotel plus plenty of extras. There are not many of these in Wyoming

Room rates vary as much with locale as with quality. Some of the trendier destinations have no rooms at all in the budget price range. In other communities—those where rates are set with truck drivers in mind and those in out-of-the-way small towns—every motel falls into the budget category, even though accommodations may range from $19.95 at rundown, spartan places to $45 or so at the classiest motor inn in town. The price categories listed in this book are relative, designed to show you where to get the most out of your travel budget, however large or small it may be.

DINING

Fine dining in Wyoming tends to focus on the region's traditional cuisine: beef and trout. Buffalo steaks and wild-game dishes are also popular throughout the state. Most cities have Italian, Mexican and Chinese restaurants, but only in more sophisticated towns like Jackson and Laramie will you find a wide selection of gourmet foods. If your idea of an ideal vacation includes savoring epicurean delights, then by all means seize opportunities whenever they arise. When traveling in Wyoming, you can go for days between gourmet meals.

Restaurants listed in this book generally offer lunch and dinner unless otherwise noted. Dinner entrées at *budget* restaurants usually cost $7 or less. The ambience is informal, service usually speedy and the crowd often a local one. *Moderate*-priced restaurant entrées range between $7 and $12 at dinner; surroundings are casual but pleasant; the menu offers more variety and the pace is usually slower than at budget restaurants. *Deluxe* establishments tab their entrées from $12 to $20; cuisines may be simple or sophisticated, depending on the location, but the decor is plusher and the service more personalized than at moderate-priced restaurants. *Ultra-deluxe* dining rooms, where entrées begin at $20, are virtually nonexistent in Wyoming; here cooking is viewed as a fine art and the service should be impeccable.

Some restaurants change hands often and are occasionally closed in low seasons. Efforts have been made in this book to include places with established reputations for good eating. Compared to evening dinners, breakfast and lunch menus vary less in price from restaurant to restaurant.

DRIVING NOTES

Some first-time visitors to the Rocky Mountains wonder why so many mountain roads do not have guardrails to separate motorists from thousand-foot dropoffs. The fact is, highway safety studies have found that far fewer accidents occur where there are no guardrails. Statistically, edgy, winding mountain roads are much safer than straight, fast interstate highways. Unpaved roads are another story. While many are wide and well graded, weather conditions or the wear and tear of heavy seasonal use can create unexpected road hazards. Some U.S. Forest Service and Bureau of Land Management roads are designated for four-wheel-drive or high-clearance vehicles only. If you see a sign indicating four-wheel-drive only, believe it. These roads can be very dangerous in a standard passenger car without the high ground clearance and extra traction afforded by four-wheel drive . . . and there may be no safe place to turn around if you get stuck.

Wyoming has its share of those straight, fast highways, especially in the eastern prairies. When the federal government repealed its mandated speed restrictions in 1995, Wyoming raised its limits. You must not drive faster than 75 miles per hour on interstate highways, 55 or 65 on other roads, 35 in construction zones. Violators are subject to fines, of course.

Some side roads will take you far from civilization, so be sure to have a full radiator and a full tank of gas. Carry spare fuel, water and food. Should you become stuck, local people are usually helpful about offering assistance to stranded vehicles, but in case no one else is around, a CB radio or car phone is a handy travel companion for long backcountry drives.

Wyoming gets a lot of snow in the winter months. Mountain passes, not to mention the prairies, frequently become snow-packed. Under these conditions, tire chains are always advised and often required, even on main highways. State patrol officers may make you turn back if your car is not equipped with chains, so make sure you carry them. At the very least, studded tires are recommended. In winter it is wise to travel with a shovel, gravel or cat litter for traction, and blankets or sleeping bags in your car.

A CB radio or car phone is not a bad idea for extended backcountry driving.

If your car does not seem to run well at high elevations, you should probably have the carburetor adjusted at the next service station. The air at Rocky Mountain altitudes is "thin"—that is, it contains considerably less oxygen in a given volume than air at lower altitudes. The carburetor or fuel injection unit should be set leaner to achieve an efficient fuel-to-air mixture. Another common problem when climbing mountain passes is vapor lock, a condition in which low atmospheric pressure combined with high engine temperatures causes gasoline to evaporate in the fuel lines, making bubbles that prevent the fuel pump from functioning. The result is that your car's engine coughs and soon stops dead. If this occurs, pull over to the side of the road and wait until the fuel system cools down. A damp rag held against the fuel line will speed up the process and get you back on the road more quickly. Remember, however, to readjust the carburetor or fuel injection unit when returning to the lowlands. An excessively lean mix can quickly damage your engine.

You can get full information on statewide road conditions for Wyoming at any time of year by calling 307-772-0824. You may also contact the American Automobile Association's Cheyenne office at 307-634-8861.

Any place that has wild animals, cowboys and Indians, rocks to climb and limitless room to run is bound to be a hit with youngsters. Plenty of family adventures are available in Wyoming, from manmade attractions to experiences in the wilderness. A few simple guidelines will help make traveling with children a pleasure.

TRAVELING WITH CHILDREN

Book reservations in advance, making sure that the places you stay accept children—many bed and breakfasts do not. If you need a crib or extra cot, arrange for it ahead of time. A travel agent can be of help here, as well as with almost all other travel plans.

If you are traveling by air, try to reserve bulkhead seats where there is plenty of room. Bring diapers, changes of clothing, snacks, toys and small games. When traveling by car, be sure to bring these extras, too. Make sure you have plenty of water and juices to drink; dehydration can be a subtle but serious problem. Larger towns, and some smaller ones, have all-night convenience stores that carry diapers, baby food, snacks and other essentials; national parks also have such stores, though they usually close early.

A first aid kit is essential for any trip. Along with adhesive bandages, antiseptic cream and something to stop itching, include any medicines your pediatrician might recommend to treat allergies, colds, diarrhea or any chronic problems your child might have. Mountain sunshine is intense, so take extra care to limit youngsters' exposure for the first few days. Children's skin is usually more tender than adults', and severe sunburn can happen before you realize. A hat is a good idea, along with a reliable sunblock.

Many national parks, monuments and historic sites offer special activities just for children; some state parks do, too. Visitors-center film presentations and rangers' campfire slide shows can help inform children about natural history, and head off some questions. Still, kids tend to find a lot more things to wonder about than adults have answers for. To be as prepared as possible, seize every opportunity to learn more—particularly about wildlife, a consistent curiosity for young minds.

TRAVELING WITH PETS   Wyoming is Big Dog Country. Throughout the Rockies, you may notice more vacationers traveling with their pets than in other parts of the country. Pets are permitted on leashes in virtually all campgrounds. But few bed and breakfasts or guest ranches will accept them, and more run-of-the-mill motels seem to be adopting "no pets" policies with each passing year.

Otherwise, the main limitation of traveling with a canine companion is that national parks and monuments prohibit pets on trails or in the backcountry. You are supposed to walk your dog on the roadside, pick up after it, then leave it in the car while you go hiking. Make sure the dog gets adequate shade, ventilation and water. Fortunately, dogs are free to run everywhere in national forests, and leashes are required only in designated camping and picnic areas.

Wildlife can pose special hazards in the backcountry. At lower elevations in the plains and foothills, campers should not leave a cat or small dog outside at night: Coyotes may attack it. In remote forest areas, it's especially important to keep on eye on your dog at all times. Bears are upset by dogs barking at them and may attack even very large dogs. Porcupines, common in pine forests, are tempting to chase and slow enough to catch; if your dog does catch one, a mouthful of quills means painfully pulling them out one by one with pliers, or making an emergency visit to a veterinary clinic in the nearest town.

WOMEN TRAVELING ALONE   Traveling solo grants an independence and freedom different from that of traveling with a partner, but single travelers are more vulnerable to crime and must take additional precautions.

It's unwise to hitchhike and probably best to avoid inexpensive accommodations on the outskirts of town; the money saved does not outweigh the risk. Bed and breakfasts, youth hostels and

YWCAs are generally your safest bet for lodging, and they also foster an environment ideal for bonding with fellow travelers.

Keep all valuables well-hidden and clutch cameras and purses tightly. Avoid late-night treks or strolls through undesirable parts of town, but if you find yourself in this situation, continue walking with a confident air until you reach a safe haven. A fierce scowl never hurts.

These hints should by no means deter you from seeking out adventure. Wherever you go, stay alert, use your common sense and trust your instincts. If you are hassled or threatened in some way, never be afraid to call for assistance. It's also a good idea to carry change for a phone call and to know a number to call in case of emergency.

For more helpful hints, get a copy of *Safety and Security for Women Who Travel* (Travelers' Tales, 1998).

GAY & LESBIAN TRAVELERS

Wyoming is a conservative state, and not among the more sympathetic to sexual minorities. Nonetheless, you'll find social and support groups in a handful of towns, especially the year-round resort town of Jackson, the liberal campus of the University of Wyoming in Laramie, and the state capital of Cheyenne.

SENIOR TRAVELERS

Wyoming is a friendly and hospitable state for senior citizens to visit, especially in the mountains in summer, when cool and sunny weather offers respite from the hot, humid climate of many other parts of the country. Many hotels, restaurants and attractions offer senior discounts that can cut a substantial chunk off vacation costs.

The national park system's Golden Age Passport allows anyone 62 or older free admission to the numerous national parks, monuments and historic sites in the region; apply in person at any national-park unit that charges an entrance fee. The passports are also good for a 50 percent discount on fees at most national-forest campgrounds. Many private sightseeing companies also offer significant discounts for seniors.

The **American Association of Retired Persons** (AARP) offers membership to anyone age 50 or over. AARP's benefits include travel discounts with several firms and escorted tours on Gray Line buses. ~ 601 E Street NW, Washington, DC 20049; 800-424-3410.

Elderhostel offers all-inclusive packages with educational courses at colleges and universities, some in Wyoming. ~ 75 Federal Street, Boston, MA 02110; 617-426-7788.

Be extra careful with your health. High altitude is the biggest risk factor. Since some driving routes through Wyoming cross mountain passes that exceed 9000 feet in elevation, it's advisable to ask your physician if high altitude is a problem for you. People with heart problems are commonly advised to avoid all physical exertion above 10,000 feet, and those with respiratory conditions such as emphysema may not be able to visit high altitudes at all. In the changeable climate of the Rockies, seniors are more at risk of suffering hypothermia. Tourist destinations may be a long way from any hospital or other health care facilities.

In addition to the medications you normally use, it's wise to bring along your prescriptions in case you need replacements. Consider carrying a medical record with you, including your history and current medical status as well as your doctor's name, phone number and address. Make sure that your insurance covers you while you are away from home.

DISABLED TRAVELERS   Wyoming is striving to make more destinations, especially public areas, fully accessible to people with disabilities. Parking spaces and restroom facilities for the physically challenged are provided according to both state law and national-park regulations. National parks and monuments also post signs that tell which trails are wheelchair-accessible. Some national-forest recreation areas even have Braille nature trails, with marked points of interest appealing to the senses of touch and smell.

Golden Access Passports, good for free admission to all national parks and monuments as well as discounts at most federal public campgrounds, are available at no charge to those who are blind or have a permanent disability. You may apply in person at any national park unit that charges an entrance fee.

The **Society for the Advancement of Travelers with Handicaps** at 347 5th Avenue, Suite 610, New York, NY 10016, 212-447-7284; and the **Travel Information Service** at 1200 West Tabor Road, Philadelphia, PA 19141, 215-456-9600, www.mossresource net.org, provide information for disabled travelers.

Flying Wheels Travel is a travel agency specifically for disabled people. ~ 143 West Bridge Street, Owatonna, MN 55060; 800-535-6790, fax 507-451-1685. You can also contact **Travelin' Talk**, a networking organization. ~ P.O. Box 3534, Clarksville, TN 37043; 931-552-6670.

FOREIGN TRAVELERS   **Passports and Visas**   Most foreign visitors, other than Canadian citizens, must have a valid passport and tourist visa to enter the United States. Contact your nearest U.S. embassy or consulate well in advance to obtain a visa and to check on any other entry requirements.

Customs Requirements   Foreign travelers are allowed to import the following: 200 cigarettes (1 carton), 50 cigars or 2 kilograms (4.4 pounds) of smoking tobacco; one liter of alcohol for personal use only (you must be at least 21 years old to bring in alcohol); and US$100 worth of duty-free gifts that can include an additional 100 cigars. You may bring in any amount of currency, although amounts in excess of US$10,000 require a declaration form. Carry any prescription drugs in clearly marked containers; you may have to provide a written prescription or doctor's statement to clear customs. Meat or meat products, seeds, plants, fruit and narcotics must not be brought into the United States, and there is a long list of other contraband items, from live birds and snakes to switchblade knives, which vacationers rarely have with them. For further information, contact the **United States Customs Service**. ~ 1300 Pennsylvania Avenue NW, Washington, DC 20229; 202-927-1770.

Driving   If you plan to rent a car, an international driver's license should be obtained prior to arrival. United States driver's licenses are valid in Canada and vice versa. Some rental car companies require both a foreign license and an international driver's license along with a major credit card and require that the lessee be at least 25 years of age. Seat belts are mandatory for the driver and all passengers. Children under the age of 5 or 40 pounds should be in the back seat in approved child safety restraints.

Currency   U.S. money is based on the dollar. Bills generally come in denominations of $1, $5, $10, $20, $50 and $100. Every dollar is divided into 100 cents. Coins are the penny (1 cent), nickel (5 cents), dime (10 cents) and quarter (25 cents). Half-dollar and dollar coins exist but are rarely used. You may not use foreign currency to purchase goods and services in the United States. Consider buying travelers' checks in dollar amounts. You may also use credit cards affiliated with an American company such as American Express, VISA, Barclay Card and Interbank.

Electricity and Electronics   Electric outlets use currents of 110 volts, 60 cycles. For appliances made for other electrical systems, you need a transformer or other adapter. Travelers who use laptop computers for telecommunication should be aware that modem configurations for U.S. telephone systems may differ from their European counterparts. Similarly, the U.S. format for videotapes is different from that in Europe; U.S. National Park Service visitor centers and other stores that sell souvenir videos often have them available in European format.

Weights and Measurements   The U.S. uses the English system of weights and measures. American units and their metric equivalents are as follows: 1 inch = 2.5 centimeters; 1 foot (12 inches) = 0.3 meter; 1 yard (3 feet) = 0.9 meter; 1 mile (5280 feet) = 1.6 kilometers; 1 ounce = 28 grams; 1 pound (16 ounces) = 454 grams or 0.45 kilogram; 1 quart (liquid) = 0.9 liter.

▼▼▼▼▼▼▼▼▼▼▼▼▼▼
Outdoor Adventures

CAMPING

Tent or RV camping is a great way to tour Wyoming's national and state parks and forests during the summer months. Besides probably saving substantial sums of money, campers enjoy the freedom to watch sunsets from beautiful places, spend nights under spectacular starry skies, and wake up to find themselves in lovely surroundings that few hotels can match.

Most towns have some sort of commercial RV parks, and longterm mobile-home parks often rent spaces to RVers by the night. But unless you absolutely need cable television, none of these places can compete with the wide array of public campgrounds available in government-administered sites.

Federal campgrounds are typically less developed. You won't find electric, water or sewer hookups in campgrounds at national forests, national monuments or national recreation areas (except for one campground in Bighorn Canyon National Recreation Area), nor in state parks. As for national parks, there are more than 300 RV hookups in Yellowstone and more than 100 in Grand Teton. The largest campgrounds offer tent camping loops separate from RV loops. Hike-in backcountry camping is granted by permit.

You won't find much in the way of sophisticated reservation systems. In July and August, the largest campgrounds in Yellowstone National Park require reservations by calling 800-365-2267 (credit cards only); reservations are not accepted at Grand Teton National Park or at most Yellowstone campgrounds. The general rule in public campgrounds is still first-come, first-served, though they fill up practically every night during peak season. For campers, this means traveling in the morning and reaching your intended campground by early afternoon—or, during peak season at Yellowstone, by late morning. In the national parks, campers may find it more convenient to keep a single location for as long as a week and explore surrounding areas on day trips.

For a list of state parks with camping facilities, contact the **Wyoming Division of State Parks & Historic Sites**. ~ 125 West 25th Street, Herschler Building 1E, Cheyenne, WY 82002; 307-777-6323. For information on camping in Wyoming's national forests, call 800-280-2267 or contact the regional office of the U.S. **Forest Service**. ~ 2501 Wall Avenue, Ogden, UT 84401; 801-625-5306. For information on camping in national parks, monuments and recreation areas, contact the **National Park Service–Inter-Mountain Regional Headquarters**. ~ P.O. Box 25287, Denver, CO 80225; 303-969-2000. For information on camping on public lands administered by the Bureau of Land Management, contact the BLM. ~ 5353 Yellowstone Avenue, Cheyenne, WY 82009; 307-775-6256.

WILDERNESS AREAS AND PERMITS   The passage of the Wilderness Act of 1993 represented a major expansion of federal wilderness protection. Today more than 2.6 million acres of national forest land in Wyoming has been designated as wilderness. To be considered for federal wilderness protection, an area must comprise at least five contiguous square miles without a road of any kind. Once it has been declared a wilderness area, the land is limited to uses that existed as of the date of declaration. Since most wilderness areas in Wyoming were created quite recently, since 1978, it is generally the highest peaks, where roads are few and far between, that qualify for wilderness status. Besides protecting ancient forests from timber cutting by newly developed methods like skylining or helicopter airlifting, federal wilderness designation prohibits all mechanized transportation: No Jeeps, motorcycles or all-terrain vehicles and, after years of heated controversy, no mountain bikes. Wilderness areas usually have well-developed trail networks for hiking, cross-country skiing and pack trips using horses or llamas.

> The general rule in public campgrounds is first come, first served. They fill up practically every night during peak season.

You do not need a permit to hike or camp in most wilderness areas. But plan to stop at a ranger station anyway for trail maps and advice on current conditions and fire regulations. Tent camping is allowed without restriction in wilderness areas and almost all other backcountry areas of national forests, except where posted signs prohibit it. Throughout the national forests in dry season and in certain wilderness areas at all times, regulations may prohibit campfires and sometimes ban cigarette smoking, with stiff enforcement penalties.

For backcountry hiking in Yellowstone and Grand Teton national parks and most other National Park Service-administered sites, you must first obtain a permit from the ranger at the front desk in the visitors center. The permit procedure is simple and free. It helps park administrators to measure the impact of hiking in sensitive ecosystems and to distribute use evenly among major trails.

BOATING & RAFTING

Many of Wyoming's large natural lakes and manmade reservoirs have large sections administered by federal or state agencies. Flaming Gorge Reservoir and Bighorn Lake, for instance, are contained within national recreation areas; Yellowstone and Jackson lakes are part and parcel of national parks; Buffalo Bill, Boysen, Seminoe, Glendo and Keyhole reservoirs have state parks on their shores; other reservoirs are largely surrounded by BLM lands. Federal boating safety regulations may vary slightly from state regulations. More significant than any differences between federal and state regulations are the local rules in force for any particular lake. These are posted near boat ramps. Ask for applicable boating regulations at a local marina or fishing supply store, or use the addresses and phone numbers listed in "Parks" or other sections of each chapter in this book to contact the headquarters about lakes where you plan to use a boat. The same is true if you're planning a trip on the North Platte River, Wyoming's major navigable stream.

Boats, from small motorized skiffs to big, fast bass boats, may be rented by the half-day, day, week or longer at marinas on many of the larger lakes. At most marinas, you can get a boat on short notice on a weekday, since much of their business comes from weekend recreationists.

If you're planning to camp in the mountains during the summer months, don't forget to pack lots of mosquito repellent.

Whitewater rafting is a very popular sport in many corners of Wyoming, notably the Snake River near Jackson, the Shoshone River near Cody, the Wind River Canyon between Riverton and Thermopolis, the Green River near Pinedale, and the upper North Platte and Laramie rivers. Independent rafters are welcome, but because of the bulky equipment and specialized knowledge of river hazards involved, most adventurous souls stick with group tours offered by the many rafting companies located throughout the state (see "Outdoor Adventures" in the appropriate chapters). State and federal regulations require rafters (as well as people using canoes, kayaks, sailboards or inner tubes) to wear life jackets.

FISHING

Since the boost given fly-fishing by the 1992 Robert Redford movie, *A River Runs Through It*, based on Norman Maclean's book, Rocky Mountain angling has received the kind of attention it has always deserved. Although Maclean's story was set in Montana, Wyoming also has thousands of miles of streams and dozens of lakes. The more accessible a shoreline, the more anglers you'll find there, especially in summer. You can beat crowds by hiking a few miles into the backcountry or, to some extent, by fishing on weekdays.

Fish hatcheries stock mountain streams with trout—especially rainbows, the Rockies' most popular game fish. Many coldwater lakes also offer fishing for cutthroat and golden trout, kokanee salmon and mountain whitefish. Catch-and-release flyfishing is the rule in some popular areas, allowing more anglers a chance at bigger fish. Be sure to inquire locally about eating the fish you catch, since some seemingly remote streams and rivers have been contaminated by old mines and mills.

In some of Wyoming's lower-elevation lakes and reservoirs, including those of the North Platte River system, the most popular game fish is walleye, a large and hard-fighting member of the perch family. There are also largemouth and smallmouth bass, catfish and various other species.

For copies of the state's fishing regulations, inquire at a local fishing supply or marina, or contact the **Wyoming Game & Fish Department**. ~ 5400 Bishop Boulevard, Cheyenne, WY 82006; 307-777-4600. Wyoming state fishing licenses are required for fishing in national forests and national recreation areas, but not on the Wind River Indian Reservation, where daily permits are sold by the tribal governments. Yellowstone National Park has its own seven-day fishing license, sold at any park visitors centers for $5.

An annual nonresident fishing license is costly compared to the resident fee. Short-term licenses (ten days or less) are the best bet for nonresident visitors. Nonresident children normally fish free with a licensed adult. High-lake and stream fishing seasons begin in late spring and run through the fall; most lower-elevation lakes and reservoirs are open year-round for fishing.

Downhill and cross-country skiing and snowmobiling all are very popular in Wyoming in the winter. There are also some less common cold-weather sports, such as dog-sledding and cutter racing (in which pairs of horses pull wheeled chariots).

WINTER SPORTS

Wyoming has nine downhill ski resorts; the largest are Jackson Hole and Grand Targhee, both within a short drive of Jackson. There are more than a dozen groomed cross-country trails in five national forests, extensive backcountry trail systems in Yellowstone and Grand Teton national parks, and several lodges that cater specifically to nordic adventurers. Additionally, 13 designated snowmobiling areas in the state connect more than 1300 miles of groomed trails, with another 600 just outside of Yellowstone National Park at the self-proclaimed "snowmobile capital of the world," West Yellowstone, Montana.

Vehicle "snow parks" in national forests and other recreation areas are closely monitored. Before you can use these to unload your skis or snow machine and head into the backcountry, you must buy a season parking permit, available at most sporting-goods shops. The permit fee is much less than the fine you'll pay if you park without one.

The best way to assure the reliability of the folks guiding you into the wilderness by horse, raft or cross-country skis is to choose someone who has met the standards of a statewide organization of their peers. For a membership list of hunting outfitters (many of which also organize other activities), contact the **Wyoming State Board of Outfitters and Professional Guides**. ~ 1750 Westland Road, Cheyenne, WY 82002; 307-777-5323. For guides and outfitters in Yellowstone Park, contact the **National Park Service**. ~ Yellowstone National Park, WY 82190; 307-344-7311.

GUIDES & OUTFITTERS

TWO

Yellowstone National Park

Yellowstone, the world's first national park, remains first on nearly every visitor's list of Most Remarkable Places. Nowhere else on earth is there as large and varied a collection of hydrothermal features: erupting geysers, bubbling mud caldrons, hissing fumaroles, gurgling mineral springs. The park is estimated to contain 10,000 thermal features, including more than 200 active geysers. Sites like Old Faithful Geyser and Mammoth Hot Springs have become part of the American lexicon, if not the American identity.

No other place in the contiguous 48 states has as great a concentration of mammals as does Yellowstone, or as extensive an interactive ecosystem. The park is home to an amazing five dozen species of mammals, including eight hoofed animals (bighorn sheep, pronghorn antelope, mountain goat, bison, elk, moose, mule deer and white-tailed deer) and two bears (black and grizzly).

Then there's the magnificent Grand Canyon of the Yellowstone, with its spectacular waterfalls; 136-square-mile Yellowstone Lake, the largest lake in North America at so high an elevation; rugged mountains reaching above 10,000 feet in all directions. It's no wonder city folk didn't believe the first stories they heard coming out of the West.

The park's 2.2 million acres were set aside by Congress as a national park on March 1, 1872. But convincing Washington had not been easy.

The heart of Yellowstone was once a giant volcanic caldera, 28 miles wide, 47 miles long and thousands of feet deep. Some geologists think the explosion that created this crater 600,000 years ago may have been 2000 times greater than Mount St. Helens' in 1980. Three ice ages sculpted the modern landscape, but they couldn't quiet the earth beneath. Nomadic tribes, who lived and hunted in the area for thousands of years thereafter, apparently avoided the most active geothermal areas, as did the Lewis and Clark expedition of 1804. Ever respectful of native superstition, William Clark noted that Indians who visited the region had "frequently heard a loud noise like thunder, which makes the earth tremble. . . . They conceive it possessed of spirits, who were adverse that men should be near them."

John Colter, a wayward member of the Lewis and Clark party, spent the winter of 1807 trapping and wandering throughout the area; he apparently was the first white man to observe the natural wonders of Yellowstone. But no one back East believed him. It didn't help when Jim Bridger, a mountain man as famous for his tall tales as for his knowledge of wilderness survival, claimed that "a fellow can catch a fish in an icy river, pull it into a boiling pool, and cook his fish without ever taking it off the hook."

Finally, in 1870, a group of respected Montana citizens set out to explore the area and put an end to rumor. Astonished by its discoveries (including Old Faithful), this Washburn-Langford-Doane party convinced Dr. Ferdinand Hayden, U.S. Geological Survey director, to investigate. In June 1871, Hayden took a survey party of 34 men, including painter Thomas Moran and photographer William Henry Jackson, to northwestern Wyoming. Their visuals and Hayden's 500-page report helped convince Congress to set aside this remarkable wilderness the following year. By the early 20th century, when rail access to the north entrance became possible, tourists were flooding in.

With 3472 square miles of terrain, Yellowstone—its name derives from the yellow rock cliffs of the Yellowstone River, which originates in the park—measures 54 miles east to west and 63 miles north to south, making it bigger than the state of Delaware. Its elevation ranges from 11,358 feet, atop Eagle Peak in the Absarokas, to 5314 feet, at the north entrance. The park has 370 miles of paved roads and more than 1200 miles of marked backcountry trails. In summer, when three million tourists visit, its population is greater than that of St. Louis or Cleveland. Its rainfall varies from 80 inches a year, in the southwestern Falls River Basin, to ten inches at Mammoth Hot Springs. Snow can fall in any month of the year.

Generally speaking, the park is open only from May through October, and many of its lodges and campgrounds have shorter seasons than that. But a second, winter season—running from mid-December to mid-March—attracts snowmobilers and cross-country skiers to the Old Faithful and Mammoth Hot Springs areas. Ironically, although 96 percent of the park is in Wyoming, only two of its five entrances—from Jackson (south) and Cody (east)—are in this state. Three entrances—West Yellowstone (west), Gardiner (north) and Cooke City (northeast)—are in Montana, which contains only 3 percent of the park. Idaho has the other 1 percent.

The following touring itinerary assumes that you're heading north from Jackson and Grand Teton National Park. From the West Thumb junction, on Yellowstone Lake, it proceeds clockwise around the park circuit for 141 miles and returns to West Thumb (which sits at six o'clock). The agenda can be easily picked up from any other gateway.

SIGHTS

GRANT VILLAGE–WEST THUMB AREA   Plan to spend about 90 minutes on the 64-mile drive from Jackson up Route 89/191 to

South Entrance, even if you have already made your long detour through Grand Teton National Park. The **John D. Rockefeller, Jr., Memorial Parkway**, is a busy highway with lots of junctions and turnouts. Once you're on Yellowstone National Park roads, you'll reduce your speed even more.

About three miles before South Entrance, you'll pass **Flagg Ranch Village**. Once a simple fishing camp on the banks of the Snake River, this private enterprise is now also a center for river float trips in summer, cross-country skiing and snowmobiling in winter. It has a riverside motel and campground, restaurant and saloon, and the last service station for 25 miles.

Just past the South Entrance ranger station, the road leaves the by-now slowly meandering Snake River and traces the steep-sided canyon rim of the tributary **Lewis River**, its black lava walls 600 feet high. Look for turnouts for **Moose Falls**, a split water-fall that enters the Lewis from Crawfish Creek, and **Lewis Falls**, a 37-foot drop.

Now you're on the east shore of **Lewis Lake**, a pretty three-mile-long, two-mile-wide favorite of fishermen. (The namesake of the lake is explorer Meriwether Lewis although he never set foot within 100 miles of it.) The lake lies just within the ancient Yellowstone caldera.

Six miles north of Lewis Lake, after crossing the Continental Divide for the first of three times in the next 15 miles, turn off a mile east to **Grant Village**, on the shore of **Yellowstone Lake**. The southernmost park community was named for Ulysses S. Grant, who as president signed the bill that created Yellowstone National Park in 1872. It has a 299-room hotel, restaurants, campgrounds, boat ramps, several shops, service station, post office and other facilities.

Much of southern Yellowstone still bears the scars of the terrible 1988 forest fires that ravaged about 36 percent (793,000 acres) of the park's vegetation and that took 25,000 firefighters about three months and $120 million to quell. But exhibits at the **Grant Village Visitors Center** (307-242-2650), beside the lakeshore amphitheater, explain fire's role not only as a destructive force but also as a creative one—clearing areas for the growth of new vegetation, which in turn nurtures a greater diversity of wildlife. Naturalists say major fires such as these occur once or twice a century when nature is allowed to take its course.

Grant Village lies on Yellowstone Lake's **West Thumb**, a bay so named because early surveyors thought the lake was shaped like a hand. (In my opinion, it's shaped more like a tired backpacker, and this bay is his or her drooping head.) Measuring 20 miles from north to south, 14 miles from east to west, and with 110 miles of shoreline, this is the highest (7733 feet) large lake in the Western Hemisphere outside of South America's High Andes.

The **West Thumb Geyser Basin,** noted for the vivid colors of its springs, is less than two miles north of Grant Village on the lakeshore. A walkway winds past features like the Thumb Paint Pots, the intensity and hue of whose colors seem to change seasonally with the light; Abyss Pool, with a deep, cobalt blue crater of remarkably clear water; Fishing Cone, a spring whose volcano-like mound is surrounded by lake water; and Lakeshore Geyser, which spouts up to 60 feet high when it's not submerged by Yellowstone Lake.

West Thumb is at the south junction of the Grand Loop Road. You should take the westbound fork, which crosses the Continen-

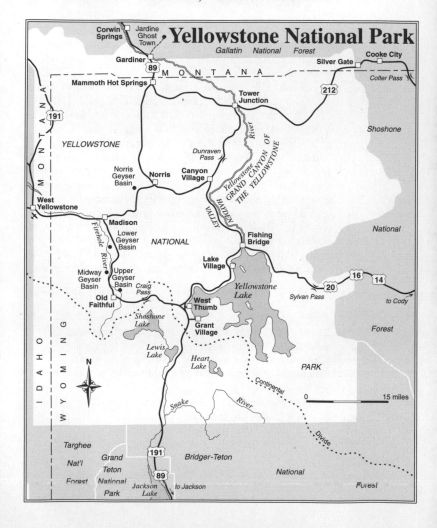

tal Divide twice more—the first time at 8391 feet elevation—en route to Old Faithful.

(If you turn right here, you'll follow the north shore of Yellowstone Lake to its outlet near Lake Village. According to this itinerary, you will return from that direction 122 miles from here.)

OLD FAITHFUL AREA   In a saddle between the crossings of the Divide, you can turn off at Shoshone Point for a view down Delacy Creek to Shoshone Lake, the park's second-largest body of water, three miles south. This is moose country. In the far distance, on clear days, you can see the towering spires of the Grand Tetons.

At Craig Pass, straddling the Divide, is tiny, spring-fed **Isa Lake**, whose waters drain west (via the Lewis, Snake and Columbia rivers) to the Pacific Ocean and east (via the Firehole, Madison, Missouri and Mississippi rivers) to the Gulf of Mexico and the Atlantic Ocean. Brilliant water lilies cover the lake's surface in midsummer.

About 15 miles from West Thumb is a wooden platform from which you can view the **Keppler Cascades**. This series of falls and rapids near the headwaters of the Firehole River plunges more than 100 feet between nearly vertical canyon walls.

It's only another two miles to the cloverleaf junction for Old Faithful Geyser, Yellowstone's best-known sight and the world's most famous geyser. While not the largest, the highest nor the most regular geyser in the park, Old Faithful has demonstrated remarkably consistent behavior since its 1870 discovery. It erupts 19 to 21 times per day at intervals averaging about 82 minutes, varying by 30 minutes on either side. Eruptions, lasting from 90 seconds to five minutes, eject between 4000 and 8000 gallons of boiling water to heights of up to 180 feet. The **Old Faithful Visitors Center**, next to the Old Faithful Inn by the west parking area,

---

✔ CHECK THESE OUT

- Marvel at the dozens of elk that bed down in the steaming limestone terraces of colorful **Mammoth Hot Springs.** *page 49*
- Rest your body in the largest log structure in the world: the massive **Old Faithful Inn**, a National Historic Landmark built of native pine and volcanic rock. *page 56*
- Enjoy a view of vast Yellowstone Lake with gourmet cuisine at the 1891 **Lake Yellowstone Hotel Dining Room.** *page 59*
- Descend past osprey nests into the Grand Canyon of the Yellowstone as you hike the **Seven Mile Hole Trail** from Inspiration Point. *page 71*

can tell you when to expect the next discharge. Normally, the shorter the last eruption, the less time you'll have to wait before for next one.

The park community of Old Faithful is one of Yellowstone's largest villages, with three overnight lodges; several restaurants, cafeterias and snack bars; numerous stores and shops; a full-service garage; a 24-hour medical clinic; a post office and other community facilities.

It's also the focal point of Yellowstone's spectacular **Upper Geyser Basin**, the world's single largest concentration of geysers. Weaving from the visitors center through the basin, on either side of the aptly named **Firehole River**, are about four miles of board-walks and paved, wheelchair-accessible trails as well as many more miles of dirt paths. The geysers of Upper Geyser Basin are a motley group of predictable and unpredictable, large and small gushers.

◄ *HIDDEN*

Directly opposite Old Faithful, overlooking the northeast bank of the river, is the Geyser Hill Group. It includes the **Anemone Geyser**, which bubbles explosively every 15 minutes; the **Plume Geyser**, which has erupted to 25 feet high every 30 to 50 minutes since 1942, when it first became active; the **Beehive Geyser**, which shoots water 150 feet or higher at irregular intervals of one to ten days; the two **Lion Geysers**, connected underground, which gush two or three times a day; and the **Giantess Geyser**, which erupts violently once or twice an hour, during a half- to two-day period, two to six times a year, and returns to dormancy in between.

Downstream is the **Castle Geyser**, possibly the oldest in the park. Its ancient cone is 120 feet around. Castle's twice-daily ex-plosions rise to 90 feet, last about 20 minutes and are followed by another 30 to 40 minutes of furious steaming. Nearby **Grand Geyser**, the world's tallest predictable geyser, erupts like a foun-tain up to 170 feet high every seven to 15 hours.

Farther down the trail, keep your eyes out for the **Giant Gey-ser**, one of Yellowstone's largest (up to 250 feet) and least active (it can be dormant for years at a time); the **Grotto Geyser**, whose weirdly shaped cone has absorbed the tree trunks that once sur-rounded it; and **Riverside Geyser**, whose 75-foot column of water arches over the Firehole River for 20 minutes every seven hours or so.

Upper Geyser Basin also includes several attractive springs and pools, the best known of which is **Morning Glory Pool**, reached by a one-and-a-half-mile stroll from the visitors center. Labeled in 1880 for its likeness to its namesake flower, the hot spring began to cloud because of vandalism (mainly trash thrown in the pool). Other notable springs include **Doublet Pool**, with a com-plex series of ledges, in the Geyser Hill Group; the **Beauty Pool**, framed by rainbow hues; and constantly bubbling **Crested Pool**, both in the Castle-Grand Group. The vivid colors of these pools —yellow, orange, brown and green—are due to the presence of photosynthetic bacteria on the submerged earth.

> The park's tallest geyser is the Giant, in the Upper Geyser Basin, which spurts as high as 250 feet for 90 to 120 minutes during its rare eruptions.

There are several more geyser basins along the Grand Loop Road as it proceeds north from Old Faithful toward the Madison junction.

Black Sand Basin, on Iron Creek just a mile south of Old Faithful village, is so named for its obsidian sand. It includes the **Emerald Pool**, whose deep-green center is bordered by orange and brown, and **Cliff Geyser**, a wildly unpredictable feature whose frequent eruptions vary in length from minutes to hours.

Biscuit Basin, another 1.7 miles north, got its name from a now-defunct feature of **Sapphire Pool**. Prior to the earthquake of 1959, this pool was a small geyser surrounded by biscuitlike mounds of geyserite, the hardened deposits of mineral water ejected by the geyser. Immediately after the quake, Sapphire Geyser staged a series of huge and violent eruptions, scattering the biscuits far across the basin. It hasn't erupted since. But nearby **Jewel Geyser**, surrounded by gemlike balls of geyserite set in colorful bacteria, erupts four or five times an hour.

The principal features of **Midway Geyser Basin**, about three miles north of Biscuit Basin, are **Excelsior Geyser** and **Grand Prismatic Spring**. Excelsior Geyser erupted in 1888 (to a height of 300 feet) and again in 1985 (nonstop for two days, to a height of 55 feet). If you missed it then, don't hold your breath). At all other times, it's like a pot of scalding water that continually boils over . . . at a rate of five million gallons *per day*. When the air cools at sunset, the geyser's steam fills the entire basin. Grand Prismatic Spring is North America's largest hot spring at 370 feet in diameter; it has azure blue water at its center, colorful bacteria around its edges.

Two miles past Midway, a turnoff down the three-mile, one-way **Firehole Lake Drive** marks the beginning of **Lower Geyser Basin**. This basin covers more ground than some of the others but its geysers are not as striking, with the exception of the **Great Fountain Geyser**, whose hour-long eruptions reach heights of 100 to 230 feet; intervals between eruptions vary from seven to 15 hours. Where the drive rejoins the Grand Loop Road you'll see the **Fountain Paint Pots**, a multicolored collection of gurgling mud pools that vary in size, color and intensity.

MADISON AREA–WEST ENTRANCE   Grand Loop Road follows the Firehole River downstream another six and a half miles to Madison. Two miles before Madison, the river drops into a deep, dark canyon. Coming from the south, you must proceed to a turn-off for one-way **Firehole Canyon Drive**, about a half mile from Madison, and then backtrack. The two-mile route penetrates the 800-foot, black lava walls of the canyon, reaching its climax where the 40-foot **Firehole Falls** tumble and churn into the **Firehole Cascades**. Above the falls is a big swimming hole; the miles of geothermal activity upstream raise the river's temperature about 30° higher than normally would be expected at this elevation and latitude.

National Park Mountain, actually a 7491-foot bluff at the edge of the Madison Plateau, rises only about 700 feet above **Madison**. It wouldn't be a remarkable landmark, but at its foot, where the Firehole and Gibbon rivers join to form the Madison, the Washburn-Langford-Doane party set up camp in 1870 and formulated the first serious proposal to create Yellowstone National Park.

Madison is one of the park's smaller communities. It doesn't offer overnight lodging, stores or service stations, but it does have a campground, a ranger station, an amphitheater, an information station and a bookstore. ~ 307-344-7381.

If you're ready for a sidetrip, a left turn at the junction will take you down the **West Entrance Road** 14 miles to the bustling town of West Yellowstone, Montana (see "Montana Gateway Communities," later in this chapter). The route closely parallels the Madison River and is excellent for wildlife viewing. In particular, keep an eye open for rare trumpeter swans at **Seven Mile Bridge** (their unmistakable, blaring cry when in flight can be heard from two miles away) and for elk and mule deer in the meadows.

To continue your tour, turn right at Madison and remain on the park's Grand Loop Road. About four and a half miles ahead, and right beside the highway, is **Gibbon Falls**, a veil-like 84-foot drop over a rock face. The route continues to ascend through the minor Monument and Gibbon geyser basins to Norris, 14 miles northeast of Madison.

NORRIS AREA   For many visitors, Yellowstone's most intriguing thermal area is not the Upper Geyser Basin around Old Faithful but the **Norris Geyser Basin**. In a walk of less than two miles beginning just a few hundred yards west of the road junction, you can take in dozens of geysers, hot springs, mud pools and silica terraces in "one of the most extreme environments on earth," as it's called by some park publications. The basin is pervaded by the perpetually pungent smell of hydrogen sulfide.

◄ HIDDEN

Thermal activity seems to be on the increase here. After a moderate earthquake struck the area in March 1994, long-dormant geysers surged back to life, and geologists monitored dramatic increases in ground temperature in certain parts of the basin.

Start your visit at the rustic **Norris Geyser Basin Museum**, where displays interpret hydrothermal geology. Then set out on the one-and-a-half-mile loop trail through patchily forested Back Basin (to the south) or the three-quarter-mile loop around the more open Porcelain Basin (to the north). ~ 307-344-2812.

The Porkchop Geyser in Norris Basin spouted continuously from 1985 to 1989, when it exploded; the geyser is now a gently boiling hot spring.

Back Basin has two highlights. **Steamboat Geyser** is the world's tallest active geyser when it is, indeed, active. Its eruptions, though spectacular, are *highly* unpredictable. After its 1969 eruption, Steamboat lay dormant for nine years, until 1978; it spewed several times between then and 1991 but has again been dormant up to the time of this writing, in 1999. When the geyser does blast, it sends a shower of water 300 feet into the air for as long as 40 minutes.

Echinus Geyser is far more dependable. Its explosions come every 35 to 75 minutes, and they last anywhere from six minutes to an hour, with water rising skyward 40 to 60 feet. Small crowds gather on benches around its cone much as they do (on a larger scale!) around Old Faithful. Echinus is also the largest acid-water geyser known, with a pH level between 3.3 and 3.6: almost as high as vinegar. Acid-water geysers are extremely rare; most of those known to exist on earth are in the Norris Geyser Basin.

Even more acidic (though not a geyser) is **Emerald Spring**, which has a pH of 4.5—nearly that of tomato juice. Its water, however, is crystal clear and green in color when bright sunlight filters through to its sulfur-coated floor, 27 feet deep. This is an extremely hot pool, normally about 194°, just 5° below the boiling point at this elevation.

From an overlook northeast of the Norris museum you can get a good panorama of **Porcelain Basin**, which appears as a steaming sheet of whitish rock. Silica and clay are responsible for the milky color characteristic of this area's various springs and geysers; some are rimmed with orange, indicating the presence of iron compounds. This is a very dynamic basin whose features come and go every few years. The **Dark Cavern Geyser**, which erupts several times an hour to heights of 15 to 20 feet, is among the more constant.

From Norris junction, the **Norris Canyon Road** proceeds 12 miles east to Canyon Village, effectively dividing the Grand Loop Road into two smaller loops. En route, about three miles east of Norris, it passes the pretty **Virginia Cascades**, where the Gibbon River slides through a narrow canyon and drops 60 feet. Most of the route is densely forested.

Less than a mile north of the junction, at the entrance to the Norris campground, is the **Museum of the National Park Ranger**. Housed in a restored log cabin built in 1897 as a U.S. Army outpost, the museum contains exhibits explaining how park protection began as a domestic military function and evolved into the highly specialized occupation it is today. ~ 307-344-7353.

The Grand Loop Road north from Norris to Mammoth Hot Springs, a distance of 21 miles, passes several interesting geothermal features. Vents in the slopes of **Roaring Mountain**, five miles from Norris, hiss and steam at the side of the road. A glossy black volcanic glass from which ancient American Indians made utensils and tools forms 200-foot-high **Obsidian Cliff**, nine miles from Norris. **Sheepeater Cliff**, 14 miles from Norris, is composed of pentagonal and heptagonal columns of basalt, another volcanic byproduct.

This region of low-lying streams and small lakes is a favorite of moose, who feed on willow shrubs and underwater plants, and who often wander through the **Indian Creek campground**, located just to the southwest of Sheepeater Cliff.

MAMMOTH HOT SPRINGS AREA   The Grand Loop Road begins its descent to Mammoth Hot Springs and the park's north entrance at **Golden Gate Canyon**, so named for the yellow lichen that paints its otherwise-barren rock walls. Where Glen Creek tumbles out of Swan Lake Flat, **Rustic Falls** drop 47 feet into the canyon. To the east, one-way **Bunsen Peak Road** winds around the base of Bunsen Peak, following the rim of the Gardiner River's 800-foot **Sheepeater Canyon**. Trails leave this road for the summit of 8564-foot Bunsen Peak and the foot of pretty **Osprey Falls**, deep in Sheepeater Canyon.

The **Mammoth Hot Springs**, truly one of Yellowstone's highlights, are a spectacular series of steaming travertine terraces in a steady state of metamorphosis. Super-heated ground water rises to the surface as carbonic acid, dissolving great quantities of natural limestone. As it seeps through cracks in the earth, it deposits the limestone, which solidifies again as travertine (calcium carbonate). This white mineral provides a habitat for colorful bacterial algae (cyanobacteria), whose varying pastel hues reflect the temperature of the water they inhabit: White bacteria live in the hottest water, followed, in descending order, by yellow, orange, brown and, in the coolest, green.

The result of this thermal dynamism on the lower slopes of Terrace Mountain is a lopsided wedding cake of a hillside. About 500 gallons of water flow from the springs per minute; by some estimates, two tons of dissolved limestone are deposited each day. But the springs and terraces are constantly changing, new ones emerging while others become dormant.

Visitors coming from the south will get their first glimpse of Mammoth Hot Springs from the one-and-a-half-mile Upper Terrace Loop Drive, a narrow, one-way route that turns left off the Grand Loop Road about a mile and a half south of Mammoth village. The thermal landscape here is highly varied: Some terraces have been inactive for five centuries, others (such as the pure white **Angel Terrace**) have come back to life after decades of dormancy, and still others (such as **New Highland Spring**) have erupted from verdant forest in relatively recent times—even as park rangers and frequent visitors watched.

Bath Lake, in Mammoth's Upper Terraces, got its name in the 1880s when soldiers posted here used it for washing.

Probably the best place to view the entire Mammoth area is from the **Lower Terrace Overlook** off the Upper Terrace Loop Drive. Boardwalk trails lead a half mile downhill through the main terrace region to the village beyond. Features like **Minerva Spring** and **Jupiter Spring** go through cycles of activity and dormancy lasting years at a time. **Opal Terrace**, at the foot of the hill, deposits as much as a foot of travertine per year in its most active periods. **Liberty Cap**, a cone formed by a long-extinct hot spring, marks the north end of the Mammoth Hot Springs; it is 37 feet high and 20 feet in diameter at its base.

One of the most surprising aspects of these hot springs is their apparent allure to elk. Dozens of the magnificent antlered creatures bed down in the terraces, seemingly oblivious to tourists who pass within a few feet. Keep in mind, however, that these are dangerous animals—it is illegal to approach within 25 yards of an elk.

Mammoth was the first settlement in Yellowstone National Park. Park headquarters are lodged in the gray stone buildings of the former **Fort Yellowstone**, a cavalry post during the three decades the park was administered by the U.S. Army, from 1886 to 1917. ~ 307-344-7381. Also in the historic fort is the **Horace M. Albright Visitors Center**, whose exhibits explain the army's role during those early years. There are also excellent wildlife displays and a slide program on park ecology, philosophy and history. ~ 307-344-2263.

Other village facilities, open year-round, include restaurants, a general store and other shops, a gas station with repair services, a medical clinic, a post office, a campground and an amphitheater for evening programs. There's even a corral for trail riders. For park visitors planning to complete a circuit of the Grand Loop Road in two days, this is a good halfway point for food and lodging on the tour from Grant Village.

The **North Entrance Road**, which connects Mammoth Hot Springs with Gardiner, Montana (see "Montana Gateway Communities"), five miles to the north, is the only route into the park that is open year-round. (The Northeast Entrance Road is open beyond the park boundary to Cooke City, Montana, but the Beartooth Highway beyond that point is closed from mid-October through May.)

The North Entrance Road passes through 600-foot-deep **Gardiner Canyon** and swings by the steaming, subterranean outlet where the **Boiling River** flows into the Gardiner River. At the north entrance, the route passes beneath the 30-foot stone **Roosevelt Arch**, dedicated in 1903 by President Theodore Roosevelt and inscribed, "For the Benefit and Enjoyment of the People."

East of Mammoth Hot Springs, the Grand Loop Road continues 18 miles to Tower Junction. En route, about four miles from Mammoth, it passes **Undine Falls**, which drop 60 feet between perpendicular cliff walls on Lava Creek.

TOWER JUNCTION–ROOSEVELT AREA The saddle between Mammoth and Tower Junction is known as the **Blacktail Deer Plateau**. Nature lovers may spot the mule deer from which it gets its name on **Blacktail Plateau Drive,** a one-way, six-and-a-half-mile eastbound dirt road that leaves the main road about ten miles east of Mammoth (eight miles west of Tower Junction) to traverse forests of fir, spruce, pine and aspen, and hills covered with sagebrush and wildflowers.

If you stay on the Grand Loop Road, about three and a half miles before Tower Junction—just north of Elk Creek (yes, there are lots of those creatures here, too)—you'll pass **Garnet Hill**. The rocks here are Precambrian granite gneiss estimated to be roughly 2.7 billion years old, formed before the first primitive lifeforms even began to appear on the planet. Imperfect garnets can be found in this ancient formation.

A short side road a little over a mile west of Tower Junction leads to a **petrified tree**, enclosed by a tall iron fence to prevent the vandalism that consumed its former neighbors. Petrified trees —like this upright 20-foot redwood stump—were fossilized 50 million years ago after falling volcanic ash covered them. They can be found in isolated locations throughout northern Yellowstone, especially nearby **Specimen Ridge**, where between nine and twelve separate petrified forests—one on top of another—have been identified.

◄ *HIDDEN*

Tower Junction takes its name from the unusual basalt pinnacles that rise above the Yellowstone River canyon just south of here. They include **Overhanging Cliff**, a columnar formation that actually hangs over the road, and **The Needle**, a 260-foot spire of volcanic breccia.

Tower Fall is about two miles south of the junction off the Grand Loop Road; it plummets 132 feet from the palisades into **The Narrows**, at 500 feet the deepest part of this section of the canyon, and its most confined. A trail that leads to the foot of the waterfall reveals more steam vents and hot springs, including **Calcite Springs**, where the geothermal waters deposit calcite, gypsum and sulfur.

At Tower Junction itself are a ranger station, a service station, horse corrals and the **Roosevelt Lodge**, a rustic 1920s log building (with cabins and a restaurant) named for Teddy Roosevelt. The environmentalist president favored this area's rolling hills for camping around the turn of the 20th century.

Granite boulders scattered through the Lamar River Valley were left behind by an Ice Age glacier 10,000 years ago.

There are really two junctions at Tower Junction: that of the Grand Loop Road with the **Northeast Entrance Road**, and that of the **Lamar River** with the Yellowstone River. The Northeast Entrance Road follows the Lamar Valley upstream for the first half of its 29-mile run to the park's Northeast Entrance, closely paralleling an old American Indian route, the Bannock Trail. Bison and elk winter in the broad, open meadows of this glacial valley. **Buffalo Ranch**, ten miles east of Tower Junction, was used as a breeding preserve for bison for a half century after its establishment in 1907, during which time it helped Yellowstone's once-rare bison population increase from 25 to a modern estimate of 2500. It's now home to the **Yellowstone Institute**, a nonprofit academy specializing in wildlife and natural-history education for day or resident students. Some courses earn university credit. ~ 307-344-2294.

There are two park campgrounds along this route. **Slough Creek campground**, Yellowstone's smallest with 29 sites, is about eight miles northeast of Tower Junction at the end of three-mile Slough Creek Road. The trout fishing is said to be excellent in this area. **Pebble Creek campground**, with 36 sites, is about 18 miles east of Tower Junction at the mouth of Pebble Creek Canyon.

The Northeast Entrance Road turns away from the Lamar River about three miles past Buffalo Ranch and follows **Soda Butte Creek** for the next 20 miles. **Soda Butte** itself, on the south side of the highway about five miles from Buffalo Ranch, is a long-dead travertine terrace not unlike those of Mammoth Hot Springs. The route climbs through the Absaroka Range, cutting a path between 10,928-foot **Abiathar Peak** and 10,404-foot **Barronette Peak**, en route to the Northeast Entrance, just across the Montana state line. Beyond are the isolated communities of Silver Gate and Cooke City (see "Montana Gateway Communities") and the rugged Beartooth Plateau.

South of Tower Junction, the Grand Loop Road passes Tower Fall, then begins a 12-mile ascent into the Washburn Range, a stretch that is Yellowstone's highest road. The area southeast of the highway, between Antelope Creek and the rim of the Yellowstone canyon, is a refuge for grizzly bears. Any human travel (even by foot) is prohibited in the area.

Trails from 8859-foot **Dunraven Pass** lead through groves of gnarled whitebark pine and subalpine fir to the fire lookout atop 10,243-foot **Mount Washburn**, a summer range for bighorn sheep.

There are magnificent views from here across the Yellowstone caldera to the Red Mountains, 35 miles away, and on clear days to the Teton Range, 100 miles to the southwest.

CANYON AREA   From Dunraven Pass the Grand Loop Road makes a five-mile descent through dense stands of lodgepole pine to **Canyon Village**.

The lodge here is among the park's newest; visitors also find dining facilities and a lounge, a campground and an amphitheater, riding stables and a general store, service station, post office and ranger station. The **Canyon Visitors Center** features a history of bison. A future exhibit will portray the creation of the Yellowstone River canyon by lava, glaciers and floods as well as other aspects of park geology. ~ 307-242-2550.

While the **Grand Canyon of the Yellowstone** extends 24 miles to The Narrows, just past Tower Fall at its northern end, the truly "grand" part is its first couple of miles, which include the Upper and Lower Yellowstone Falls. For your first view of the falls (you'll want more than one), take the two-and-a-half-mile, one-way North Rim Drive east and south from Canyon Village.

Your first stop is **Inspiration Point**, where you can park and descend several dozen steps to a lookout. To the southwest (about 1.4 miles) is the **Lower Falls**, at 308 feet Yellowstone's highest waterfall. (Around the corner to the south, out of view from this point, are the 109-foot **Upper Falls**.) The canyon is about 1000 feet deep at this point (it ranges from 800 to 1200), while the distance from here to the South Rim is about 1500 feet. Farther downriver are places where it widens out to about 4000 feet.

The vivid hues of the canyon walls—yellow, red, orange, brown and even blue—are proof of ancient hydrothermal action on rhyolite, a fine-grained volcanic rock heavy in silica, and its mineral oxides. Though the cliffs still exude steam and seem forbidding, they make a fine home for ospreys, which scan for fish from their huge summer nests built on rock porches high above the Yellowstone River, and violet-green swallows, which help keep down the populations of flying insects.

Southwest of Inspiration Point, nearer Lower Falls, there are additional viewing points off North Rim Drive at **Grandview Point, Lookout Point** and **Red Rock Point.** A parking area just before the drive rejoins the Grand Loop Road signals a three-quarter-mile paved trail that switchbacks 600 feet downhill to the lip of the Lower Falls.

Less than a half-mile south, after Grand Loop Road crosses Cascade Creek (whose own **Crystal Falls** empty into the Yellowstone just below this point), look for a turnout to the Upper Falls. The trail to the brink of these falls is almost a stairway, and it's only a couple of hundred yards in either direction.

Just over a half mile from the Upper Falls turnout, and about 2.3 miles south of Canyon Village, cross the Chittenden Bridge to Artist Point Road, which branches northeast along the canyon's South Rim. It ends .8 mile beyond at **Artist Point**, directly opposite Grandview Point but with a strikingly different perspective on the canyon. En route, you'll pass a parking area for a network of trails that head out for closer views of both waterfalls and the canyon. Among them is **Uncle Tom's Trail,** named not for a Harriet Beecher Stowe character but for Tom Richardson, who built the first trail into the canyon in 1890.

> Black Dragon's Caldron broke out in 1948 with seething bubbles of pitch-black earth that burst with such force that they flung the sticky, rubbery mud into nearby trees.

The contrast between the reckless river that rushes through the Yellowstone canyon and the tranquil stream that meanders through the **Hayden Valley** is quite striking. Yet only about three miles separate these two opposite faces of the Yellowstone River. Whereas the canyon is hostile to most wildlife, the lush, six-mile valley between Alum and Trout creeks is a natural sanctuary.

Bison, moose, elk, bear and other large animals wander the former lakebed, whose rolling hills, meadows and marshlands are a veritable garden of tasty grasses and shrubs. Trumpeter swans, sandhill cranes, great blue herons, white pelicans and other stately waterfowl abound in the marshes. Fishing is prohibited in the valley—for the peace of the animals and the safety of the anglers.

Numerous roadside parking areas have been created to accommodate wildlife viewing. Nevertheless, traffic jams are common. Park officials continually warn visitors to view large animals only from a distance, even if they're in their cars. The ferocity of grizzly bears is well documented, but bison, though they may seem docile, can be unpredictable and temperamental as well.

An intense thermal area beyond Elk Antler Creek marks the south end of the Hayden Valley, about 11 miles from Canyon Village. The varied features here are arguably the park's most foul smelling. The stench of hydrogen sulfide gas emanates from the constantly churning caldron of murky **Mud Volcano**. Rising volcanic gases continually bubble to the surface of **Black Dragon's Caldron,** which erupted in 1948 with such frenzy that it flung pitch-black mud dozens of feet around; Sour Lake, whose acid water has killed nearby trees; Dragon's Mouth, whose bursts of steam roar and echo within its cavern; and Sulphur Caldron, its water yellow with sulfur.

YELLOWSTONE LAKE AREA   Spawning cutthroat trout leap up the cascades at **Le Hardy Rapids** on the Yellowstone River in June and July, making their final approach to nearby Yellowstone Lake. **Lake Junction** is just three miles south from this point.

The first of three communities situated along the lake's northwest shore is **Fishing Bridge**, whose facilities (just east of Lake Junction) include a full-service garage, a general store, a hotel, a ranger station and a park for hard-sided recreational vehicles. A camping restriction was imposed because of the area's popularity among park bears.

Despite its name, the bridge—which spans the Yellowstone River at its outlet from Yellowstone Lake—was closed to fishing in 1973. Visitors now use it primarily for watching the summer spawning spectacular of native cutthroat trout returning to the river to lay their eggs. Pelicans, gulls and even bears are a part of the show. Exhibits at the **Fishing Bridge Visitors Center** focus on the geology and bird and fish life of the Yellowstone Lake area. ~ 307-242-2450.

The turnoff from the Grand Loop Road to **Lake Village** is less than two miles south of Lake Junction. Lake Village is the home of the park's oldest lodging, the **Lake Yellowstone Hotel**, which opened to visitors in 1891. Though renovated, it has kept its historic flavor and is still going strong. Lake Village also has cabins, restaurants, stores, a ranger station and a hospital.

Another two miles south is **Bridge Bay**, the lake's primary abode for tent campers and, with 420 sites, the park's largest campground. Besides a ranger station, amphitheater and store, Bridge Bay boasts a marina. You will need permits both to fish and to operate your boat; obtain them at ranger stations. You can swim without a permit, but be cautious: The average lake surface temperature, even in mid-August, is about 60°.

As you follow the lakeshore south and west from Bridge Bay to West Thumb, a distance of about 17 miles, passing a half-dozen picnic sites en route, you'll get a feeling for the breadth of this huge mountain lake: It covers 136 square miles and has an average depth of 139 feet, though at its deepest point it's 390 feet. Of five islands in the lake, three—Stevenson, Dot and Frank—are easily visible from this lakeshore drive.

West Thumb, at the junction of South Entrance Road, is where this tour route began. If you want to head out the park's **East Entrance Road** toward Cody, Wyoming, 77 miles from Lake Junction, you'll need to retrace your treadmarks to Fishing Bridge. It's 26 miles from there through the dense evergreen forests surrounding 8530-foot Sylvan Pass in the Absaroka Range, to the East Entrance station.

For its first nine miles, the East Entrance Road traces the north shore of Yellowstone Lake. Moose occasionally browse in the fens and sedge meadows of the **Pelican Creek Flats**, one to three miles east of Fishing Bridge. Although there's no immediate cause for alarm, the earth in this area is rising by as much as an inch per year—a warning of future volcanic activity, perhaps along the line of what exists in the Norris Geyser Basin today.

It wasn't long ago, in geological terms, that hydrothermal explosions created the craters now filled by **Mary Bay** and adjacent **Indian Pond**. The bottom sediment in Mary Bay is still very warm, and a fault line that runs along Yellowstone Lake's northeastern shore continues to feed hot springs, among them **Beach Springs** (at Mary Bay), **Steamboat Springs** (at Steamboat Point) and **Butte Springs** (at the foot of Lake Butte). There are picnic areas at each of these thermal locations, which are five, six and seven miles, respectively, from Fishing Bridge.

A short spur road climbs 600 feet to the **Lake Butte Overlook** for one last panoramic glimpse of Yellowstone Lake. Then it's back to the East Entrance Road and up the west side of the Absaroka Range. Look for marmots and pikas on the rocky slopes at higher elevations. Beyond **Sylvan Pass**, 20 miles from Fishing Bridge, the highway descends nearly 1600 feet in seven miles to **East Entrance**.

Several guest ranches, campgrounds and other tourist-oriented facilities are located just a few miles outside the park boundary in the Wapiti Valley, along the North Fork Shoshone River. This route is described in Chapter Four, "The Big Horn Basin."

LODGING   Yellowstone National Park probably offers more accommodations and more hotels of historic value than any other park. In all, Yellowstone boasts nine properties with 1043 hotel rooms and 1159 cabin units. *Note:* All accommodations must be booked through **AmFac Parks & Resorts.** ~ Yellowstone National Park, WY 82190; 307-344-7311, fax 307-344-7456.

Grant Village, built in 1984, offers 299 standard rooms, all with private bathrooms and showers. Facilities include a dining room and separate steakhouse, a lounge, a gift shop and a guest laundry. Closed late September to late May. ~ West Thumb; 307-344-7311. MODERATE TO DELUXE.

The massive yet rustic **Old Faithful Inn** was acclaimed a National Historic Landmark in 1987. Built of pine logs from the surrounding forests and volcanic rock from a nearby quarry, this 325-room hotel is said to be the largest log structure in the world. The gables on its steeply pitched roof were a trademark of architect Robert Reamer. In the enormous lobby are a stone fireplace and a clock handcrafted from copper, wood and wrought iron. The inn has deluxe-priced suites, moderate-priced rooms with private baths and budget-priced rooms with shared toilets and showers down the hall. Closed mid-October through April. ~ Old Faithful; 307-545-4600. BUDGET TO ULTRA-DELUXE.

From the **Old Faithful Lodge Cabins**, just a couple of hundred yards south of the famous geyser, it seems as if you can reach out and touch the park landmark. The 132 rustic cabins include "pioneer" units, with private toilets and showers, and "budget" units that share a common bathhouse. Closed mid-September to mid-May. ~ Old Faithful; 307-344-7311. BUDGET.

Winter activities in this thermal basin center around the **Old Faithful Snow Lodge & Cabins,** with 69 rooms. Most cabins have private baths; the lodge has rooms with private baths. Closed mid-March to mid-May and early October to mid-December. ~ Old Faithful; 307-344-7311. MODERATE TO DELUXE.

The only other park accommodation open in both winter and summer is the **Mammoth Hot Springs Hotel,** built in 1937, which incorporates a wing of an earlier inn from 1911 (during the heyday of Fort Yellowstone). Its 223 rooms and cabin units come either with (moderate) or without (budget) private baths; four deluxe suite-style cabins have private hot tubs. Facilities include a dining room, fast-food outlet, lounge and gift shop. A decorative highlight is a huge United States map made of 15 woods from nine different countries. Closed early March to mid-May and November to mid-December. ~ Mammoth Hot Springs; 307-344-5400. BUDGET TO ULTRA-DELUXE.

The rustic **Roosevelt Lodge Cabins,** so named because of their proximity to President Teddy Roosevelt's favorite camping areas, have the feel of an earlier era. The 69 cabins are of simple frame construction; some have electric heat and private baths, but most have wood-burning stoves and share a bathhouse. In the main lodge are two stone fireplaces, a family-style restaurant, a lounge and a gift shop. Closed early September to mid-June. ~ Tower Junction; 307-344-7311. BUDGET TO MODERATE.

Not far from the Grand Canyon of the Yellowstone is the 609-room **Canyon Lodge & Cabins.** The two three-story lodges have hotel-style rooms with private baths; cabins are single-story four-plex units, all with private toilets and showers. In the main lodge are a dining room, cafeteria, snack shop, lounge and gift shop.

◆◆◆

WHO'S AFRAID OF THE BIG GRAY WOLF?

When 14 gray wolves from Canada were released in Yellowstone National Park in March 1995, they became the first wolf pack in this ecosystem since the species was exterminated in the 1930s. Having once been regarded as carnivorous villains, wolves were now an endangered species considered vitally important to the natural order. More wolves were released in 1996 and 1997. It is anticipated that two decades must pass before the animals, which are doing well in the northeast part of the park, reestablish stable territories.

Closed late August to early June. ~ Canyon Village; 307-344-7311. BUDGET.

The grande dame of Yellowstone hostelries is the **Lake Yellowstone Hotel & Cabins**. First opened in 1891 and listed on the National Register of Historic Places, the 296-room hotel has been fully renovated and again boasts its long-sequestered 1920s wicker furniture. The Sun Room, which has great lake views (especially at sunrise!), has evening cocktail service and frequent piano or chamber-music performances. Other facilities include a lakeside dining room, deli and gift shop. Guests choose between deluxe hotel rooms, less expensive annex rooms or cabins with private baths. Closed early October to mid-May. ~ Lake Village; 307-344-7311. MODERATE TO DELUXE.

Relax in rocking chairs on the lodge porch of the **Lake Lodge Cabins** to take in a sweeping view of Yellowstone Lake to the east. The Lake Lodge has 186 cabins: some cozy, some spacious, all with private baths. In the classic log lodge are a big fireplace, a cafeteria, a lobby bar and a gift shop. There's also a guest laundry. Closed mid-September to mid-June. ~ Lake Village; 307-344-7311. BUDGET TO MODERATE.

Flagg Ranch Village, located on Rockefeller Parkway between Yellowstone's South Entrance and the north entrance to Grand Teton National Park, has 92 rooms in cabin-like buildings scattered throughout the woods. Open summer (mid-May to mid-October) and winter (mid-December through mid-March) seasons, it's a mecca for anglers, rafters, cross-country skiers and snowmobilers. Facilities include a restaurant (serving three meals a day), cocktail lounge, service station and campground. ~ Route 89/191, Moran; 307-543-2861, fax 307-543-2356. MODERATE.

DINING

Most restaurants within Yellowstone National Park are in the hotels and lodges themselves. Reservations are highly recommended at hotel dining rooms and the Old West Dinner Cookout.

The Lakehouse serves up pizzas, pastas, seafood and chicken entrées along with a sterling view across Yellowstone Lake. Full breakfasts are served as well. ~ Grant Village, West Thumb; 307-344-7311. MODERATE.

The **Old Faithful Inn Dining Room** offers a gourmet menu of prime rib, steak, seafood and poultry beneath the log beams and braces of this immense lodge. Etched glass panels are replicas of carved-wood murals. Three meals a day are served. MODERATE. The hotel's **Pony Express** serves a take-out lunch and dinner menu. ~ Old Faithful Inn, Old Faithful; 307-344-7311. BUDGET.

Fast food, homemade soup and other light fare are the specialties of the **Four Seasons Snack Shop**. ~ Near Old Faithful Snow Lodge, Old Faithful. BUDGET.

Patrons of the **Mammoth Hotel Dining Room** can enjoy three American-style meals a day amid the steaming travertine terraces for which the area is named. ~ Mammoth Hot Springs; 307-344-7311. MODERATE. In the same lodge, **The Terrace Grill** dishes up cafeteria-style fast food and snacks. BUDGET.

For a taste of how things used to be, look no further than the **Old West Dinner Cookout**. Adventurous diners mount horses or clamber aboard a wagon and ride a short distance to Yancey's Hole, where they are served a hearty chuck-wagon dinner of steak, corn, watermelon, baked beans, corn muffins, cole slaw and more. ~ Roosevelt Lodge, Tower Junction; 307-344-7311. MODERATE.

The **Canyon Lodge Dining Room** offers American-style breakfasts and steak-and-seafood dinners daily in a forested setting just a half mile from the north rim of the Grand Canyon of the Yellowstone. ~ Canyon Village; 307-344-7311. MODERATE.

Yellowstone's top-end culinary experience is at the **Lake Yellowstone Hotel Dining Room**. Prime rib, steak, seafood, chicken and vegetarian meals, as well as daily specials, are served in a classic lakeside setting of etched glass and wicker furniture. Breakfast and lunch are also available. ~ Lake Yellowstone Hotel, Lake Village; 307-344-7311. DELUXE.

SHOPPING

Nine of Yellowstone's lodging facilities have gift shops for your souvenir needs. In addition, there's **Hamilton Stores, Inc.** Headquartered in Bozeman and West Yellowstone, Montana, this company operates all general stores, photography shops and tackle shops within the park. That means prices don't differ from one location to another. They're open year-round at Mammoth Hot Springs (307-344-7702) and seasonally at Grant Village (307-242-7390), Old Faithful (307-545-7282 or 307-545-7237), Tower Fall (307-344-7786), Canyon Village (307-242-7377), Fishing Bridge (307-242-7200), Lake Village (307-242-7563) and Bridge Bay (307-242-7326).

NIGHTLIFE

Clearly, no one comes to Yellowstone Park for its nightlife, which is mostly limiting to lounging around a lodge fireplace or swapping stories around a campfire. For more social interaction, there are comfortable lounges with full bar service at Grant Village, Old Faithful Inn, Mammoth Hot Springs Hotel, Roosevelt Lodge, Canyon Lodge, Lake Yellowstone Hotel and Lake Lodge.

YELLOWSTONE NATIONAL PARK

PARKS

Superlatives rule in Yellowstone's 2.2 million acres: the largest and most varied hydrothermal region on earth, the largest lake in North America at so high an elevation (7700 feet), the greatest diversity of wildlife in the Lower 48—the list goes on.

Within the park are nine overnight lodges, 31 restaurants and snack shops, 11 general stores and numerous other shops, 49 picnic areas, restrooms, five visitors centers, two museums, 11 amphitheaters, a marina, 1200 miles of hiking and horse trails with 97 trailheads (permits required on some trails); $20 weekly vehicle pass (includes Grand Teton National Park). Swimming is prohibited in thermal features and discouraged in Yellowstone and other lakes because of the risk of hypothermia from the cold waters. Park fishing permits ($10 for ten days) can be obtained at ranger stations, visitors centers and general stores. Regulations vary in park waters; for example, no fishing is allowed in a six-mile stretch of the Hayden Valley. Boating permits can be obtained at the South Entrance, Lewis Lake campground, Grant Village Backcountry Office, Bridge Bay Marina and the Lake Ranger Station. Cutthroat trout and mountain whitefish are native to Yellowstone waters, and rainbow trout have been introduced to all. ~ There are five park entrances: South (via Route 89/191 from Jackson and Route 287 from Dubois); West (via West Yellowstone, Route 20 from Idaho Falls, Route 191 from Bozeman and Route 287 from Ennis); North (via Gardiner, Route 89 from Livingston); Northeast (via Cooke City, Route 212 from Red Lodge and Billings); and East (Route 14/16/20 from Cody); 307-344-7381.

▲ There are 2189 units (1849 for tents or RVs, 340 for RVs only) at 12 campgrounds (hookups at Fishing Bridge only), plus 300 backcountry campsites (tents only). Numbers of sites, open dates and fees are listed below. National Park Service campgrounds: *Lewis Lake* (85, early June to October 31, $10); *Norris* (116, mid-May to late September, $12); *Indian Creek* (75, early June to mid-September, $10); *Mammoth* (85, year-round, $12); *Tower Fall* (32, mid-May to late September, $10); *Slough Creek* (29, mid-May to October 31, $10); *Pebble Creek* (32, early June to late September, $10). AmFac Parks and Resorts campgrounds: *Grant Village* (425, mid-June to late October, $15); *Madison* (280, early May to late October, $15); *Canyon* (271, early June to early September, $15); *Bridge Bay* (429, mid-May to mid-September, $15; reservations for stays from early June to Labor Day through AmFac Parks and Resorts [P.O. Box 165, Yellowstone National Park, WY 82190; 307-344-7311]); *Fishing Bridge* (340, RVs only, full hookups, mid-May to mid-September, $27). Funding restrictions may force the National Park Service to temporarily close down some of these campgrounds or raise their fees significantly.

WINEGAR HOLE WILDERNESS 🚶 🐎 🛶 ⏛ A tiny (by wilderness standards), 11,000-acre grizzly-bear sanctuary, Winegar Hole is bordered by Yellowstone National Park to the north and Idaho to the west. It comprises a mountain wetland pockmarked with small lakes and streams, rich in natural vegetation. Access is difficult, as only two small trails penetrate the wilderness. ~ The most direct trail is off Targhee National Forest Road 124, which turns off Cave Falls Road 22 miles east of Ashton, Idaho. Forest Road 261 traces the southern boundary of the wilderness; 208-354-2431.

▲ Primitive only.

Just outside the three Montana entrances to Yellowstone National Park are a handful of small towns that serve a year-round coterie of tourists and outdoor-sports lovers. They are West Yellowstone, at the park's west entrance; Gardiner, at the north entrance; and Cooke City and Silver Gate, at the northeast entrance.

Montana Gateway Communities

WEST YELLOWSTONE With about 900 full-time residents, West Yellowstone is the park's primary "suburb," as it were. Founded in 1909 as a Union Pacific railroad terminus where Yellowstone visitors could transfer to stagecoaches for their tour of the national park, it gradually grew into the tourism- and outdoor recreation-focused community it is today.

SIGHTS

The train stopped running to West Yellowstone as private automobiles came into common use after World War II. The imposing stone Union Pacific Depot, damaged by the massive 7.1-magnitude 1959 earthquake but restored in 1972, is now the **Museum of the Yellowstone**. Permanent displays on regional history and wildlife are complemented by annually changing exhibits; there's also a bookstore and a theater showing documentary videos. Closed November through March. Admission. ~ Yellowstone and Canyon avenues, West Yellowstone; 406-646-7814.

Almost across the street, the **Yellowstone IMAX Theatre** presents *Yellowstone* on its six-story screen with Dolby sound, as well as three to five other films, which change from year to year. The films are shown hourly from June through September; times vary the rest of the year. Admission. ~ 101 South Canyon Street, West Yellowstone; 406-646-4100.

Next door to the theater, on the south side, is the **Grizzly Discovery Center** where visitors can observe the natural behavior of grizzly bears in an outdoor viewing area constructed with minimal barriers. Several bears reside here; they have been orphaned, born in captivity or taken in as a habitual "problem" bear. The center also has museum displays and a gift shop. Admission. ~ Canyon Street, West Yellowstone; 406-646-7001.

North of West Yellowstone, two miles up Route 287, is the **Interagency Aerial Fire Control Center**, where summer visitors can make reservations for a facility tour, including a closer look at smokejumping techniques. Closed October through May. ~

Route 287 at the Yellowstone Airport, West Yellowstone; 406-646-7691.

The **West Yellowstone Visitor Information Center**, open year-round, is one of the most comprehensive you'll find. Besides providing basic information on West Yellowstone and the national park, chamber-of-commerce representatives locate lodging for tourists who arrive without reservations, and forest rangers advise on nearby camping when "Full" signs cover the campground board at Yellowstone's west entrance. Reduced hours in fall and winter. ~ 100 Yellowstone Avenue, West Yellowstone; 406-646-7701; www.wyellowstone.com.

After Yellowstone, the world's most active thermal areas are in Iceland, New Zealand, Chile and Russia's Kamchatka Peninsula.

One of the most popular places to send campers is **Hebgen Lake**, less than five miles northwest of the town. Numerous recreation areas and campgrounds speckle the south and west shores of the 15-mile-long lake, created by the damming of the Madison River. Hebgen is especially popular among boaters, fishermen and wildlife watchers, who keep their eyes peeled for moose and trumpeter swans. The great earthquake of August 17, 1959, had its epicenter just west of Hebgen Lake. The tremor dropped Hebgen's north shore 18 feet and caused a landslide that blocked the Madison River canyon, forging adjacent Quake Lake. Twenty-eight campers died. The **Madison Canyon Earthquake Area and Visitor Center**, at the west end of Quake Lake, commemorates the epicenter of the earthquake. Closed September to Memorial Day. ~ Route 287; 406-646-7369.

GARDINER Located astride the Yellowstone River just five miles north of Mammoth Hot Springs, Gardiner began life as an entertainment boom town for soldiers stationed at Mammoth in the late 19th century. By the time the army turned over its responsibilities to the National Park Service during World War I, the saloons, gambling halls and cigar factory were less important to Gardiner than its position as a terminus for the Yellowstone rail spur from Livingston. As at West Yellowstone, tourists changed from train coaches to stagecoaches at Gardiner to explore the park.

Today, more than one million visitors a year stream through the Roosevelt Arch to the north entrance, the only park entrance open year-round. The town, while retaining some of its Wild West flavor, has a tidy tourist infrastructure of motels, restaurants, bars, a cinema and plenty of outfitters. For more information contact the **Chamber of Commerce**. ~ P.O. Box 81, Gardiner, MT 59030; 406-848-7971; www.gomontana.com/gardinerchamber.html.

HIDDEN ▶

Six miles northeast of Gardiner on a rutted dirt road is the old mining village of **Jardine**, where prospectors struck gold in 1866. Various century-old mining structures can be seen by ambitious visitors to this not-quite-a-ghost town: Since 1989, the Mineral Hill Mine has pulled about 42,000 ounces of gold a year from the side of Palmer Mountain. The mine is now defunct. ~ Forest Road 493.

THE BEARTOOTH PLATEAU   Yellowstone's northeastern gateway route is the **Beartooth Highway** (Route 212 West). Officially opened in 1936, this 70-mile designated scenic byway through Custer and Shoshone national forests and Red Lodge, Montana, has been called "the most beautiful drive in America" by CBS television correspondent Charles Kuralt. The trip through isolated Cooke City to the park entrance may take up to three hours because of the highway's elevation (nearly 11,000 feet at its high point) and its prodigious number of switchbacks.

But *breathtaking* is not the only descriptive word that applies here. Numerous trails leave the highway to enter the Beartooth Plateau portion of the **Absaroka-Beartooth Wilderness**. Nearly a million acres in size, this wilderness area includes some two dozen mountains over 12,000 feet in elevation. Traveling around the rim and over the top of the Beartooth Plateau, visitors get spectacular vistas across magnificent glaciated peaks and pristine alpine lakes.

Snow stays late and returns early, so the Beartooth Highway is normally open only from June to the middle of October. That leaves **Cooke City**, four miles from Yellowstone's northeast entrance, in peaceful seclusion for most of the year. Only a few hundred people live here and in the hamlet of **Silver Gate**, three miles west. From mid-October through May, the towns are only reachable from via Mammoth Hot Springs and Tower Junction.

Cooke City is perhaps best regarded as a stepping-off point for wilderness excursions. There's fishing, hunting and mountain climbing in the adjacent mountains, as well as horseback and backpacking trips. The town also has a **Yellowstone Wildlife Museum** that displays more than 100 animals and birds in lifelike dioramas. Closed October through Memorial Day. Admission. ~ Route 212; 406-838-2265. For more information, contact the **Cooke City Chamber of Commerce**. ~ P.O. Box 1071, Cooke City, MT 59020; 406-838-2272, 406-838-2495.

Of particular note is the 14-mile trail to **Grasshopper Glacier**   ◀ HIDDEN in the Absaroka-Beartooth Wilderness Area. The glacier, one of the largest ice fields in the contiguous United States, takes its name from the millions of grasshoppers (of a now-extinct species) frozen in a sheer 80-foot cliff of glacial ice. Nearby is **Granite Peak**, at 12,799 feet Montana's tallest.

In 1996, U.S. President Bill Clinton negotiated a solution to a potential environmental crisis that had made Cooke City a center of discussion in the northern Rockies for many years. A Canadian mining conglomerate obtained rights to Custer National Forest land just outside the Absaroka-Beartooth Wilderness Area, two and a half miles from Yellowstone Park, and planned to begin extracting gold, silver and copper from 10,000-foot Crown Butte. Led by the Bozeman-based Greater Yellowstone Coalition, conservationists maintained that mining in so fragile an ecosystem would severely pollute three major tributaries of the Yellowstone River, all of which have their sources on or near Crown Butte. Clinton, a regular visitor to nearby Jackson Hole, Wyoming, succeeded in trading land in less sensitive precincts for the Beartooth Plateau property.

LODGING   Doing Yellowstone on the cheap? The **Madison Hotel Youth Hostel** is a good place to start. Open Memorial Day weekend to October 10, the hotel can accommodate two dozen backpackers in dormitories and hotel and motel rooms. Shared facilities include toilets and showers, a TV lounge and a coffee bar. There's no kitchen, unfortunately. ~ 139 Yellowstone Avenue, West Yellowstone; 406-646-7745, 800-838-7745, fax 406-646-9766; www. wyellowstone.com/madisonhotel. BUDGET TO MODERATE.

West Yellowstone's best bet is the **Travelers Lodge**. This two-story motor hotel has 46 rooms of varying sizes: from small units by the park entrance to suites with king-size beds. All have TVs and room safes; some have refrigerators. Facilities include a sauna, a whirlpool, a heated pool, and a coin laundry. In winter, the lodge offers snowmobile rentals. ~ 225 Yellowstone Avenue, West Yellowstone; 406-646-9561, fax 406-646-4478. MODERATE.

The **Yellowstone Inn** is one of the nicest motels around. A shingle-roofed lodging with a rock facade and a balcony that surrounds its large, knotty pine–paneled lobby and stone fireplace, it looks as if it came straight out of a storybook. The 87 guest rooms are cozy but nicely decorated. The inn has an upscale dining room, coffee shop, casino-lounge, spa and sauna, and guest laundry. ~ 209 Madison Avenue, West Yellowstone; 406-646-7381, 800-842-2882, fax 406-646-9575; www.yellowstoneinn. com. MODERATE TO DELUXE.

Sleepy Hollow Lodge serves as the home away from home for countless anglers and vacationing families. Thirteen log cabins are appointed with handmade furniture, refrigerators and coffeemakers; some are equipped with kitchens. Call for winter hours. ~ 134 Electric Street, West Yellowstone; 406-646-7707; www. wyellowstone.com/sleepyhollow. MODERATE.

Six miles north of Mammoth Hot Springs, the two-story **Yellowstone Village Motel** is all rustic wood on the outside but virtually brand-new inside (it opened in 1992). The guest rooms include 43 standard-size units and three family condominium suites with full kitchens. The motel also has an indoor pool and sauna and a guest laundry. ~ Route 89 North, Gardiner; 406-848-7417,

800-228-8158, fax 406-848-7118; www.gomontana.com/yellow stoneinn.html. MODERATE.

In Cooke City, the **Soda Butte Lodge** has a little of everything. Most of the 32 rooms have queen-size or double beds; all have full baths and Western-style decor. Family suites are also available. The lodge restaurant is open for three meals daily, and there's a casino, hot tub and heated indoor pool. Snowmobile rentals are available. ~ Route 212, Cooke City; 406-838-2251, 800-527-6462, fax 406-838-2253. MODERATE TO DELUXE.

Regional game dishes—including elk and buffalo—are available outside the park's west entrance at the **Rustler's Roost**, in the Big Western Pine Motel. Rainbow trout, chicken and prime rib are also on the menu at this family establishment, which offers a soup-and-salad bar and a children's menu as well. Three meals a day during summer. ~ 234 Firehole Avenue, West Yellowstone; 406-646-7622. MODERATE.

DINING

The **Three Bear Restaurant**, located in a motor lodge of the same name, serves breakfasts and dinners daily from mid-May to mid-October and from mid-December through mid-March. The nonsmoking, family-style restaurant touts its salad bar, prime rib and homemade pastries. The Grizzly Lounge is attached. ~ 306 Yellowstone Avenue, West Yellowstone; 406-646-7811. BUDGET TO DELUXE.

Alice's Restaurant is eight miles west of the park entrance on Route 20, but many folks find it worth the drive for its old-time gas station atmosphere and menu of roadside standards like rib-eye steak and turkey dinners. The restaurant is located at the foot of the Continental Divide just east of the Idaho border. Closed mid-October through December. ~ 1545 Targhee Pass Highway, West Yellowstone; 406-646-7296. MODERATE.

◄ **HIDDEN**

At the north entrance of the park, the **Yellowstone Mine Restaurant**, in the Best Western by Mammoth Hot Springs, offers a fine steak-and-seafood menu amid the re-created ambience of a 19th-century mine. There's a children's menu, and breakfast is served as well. The Rusty Bale Lounge is adjacent. ~ Route 89 at Hellroaring Street, Gardiner; 406-848-7336. DELUXE.

Beyond the park's remote northeast corner is **Joan & Bill's Restaurant**, certainly a throwback to another era. Three meals are served daily in a relaxed and rustic family-style atmosphere in the heart of the old mining town of Cooke City. Closed September through December and April to late May. ~ Route 212; 406-838-2280. BUDGET TO ULTRA-DELUXE.

Outside the park's west entrance in West Yellowstone, check out **Eagle's Store** for Western wear, outdoor equipment and American Indian crafts. Closed April and November. ~ 3 Canyon Street;

SHOPPING

406-646-9300. The **Madison Gift Shop** has a large selection of souvenirs. Closed October 10 through Memorial Day. ~ 139 Yellowstone Avenue; 406-646-7745. **Oak N Pine** is renowned for its custom lodge-style furniture and handmade quilts. Closed mid-October through December. ~ 120 Canyon Street; 406-646-9657. The **Book Peddler** carries volumes about the West as well as espresso and baked goods. ~ 106 Canyon Street; 406-646-9358.

In Gardiner, **Kellem's Montana Saddlery** may be the most intriguing store outside the north entrance; its inventory runs from handmade saddles and other cowboy gear to clothing, silver jewelry and Montana-made gifts. ~ 222 Main Street, Gardiner; 406-848-7776. The **Yellowstone Outpost Mall** puts ten shops, restaurants and the Chamber of Commerce under one roof at the north end of town. ~ Route 89 at Hellroaring Street; 406-848-7220. For reading material and espresso, try **High Country Books**. ~ Park Street; 406-848-7707.

NIGHTLIFE   Theater is growing in popularity in the gateway communities. West Yellowstone, in fact, has two stages. The **Playmill Theatre** has presented a summer season of melodrama and musical comedy since 1964. Admission. ~ 29 Madison Avenue, West Yellowstone; 406-646-7757.

For pure imbibing, travel nine miles north of West Yellowstone on Route 191 (just past the Route 287 junction) to **Eino's Tavern**, which has a grill alongside Hebgen Lake, big-screen TV and even fuel for snowmobilers. Closed for two weeks after Thanksgiving. ~ 8955 Gallatin Road, West Yellowstone; 406-646-9344.

The most historic bar in the greater Yellowstone area is Gardiner's **Two-Bit Saloon**, a mining-era relic that is open 18 hours a day. Occasional live bands. Occasional cover. ~ Route 89, Gardiner; 406-848-7743.

PARKS   **HENRY'S LAKE STATE PARK** 🚶 🚲 🎣 ⛺ 🛥 🏊 ⛵
Henry's Lake is a quiet mountain oasis just 15 miles west of West Yellowstone, on the Idaho side of Targhee Pass. Sheltered on three sides by the Continental Divide, the lake fills an alpine valley of about 12 square miles. The 585-acre park, on the southeast shore near its outlet to Henry's Fork of the Snake River, is ideal for trout-fishing enthusiasts. There are picnic areas and restrooms. Closed November through mid-May. Day-use fee, $3. ~ From West Yellowstone, take Route 20 west 13 miles to Henry's Lake Road; turn west two miles to the park entrance; 208-558-7532.

▲ There are 45 RV/tent sites, 28 with hookups; $16 per night for RVs, $12 for tents; 15-day maximum stay. Closed November to Memorial Day.

ABSAROKA-BEARTOOTH WILDERNESS AREA 🏃🏇🚵🎣

Abutting Yellowstone National Park on its northern edge, and nearly half as large as the park itself, this 944,000-acre wilderness comprises two distinctly different mountain ranges: in its western half, the rugged, forested Absarokas; in the east, near Red Lodge, the alpine meadows and plateaus of the Beartooths. Several Absaroka peaks top 11,000 feet, but more than two dozen Beartooth summits exceed 12,000, including Granite Peak, Montana's highest mountain at 12,799 feet. A unique feature is the Grasshopper Glacier, a remote ice field named for the millions of ancient grasshoppers frozen into the face of a sheer 80-foot ice cliff. Seven species of trout inhabit the small lakes of the Beartooth Plateau. The wilderness features nearly 1000 alpine lakes and more than 700 miles of hiking trails. Horseback riders are welcome; vehicles are not. ~ The Absaroka-Beartooth has many gateways, including Mill Creek Road, off Route 89 south of Livingston; the Boulder River road from McLeod, south of Big Timber; East and West Rosebud roads, off Route 78 south of Absarokee; and Route 212 (the Beartooth Highway) southwest of Red Lodge; 406-222-1892.

> The highest elevation in Yellowstone Park is Eagle Peak, 11,358 feet, located in the Absaroka Range on the park's southeast boundary.

▲ Primitive only.

Outdoor Adventures

FISHING

Within the boundaries of Yellowstone National Park, all anglers regardless of residency must buy a ten-day park license, which costs $10. Anyone fishing elsewhere in Wyoming must obtain a state license: Contact the **Wyoming Game and Fish Division**. ~ 5400 Bishop Boulevard, Cheyenne, WY 82006; 307-777-4600, 307-733-2321. If you're planning to fish outside park boundaries in Montana, you'll need a license for that state: Contact the **Montana Department of Fish, Wildlife & Parks**. ~ 1420 East 6th Avenue, Helena, MT 59620; 406-444-2535.

Yellowstone Lake is renowned for its cutthroat trout, as is the upper portion of the Yellowstone River between Fishing Bridge and the Hayden Valley. Rainbow and brook trout and grayling are native to waters on the west side of the Continental Divide, including Shoshone and Lewis lakes, the Gallatin and Madison rivers and their tributaries, and Hebgen Lake, outside the park near West Yellowstone, Montana.

Within the park, you can buy or rent complete fishing gear at marinas on Yellowstone Lake; guides are generally available at the marinas as well. **Bridge Bay Marina** rents rods and reels. ~ Bridge Bay Marina; 307-344-7381. Or try **Grant Village** for your supplies. ~ West Thumb; 307-242-3400. Tackle is also available at **Hamilton Stores** located throughout the park. ~ Mammoth Hot Springs; 307-344-7702.

Outfitters in the gateway communities include **Bud Lilly's Trout Shop**, a full-blown fly shop that offers guide services and organizes trips. ~ 39 Madison Avenue, West Yellowstone, MT; 406-646-7801. Or try **Jacklin's Outfitters for the World of Fly Fishing** for trout guides. ~ 105 Yellowstone Avenue, West Yellowstone, MT; 406-646-7336. **Parks' Fly Shop** also has fishing equipment, guides and information. ~ 2nd Street, Gardiner, MT; 406-848-7314.

BOATING

Yellowstone Lake marinas offer full boat-rental services and guided lake trips. Forty-passenger excursion boats leave the **Bridge Bay Marina** several times daily on lake cruises; there are also twilight trips and individual motorboat rentals. Closed October through May. ~ Bridge Bay; 307-344-7381. Ranger stations provide boat-operating permits on request.

RIVER RUNNING

Most Yellowstone National Park streams, and some lakes, are closed to all boats. Shoshone Lake, as well as the South, South East and Flat Mountain arms of Yellowstone Lake, are restricted to "hand-propelled" vessels: canoes, kayaks and rowboats.

The best place for canoeing is the Lewis River Channel, which connects Shoshone and Lewis lakes; launch your craft from the northeastern shore of Lewis Lake, off the park highway south of West Thumb, and follow the shoreline west to the channel.

The best rivers in the greater Yellowstone area for whitewater rafting and kayaking are the Snake, south of Jackson, and the Gallatin, north of Yellowstone in Montana. For tranquil float trips or easy canoeing with spectacular scenery and abundant wildlife, it is hard to top the upper Snake River through Grand Teton National Park.

Most of the rafting outfitters that operate in the Montana rivers north of Yellowstone are based in Bozeman, Livingston or Big Sky. An exception is the **Yellowstone Raft Company**, which runs the Yellowstone, Gallatin and other rivers on the north side of the park. ~ P.O. Box 46, Gardiner, MT 59030; 406-848-7777.

RIDING STABLES

Three stables in Yellowstone National Park offer park visitors ample opportunities for one- and two-hour guided rides in off-the-road wilderness. Private outfitters throughout the region provide many more options. Half-day, full-day and extended overnight trips are available. Some outfitters offer riding lessons; more commonly, novice riders will be matched with gentler horses.

One- and two-hour guided trail rides depart from corrals at **Mammoth Hot Springs** (307-344-5400), **Roosevelt Lodge** (307-

Winter
Wonderland

The natural wonders of Yellowstone National Park are more spectacular in winter than in summer. Imagine, for instance, the steam from hot springs and geysers filling the frigid Rocky Mountain air as snow falls all around.

From mid-December to mid-March, Yellowstone is a paradise for cross-country skiers, snowmobilers and snowshoers. Although the park is accessible by car only at its north entrance, via Gardiner, Montana (this route, through Mammoth Hot Springs to Tower Junction and Cooke City, Montana, on the Beartooth Plateau, is kept open year-round) there are other ways to get there.

Heated ten-passenger snowcoaches run from the south and west entrances and from Mammoth Hot Springs. **AmFac Parks and Resorts** coaches depart from the south entrance for Old Faithful every afternoon, returning every morning. ~ Mammoth Hot Springs; 307-344-7311. Similar trips connect Old Faithful and Canyon Village with West Yellowstone and Mammoth Hot Springs. Other snowcoaches are run by **Yellow Alpen Guides**. ~ 555 Yellowstone Avenue, West Yellowstone; 406-646-9591.

Mammoth Hot Springs Hotel and Old Faithful Snow Lodge are the only park accommodations open during winter, although warming huts throughout the park provide shelter. Like the rest of the park, Old Faithful can be reached only across snow. But like the Mammoth hotel, the Snow Lodge serves three good meals daily and offers both nordic skiing and snowshoeing equipment rentals and lessons. It's a good base for winter exploration of the park.

Hundreds of miles of cross-country ski trails are marked in Yellowstone, and the most popular are groomed. Maps are available at visitors centers.

Just outside the park boundaries, West Yellowstone's **Rendezvous Ski Trails** offer 30 kilometers of groomed trails. The U.S. national cross-country and biathlon (skiing and shooting) teams train here each year. ~ 406-646-7701. **Yellowstone Expeditions** leads cross-country skiing tours through Yellowstone from their yurt camp. ~ P.O. Box 865, West Yellowstone, MT 59758; 406-646-9333, 800-728-9333. For ski, pole and boot rentals call **Freeheel & Wheel**. ~ 40 Yellowstone Avenue, West Yellowstone; 406-646-7744.

Much to the chagrin of cross-country skiers and other "purists," snowmobiling has become the sport of choice of many winter visitors to Yellowstone National Park. Snowmobiles are restricted to 300 miles of park roads, groomed daily. Expect a four-foot snowpack beside highways. AmFac Parks and Resorts rents snowmobiles with helmets and all appropriate clothing.

Ice skaters enjoy the **Mammoth Hot Springs Hotel**, which has an outdoor rink with skate rentals. ~ Mammoth Hot Springs; 307-344-5400.

344-5273) and **Canyon Village** throughout the day. Roosevelt visitors can also ride to Yancey's Hole for an Old West dinner cookout or hop aboard a horse-drawn stagecoach for half-hour rambles around the Tower Junction area. Schedules vary; the summer riding season is longest at lower-lying Mammoth than at the other two sites.

Families with tiny tots can enjoy a trail ride through Gallatin National Forest with **Diamond P Ranch**. Closed December through April. ~ 2865 Targhee Pass Highway, West Yellowstone, MT; 406-646-7246.

PACK TRIPS & LLAMA TREKS   Contact **Hell's a Roarin' Outfitters**, who have more than 300 horses in their stables. Closed September through May. ~ Route 89 North, Gardiner, MT; 406-848-7578. **Wilderness Connection** is another option, with horseback treks to prime fishing spots in the Yellowstone backcountry. ~ 21 Shooting Star Road, Gardiner, MT; 406-848-7287. **Beartooth Plateau Outfitters** specializes in five-day-long fishing trips on horseback from June through September; all supplies and gear are included. ~ Main Street, Cooke City, MT; 406-838-2328, 800-253-8545. Visitors centers can offer extensive lists of additional outfitters serving the nearby Absaroka-Beartooth and other wilderness areas.

The llama is more a hiking companion than a mode of transportation; it carries all the gear while you proceed on foot. Guided four- and five-day llama treks through Yellowstone Park, mid-July through September, are the specialty of **Jackson Hole Llamas**. Routes range from easy to strenuous. ~ P.O. Box 12500, Jackson, WY 83002; 800-830-7316. Llama trekking through backcountry Yellowstone, the Crazy Mountains and the Tobacco Root Range is also offered by **Yellowstone Llamas**. ~ P.O. Box 5042, Bozeman, MT 59717; 406-586-6872, fax 406-586-9612; e-mail llamas@mcn.net.

BIKING   Bicycling through Yellowstone can be an exhilarating experience, but it is not without peril. For the most part, there are no bicycle lanes along park roads, and because roads are narrow and winding, high-visibility clothing, helmets and rear-view mirrors are recommended. Essential accessories include a small tool kit and a first-aid kit. Keep an eye out for campers and RVs passing you from behind; their projecting mirrors pose a particular safety threat. Though a few bike paths do exist around park communities, bicycles are not permitted on boardwalks or backcountry trails.

Bike Rentals   A good full-service bicycle shop is **Yellowstone Bicycles**. ~ 132 Madison Avenue, West Yellowstone, MT; 406-646-7815. The full-service **Freeheel & Wheel** rents mountain, tour and kid's bikes that come with helmets. ~ 40 Yellowstone Avenue, West Yellowstone; 406-646-7744.

The greater Yellowstone ecosystem is one of the most environmentally remarkable in North America, with its mountains and river canyons, hot springs and alpine meadows, and its vast array of wildlife. Hikers can access the backcountry in a way that drivers never will. And in adjacent national forests, they have the opportunity to stay in several dozen recreational cabins available (by reservation) from the U.S. Forest Service at a cost of $15 to $30 per night. Contact specific National Forest offices.

HIKING

Following are a few of the region's more popular trails. All distances listed are one way unless otherwise noted.

YELLOWSTONE NATIONAL PARK   Yellowstone contains more than 1200 miles of marked hiking trails and 97 trailheads. Trails include the boardwalks and handicapped-accessible trails at **Upper Geyser Basin** (Old Faithful), **Norris Geyser Basin** and **Mammoth Hot Springs**, among others.

For youngsters, the **Fountain Paint Pot Nature Trail** (.5 mile) in the Lower Geyser Basin and the **Children's Fire Trail** (.5 mile) east of Mammoth Hot Springs have several interpretive stations to help teach about thermal activity and forest fires, respectively.

Backcountry permits are required for all overnight hikes and some day hikes in Yellowstone Park. They can be obtained from ranger stations or in advance (Backcountry Office, P.O. Box 168, Yellowstone National Park, WY 81290) within 48 hours before you start your hike. They are $15. Topographic maps are sold at Hamilton Stores.

Avalanche Peak Trail (2.5 miles) is a strenuous ascent to a 10,566-foot summit, a mile west of Sylvan Pass on the East Entrance Road. Look for the unsigned trailhead opposite the Eleanor Lake picnic area. The trail transits several eco-zones before achieving the peak, which provides spectacular views across Yellowstone Lake to the Tetons and beyond.

Mount Washburn Trail (3 miles) leads to another panoramic point, but the climb isn't as steep as Avalanche Peak. Bighorn sheep are often seen on top. There are trailheads on the Grand Loop Road (north of Canyon Village) at the Dunraven Pass picnic area and the Chittenden Road parking area.

Seven Mile Hole Trail (5.5 miles) offers an impressive way to see the Grand Canyon of the Yellowstone . . . close up. Beginning on the Inspiration Point spur road a mile east of Canyon Village, it clings to the rim of the gorge for the first mile and a half, then swings into the pine forest and drops rapidly for three miles to the canyon floor near Sulphur Creek. Perhaps needless to say, the return climb is harder than the descent.

Bechler River Trail (32 miles) traverses the park's rarely visited southwest corner. It begins at Old Faithful, crosses the Continental Divide three times and then descends steep-sided Bechler Canyon, passing dazzling waterfalls and hot springs. The trail crosses Bechler Meadows, a low-lying haven for moose, black bear and trumpeter swans, and ends at Bechler River Ranger Station, off Cave Falls Road 25 miles east of Ashton, Idaho. Moderate.

WEST YELLOWSTONE AREA   The **Skyline Ridge Trail** (21 miles) transits the Cabin Creek Recreation and Wildlife Management Area north of Hebgen Lake. This track, which follows the base of a 10,000-foot ridge across an alpine meadow, is reached via Forest Road 986 (off Route 191) or Forest Road 985 (off Route 287). Difficult.

▼▼▼▼▼▼▼▼▼▼▼
Transportation

Interstate highways surround, but don't invade, northwestern Wyoming. A broad choice of highways provide easy access from all directions, however: No fewer than seven routes meet in Yellowstone National Park.

CAR

To reach Yellowstone, take **Route 89/191** north from Jackson; **Route 14/16/20** west from Cody; **Route 212** southwest off Route 90 near Billings, Montana; **Route 89** south at Livingston, Montana, or **Route 191** south at Bozeman, Montana, off 90; **Route 287** southeast off 90 near Butte, Montana; or **Route 20** northeast off **Route 15** at Idaho Falls.

AIR

The region's primary airport is in Jackson. West Yellowstone is served by commuter airlines in summer.

Jackson Hole Airport has regular daily nonstop arrivals from and departures to Denver and Salt Lake City, with connecting flights from many other cities. It is served by American Airlines, SkyWest Airlines, United and United Express. Regional charters and scenic flights are available at the aviation center adjacent to the airport.

From May to September, the **West Yellowstone Airport**, near the west entrance to Yellowstone Park, is served by regular SkyWest commuter flights and by charters. The airport closes from mid-October to mid-May.

Limousines and taxis take visitors to and from the airports. In Jackson, call **All Star Taxis**, especially if you need a longer ride. ~ 307-733-2888. Or try **Buckboard Cab**. ~ 307-733-1112. In West Yellowstone, call **The 4 by 4 Stage**. ~ 406-388-6404, 800-517-8243.

BUS

Greyhound Bus Lines serves West Yellowstone, Montana (between Idaho Falls, Idaho, and Bozeman, Montana), in summer. ~ 800-231-2222.

Gray Line (800-733-2304) offers seasonal charter service and guided tours through Yellowstone Park. One office is in Jackson Hole. ~ 330 North Glenwood Street, Jackson; 307-733-4324. Another is in West Yellowstone. ~ 633 Madison Avenue, West Yellowstone; 406-646-9374.

Access Tours offer multiday van tours of the northwestern Wyoming region and elsewhere in the Rockies for travelers with disabilities. ~ Both at P.O. Box 2985, Jackson, WY 83001; 307-733-6664.

Rental agencies at the Jackson Hole Airport are **Alamo Rent A Car** (800-327-9633), **Avis Rent A Car** (800-331-1212), **Budget Rent A Car** (800-527-0700) and **Hertz Rent A Car** (800-654-3131). **CAR RENTALS**

In West Yellowstone, you'll find **Avis Rent A Car** (800-331-1212) at the Yellowstone Airport. **Big Sky** (429 Yellowstone Avenue; 406-646-9564) and **Budget Rent A Car** (131 Dunraven Street; 800-527-0700) are in town.

Guided all-day motorcoach tours of Yellowstone National Park are offered from various park lodgings by **AmFac Parks and Resorts**. ~ 307-344-7311. **PUBLIC TRANSIT**

THREE

Jackson Hole and the Tetons

Recipe for a great trip: Start with what may be North America's most spectacular mountain range, the Tetons. Add generous portions of history and culture, from Shoshone Indians and "mountain men" to John D. Rockefeller, Jr. Mix with the Old West flavor of a bustling modern resort town. Liberally season with fishing, hiking, skiing, rafting, horseback riding and other outdoor activities. Stir in a dash of rodeo and guest ranches. Garnish with the dramatic scenery and rich wildlife of the world's oldest and best-known national park, Yellowstone, little more than an hour's drive up the road. *Voila!* You have Jackson Hole. Come prepared with an appetite for adventure.

The glories of this corner of the earth weren't lost on several thousand Teton and Wind River Shoshone Indians, who traditionally wintered in the Snake and Green river valleys but found a fertile hunting ground in Jackson Hole and other mountain dales after the annual snowmelt. The intrepid John Colter, who had gone to the Pacific with Lewis and Clark but soloed his return, was apparently the first white man to see Jackson Hole, and the Tetons after he passed through the Yellowstone basin in 1807. It wasn't long before mountain men and fur trappers penetrated the region in search of beaver and other pelts that were earning top dollar on the East Coast. In 1819, French Canadian trappers, with the coarse humor typical of their breed, named the craggy peaks overlooking Jackson Hole *Les Trois Tétons*: "the three breasts."

After 1845, the demand for furs diminished, the trappers moved out, and northwestern Wyoming briefly settled back into splendid isolation. The remoteness of the Teton country left it relatively un-pioneered until the end of the century, and even today its population remains sparse. Jackson, the "metropolis" of the region, has only about 5000 year-round residents.

Despite the town's relatively small size, no other community in the northern Rockies is as much of a tourist mecca. (There are some 2700 hotel rooms in Jackson alone, with another 1300 in the surrounding valley and Grand Teton National

Park. By contrast, Boise, Idaho, with a county population 20 times that of Jackson and Teton County, has about the same number.)

Jackson is a perfect place to begin a vacation in northwestern Wyoming. Situated in the shadow of the Tetons at the southern gateway to Yellowstone, it is surrounded by year-round recreational sites, including one of North America's leading ski resorts. The town itself is the very embodiment of an Old West town in the late 20th century, with mock gunfights in the streets, barstool saddles in the saloons and a seemingly endless choice of fine shops and restaurants.

North of Jackson is Grand Teton National Park, climaxed by the remarkable spire of the 13,772-foot Grand Teton itself. A half-dozen pristine piedmont lakes nestle at the foot of the peaks, framing the reflections of their glaciated summits in eternally green pine forests. But whereas Yellowstone Park can be seen fairly easily by driving, the best features of Grand Teton require getting out of your car and walking . . . or at the very least, going for a horse or boat ride. This is no place to be timorous.

▼▼▼▼▼▼▼▼▼▼

Jackson Hole

Let's start from the top: Jackson Hole is the valley. Jackson is the town. Framed on the west by the Tetons and on the east by the Gros Ventre Range, Jackson Hole (a name bestowed by early-19th-century fur trappers to honor Davey Jackson, a mountain man who trapped in this area during the early 1800s) encompasses about 400 square miles near the headwaters of the Snake River. Lying just west of the Continental Divide, it was created by the same faulting and geological upthrust that is still forcing the Teton Range ever heavenward.

The valley, about 48 miles long, includes the big lakes of Grand Teton National Park as well as Jackson and its smaller neighboring communities. Located at the convergence of trails from seven different passes and canyons, it is near an important annual trade rendezvous site for mountain men, fur traders and American Indians in the 1830s.

Jackson, with an elevation of about 6200 feet, is near the south end of the valley. Ironically, the town is one of the few places within Jackson Hole from which you *cannot* see the Tetons. Low-lying East Gros Ventre Butte effectively shields the community from that northwesterly perspective. Snow King Mountain anchors Jackson on the south; Jackson Peak, in the Gros Ventre Wilderness, rises to the east.

SIGHTS

It's only to the northeast, in the flats of the **National Elk Refuge**, that there's a sense of the broader valley. As many as 9000 American elk winter in the 24,700-acre refuge, which preserves about one-quarter of the original winter Jackson Hole elk range. The elk herd consumes seven to eight pounds of pelleted alfalfa hay per animal each day in the winter, about 30 tons per day for the entire herd for 10 to 11 weeks. In late spring they migrate to the higher alpine meadows of Grand Teton and Yellowstone national parks and adjacent Bridger-Teton National Forest, where they give birth to their young, then return to Jackson Hole in mid-autumn. Although the refuge is open year-round, don't expect to see *Cervus canadensis* if you drive through in summer. (You will, on the other hand, be rewarded with sightings of a wide variety of bird life in the wetlands, perhaps including trumpeter swans.)

The best time to see elk—as well as moose, bison, bighorn sheep and mule deer—is from November through mid-April, when the visitors center is open and guided 40-minute **sleigh rides** take warmly dressed nature lovers to a special viewing area. Admission. Get there by following Broadway east from Jackson Town Square about a mile to its end, just past refuge headquarters; then turn north onto Elk Refuge Road and continue for four miles. ~ Elk Refuge Road; 307-733-3582.

It's no accident that the arches at the four corners of **Jackson Town Square**, in the heart of the town's bustling shopping district, are made up of hundreds of elk antlers. Each spring, local Boy Scouts scour the refuge for antlers shed by adult males . . . who promptly begin growing a new set for the autumn mating season (the elk, not the Scouts). White antlers are used in the arches; others are auctioned to earn money for the Scouts and the refuge, which uses most of the funding to buy supplemental winter feed for the elk.

Another ritual, straight out of the Old West, takes place at the southeast corner of Town Square from Memorial Day to Labor Day. The **Jackson Hole Shootout** climaxes an almost-nightly confrontation (the gunfighters rest on Sundays) that may soon supplant the Hatfield–McCoy vendetta as the nation's longest running feud. Local merchants created the 20-minute show back in 1955. Then, as now, it involves a 6:30 stagecoach robbery, a female hostage, an old grudge, blazing six-guns and perhaps a bad haircut, all portrayed in highly melodramatic fashion by a troupe of about ten local actors and townspeople costumed in 19th-century garb. The irony here, of course, is that Jackson was settled *after* the rough-and-ready era romanticized by filmdom and never experienced the sort of action depicted here.

A good starting point for explorations of Jackson and Jackson Hole, the parklike Town Square (bounded by Broadway and Deloney, Cache and Center streets) is surrounded on all sides by false-fronted shops, restaurants and saloons: like the celebrated **Million Dollar Cowboy Bar** on the west side (of course). With saddles for barstools and silver dollars inlaid into its bar, it was a well-known watering hole long before Clint Eastwood filmed scenes from *Any Which Way You Can* here in the 1970s. ~ 25 North Cache Street, Jackson; 307-733-2207.

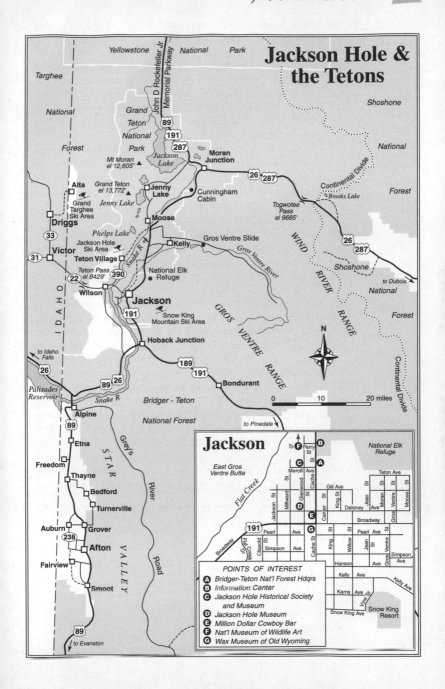

Jackson Hole & the Tetons

Yellowstone National Park

Targhee

National

Forest

Grand Teton National Park

John D Rockefeller Jr Memorial Parkway

Shoshone

89
191
287

Mt Moran el 12,605'

Jackson Lake

Moran Junction

National

26 287

Continental Divide

Brooks Lake

Forest

Alta

Grand Teton el 13,772'

Grand Targhee Ski Area

Driggs

Jenny Lake

Jenny Lake

Cunningham Cabin

Togwotee Pass el 9685'

33

Phelps Lake

Moose

26

287

Victor

Jackson Hole Ski Area

Kelly

Gros Ventre Slide

Gros Ventre River

WIND

Shoshone

31

Teton Village

National

Teton Pass el 8429'

390

National Elk Refuge

to Dubois

RIVER

Forest

22

Wilson

Jackson

GROS

RANGE

Snow King Mountain Ski Area

191

Hoback Junction

VENTRE

N

to Idaho Falls

RANGE

Palisades Reservoir

89 26

189
191

Bondurant

Continental Divide

Alpine

Snake R

Bridger - Teton

0   10   20 miles

89

Etna

National Forest

to Pinedale

Freedom

STAR

Thayne

Bedford

Grey's

Jackson

To F Perry St

B

National Elk Refuge

Turnerville

River

East Gros Ventre Butte

Mercill Ave

C

A

Teton Ave

Auburn

Grover

Flat Creek

St

St

Glenwood

St

Gill Ave

238

VALLEY

Millward

St

D

Center

King St

Deloney

Jean

Ave

Moran

Ventre

Moose

Afton

E

Fairview

Road

Broadway

191

Pearl

Ave

G

St

St

Pearl Ave

St

King

Willow

Jean

Gros Ventre

Smoot

Simpson

Ave

Cache Ave

St

Simpson Ave

Hanson

Ave

89

to Evanston

Kelly

Ave

Karns

Ave

Dr

Kelly Ave

Snow King Ave

Vine

Snow King Resort

POINTS OF INTEREST

A Bridger-Teton Nat'l Forest Hdqrs
B Information Center
C Jackson Hole Historical Society and Museum
D Jackson Hole Museum
E Million Dollar Cowboy Bar
F Nat'l Museum of Wildlife Art
G Wax Museum of Old Wyoming

A block west of Town Square's northwest corner via Deloney Street, the **Jackson Hole Museum** has exhibits depicting the valley's American Indian prehistory and the fur trade and homesteader eras, as well as displays of early cowboy memorabilia and century-old photography. The museum sponsors summer walking tours of an eight-block area of downtown Jackson, including 19 historic buildings, every Tuesday, Thursday and Saturday. Closed October through May. Admission. ~ 105 North Glenwood Street, Jackson; 307-733-2414.

The museum is associated with the **Jackson Hole Historical Society and Museum,** two blocks farther north on Glenwood. The historical center is primarily an archive and research facility, but a few seasonal exhibits are on display here. Closed Saturday and Sunday. ~ 105 West Mercill Street, Jackson; 307-733-9605.

A half-block south of the square, the **Wax Museum of Old Wyoming** contains 27 dioramas illustrating regional history, like Sacajawea guiding the Lewis and Clark expedition and Butch Cassidy and his Wild Bunch counting their take from an 1890s stagecoach robbery. Admission. ~ 55 South Cache Street, Jackson; 307-733-3112.

As you head north from Town Square on Cache Street, you pass on your right, after about two blocks, the **Bridger-Teton National Forest Headquarters**. This is the place to learn about recreational opportunities in the 3.5 million acres of federal land that flank Jackson on the east and south. Bridger-Teton itself, encompassing nearly 1.7 million acres, is the largest national forest in the United States, excluding those of Alaska. ~ 340 North Cache Street, Jackson; 307-739-5500. About two blocks farther is the modern **Jackson Hole and Greater Yellowstone Information Center,** operated by the Jackson Hole Chamber of Commerce. The center has some interesting displays on the region's natural attractions, as well as a lodging reservation service and more brochures than any traveler truly needs. ~ 532 North Cache Street, Jackson; 307-733-3316; www.jacksonholechamber.com.

ANTLERS ON AUCTION

On the third Saturday in May, Jackson hosts an elk-antler auction to earn money for the Boy Scouts and the U.S. Fish and Wildlife Service. An elk antler weighs an average of 10 to 12 pounds and can be expected to bring $100 or more; the take can exceed $75,000. The principal buyers are Chinese and Koreans, who powder the antlers and sell them as aphrodisiacs in Asian herbalists' shops. Craftspeople and Western export houses also are leading bidders.

It's three miles from Town Square to the excellent **National Museum of Wildlife Art** housed in a rock castle that overlooks the elk refuge. Considered America's finest public collection of fine art devoted specifically to animals and birds, the museum was established in downtown Jackson in 1987 before moving to this magnificent 51,000-square-foot facility in 1994. Fourteen galleries showcase original works by such noted artists as John J. Audubon, Robert Bateman, Albert Bierstadt, Karl Bodmer, George Catlin, John Clymer, Charles Russell, Carl Rungius, Conrad Schwiering and Ernest Thompson Seton. There are also contemporary and historic photography displays, an outdoor sculpture garden and traveling exhibits whose subjects range from 19th-century African wildlife to Navajo weaving. The museum contains a children's activity center, a café, a bookstore and gift shop, an auditorium, film and research libraries. Admission. ~ Rungius Road, Jackson; 307-733-5771.

A few miles farther, the northward highway enters the domain (but not the fee area) of Grand Teton National Park. Turn off the highway at Gros Ventre Junction (about seven miles from Jackson), to reach the tiny community of **Kelly**. The town, a ranching center established around the turn of the century, was vying with Jackson to become the Teton County seat until natural disaster played its hand in 1925. Just five miles east of Kelly in Bridger-Teton National Forest, the **Gros Ventre Slide** dumped 50 million cubic yards of sandstone—the entire north slope of Sheep Mountain—into the Gros Ventre River, damming the stream in minutes and creating five-mile-long Lower Slide Lake. Two years later, part of the natural dam collapsed, sending a wall of water, mud and rock upon Kelly and wiping the town off the map. Six people and hundreds of animals died.

Today, the partially reconstructed village is the home of the **Teton Science School**, which offers summer adult seminars in areas such as natural history and nature photography. Its **Murie Memorial Museum**, which displays thousands of mammal, bird and plant specimens collected by field biologists, is open by appointment only. ~ 1 Ditch Creek Road, Kelly; 307-733-4765.

The Gros Ventre River—the name, incidentally, is pronounced "Grovont," and is a French trapper-ism meaning "big belly"— traces the northern boundary of the **Gros Ventre Wilderness,** one of three wilderness areas within Bridger-Teton National Forest.

Jackson Hole has two popular ski resorts and a third nearby. The **Snow King Resort**, established in 1939 as Wyoming's first ski resort, is actually right in Jackson, nine blocks southeast of Town Square. Summer visitors can take a 20-minute chairlift ride to the 7800-foot level of 8420-foot Snow King Mountain, then descend a half-mile through forest and meadow on an alpine slide. A hotel at the foot of the mountain offers riding stables in summer, skiing and skating rentals in winter. Admission for activities. ~ 400 East Snow King Avenue, Jackson; 307-733-5200.

Better known is the **Jackson Hole Mountain Resort**, 12 miles west of Jackson. Its aerial tramway—two and a half miles long—ascends to the crest of 10,450-foot Rendezvous Peak in the Teton Range. The vertical rise of 4139 feet from the valley floor is the greatest of any ski area in the United States. Summer visitors can take the 63-passenger tram to the summit in just 12 minutes and ride or hike down. Admission for activities. ~ Route 390, Teton Village; 307-733-2660.

At the foot of Rendezvous Peak is **Teton Village**, a community that came into its own with the resort's development in the 1960s. The 100-foot clock tower of the tramway's base facility, Valley Station, is surrounded by hotels and condominiums, restaurants and bars, shops and the Walk Festival Hall where each summer, for eight weeks beginning in late June, the **Grand Teton Music Festival** takes place. Concerts by the likes of the Moscow String Quartet and members of the New York Philharmonic Orchestra highlight the festival. Admission. ~ P.O. Box 490, Teton Village, WY 83025; 307-733-1128.

A third major resort, the **Grand Targhee Ski & Summer Resort,** is almost directly over the back side of the Teton Range from Jackson Hole Ski Area. Though political boundaries place it in Wyoming, it can be reached only through Driggs, Idaho. The resort, which opened in 1970, has lodges, condos, restaurants and some of the finest powder skiing in the Rocky Mountains during its November-to-April season. In summer, it hosts popular rock and bluegrass music festivals. ~ Ski Hill Road, Alta; 307-353-2300.

Those who make the 42-mile trek from Jackson to Targhee must scale 8429-foot **Teton Pass**, the only road passage through the Teton Range. Route 22 switchbacks over the state line from

✔ **CHECK THESE OUT—UNIQUE SIGHTS**

- Take a winter sleigh ride through the **National Elk Refuge**, where 9000 of the magnificent antlered creatures pass the colder months. *page 75*
- Cheer and hiss as a stagecoach is robbed and six-guns blaze at the **Jackson Hole Shootout** in Town Square summer evenings. *page 76*
- Slide into a saddle and lean across a bar inlaid with silver dollars to order a beer at the **Million Dollar Cowboy Bar**. *page 76*
- Drink in the image of towering Mt. Moran reflected in the crystal waters of Jackson Lake from atop **Signal Mountain** in Grand Teton National Park. *page 92*

the village of Wilson, affording spectacular panoramas of Jackson Hole if you can unclench your teeth long enough to find a roadside turnout from which to appreciate the views. The path was blazed in 1811 by Oregon-bound Astorian fur traders.

Wilson, named for "Uncle Nick" Wilson, patriarch of a very extended Mormon family that settled in Jackson Hole about 1889, lies about eight miles from Jackson and a mile west of the Teton Village junction. From here there is ready access to Bridger-Teton and the bordering **Targhee National Forest** to the **Jedediah Smith Wilderness** (a parcel of Targhee that bounds Grand Teton National Park on its west side), and to the meandering ribbons of the **Snake River**'s upper portion.

The 1038-mile Snake, of course, is the main tributary of the Columbia River. Its source is in the Teton Wilderness, on the Continental Divide at the southeastern edge of Yellowstone National Park; the stream runs west and south through Jackson Lake and Grand Teton National Park, draining Jackson Hole, before rushing westward through the **Snake River Canyon**. Through the Hole, the Snake weaves a broad, flat plain that teems with wildflowers and wildlife through much of the year. Then it hits the canyon about 13 miles south of Jackson.

The 22-mile stretch southwest from **Hoback Junction** to **Palisades Reservoir,** on the Idaho border, is a paradise for river runners. There are several put-in and take-out spots for rafters and kayakers along Route 26/89, which closely follows the Snake's course. Also on this highway, at the river's edge four miles from Hoback, the **Astoria Hot Springs** bubble from the earth at 104°F. (They're cooled to 90° for swimming.) Admission. ~ 12500 South Route 89, Hoback Junction; 307-733-2659.

Accommodation prices tend toward the high end in Jackson Hole, and with so many deluxe properties, it's hard to recommend one over another. The following list is merely a sampling of what's available in different lodging categories, different price ranges and different parts of the valley. Summer (June to mid-September) is the high season in Jackson, with winter (mid-December to March) priced somewhat lower. You'll get the best prices during spring and fall shoulder seasons.

LODGING

In Jackson itself, the most elaborate hotel is the **Snow King Resort Hotel**, nine blocks southeast of Town Square. Located at the base of Snow King Mountain, the modern chalet-style hotel has 195 rather ordinary rooms and suites. But guests don't come to stay in their rooms; they come to ski in winter, hike or ride horses in summer, and enjoy the hotel's outdoor swimming pool and two hot tubs, sauna and fitness center. The hotel's restaurants offer gourmet dining and more standard fare; there's also live music and dancing in the saloon. Laundry facilities are available.

~ 400 East Snow King Avenue, Jackson; 307-733-5200, 800-522-5464, fax 307-733-4086. DELUXE.

For historic flavor in Jackson, there's the **Wort Hotel**. A downtown landmark at the corner of Broadway for more than a half-century, it was rebuilt after a 1980 fire, its gabled architecture intact. Its 60 bright, spacious rooms and suites have full baths. The Wort is perhaps best known for its bar, and its grill is among Jackson's best restaurants. Facilities include a hot tub and fitness center. ~ 50 North Glenwood Street, Jackson; 307-733-2190, 800-322-2727, fax 307-733-2067; www.worthotel.com. ULTRA-DELUXE.

Bed and breakfasts are increasingly a part of the Jackson Hole scene. The **Nowlin Creek Inn**, opposite Elk Refuge headquarters and six blocks east of Town Square, sets a tough standard for others to follow. The five rooms of this nonsmoking inn face either the refuge or Snow King Mountain. All have private baths with pedestal-style sinks and Western-style furnishings. There's also a cabin available for rent. There's a sun deck, hot tub and library with a collection of regional literature. A gourmet breakfast is served each morning in the dining room. ~ 660 East Broadway, Jackson; 307-733-0882, 800-542-2632, fax 307-733-0106. DELUXE TO ULTRA-DELUXE.

The **49er Inn** is one of many centrally located motels. A member of the Quality Inn chain, it has 114 first- and second-story rooms with desks, private baths and other standard amenities. Rooms are a little dark, but the front office keeps coffee on in the lobby and provides complimentary daily newspapers. The motel has a sauna and a hot tub, and is adjacent to a Mexican restaurant and bar. ~ 330 West Pearl Street, Jackson; 307-733-7550, 800-451-2980, fax 307-733-2002; www.townsquareinns. com. MODERATE TO DELUXE.

✔ **CHECK THESE OUT—UNIQUE LODGING**

- *Budget to moderate:* Bunk down in **The Hostel**, an old-time Teton Village ski lodge with a fireside lounge where schussers swap tall tales. *page 83*
- *Moderate to deluxe:* Reserve a log cabin at **Signal Mountain Lodge** for easy exploration of Grand Teton National Park. *page 94*
- *Deluxe:* Soak away an action-packed day in a hot tub at **Snow King Resort Hotel**, at the foot of Snow King Mountain. *page 81*
- *Ultra-deluxe:* Take a pre-breakfast horseback ride around the 1000-acre grounds of **Spring Creek Resort** and watch as the early-morning sun awakens the stark crest of the Grand Teton. *page 83*

Budget: under $50   Moderate: $50–$90   Deluxe: $90–$130   Ultra-deluxe: over $130

The **Angler's Inn** is a small, family-run operation beside Flat   ◄ *HIDDEN*
Creek at the north end of downtown. Within the two-story wood-
frame motel are 28 rooms with lodge-style furnishings, microwaves, coffeemakers and refrigerators, as well as private baths,
cable TV and air conditioning. A bargain at the price. ~ 265 North
Millward Street, Jackson; 307-733-3682, 800-867-4667, fax 307-
733-8662; e-mail innsoftetons@wyoming.com. DELUXE.

There are several luxury resorts in the area, including Teton
Pines and the Jackson Hole Racquet Club, both south of Teton
Village on Route 390. But if we had to choose just one, it would
be the **Spring Creek Resort**, with a view across Jackson Hole to
the high Tetons. Set on 1000 acres atop East Gros Ventre Butte,
the modern rustic resort offers accommodations with handmade
lodgepole furniture, vaulted ceilings and stone fireplaces. Its Gran-
ary restaurant is highly regarded for creative game and seafood
preparations. The resort also has a lounge, swimming pool and
jacuzzi, tennis courts and riding stables. ~ Spring Gulch Road,
Jackson; 307-733-8833, 800-443-6139, fax 307-733-1524; www.
springcreekranch.com. ULTRA-DELUXE.

Several lodges cluster in Teton Village beneath Rendezvous
Peak. **The Inn at Jackson Hole** is an elegant hotel just 100 yards
from the aerial tramway terminal. It has 83 rooms, all with private baths and some with fireplaces and kitchenettes. The outdoor
swimming pool is kept heated year-round; there's also a sauna and
hot tubs, two restaurants and a bar. The Inn is a Best Western
property; its sister motel in Jackson, the sophisticated Lodge at
Jackson Hole, handles winter overflow. ~ 3345 West McCollister
Drive, Teton Village; 307-733-2311, 800-842-7666, fax 307-733-
0844; www.innatjh.com. ULTRA-DELUXE.

The Hostel attracts hard-core skiers who would rather spend   ◄ *HIDDEN*
extra days on the slopes than splurge on a hotel room. An old-
time family-owned ski lodge at the foot of Jackson Hole's slopes,
it has 54 rooms that sleep from one to four people. Rooms are
extremely simple; all have private baths, dressers and bedside tables but little else. Guests share a fireside lounge, game rooms, a
coin-op laundry, a ski-waxing room and an equipment storage
area. ~ 3315 McCollister Drive, Teton Village; 307-733-3415,
fax 307-739-1142; www.hostelx.com. BUDGET TO MODERATE.

Grand Targhee Ski & Summer Resort has rooms in three alpine lodges at 8000 feet. All have southwestern decor with handcrafted lodgepole furnishings and private baths. The Targhee
Lodge has moderate motel-style rooms; the Teewinot Lodge has
hotel-style rooms; the condo-style Sioux Lodge features bunk
beds, kiva fireplaces and kitchenettes. All are an easy walk from
restaurants, lounges, shops and sports facilities. Rates are lowest
in summer, highest on holidays in the peak ski season. ~ Ski Hill
Road, Alta; 307-353-2300, 800-827-4433, fax 307-353-8148;
www.grandtarghee.com. MODERATE TO ULTRA-DELUXE.

DINING   Arguably the finest restaurant in downtown Jackson is **The Range**, located in a spacious upstairs room of rustic elegance two blocks north of Town Square. Creative regional cuisine is prepared in an open kitchen; the menu might include an appetizer of carmelized onion polenta with a basil–wild mushroom sauce and an entrée of rack of lamb with artichoke heart–mint risotto, roasted tomatoes and dijon demiglaze. Closed mid-April to mid-May. ~ 225 North Cache Street, Jackson; 307-733-5481. DELUXE TO ULTRA-DELUXE.

You can't go wrong at the delightful **Cadillac Grille**, which re-creates a 1940s art deco ambience opposite Town Square. A creative menu of fresh fish and game entrées is complemented by steaks, poultry and pasta. The list changes daily; selections have included medallions of elk and seared ahi tuna with a sauce of shiitake mushrooms, ginger and soy cream. Fine wines are served by the glass in the adjacent lounge. ~ 55 North Cache Street, Jackson; 307-733-3279. DELUXE TO ULTRA-DELUXE.

Creativity is afoot at **The Blue Lion**, where dishes like pheasant cakes served with chipotle mayonnaise, chicken *fragelico*, tempeh crepes and elk *au poivre* are served in a casual but elegant atmosphere. The outdoor patio is packed on summer evenings; diners who arrive within the first half-hour after opening get early-bird discounts. Breads and desserts are prepared in-house by a pastry chef. ~ 160 North Millward Street, Jackson; 307-733-3912. DELUXE TO ULTRA-DELUXE.

The Cajun and Creole dishes presented next door at **The Acadian House,** from étouffée and filé gumbo to blackened catfish and crawfish jambalaya, are as authentic as you'll find this far north of Bayou country. The wine list is short but enlightened, and the elegant decor is worthy of a New Orleans–style restaurant. ~ 180 North Millward Street, Jackson; 307-739-1269. MODERATE TO DELUXE.

Diners at the **Snake River Grill** can survey Town Square from rooftop tables in summer or sit inside and gaze at Snow King Mountain's floodlit slopes in winter. Located upstairs in the Crabtree Corner complex, the restaurant serves American roasts and grills (such as fresh fish and free-range chicken) and Italian cuisine (pastas and pizzas from a wood-fired oven). There's a sophisticated wine list and a lighter bar menu. Closed April and November. ~ 84 East Broadway, Jackson; 307-733-0557. DELUXE TO ULTRA-DELUXE.

Beef eaters are always delighted at **The Gun Barrel Steak and Game House,** at the south end of town. Housed in a former taxidermy museum, the cavernous log structure still boasts many of its game trophies and antique cowboy artifacts. Steaks include a rib-eye and New York strip while wild-game dishes list elk, buffalo and wild boar as choices. Tamer offerings of chicken, fish and pasta are also available. The Gun Barrel's bar claims Wyoming's largest selection of scotches, bourbons and draft beers. Closed from late October to early December and from April to early May. ~ 862 West Broadway, Jackson; 307-733-3287. MODERATE TO DELUXE.

Dine amid mash tubs, wort kettles and beer storage tanks at the **Jackson Hole Pub & Brewery**, where the emphasis is on custom ales, bitters, stouts, porters and other microbrews, as well as on stick-to-your-ribs meat dishes, pizzas baked in wood-burning ovens and pastas. An outside deck appeals to summer diners. ~ 265 South Millward Street, Jackson; 307-739-2337. MODERATE.

One of Jackson's original log cabins is an appropriate home for **Jedediah's Original House of Sourdough**, shaded by giant cottonwoods and located a block east of Town Square. Hearty home-style breakfasts (sourdough pancakes are a specialty), lunches (thick soups, buffalo burgers) and dinners (steaks, chops, trout) are served in a rustic atmosphere complete with old photographs and pioneer artifacts. Dinner only in summer. ~ 135 East Broadway, Jackson; 307-733-5671. BUDGET TO MODERATE.

The Bunnery serves up Jackson's best breakfast. All manner of omelets and pastries are available here, along with Mexican-style day-starters (*chilaquiles, huevos rancheros*) and homemade waffles and French toast. There's a great sandwich selection at lunch as well. Dinner is served in the summer. ~ 130 North Cache Street, Jackson; 307-733-5474. BUDGET.

Some of the valley's finest dining is ten miles from town, out toward the Jackson Hole Ski Area. **The Grille at the Pines**, in the Teton Pines Country Club & Resort clubhouse, specializes in fresh fish, beef and local game dishes, as well as homemade pastas, breads and desserts. The atmosphere is casual, yet the service is impeccable. Closed Sunday, November and April. ~ Teton Village Road, Wilson; 307-733-1005. DELUXE TO ULTRA-DELUXE.

✔ CHECK THESE OUT—UNIQUE DINING

- *Budget to moderate:* Feast on sourdough pancakes or buffalo burgers at **Jedediah's Original House of Sourdough**, occupying one of Jackson's original 19th-century log cabins. *page 85*
- *Moderate to deluxe:* Enjoy branded steaks at **The Gun Barrel Steakhouse**, located in an old taxidermy museum. *page 84*
- *Deluxe:* Dine à la chuckwagon while cowboy musicians serenade you at the **Bar-J Chuckwagon**. *page 86*
- *Deluxe to ultra-deluxe:* Imagine yourself in the Tyrolean Alps at **Stiegler's**, where your meal may include *Leberknödelsuppe*. *page 86*

Budget: under $7   Moderate: $7–$12   Deluxe: $12–$20   Ultra-deluxe: over $20

Alpinists feel right at home at **Stiegler's Restaurant & Bar** at the Jackson Hole Racquet Club. The fare here is Austrian/Continental: You can start with *Leberknödelsuppe* (liver-dumpling soup), follow with *Bauernschmaus* (a sauerkraut-and-pork concoction), and finish with *Palatschinken* (crêpes) in an atmosphere of *Gemütlichkeit* (warmth and friendliness). Wild game, fish and pasta, and a lighter menu are also available. Closed Monday, November, April and May. ~ Teton Village Road, Wilson; 307-733-1071. DELUXE TO ULTRA-DELUXE.

For a family night out, you can't top the **Bar-J Chuckwagon**. A cowboy musical revue featuring the ranch's own Bar J Wranglers follows an all-you-can-eat chuckwagon dinner of barbecued beef or chicken served at 7:30 every night throughout the summer. A very reasonable price tag includes dinner and show, tax and tip. ~ Teton Village Road, Wilson; 307-733-3370. DELUXE.

Jackson locals who want to avoid the tourist scene often drive ten minutes south to **Horse Creek Station**, a casual oasis where steaks and barbecue are the house specialties. A collection of antique fishing gear on the walls is a reminder that fresh seafood is also served. An adjacent saloon offers a sandwich menu. ~ Route 89 South, Hoback Junction; 307-733-0810. BUDGET TO MODERATE.

SHOPPING   Most of Jackson's two dozen or so art galleries specialize in Western art and regional landscapes. Many are clustered around Town Square. My favorite is the **Sun 3 Studio**, where working cowboy Doug Lindauer documents the Western lifestyle. Closed Sunday. ~ 47 South Glenwood Street; 307-733-0660. **Sacred Trails** displays American Indian art. ~ 81 South King Street; 307-733-8874. The **Center Street Gallery** contains numerous rooms that exhibit contemporary and abstract art. ~ 172 Center Street; 307-733-1115.

If you're a serious collector, consider attending the annual **Jackson Hole Fall Arts Festival**, which runs for 17 days beginning the third Friday of September and includes the all-day Western Art Symposium.

Visitors who get a hankering to dress just a little more "cowboy," a little more Wyoming, can readily indulge themselves at a couple of dozen Jackson stores. Check out **Buckskin Mercantile** for traditional Western wear. ~ 125 North Cache Street; 307-733-3699. Try **Cattle Kate** for 1990s clothing in 1890s designs. Closed Saturday and Sunday. ~ 3530 South Park Drive; 307-733-7414. For outdoor wear, you won't go wrong at **Wyoming Outfitters**. ~ 12 Center Street; 307-733-3877.

The **Bitterroot Trading Co.** is a traditional trading post that sells antique firearms, hides, furs and American Indian art and jewelry. Closed Sunday, except in summer. ~ 170 West Broadway;

307-733-4192. The **Jackson Trading Company** has more contemporary Western furnishings and gifts. ~ 25 West Broadway; 307-733-5714. **Lodgepole Furniture Manufacturing** sells log and rawhide furnishings. Closed Sunday. ~ 6740 South Henry's Road; 307-733-3199. **Cayuse Western Americana** specializes in cowboy and American Indian antiques, as well as Yellowstone memorabilia and photos from decades past. Closed Sunday from November through May. ~ 255 North Glenwood Street; 307-739-1940.

You can get vintage home decorative pieces such as lamps, linens, candles and rugs at the **Back Porch**. Primitive antiques also number among the finds here. Closed Sunday. ~ 145 East Pearl Street; 307-733-0030.

If you're looking for a good book, try **Valley Bookstore**. ~ 125 North Cache Street; 307-733-4533. The **Teton Bookshop** specializes in volumes on Wyoming and the West. ~ 25 South Glenwood Street; 307-733-9220. The work of outstanding wildlife photographer Thomas Mangelsen is displayed and sold at the **Images of Nature Gallery**. ~ 170 North Cache Street; 307-733-9752.

The first movie in which John Wayne had a speaking role was *The Big Trail*, filmed in Jackson Hole in 1932. This was also reputedly the first time Wayne ever rode a horse.

NIGHTLIFE

Jackson is a summer mecca of the performing arts. Its best-known event is the **Grand Teton Music Festival**, held at Teton Village's Walk Festival Hall for eight weeks beginning in late June. The orchestra consists of more than 200 artists whose names read like a *Who's Who* of symphonic music. Chamber music recitals are offered Tuesday through Thursday nights; the full festival orchestra performs on Friday and Saturday. Several concerts are also performed during the winter. ~ P.O. Box 490, Teton Village, WY 83025; 307-733-1128, fax 307-739-9043.

Each July, the locally based Dancers' Workshop presents the three-week **Jackson Hole Summer Dance Festival** under a tent at Snow King Resort. The festival includes dance classes, children's shows, and evening concerts with guest artists performing modern dance and classical ballet. ~ 49 West Broadway; 307-733-3810.

Jackson's live theater runs the gamut from serious musicals to tongue-in-cheek melodramas. The **Grand Teton Main Stage Theatre**, in Pink Garter Plaza, presents Western-themed musical comedies year-round. ~ 49 West Broadway; 307-733-3670. The **Jackson Hole Playhouse** presents classic Western musicals (*Oklahoma*, *Calamity Jane*, *Paint Your Wagon*) in an equally classic old-time theater, complete with popcorn and sarsaparilla concessions. Dinner packages are available. ~ 145 West Deloney Street; 307-733-6994.

Rodeo and country-and-western music are at the forefront of the popular entertainment scene in this "cowboy" town. Twice a week on summer evenings, the **JH Rodeo Company** stages a rodeo—complete with bronco busting, bull riding and calf roping —at the Teton County Fair Grounds. Midway through the event, kids from 4 through 12 years are invited to enter a "calf scramble" on the arena floor. Admission. ~ Snow King Avenue at Flat Creek Drive; 307-733-2805 (summer), 435-652-0510 (winter).

Headquarters for two-steppers and Tennessee waltzers is the **Million Dollar Cowboy Bar**, on the west side of Town Square. Country bands play dance music nightly. Even if you don't dance, drop by for a beer and sit in a saddle-seated barstool. ~ 25 North Cache Street, Jackson; 307-733-2207.

Other spots heavy on C&W include **Rancher Spirits and Billiards**, on the south side of Town Square, with nine very busy billiards tables upstairs. ~ 20 East Broadway, Jackson; 307-733-3886. The **Stagecoach Bar** is popular among locals especially on Sunday, when the venerable Stagecoach Band pumps out melodies, and on disco-night Thursday. ~ Route 22, Wilson; 307-733-4407.

The **Mangy Moose** is the leading venue for live funk, blues, bluegrass, rockabilly and alternative rock. *Snow Country* magazine has rated it the "number one après ski bar in North America." On a given night, you might hear Leo Kottke, Big Head Todd or Chris Duarte perform. ~ 3285 West McCollister Drive, Teton Village; 307-733-4913. In town, the Snow King Resort's **Shady Lady Saloon** presents low-key live jazz, cover bands and contemporary rock for dancing and listening. They have live music on Wednesday and some weekends. ~ 400 East Snow King Avenue; 307-733-5200. **Spirits of the West** is a sports bar with 11 big screen TVs and a satellite system. There are also pool tables and game tournaments (darts, foosball, cribbage). ~ 385 West Broadway; 307-733-3854.

If it's Old West atmosphere you want, **JJ's Silverdollar Bar** will return you to those thrilling days of yesteryear at its historic bar inlaid with 2032 silver dollars. Monday is jazz night, a ragtime pianist plays Wednesday and Thursday, and country or bluegrass bands perform Friday and Saturday. ~ Wort Hotel, 50 North Glenwood Street, Jackson; 307-733-2190. For drinks and conversation, try the **Log Cabin Saloon**, a rustic local favorite. ~ 435 North Cache Street, Jackson; 307-733-7525.

Cowboy country doesn't often embrace gay visitors, but the **Jackson Hole Gay & Lesbian Association** holds a social event once a week. ~ P.O. Box 2424, Jackson, WY 83001.

PARKS

BRIDGER-TETON NATIONAL FOREST 🏃 🚴 🐎 ⛷ 🏂 🏊 ⛷
🚣 🛶 🛥 🎣 Stretching south for 135 miles from Yellowstone National Park through five mountain ranges, this 3.4-million-acre

forest is America's largest outside of Alaska. It contains three wilderness areas, three national scenic byways, several hot springs and the geologically intriguing Gros Ventre Slide. In the Wind River Range, on Bridger-Teton's border with Shoshone National Forest, are the state's highest mountain—13,804-foot Gannett Peak—and seven of the ten largest active glaciers in the continental United States. There are picnic areas and restrooms; swimming at the Granite Hot Springs pool, 27 miles southeast of Jackson. ~ From Jackson, take Route 189 southeast for Pinedale and access to the Wind River Range; Route 89 South for Afton and the Salt Range; Route 26 North for Moran and the northern part of the national forest; 307-739-5500.

▲ There are 585 sites in 46 campgrounds (no hookups); no charge to $9 per night; 16-day maximum stay. Most of the campgrounds are open only from June to September.

GROS VENTRE WILDERNESS AREA 🚶🏇 🏊 ⛵ This 287,000-acre wilderness, which encompasses the rugged Gros Ventre Mountains, begins within a mile of Jackson's eastern city limits. More than 200 miles of trails rise from sagebrush-cloaked foothills through aspen and spruce forests to open alpine meadows. Numerous summits surpass 10,000 feet, capped by 11,750-foot Doubletop Peak. This is prime habitat for deer, elk, moose, bighorn sheep and black bear. Mountain whitefish, brown and cutthroat trout can be taken from lakes and streams. ~ Direct trail access from Forest Service roads that run east out of Jackson at Flat Creek, Curtis Canyon and Cache Creek. There are short, steep southerly approaches from Granite Creek Road, off Route 189/191 east of Hoback Junction; and long, gradual northerly approaches from Gros Ventre Road east of Kelly, especially near Upper Slide Lake; 307-739-5500.

▲ Primitive only.

TARGHEE NATIONAL FOREST 🚶 🚴 🏇 🎿 🏊 ⛵ 🛶 Grand Teton National Park forms the eastern boundary of this 1.8-million-acre forest, most of which lies in Idaho. The Wyoming portion encompasses the western slope of the Teton Range (most of it in the Jedediah Smith Wilderness) from Yellowstone Park to Palisades Reservoir, on the Snake River at Alpine. It includes the Grand Targhee ski resort. Facilities are limited to picnic areas and restrooms. ~ From Jackson, the westbound Teton Pass Highway (Route 22) passes through Targhee en route to Idaho. Several roads enter the forest from the Idaho side. Or take Route 26 southwest through Alpine to the Palisades Reservoir area; 208-624-3151.

▲ In Wyoming, 96 RV/tent units in four campgrounds (no hookups); $5 to $8 per night. 14-day maximum stay. Closed September through May.

JEDEDIAH SMITH WILDERNESS AREA 🧍🐎🛶🚣 A mirror image of the Grand Teton National Park backcountry without its large lakes, this 116,535-acre wilderness, named for a famous mountain man of the early 1800s, extends 43 miles from north to south on the west side of the Teton Range. Included are 300 miles of hiking and horse trails through such areas as the Alaska Basin, a lake-speckled alpine meadow at 9500 feet elevation on the back side of the Grand Teton. ~ Access is around the back side of Rendezvous Peak off the Teton Pass Highway (Route 22); otherwise by forest road from Idaho, or by westbound trail through the national park; 208-354-2431.

▲ Primitive only.

▼▼▼▼▼▼▼▼▼▼▼▼▼▼▼▼▼▼▼

Grand Teton National Park

Anyone who has ever laid eyes upon the stunning heights of the Teton Range has come away awestruck. Even people whose only glimpse of these dramatic mountains has been in photographs or paintings find themselves haunted by their beauty.

SIGHTS   Climaxed by the 13,772-foot **Grand Teton**, this commanding range boasts 16 peaks of 11,000 feet or higher in a north–south stretch of less than 20 miles, towering over a string of conifer-shrouded lakes.

The geological forces that created the Tetons are still actively sculpting these peaks, which in Cenozoic terms might be considered teenagers. Some five million years ago, massive earthquakes began occurring (about every 1000 years) along a fault line where the mountains today meet the valley of Jackson Hole. Over the course of time, the mountain block on the west uplifted while the valley block dropped, so that today the Grand Teton rises about 6000 feet above Jenny Lake on the valley floor. Wind, water and late–Ice Age glaciation (only about 10,000 to 15,000 years ago) have continued to chisel the mountains' features.

The mountains and six piedmont lakes were within the national park's original boundaries in 1929. But extension of those borders to include the upper Jackson Hole, including the Snake River, induced a grim battle between conservationists and ranchers. A key player in the drama was philanthropist John D. Rockefeller, Jr., who bought up many of the ranch properties beginning in the late 1920s, then donated them to the National Park Service for a national monument that was created in 1943 and annexed to the national park in 1950. The highway corridor and adjacent lands that today connect Grand Teton and Yellowstone national parks have been named the **John D. Rockefeller, Jr., Memorial Parkway** in his honor.

Grand Teton National Park now covers an area of 485 square miles. Despite its close proximity to Yellowstone National Park, Grand Teton is very different from its famous sister. Yellowstone has premier attractions like Old Faithful Geyser and Mammoth Hot Springs, easily accessible either by car or by a short walk. Grand Teton's allure, on the other hand, is scenery that seems so close that you can reach out and touch it, but the park in fact demands active effort to fully appreciate it.

America's *Voyager II* spacecraft, launched in 1977 "to go where no one has gone before," carries within its cargo an Ansel Adams photo of Jackson Hole and the Tetons.

Teton Park Road skirts the shores of Jenny Lake, at the foot of the Grand Tetons, and Jackson Lake, a natural glacial lake whose size was increased significantly in 1911 by an earthen dam (since rebuilt) on the Snake River. Several park lodges are on or near the lakeshores. But rather than destinations in themselves, the lodges are best considered starting points for more energetic explorations of the park by foot, by boat, by horseback or by snowshoe.

Heading north from Jackson, the Rockefeller Parkway (Route 26/89/191) enters the national park about four miles north of Jackson. But you won't be charged a fee for passing through this area, the Antelope Flat corridor, unless you turn off onto the Teton Park Road at **Moose**, 12 miles north of Jackson, or Moran, 26 miles from Jackson. The former is the principal route for park explorers; the latter bypasses the Jackson Lake Lodge and heads more or less directly for the south entrance of Yellowstone Park.

At Moose, on the west side of the Snake River, are the park headquarters and **Moose Visitors Center**, with a variety of displays and information on park activities. ~ Teton Park Road, Moose; 307-739-3399. A general store and tackle shop, snack bar and service station are also located here. Nearby **Dornan's**, on the east side of the river, offers log-cabin accommodations and two restaurants. Fishing and mountaineering shops, mountain bike and canoe rentals make this a center for outdoor-sports lovers. ~ Teton Park Road, Moose; 307-733-2415.

Moose, named for the ungainly looking creatures often seen browsing on willows beside the Snake, lies at the junction of Teton Park Road and **Moose-Wilson Road**, which winds through the national park's southwestern section. It passes trailheads for Phelps Lake and Death Canyon, then reaches Teton Village and the Jackson Hole Ski Area after about eight miles. Part of the road is unpaved.

Upriver from Moose, a half-mile north on Teton Park Road, then a half-mile east, is the log-built **Chapel of the Transfiguration**, whose altar window frames the Grand Teton. A short trail leads

HIDDEN ► to **Menor's Ferry**, once the only crossing of the Snake for miles in either direction. The homestead cabin of Bill Menor contains a replica of his late-19th-century ferry; Bill's brother, Holiday, lived on the opposite side of the Snake. Like the *Grumpy Old Men*, the bachelor brothers were not on speaking terms.

Jenny Lake, eight miles north of Moose, is Teton Park's second-largest lake, filling a glacial trough a mile wide and a mile and a half long. There are two ways to approach the lake: from South Jenny Lake Junction or, for those with a bit more time, via the Jenny Lake Scenic Drive.

South Jenny Lake is the park's number-one focal point for backcountry hikers and mountaineers. The campground here is for tenters only. Ascents of the Grand Teton begin with registration at the Jenny Lake Ranger Station here; trails to a chain of lakes north (Leigh and String) and south (Bradley and Taggart) of Jenny Lake also begin at South Jenny.

A six-mile trail circles Jenny Lake. From **Hidden Falls**, at Jenny's west end (two and a half miles from the South Jenny Lake trailhead), another trail follows U-shaped **Cascade Canyon** seven miles upstream to Lake Solitude, one of the park's most popular backcountry destinations. The 200-foot Hidden Falls are the most notable cascade on Cascade Creek, which runs through the canyon; the falls are secluded by a grove of 400-year-old Engelmann spruce, pines and firs.

Jenny Lake Scenic Drive begins as a two-way route from Teton Park Road, four miles north of South Jenny, to canoeing put-ins for String and Leigh lakes; but at the **Jenny Lake Lodge**, a community of secluded log cottages that were once part of a dude ranch, it becomes a one-way southbound road, emerging back on Teton Park Road on the north side of South Jenny Lake Junction. The road offers serene views of Jenny Lake with the Grand Teton and its neighboring peaks rising behind.

It's eight miles from the Jenny Lake Scenic Drive junction (near the lake's north end) to **Signal Mountain Summit Road**, a steep and narrow byway that winds five miles to the top of **Signal Mountain**. From the summit, 800 feet above the surrounding country, visitors coming from the south can get their first glimpse of **Jackson Lake**, a natural lake formed by an immense Ice Age glacier that flowed out of Yellowstone Park. The 1911 damming of the Snake—a U.S. Bureau of Reclamation project that benefits eastern Idaho potato farmers—raised the lake's water level as much as 39 feet. The lake now extends 19 miles south, from the northern edge of Grand Teton National Park, and nine miles east and west at its widest.

Looming behind Jackson Lake is massive 12,605-foot **Mount Moran**, named for artist Thomas Moran, whose 1870s paintings immortalized the Teton Range on canvas for many Americans.

Moran's close friend, photographer William Henry Jackson, did the same for the region on film. Many Jackson Holers lament that their valley was named not for William but for David Jackson, the trapper who passed through two to three generations earlier.

Four miles past the Signal Mountain Road, Teton Park Road rejoins the Rockefeller Parkway at **Jackson Lake Junction**. Northbound travelers can detour to the east here, following the Snake River downstream past **Oxbow Bend**, one of the park's richest wildlife-viewing areas, to **Moran**, where the park has its east entrance gate and a small community for park employees. East of Moran, Route 26/287 reclaims its identity as the Wyoming Centennial Scenic Byway and completes its semi-circuit of the Wind River Range from Pinedale to Dubois, 55 miles from Moran.

Near the east bank of the Snake, six miles south of Moran, the **Cunningham Cabin** preserves the log homestead of J. Pierce and Margaret Cunningham, two early residents of Jackson Hole who arrived in the valley about 1888. The cabin, built about two years later, became the cornerstone of their 560-acre Bar Flying U Ranch, which they held until 1928. A self-guided trail describes their lifestyle.

◄ HIDDEN

A few hundred yards north of Jackson Lake Junction is the **Jackson Lake Lodge**, nearly twice as large as any other hotel complex in the Jackson Hole. ~ 307-543-3100, 800-628-9988. Trails from the lodge lead to Jackson Lake (more than a mile away) and the smaller Two Ocean and Emma Matilda lakes, on the edge of the Teton Wilderness Area.

Colter Bay Village, six miles north of Jackson Lake Junction on a sheltered arm of the lake, has economy-priced log cabins (some of them settlers' cottages, remodeled and moved to this lakeside site) and a campground. The **Colter Bay Indian Arts Museum**, next to the ranger station and visitors center, houses a collection of American Indian artifacts of artistic and religious significance. Closed Thanksgiving to mid-May. ~ Colter Bay Village; 307-739-3594.

It's about 17 miles from Colter Bay, or 23 miles from Jackson Lake Junction, to the south entrance of Yellowstone Park.

The **Grand Teton Lodge Company** is the principal concessionaire in Grand Teton National Park. It operates three separate properties: the **Jenny Lake Lodge** (Jenny Lake Scenic Drive), an ultra-deluxe former dude ranch whose 37 cabins are secluded in a conifer forest near the shores of Jenny Lake; the huge **Jackson Lake Lodge** (Jackson Lake Junction), with 385 rooms in multiplex cabins and the main hotel, starting in the deluxe price range; and **Colter Bay Village** (Colter Bay Village), whose budget lodgings include 166 log cabins (some of them settlers' cottages remodeled and moved to their lakeside site), 72 tent cabins, 112 trailer sites

LODGING

and about 200 spaces for tents. Closed mid-October to mid-May. ~ Book all lodgings at P.O. Box 250, Moran, WY 83013; 307-543-3100, 800-628-9988, fax 307-543-3143; www.gtlc.com.

Also within the park are **Dornan's Spur Ranch Log Cabins**, 12 modern cottages overlooking the Snake River just west of the Moose junction. All have private baths, full kitchens, lodgepole furniture, porches and courtyards. One-bedroom cabins can sleep up to four; two-bedroom cabins can accommodate six. Dornan's also includes two restaurants, a bar, a wine shop, grocery, gift shop, service station, sporting goods stores and rental outlets. ~ Moose Lane, Moose; 307-733-2522, fax 307-739-9098; www. dornans.com. DELUXE TO ULTRA-DELUXE.

Jackson Hole offers more than a dozen guest ranches. One of the most popular is the **Gros Ventre River Ranch**, 18 miles northeast of Jackson near Kelly. Guests stay in eight log cabins with ten-foot ceilings, kitchenettes and private baths. Gourmet meals (American plan) are served with California wine in the main lodge, which also has a bar for guests' use and a recreation room. Activities include horseback riding and flyfishing in summer, cross-country skiing and snowmobiling in winter. ~ P.O. Box 151, Moose, WY 83012; 307-733-4138, fax 307-733-4272; www. ranchweb.com/grosventre. ULTRA-DELUXE.

The **Signal Mountain Lodge**, on Jackson Lake at the foot of Signal Mountain, is one of the few privately owned and operated park properties. Its 79 units include 34 log cabins (many with refrigerators and microwaves) and 45 rooms in a two-story motel building, all overlooking the lake. Boat and canoe rentals are available from the lodge marina, and raft trips on the Snake are offered. There's also a beach and campground, two restaurants, a gift shop and a lounge. Closed mid-October to mid-May. ~ Teton Park Road, Moran; 307-733-5470. MODERATE TO DELUXE.

Surrounded by mountains and trees on the eastern rim of Jackson Hole is **Cowboy Village Resort at Togwotee**. Summer guests indulge in the area's many outdoor activities, including hiking, horseback riding and flyfishing; in winter, snowmobilers make use of the groomed trails. A pine lodge comprises 35 guest rooms outfitted with two queen-sized beds; kitchenettes are available in the 54 log cabins. The lodge's dining room serves meals. Closed mid-October to mid-November and mid-April through May. ~ P.O. Box 91, Moran, WY 83013; 307-733-8800, 800-543-2847, fax 307-543-2391; www.cowboyvillage.com. DELUXE TO ULTRA-DELUXE.

DINING

In Moose, Dornan's offers two dining options. Large windows frame picture-perfect views of the Grand Tetons at **Dornan's Pizza Pasta Company**. The menu features the obvious—pizzas and pastas—but also serves salads and specials. In the summer **Dornan's Chuckwagon** serves up hearty meals prepared in cast-iron kettles. Come hungry—there are lumberjack-sized portions of barbecued ribs, vegetable stews and roast beef. ~ Moose Lane, Moose; 307-733-2415. MODERATE.

Perhaps the best of the restaurants in the national-park lodges is **The Mural Room,** whose walls are adorned with paintings that depict various episodes in the history of Jackson Hole. Three meals a day are served in smoke-free surroundings. Breakfast and lunch offer standard American fare; dinners are highlighted by a nightly outdoor barbecue from June to September. ~ Jackson Lake Lodge, Rockefeller Parkway, Moran; 307-543-2811. DELUXE TO ULTRA-DELUXE.

Seafood specialties are featured at the **Aspens Restaurant,** a few miles south down the lakeshore. Trout or other angler's takes from Jackson Lake itself may be offered, as well as steaks and other traditional American cuisine. Large windows look out upon the lake, and the smoke-free atmosphere is casual. Closed mid-October to mid-May. ~ Signal Mountain Lodge, Teton Park Road, Moran; 307-543-2831. MODERATE TO DELUXE.

There are few alternatives to lodge dining rooms and snack bars within the national park. An exception is **Leeks Restaurant Pizzeria**. With an outdoor deck overlooking Jackson Lake opposite Mount Moran, this fully licensed summer-only eatery offers pizza, salad, burgers and other sandwiches. Closed in winter. ~ Leeks Marina, Rockefeller Parkway, Moran; 307-543-2494. BUDGET.

NIGHTLIFE

Dornan's Spur Ranch has live acoustic performances every season except summer. ~ Moose Lane, Moose; 307-733-2415 ext. 200.

There are cocktail lounges in the various park lodges, but most visitors interested in an active nightlife head for the joys of Jackson. Things are decidedly quiet at night in Grand Teton.

PARKS

GRAND TETON NATIONAL PARK

The spectacular Teton Range, the string of evergreen-ringed lakes at its eastern front, and Jackson Hole itself are dominant features of this 485-square-mile park. Mountaineers are challenged by the Grand Teton and other peaks, while watersports enthusiasts enjoy floating the upper Snake River and scanning its shores for wildlife. Although Jackson Lake is extremely cold year-round, there are designated swimming beaches at Colter Bay and Signal Mountain Lodge. The park's lakes and rivers yield mountain whitefish and brown, cutthroat and lake trout, while flyfishing in the upper Snake River is an trout angler's dream. A state fishing license is required. In the winter, there's cross-country skiing and snowshoeing. Within the park are overnight lodges and restaurants, stores, picnic areas, restrooms, amphitheaters, visitors centers and marinas with boat and canoe rentals; $20 weekly vehicle pass (includes Yellowstone National Park). ~ Take Route 26 north from Jackson or Route 89/191 south from Yellowstone National Park; 307-739-3399.

▲ There are 850 RV/tent sites at five park campgrounds (trailers allowed; no hookups); $12 per night; Jenny Lake has 49 tent sites with a seven-day maximum stay; 14-day maximum stay elsewhere; open from May to October. There are 334 units at three privately owned campgrounds; $21 to $32 per night: Colter Bay RV & Trailer Park (112 trailer sites with hookups; 307-543-3100); Colter Bay Tent Village (72 sites for tents only; 307-543-3100); Grand Teton Park KOA (36 tent sites, 114 RV sites with hookups; 307-733-1980). Reservations accepted; closed September through April.

TETON WILDERNESS AREA 🚶 🐎 🛶 🎣 Bounded on the north and west by Yellowstone and Grand Teton national parks and on the east by Shoshone National Forest's Washakie Wilderness Area, this primitive 585,468-acre preserve, most of it above 8000 feet, is a paradise of alpine meadows, ridges and canyons, mountains and lakes, streams and waterfalls. A part of the Bridger-Teton National Forest, it extends from the Absaroka Range to the Rockefeller Parkway and includes Two Ocean Pass on the Continental Divide. In a geographical anomaly found nowhere else in North America, Two Ocean Creek splits in two, sending one rivulet, Pacific Creek, westward (to the Snake River) and the other, Atlantic Creek, eastward (to the Yellowstone River). ~ The wilderness directly abuts Grand Teton Park, so you can enter it from several trailheads. Pacific Creek Road, north of Moran, and Buffalo Valley Road, east of Moran, are recommended. Turpin Meadow, 15 miles east of Moran, is the busiest trailhead; 307-543-2386.

▲ Primitive only.

▼▼▼▼▼▼▼▼▼▼▼▼▼▼
Outdoor Adventures

FISHING

Jackson Lake and other Grand Teton National Park lakes have excellent cutthroat and mackinaw (lake trout) fisheries. The Snake River is considered superb for cutthroat and brook trout, and is a paradise for fly fishermen. Mountain streams and alpine lakes of the region boast mountain whitefish, arctic grayling and six species of trout: rainbow, brook, brown, bull (dolly varden), lake and the rarer golden trout. The Wyoming fishing season runs from April through October.

Anyone fishing in Wyoming must obtain a state license, except within the boundaries of Yellowstone National Park, where all anglers regardless of residency can avoid the state license requirement by obtaining a park license. For more information, call the Jackson regional office of the **Wyoming Game and Fish Division.** ~ 307-733-2321.

Nearly two dozen fishing outfitters are based in Jackson Hole to guide anxious anglers to their limits of trout. Joe **Allen's Scenic Fishing** has been leading guided trips for nearly a half-century. They guarantee fish (or your money back!). Popular destinations are the Snake, Green and Salt rivers. ~ 225 North Millward Street, Jackson; 307-733-2400.

BOATING

Marinas on Jackson Lake, in Grand Teton National Park, offer full boat-rental services and guided lake trips. The **Colter Bay Marina**, administered by the Grand Teton Lodge Company, features daily scenic and fishing boat trips, as well as breakfast and evening trips on selected days. ~ Rockefeller Parkway, Moran; 307-543-2811. You can also try the privately owned **Signal Mountain Lodge** for three-hour scenic trips on the Snake River. ~ Teton Park Road, Moran; 307-543-2831. Shuttles across little Jenny Lake are operated by the **Teton Boating Co.** ~ South Jenny Lake, Moose; 307-733-2703.

RIVER RUNNING

From late May to late September river running is in season in Wyoming. Whitewater enthusiasts love the eight-mile Snake River Canyon south of Jackson. It's a good half-day trip, exciting but not too strenuous, and it can be combined with some flatter portions of the river for a leisurely full-day excursion. **Barker-Ewing River Trips** outfits this stretch. ~ 45 West Broadway, Jackson; 307-733-1000. Also try **Mad River Boat Trips** for half-day guided scenic or whitewater tours or a full-day trip that combines the two. ~ 1255 South Route 89, Jackson; 307-733-6203. A half-dozen other outfitters also run this stretch of river. The only rapid you *really* have to look out for is the one known as Lunch Counter!

For tranquil float trips or easy canoeing with spectacular scenery and abundant wildlife, it is hard to top the upper Snake River through Grand Teton National Park. The **Grand Teton Lodge Company** offers scenic float trips, including lunch and dinner voyages, along a ten-and-a-half-mile stretch of the Snake from mid-May through September. ~ Jackson Lake Lodge, Moran; 307-543-2811. Triangle X Ranch runs other outfitters, including **Triangle X** and **National Park Float Trips**, which put in at Deadman's Bar, south of Moran, and take out at Moose Visitors Center. ~ Moose; 307-733-6445. **Fort Jackson Scenic Snake River Float Trips** is the oldest float-trip operator in the valley. They specialize in sunrise and sunset wildlife trips along a 14-mile stretch of river. ~ Jackson; 307-733-2583, 800-735-8430.

The **Snake River Kayak & Canoe School** introduces novice and intermediate paddlers to Snake River whitewater. Camping tours, by sea kayak, of the shores of Yellowstone Lake are also offered. ~ 365 North Cache Street, Jackson; 307-733-9999.

All manner of support gear can be rented or repaired at **Teton Aquatic Supplies**. ~ 145 West Gill Street, Jackson; 307-733-3127. Rentals of rafts and kayaks can also be made from **Leisure Sports**. ~ 1075 South Route 89, Jackson; 307-733-3040.

DOWNHILL SKIING

For die-hard skiers and snowboarders, there's no place like the **Jackson Hole Mountain Resort**, 12 miles west of the town of Jackson. From the top of 10,450-foot Rendezvous Peak to the base lodge at Teton Village, the vertical drop is 4139 feet, the longest of any skiable mountain in the United States. About 33 feet of snow fall annually. Runs like Corbet's Couloir, a frightening mountaintop chute, and the Hobacks, a series of steep, ungroomed, backcountry glades, make this a mecca for expert skiers like ski school director Pepi Stiegler, an Olympic gold medalist in 1964, and American hero Tommy Moe, the 1994 Olympic downhill gold medalist.

But only 50 percent of the area's 2500 acres are rated expert. There's plenty of intermediate terrain, and beginners are served by runs on adjoining Après Vous Mountain. Lifts include seven chairlifts and a 2.4-mile-long aerial tramway that carries five dozen skiers to the summit every 12 minutes. Full alpine, telemark and snowboard rentals are available. The season extends from early December through early April. ~ Route 390, Teton Village; 406-733-2292, 800-333-7766, fax 307-733-2660.

The Jackson Hole Ski Area was not the first in the Hole. That honor belongs to the **Snow King Mountain Ski Area**, established in 1939. The slopes drop 1571 feet right to the edge of town— just eight blocks southeast of Town Square, in fact. Three chairlifts and a surface tow serve 400 acres of skiable terrain, including 110 acres lit for night skiing. The snowboard park is outfitted with a half-pipe. Snow King's season runs from Thanksgiving weekend to early April. ~ 400 East Snow King Avenue, Jackson; 307-733-5200, 800-522-5464.

Also served by Jackson is the **Grand Targhee Ski & Summer Resort**, on the west side of the Teton Range. The resort gets more than 500 inches of snow (more than 40 feet) a year, and is regarded as one of America's great getaways for powder hounds. One of its two mountains, 10,230-foot Peaked Mountain, is perpetually ungroomed: Skiers are ferried there by Sno-Cat in groups of ten, accompanied by two guides. Fred's Mountain, only slightly smaller at 10,200 feet, has three chairlifts, one rope tow and 46 runs. Both mountains have 1500 acres of skiable terrain; the vertical drop is 2400 feet. Although it's in Wyoming, Grand Targhee can be reached only via Driggs, Idaho, 12 miles west.

Skiers who don't find the extremes they want at the formal ski areas can arrange to be dropped off in the Teton Range by helicopter. **High Mountain Heli-Skiing** offers packages. From mid-December to mid-April. ~ Teton Village Sports, Teton Village; 307-733-3274; www.heliskijackson.com.

Ski Rentals   For rentals outside the ski resorts themselves, try **Jack Dennis Sports**. ~ 50 East Broadway, Jackson, 307-733-3270; McAllister Drive, Teton Village, 307-733-4505; and Alpenhof Lodge, Teton Village, 307-733-6838. Also try **Teton Village Sports**. Closed April and May. ~ Crystal Springs Inn, Teton Village; 307-733-2181.

The **Jackson Hole Nordic Center** has 15 kilometers of groomed nordic trails along with full equipment rentals. ~ Teton Village; 307-739-2292. There are also trails and rentals at the **Snow King Resort**. ~ 400 East Snow King Avenue, Jackson; 307-733-5200. If you're looking to ski on a fair-weather golf course, try the **Teton Pines Nordic Ski Center**. This course has about 13 kilometers of groomed trails, rentals and instruction. Closed April through November. ~ 3450 North Clubhouse Drive, Teton Village; 307-733-1005. There's also the **Spring Creek Nordic Center**. Closed mid-March through November. ~ Spring Gulch Road, Jackson; 307-733-1004.

Some 65 kilometers of marked but ungroomed trails are open to cross-country skiers in **Grand Teton National Park**; maps are available at the Moose Visitors Center, open daily in winter. ~ Moose; 307-739-3399. Maps and information on nordic trails within **Bridger-Teton National Forest**—including the Cache Creek, Shadow Mountain, Teton Pass and Togwotee Mountain Lodge

CROSS-COUNTRY SKIING

✔ **CHECK THESE OUT—UNIQUE OUTDOOR ADVENTURES**

- Tackle the Snake River Canyon whitewater from a rubber raft, but don't lose your lunch at the rapid known as Lunch Counter! *page 97*
- Take the leap into Corbet's Couloir atop the Jackson Hole Ski Area, and continue skiing down Rendezvous Peak, whose vertical drop is the longest of any U.S. ski area. *page 98*
- Collect your ropes and pitons at South Jenny Lake and join a mountaineering expedition up the lofty Grand Teton. *page 101*
- Board the Jackson Hole Aerial Tramway to the top of Rendezvous Peak for a nature walk through Rock Springs Bowl. *page 104*

areas—are available from the National Forest visitors center. ~ 532 North Cache Street, Jackson; 307-739-5500.

Hardy adventurers can learn winter mountaineering and join hut-to-hut skiing expeditions with **Jackson Hole Mountain Guides**. ~ 165 North Glenwood Street, Jackson; 307-733-4979.

Ski Rentals   Nordic specialists with rentals available include **Skinny Skis**. ~ 65 West Deloney Street, Jackson; 307-733-6094. Contact **Wilson Backcountry Sports** for backcountry skis. ~ 1230 Ida Lane, Wilson; 307-733-5228. **Teton Mountaineering** rents cross-country skis. ~ 170 North Cache Street, Jackson; 307-733-3595.

**OTHER
WINTER
SPORTS**

The Togwotee Pass area, some 20 miles east of Moran off Route 26/287, has become a popular destination for snowmobilers near the head of Wyoming's Continental Divide Trail. (The trail extends south through national forest lands from the edge of Grand Teton National Park through Pinedale to Lander and covers more than 350 miles.) **Cowboy Village Resort** along with **Togwotee Snowmobile Adventures** provide machines for guided or self-guided trips as well as overnight tours. ~ Route 26, Moran; 307-733-8800. There are perhaps 20 places to rent snowmobiles in Jackson itself, including **Wyoming Adventures**. ~ 1050 South Route 89; 307-733-2300.

Grand Teton National Park rangers lead free snowshoeing tours along the Snake River. Tours leave the Moose Visitors Center at 2 p.m. every day except Wednesday. For information, call 307-739-3399. **The Hole Hiking Experience** provides snowshoe trips into the Bridger-Teton and Targhee national forests. ~ P.O. Box 7779, Jackson, WY 83002; 307-690-4453. Snowshoe rentals are available at several locations, including **Teton Mountaineering**. ~ 170 North Cache Street, Jackson; 307-733-3595.

Jackson Hole doesn't have Alaska's affinity for dogsledding —not yet—but it does host an annual winter dog race that draws an international group of contestants. Recreational dogsledding is offered by **Jackson Hole Iditarod Sled Dog Tours** from mid-November to mid-April. ~ 11 Granite Creek Road, Jackson; 307-733-7388. It's also available at **Moon Mountain Ranch** at the Grand Targhee Ski Resort. ~ Alta; 800-827-4433.

There's ice skating in Jackson at the **Snow King Center Ice Rink**. The indoor rink at the foot of the Snow King Mountain ski slopes offers rentals and instruction. The rink is open to the public from November to April. During June and July it is the site of the highly acclaimed Huron Hockey School. ~ 100 East Snow King Avenue, Jackson; 307-733-5200. There's also a free **outdoor rink** on Cache Street, two blocks south of Town Square, open daily in winter, weather permitting.

Climbing
the Tetons

The Teton Range is considered one of the world's finest tests for experienced climbers. Yet even first-timers can master the apparently insurmountable Grand Teton itself, given good physical strength, determination and expert instruction.

At 13,772 feet, the Grand Teton is regarded as a classic two-day ascent for skilled climbers, three or four days for the less accomplished. The easiest path to the summit is the Owen-Spalding Route originally pioneered by the peak's first conquerors in 1898; today, more climbers tackle the moderately difficult Exum Ridge route.

Mt. Moran and Mt. Owen are other oft-attempted two- to three-day climbs. Moran, at 12,605 feet, offers the range's most commanding views. It also boasts the most popular snow climb in the Tetons with a transit of Skillet Glacier.

Two of the best one-day climbs are off Hanging Canyon, a relatively short hike west of Jenny Lake. Cube Point is considered a moderate climb, while nearby Symmetry Spire is known for its long, relatively strenuous pitches.

The main climbing season in the Tetons extends from early June to mid-September, when the Jenny Lake Ranger Station registers all mountaineers and provides climbing information, including current weather forecasts, route descriptions and conditions, and equipment advice.

During other months, climbers are required to sign in and out at the Moose Visitors Center. Many adventurers, in fact, prefer the challenge of winter climbing. Ski mountaineering between alpine huts is also popular.

The area is blessed with two internationally renowned climbing schools, staffed year-round by expert instructors. Both provide everything from one-day basic or intermediate courses in rock, ice and snow climbing to full four-day guided ascents of Grand Teton or any other peak in the Teton Range.

Exum Mountain Guides & School of American Mountaineering maintains its headquarters at South Jenny Lake. ~ P.O. Box 56, Moose, WY 83012; 307-733-2297. Nearby is the **American Alpine Club's Climbers' Ranch**, where dormitory beds, showers and a community kitchen are available at minimal cost. ~ South Jenny Lake; 307-733-7271. **Jackson Hole Mountain Guides & Climbing School** offers many guided mountaineering trips as well as instruction. ~ 165 North Glenwood Street, Jackson; 307-733-4979.

To help you stay in shape, the **Teton Rock Gym** has an indoor climbing wall and a weight room. Basic climbing instruction and equipment rentals are also available. ~ 1116 Maple Way, Jackson; 307-733-0707.

Teton Mountaineering has the largest inventory of equipment and clothing in the area. ~ 170 North Cache Street, Jackson; 307-733-3595.

GOLF

Jackson Hole has some great 18-hole courses, but snow severely limits the season: It is typically May 1 to October 15.

The **Jackson Hole Golf & Tennis Club,** operated by the Grand Teton Lodging Company, has been rated by *Golf Digest* magazine as one of the top ten resort courses in the United States. Located eight miles north of Jackson, the course was redesigned by the renowned Robert Trent Jones, Jr. Facilities include a pro shop, rental carts and clubs, a driving range, putting green and a gourmet restaurant. ~ One mile west of Route 89 at Gros Ventre Junction; 307-733-3111.

The course at the semiprivate **Teton Pines Country Club & Resort,** six miles west of Jackson, is every bit the equal of the Jackson Hole Golf & Tennis Club. Designed by Arnold Palmer and Ed Seay, it is rated the number-one course in Wyoming by *Golf Digest.* A pro shop, rental carts and clubs, a driving range, putting green and an elegant restaurant complete its facilities. ~ 3450 North Clubhouse Drive, off Teton Village Road, Wilson; 307-734-3128.

Playful putters will find an 18-hole miniature golf course at **Snow King Resort.** ~ 400 East Snow King Avenue, Jackson; 307-734-3128.

TENNIS

The **Jackson Hole Golf & Tennis Club** has six Plexicushion courts. ~ Off Route 89 at Gros Ventre Junction; 307-733-7787. The **Teton Pines Tennis Center** has seven courts (plus indoor courts for winter play). ~ 3450 North Clubhouse Drive, Wilson; 307-733-9248. Both clubs offer a full range of lessons and pro shops with racquet sales, rentals and restringing service. Call ahead for court times.

RIDING STABLES

Two stables in Grand Teton National Park offer visitors ample opportunities for one- and two-hour guided rides in off-the-road wilderness. Private outfitters throughout the region provide many more options. Half-day, full-day and extended overnight trips are available for photography or wildlife watching, fishing or hunting, or simply for the joy of riding. Summer visitors can book a wagon-train trip, which may require city slickers to assist cowboys with their chores.

Some outfitters offer riding lessons; more commonly, novice riders will be matched with gentler horses. (Said one outfitter, tongue firmly in cheek: "When we get people who don't like to ride, we give them horses that don't like to be rode neither.") While most trips are guided, some stables rent horses and saddles to qualified riders for exploring on their own. Rates vary widely, but in general the smaller your group, the higher your cost.

The Grand Teton Lodging Company offers all manner of trail rides from both the **Colter Bay Village Corral** (Rockefeller Parkway, Moran; 307-543-3594) and the **Jackson Bay Lodge Corral** (Rockefeller Parkway, Moran; 307-543-2811).

Elsewhere in Jackson Hole, for short daytrips, check **Snow King Stables**, right in town. ~ Snow King Resort, 400 East Snow King Avenue, Jackson; 307-733-5200. At the **A/OK Corral**, a few miles south, non-riders can travel in covered wagons to join their horse-borne friends at chuck-wagon dinners. ~ Route 191, Hoback Junction; 307-733-6556.

Cowboy Village Resort leads one-hour to full-day trail rides into the Teton Wilderness. Closed September to late June. ~ P.O. Box 91, Moran, WY 83013; 307-733-8800, 800-543-2847, fax 307-543-2391.

Backcountry horse trips are the forté of groups like **Bridger Teton Outfitters**, which ventures into the Gros Ventre Wilderness and Wind River Range. ~ Star Route Box 347, Jackson, WY 83001; 307-733-7745. **Peterson-Madsen-Taylor Outfitters** provides horse trips and focuses on the Teton Wilderness. ~ Turpin Meadows, Moran; 307-543-2418. **Cowboy Village Resort** conducts two- and seven-day horse trips through the Teton Wilderness. Closed September to late June. ~ P.O. Box 91, Moran, WY 83013; 307-733-8800, 800-543-2847, fax 307-543-2391.

PACK TRIPS & LLAMA TREKS

Jackson Hole Llamas will take you on llama treks of three, four or five days into the Jedediah Smith Wilderness and Yellowstone National Park. ~ P.O. Box 12500, Jackson, WY 83002; 307-739-9582.

A broad, relatively flat valley surrounded on all sides by mountains, Jackson Hole is a natural for biking.

BIKING

Mountain bikes have become a common sight here in recent years, joining touring bikes on and off the roads. Many of the routes here are narrow and dangerous, so helmets and rear-view mirrors, small tool kits, first-aid kits and (if you're venturing into the backcountry) emergency survival kits are essential accessories. The season for bike tours generally runs May through September.

For a moderate day ride near Jackson, locals recommend the **Cache Creek-Game Creek** loop trail, an 18-mile circuit around Snow King Mountain southeast of Jackson in Bridger-Teton National Forest.

Grand Teton National Park roads and other valley highways are great for touring, and hundreds of miles of trails and dirt roads head into adjacent national forests. Wilderness areas are off-limits.

The 15-mile RKO **Road** in Grand Teton Park, a dirt road along a bluff on the west side of the Snake River from Signal Mountain to Cottonwood Creek, is a good bet for a moderate day ride.

Teton Mountain Bike Tours offers one-day guided tours, lasting from three to nine hours, through the Grand Teton and Yellowstone national parks, Bridger-Teton National Forest or through the National Elk Refuge. ~ P.O. Box 7027, Jackson, WY 83002; 307-733-0712. Another bicycle touring company is **Fat Tire Tours.** They offer family Elk Refuge trips and a Snow King trip for more intense riding. ~ 40 South Millward Street, Jackson; 307-733-5335.

Bike Rentals   Several Jackson Hole shops rent and repair bicycles and provide regional biking maps. For touring and mountain bikes in downtown Jackson try **Hoback Sports.** ~ 40 South Millward Street; 307-733-5335. Also try **Teton Cycle Works** for rentals. ~ 175 North Glenwood Street; 307-733-4386. Near Grand Teton National Park, you can contact **Mountain Bike Outfitters,** located at Dornan's at the south entrance to the park. ~ 10 Teton Park Road, Moose; 307-733-3314. **Teton Village Sports** rents bicycles during the summer. ~ Crystal Springs Inn, Teton Village; 307-733-2181.

HIKING   Northwestern Wyoming is crisscrossed by thousands of miles of trails—no exaggeration—and there's something for everyone here, even the elderly and the disabled. Routes vary dramatically in difficulty and length, from gentle day hikes along the shores of unspoiled lakes to arduous, multiday expeditions up steep-sided canyons and over mountain passes. All distances listed for hiking trails are one way unless otherwise noted.

JACKSON HOLE   The moderate descent of **Rendezvous Peak** (4.2 miles) is made easier by the Jackson Hole Aerial Tramway. Take it to the top; then start down through Rock Springs Bowl. Wildflowers, small mammals and birds (including large raptors) are often seen.

Goodwin Lake-Cache Creek Trail (7.5 miles) is a moderately strenuous introduction to the Gros Ventre Wilderness Area east of Jackson. Starting at the end of Curtis Canyon Road, nine miles northeast of Jackson, the trail traverses a high plateau at 10,000 feet before dropping to the headwaters of Cache Creek. If you don't have a car waiting to pick you up at the trailhead, you'll have to walk an extra five miles downhill to Jackson.

Guided interpretive hikes in the Bridger-Teton and Grand Targhee national forests are offered by **The Hole Hiking Experience.** ~ P.O. Box 7779, Jackson, WY 83002; 307-690-4453.

GRAND TETON NATIONAL PARK   **Hidden Falls Trail** (2.5 miles) is an easy two-mile walk around the southwest shore of Jenny Lake from the South Jenny ranger station and a strenuous half-mile uphill scramble to the secluded cascade. If you want to continue, there's another half-mile climb to Inspiration Point and then six and a half more through Cascade Canyon to lovely Lake Solitude. Boat shuttles across Jenny Lake are available to return tired hikers from near Hidden Falls to the South Jenny ranger station.

Two Ocean Lake Trail (12.2 miles) circles the three-mile-long lake in the park's northeastern corner, skirts adjacent Emma Matilda Lake and climbs to a panoramic outlook toward Jackson Lake at Grand View Point. It's of moderate difficulty.

Teton Crest Trail (27 miles) has many feeder trails and many spurs. One popular if strenuous circuit of the Grand Teton begins at Jenny Lake Lodge (6900 feet), climbs west on the Paintbrush Canyon Trail to Lake Solitude, then turns south along the upper slopes of Mount Owen and the high Tetons. The trail crests at about 11,000 feet before descending again on switchbacks through Death Canyon to Phelps Lake and Teton Village (6300 feet).

All overnight backcountry camping requires a permit, which can be obtained free at ranger stations.

Equipment   For more information on area trails or to obtain equipment, visit **Jack Dennis Sports**. ~ 50 East Broadway, Jackson; 307-733-3270. Or try **Wilson Backcountry Sports**. ~ 1230 Ida Lane, Wilson; 307-733-5228.

Transportation

To reach Jackson Hole, take **Route 26** west off Route 25 at Casper, or east off Route 15 at Idaho Falls, Idaho. Or take **Route 191** north at Rock Springs or **Route 189** north at Evanston off Route 80. From Yellowstone, take route 89/191/ 287 south.

CAR

Following principal routes, Jackson is 100 miles from Lake Village (Yellowstone Park) and 432 miles from the Wyoming state capital at Cheyenne.

Jackson Hole Airport has regular daily nonstop arrivals from and departures to Chicago, Denver and Salt Lake City, with connecting flights from many other cities. It is served by American Airlines, SkyWest Airlines, United and United Express. Regional charters and scenic flights are available. The airport is eight miles north of Jackson within the boundaries of Grand Teton National Park. ~ 1250 East Airport Road off Route 89 North, Jackson; 307-733-7682, 307-733-2272.

AIR

Jackson's only scheduled bus service is the **Jackson Hole Express**, which runs daily between Jackson and Salt Lake City. They also run buses to Idaho Falls. ~ 307-733-1719.

BUS

AllTrans–Gray Line offers seasonal charter service and guided tours through Yellowstone Park from Jackson Hole. ~ 1680 West Martin Lane, Jackson; 307-733-1700.

CAR RENTALS

At the Jackson Hole Airport, you can rent from **Alamo Rent A Car** (800-327-9633), **Avis Rent A Car** (800-331-1212), **Budget Rent A Car** (800-527-0700) and **Hertz Rent A Car** (800-654-3131). In town, also consider **Eagle Rent A Car**, which offers everything from minivans and Jeep Wranglers to snowmobiles. ~ 375 North Cache Drive, Jackson; 307-739-9999.

PUBLIC TRANSIT

In Jackson, the **Southern Teton Area Rapid Transit**, known as START, runs two routes between Jackson and Teton Village. ~ 307-733-4521.

TAXIS

AllTrans–Gray Line (307-733-1700), **All Star Transportation** (307-733-2888) and **Buckboard Cab** (307-733-1112) provide taxi service in Jackson Hole. Also meeting all incoming and departing flights is **Grand Limousine.** ~ 307-739-2534.

FOUR

The Big Horn Basin

The Big Horn Basin is a natural fortress. Measuring about 50 by 100 miles and averaging 4000 feet in elevation, it is surrounded on three sides by high mountain ranges and to the north by rugged foothills.

Through its heart, the Bighorn River slices a course from south to north, entering the basin through the nearly impassable Wind River Canyon and disappearing into Montana through the even more forbidding (but magnificent) Bighorn Canyon. Numerous tributaries allow an otherwise arid climate to support large cattle and sheep ranches, which have thrived in the basin since 1879.

This was the land of "Buffalo Bill" Cody, whose namesake town today is a center for ranching and tourism. A thriving community of 8000 people, Cody sits at the western edge of the basin, at the foot of the Absaroka Range and the eastern gateway to Yellowstone National Park. The highway between Cody and Yellowstone, which follows the Wapiti Valley through Shoshone National Forest, was one of the first forest areas in the western United States developed for outdoor recreation; indeed, the first ranger station ever built in this country was here, on the North Fork of the Shoshone River.

The main Big Horn Basin sweeps east from here, running from the hot-springs resort town of Thermopolis north to Lovell, headquarters town for Bighorn Canyon National Recreation Area. Beyond, a trio of highways ascend the cloud-piercing passes of the Big Horn Mountains before dropping to Sheridan and the plains of northeastern Wyoming.

This western Big Horn slope is of special interest to modern scientists for its geology, paleontology and archaeology. Shell Canyon, east of Greybull, for instance, has unveiled marine fossils in three-billion-year-old granite. And discoveries at Medicine Lodge (near Hyattville) and Medicine Wheel (east of Lovell) indicate that American Indians were writing on cliff walls and building astronomical monuments before the rise of any of the great Chinese, Egyptian or Mesoamerican civilizations.

Cody

Cody is Cowboy Country, with capital Cs: it's the chosen home of Colonel William F. "Buffalo Bill" Cody and the self-proclaimed "Rodeo Capital of the World."

Located on the Shoshone River beneath the towering 12,000-foot peaks of the Absaroka Range, Cody was founded in 1895 as a rail terminus of the Chicago, Burlington & Quincy line. A group of entrepreneurs, including Buffalo Bill himself, foresaw the commercial opportunities in tourism and recreation that such a location, 52 miles from the east entrance to Yellowstone National Park, might provide. Cody offered his name to the town, and his gracious partners concurred; he already had international name recognition.

Modern Cody has a battery of comfortable motels and restaurants serving travelers a short drive from Yellowstone—as well as considerable tourist attractions of its own.

SIGHTS

Chief among the town's tourist attractions is the **Buffalo Bill Historical Center**, certainly one of the finest museums in the Rocky Mountain region and, some say, in all of the United States. The large modern building, located at the west end of downtown Cody, is impossible to miss (not that you'd want to). Inside are four separate collections that comprise a sort of Smithsonian Institution of the American West.

The **Buffalo Bill Museum** is dedicated to Cody himself, a man who—probably more than any other—symbolized the emergence of the West from a primitive frontier to a vital and integral part of the United States. The vast assemblage includes "Lucretia Borgia," the rifle Cody used while earning the nickname "Buffalo Bill," shooting bison in the employ of the railroad; elaborate gifts he received from such royalty as Czar Alexander II of Russia; and a wide variety of clothing, saddles, trophies and photographs recalling his colorful life and those of many of his contemporaries.

The **Plains Indian Museum** depicts the cultures and lifestyles of Arapaho, Blackfoot, Cheyenne, Comanche, Crow, Gros Ventre, Kiowa, Pawnee, Shoshone, Sioux and other tribes of the northern Great Plains. Traditional clothing (including beadwork and headdresses), spiritual artifacts (such as ceremonial pipes), weapons, tools and art are all part of the extensive display of more than 5000 items. Exhibits interpret the importance of the horse and the bison to Plains Indian culture; in Tipi Hall, a portion of an 1890 Sioux camp has been recreated.

The **Whitney Gallery of Western Art** documents the American West in more than 1000 original paintings and sculptures by some of the most famous artists of the 19th and 20th centuries. There's a reconstruction of Frederic Remington's studio, early Yellowstone and Grand Teton landscapes by Albert Bierstadt and

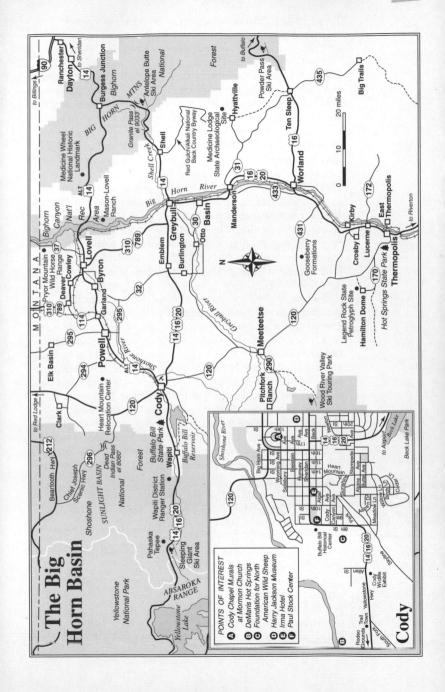

The Big Horn Basin

POINTS OF INTEREST
A Cody Chapel Murals at Mormon Church
B DeMaris Hot Springs
C Foundation for North American Wild Sheep
D Harry Jackson Museum
E Irma Hotel
F Paul Stock Center

Cody

Thomas Moran, classic works by Charles M. Russell and Andrew Wyeth and numerous contemporary works. Among the highlights is Edgar Paxson's original wall-size oil of "Custer's Last Stand."

The **Cody Firearms Museum**, originally the Winchester Arms Museum, contains more guns than you probably ever thought you'd see in one place at one time. The 4000 pieces make up the world's largest and most important collection of American arms; also on display are European firearms dating back to the 16th century and a hunting lodge with numerous world-record big-game heads. Virtually every type and manufacturer of American firearms is represented in the collection, making it possible to trace the technical and artistic evolution of the industry.

The Historical Center also includes a special exhibitions area, outdoor sculpture gardens, a café, a gift shop, and the Harold McCracken Research Library. Outside is the **Buffalo Bill Monument**, officially called *The Scout.* One of the country's largest bronze equestrian statues, the monument was sculpted and donated by Gertrude Vanderbilt Whitney in 1924. Closed Monday from November through March. Admission. ~ 720 Sheridan Avenue; 307-587-4771.

History is also the cornerstone of **Trail Town,** just off the Yellowstone Highway heading west from town. Some two dozen late-19th-century buildings from throughout northern Wyoming have been relocated to the original 1895 town site of Cody, just above DeMaris Hot Springs. Unlike other re-created frontier towns, Trail Town is almost entirely lacking in commercialism; aside from a boardwalk that extends up one side of the single street and down the other, the structures look almost exactly as they would have a century ago, down to their rustic period furnishings.

Among the buildings (many donated by pioneer families) is Butch Cassidy's 1883 "Hole-in-the-Wall" hideout cabin, a saloon, a blacksmith shop, a livery stable and a post office. The Burlington Store and the adjacent Museum of the Old West contain an

✔ **CHECK THESE OUT—UNIQUE SIGHTS**

- Explore the galleries of the **Buffalo Bill Historical Center**—some say it's the single finest museum of the American West. *page 108*
- Ponder the power of 64 million years of geologic history as you gaze into 2200-foot-deep **Bighorn Canyon.** *page 123*
- Go on a vision quest at **Medicine Wheel National Historic Landmark,** a medieval monument and sacred American Indian site that some think may have been a solstice observatory. *page 124*
- Soak your worries away at **Hot Springs State Park,** whose Big Spring produces millions of gallons of mineral-rich water daily. *page 129*

extended collection of frontier and American Indian artifacts. More than 100 old horse-drawn vehicles, including a black hearse, are on display around the grounds. In a sagebrush-landscaped cemetery at the end of town lie a handful of graves, including that of John "Jeremiah Liver Eatin'" Johnston (1824–1900), immortalized in the Robert Redford movie *Jeremiah Johnson*. Closed October through April. Admission. ~ 1831 DeMaris Drive; 307-587-5302.

DeMaris Hot Springs, just below Trail Town, are better known to some as **Colter's Hell**. Now dormant, these semiactive geysers drew health seekers throughout the 19th century after their discovery by John Colter during his 1807–08 pioneer travels through the Yellowstone region.

The original Cody town site had already been moved two miles east to its present location by the time Buffalo Bill Cody built **The Irma Hotel** in 1902. Named for the colonel's youngest daughter, it has been in continuous operation ever since. The Irma cost Cody $80,000 to build . . . not counting the cherrywood bar given to him by Queen Victoria, itself then valued at $100,000. ~ 1192 Sheridan Avenue; 307-587-4221.

The Irma is only one of many historic buildings in downtown Cody. A mile-long **Cody Historic Walking Tour** starts and ends near the Buffalo Bill Historical Center; for a brochure and map, visit the **Cody Country Chamber of Commerce** next to City Park. The chamber and the Cody Country Art League are housed in the **Paul Stock Center**, a replica of Buffalo Bill's original T. E. Ranch on the South Fork of the Shoshone River. ~ 836 Sheridan Avenue; 307-587-2297.

Off the walking tour route but of particular interest to visitors of the Mormon faith are the **Cody Chapel Murals** at the Church of Jesus Christ of Latter-Day Saints. The principal mural, by Edward Grigware, covers a domed ceiling 18 feet high and 36 feet around; it highlights the first 70 years (until 1900) of Mormon church history. In an adjoining chamber, displays and more art describe the Mormon colonization of the Big Horn Basin. ~ 1719 Wyoming Avenue; 307-587-3290.

Art of a different nature is exhibited at the **Harry Jackson Museum**. Jackson, a Cody resident since his teens, is regarded as one of the leading living sculptors of the American West. Born in the early 1920s, he was a major player in both the abstract expressionism and realism movements and now focuses on painted sculpture. Closed Saturday and Sunday. ~ 602 Blackburn Street; 307-587-5508.

◄ HIDDEN

The private **Cody Wildlife Exhibit** is a museum of taxidermy with more than 400 mounted animals and birds, including all manner of Rocky Mountain creatures and a variety of Alaskan and African mammals in natural-looking settings. Open by appointment in winter. Admission. ~ 410 Yellowstone Avenue; 307-587-2804.

At the headquarters of the **Foundation for North American Wild Sheep**, on the south side of the Buffalo Bill Historical Center, visitors can view an audiovisual presentation on conservation and wildlife management and sculptures of bighorn sheep. The foundation is driven by the sobering knowledge that two subspecies of wild sheep have become extinct in the 20th century. Closed Saturday and Sunday. ~ 720 Allen Avenue; 307-527-6261.

Poignant is the word to describe the black-granite **Wyoming Vietnam Veterans Memorial**, southeast of Cody near Yellowstone Regional Airport. The memorial lists the names of 137 Wyoming citizens killed or lost in action in the Vietnam war. ~ Greybull Highway; 307-527-7511.

LODGING   Cody hotel rates have enormous seasonal variance. High-season (June–August) rates can be more than twice what you'd pay for the same room during the long low season (October–April). Since most travelers visit during the high season, the following price designations reflect that rate level.

It's not the biggest, not the fanciest, certainly not the newest, but Buffalo Bill's very own hotel, **The Irma**, still captures the imagination of guests with its turn-of-the-century spirit. Colonel Cody spent $80,000 to have this hotel in the heart of downtown Cody built of native wood and sandstone in 1902. Named for his youngest daughter, it has 40 rooms, including 15 restored Victorian chambers (now air-conditioned, with private modern bathrooms) and 25 adjacent units, added later. The $100,000 cherrywood bar given to Buffalo Bill by England's Queen Victoria graces The Irma's restaurant; there are also two lounges. ~ 1192 Sheridan Avenue; 307-587-4221, 800-745-4762, fax 307-587-4221 ext. 21. MODERATE TO DELUXE.

The **Parson's Pillow B&B** occupies Cody's original Methodist-Episcopal house of worship, dedicated in 1902. Four guest rooms with private baths are individually decorated with Victorian antiques and lace. Full breakfasts are served in the dining room. ~ 1202 14th Street; 307-587-2382, 800-377-2348. MODERATE.

Luxuriate in one of just three rooms at the **Mayor's Inn**, a peaked-roof manse that was built by Cody's first mayor. Guest quarters are individually decorated, but all have down comforters and private baths with heated floors. ~ 1413 Rumsey Avenue; 307-587-6000, 800-587-6560, fax 307-587-8048; www.wtp.net/cghouses. DELUXE TO ULTRA-DELUXE.

Some of the 14 rooms at **The Lockhart Bed and Breakfast Inn**, on the west end of town, occupy the 1904 wood-frame home of Western novelist Carolyn Lockhart (1870–1962). Others are in an adjoining motel annex. All room have antique furnishings, including old-fashioned double beds and private bathrooms with claw-foot tubs. A full breakfast is included. ~ 109 West Yellowstone Avenue; 307-587-6074. MODERATE.

The Carriage House is a log-cabin village. Individual and duplex cabins contain 24 small units, including several with two or three bedrooms. There is air conditioning, and all rooms have full bathrooms and are decorated in a country Victorian theme. ~ 1816 8th Street; phone/fax 307-587- 2572. MODERATE.

"Absaroka" is the American Indian name for the Crow nation—which is curious, since these mountains never were Crow territory.

Near the Buffalo Bill Historical Center, the **Best Western Sunset Motor Inn** offers nicely landscaped grounds and 100 spacious rooms. Motel facilities include a restaurant, separate indoor and outdoor swimming pools, a spa, a fitness room, a playground and a guest laundry. Don't confuse the Sun*set* with the nearby Best Western Sun*rise*, which is nowhere near as nice. ~ 1601 8th Street; 307-587- 4265, 800-528-1234, fax 307-587-9029. DELUXE.

The biggest and the fanciest, if that's what you're looking for, is the **Holiday Inn-Buffalo Bill Village Resort.** This is actually three properties under common management: the modern, 190-room Holiday Inn, the rustic, 83-cabin Buffalo Bill Village, and the 75-room Comfort Inn. The two-story Holiday Inn has standard, spacious motel units built around a central courtyard and swimming pool. The Village—open May through September only—consists of 1920s-vintage log cabins; the interiors have been completely remodeled. All rooms in Inn and Village have air conditioning. The Inn has a dining room, coffee shop and lounge. ~ 1701 Sheridan Avenue; 307-587-5555, 800-527-5544, fax 307-527-7757. DELUXE.

DINING

"Kickass cowboy cuisine" like steaks, prime rib and Rocky Mountain oysters is the fare at the rustic **Proud Cut Saloon & Restaurant,** a longtime Cody stalwart in the heart of downtown. ~ 1227 Sheridan Avenue; 307-527-6905. DELUXE.

For a little twang and two-step with their victuals, locals head for **Cassie's,** not far from the rodeo grounds. This restaurant-saloon has been around since 1922 serving barbecued ribs, steak, seafood and such. There's live music most nights. ~ 214 Yellowstone Avenue; 307-527-5500. MODERATE TO DELUXE.

Cody's finest dining experience may be at **Franca's,** a small northern Italian spot a block off the main street. It serves exquisite four-course, set-menu dinners by reservation only, Tuesday through Saturday. The carefully assembled wine list has more than 100 selections. Western and Italian art hang side by side on permanent display in a back gallery. ~ 1421 Rumsey Avenue; 307-587-5354. ULTRA-DELUXE.

Steaks, seafood and pasta head the bill at **Maxwell's**, a handsome restaurant near the Buffalo Bill Historical Center with cut glass and wood decor inside, deck and patio seating outside. Soups, salads and sandwiches are also served. ~ 937 Sheridan Avenue; 307-527-7749. MODERATE TO DELUXE.

Lovers of gourmet Mexican food won't be disappointed by **La Comida**. The fajitas, the enchiladas and even the soups here are a couple of solid notches above the standard Tex-Mex hole in the wall. La Comida has outdoor patio seating. ~ 1385 Sheridan Avenue; 307-587-9556. BUDGET TO MODERATE.

SHOPPING   If every store were like the **Cody Rodeo Company**, shopping would always be a delight. From the mechanical bull near the entrance to the videos of live rodeo action playing nonstop on a screen on the far wall, this modest store is an attraction in itself. Western fashion clothing, books, household items, souvenirs and gifts—all with a cowboy theme—are the icing on the cake. Closed Sunday in winter. ~ 1291 Sheridan Avenue; 307-587-9783.

For Western clothing, jewelry, belts and boots, there's **Corral West Ranchwear**. ~ 1202 Sheridan Avenue; 307-587-2122. **Scary Mary's** offers ethnic crafts, home accents and clothing. ~ 1209 Sheridan Avenue; 307-587-9933. **Wayne's Boot Shop** has been selling boots—Western, work, hiking, hunting, snow—since 1959. Closed Sunday. ~ 1250 Sheridan Avenue; 307-587-5234. **The Plush Pony** specializes in women's clothing and accessories. ~ 1350 Sheridan Avenue; 307-587-4677.

Cody is becoming a regional art center of note, and a good place to start a gallery walk is at the **Cody Country Art League**. Located in the Paul Stock Center, it exhibits and sells paintings, sculptures and crafts by regional artists. Closed Sunday in winter. ~ 836 Sheridan Avenue; 307-587-3597.

Among the many other fine galleries in Cody is the **Big Horn Gallery**, offering classic and traditional Western art. ~ 1167 Sheridan Avenue; 307-527-7587. Another one to see is **Prairie Rose Northern Plains Indian Gallery**, featuring traditional reproductions by members of Sioux, Crow and other tribes. Closed Sunday in winter. ~ 1356 Sheridan Avenue; 307-587-8181. The **Harry Jackson Museum** features the work of a major living sculptor of Western themes. Closed Saturday and Sunday. ~ 602 Blackburn Street; 307-587-5508.

Each year, the last full weekend of June, Cody hosts the annual Cowboy Antique and Collectible Show, the largest event of its kind in the nation. A selection is available all year from one of its principal sponsors: **Old West Antiques & Cowboy Collectibles**. By appointment only in winter. ~ 1215 Sheridan Avenue; 307-587-9014.

For other sorts of gifts, Cody has a great many places to look. One interesting store in a big log cabin just up the road from the Buffalo Bill Historical Center is the **Cody Gift Shoppe**. ~ 1402 8th Street; 307-587-4205. Across the street, with a similarly wide selection, is the **Ponderosa Trading Post**. ~ 1815 8th Street; 307-587-8461.

Gift packs of buffalo sausage and salami are prettily wrapped with appropriate condiments at the **Wyoming Buffalo Company**. You'll also find gourmet Western foods and a line of Western home decor. Closed on Sunday during the winter. ~ 1276 Sheridan Avenue; 307-587-8708.

Handmade leather clothing, reproduction Indian souvenirs and tourist gift items are available from the **Old West Miniature Village & Museum**. One can also visit the on-site museum (fee) featuring a collection of Indian artifacts and dioramas that portray the history of Wyoming and Montana. By appointment only in winter. ~ 142 West Yellowstone Avenue; 307-587-5362.

The first word in Cody evening entertainment, hands down, is the **Cody Nite Rodeo**. Every night in June, July and August, battle-proven cowboys gather at Stampede Park, at the far west end of town, to test their mettle in bull riding, calf roping, bulldogging and bareback and saddle bronco competition. Other events include women's barrel racing and a free-for-all during which every child in attendance, 12 or under, is invited to scramble after a frightened calf and untie a white flag from its tail. The rodeo lasts about 90 minutes. Try to get a seat in Buzzard's Roost, above the chutes on the far side of the arena. Admission. ~ 115 West Yellowstone Avenue; box office 307-587-5155.

NIGHTLIFE

From Memorial Day through Labor Day, the **Cody Gunslingers** re-enact Western gun battles and other significant incidences in front of the Irma Hotel. The action begins at 6 p.m. ~ 1192 Sheridan Avenue; 307-587-4221.

Elsewhere in Cody, there's live country-and-western music for dancing at **Cassie's**. ~ 214 Yellowstone Avenue; 307-527-5500. Try **Angie's Saloon at the Silver Dollar Bar** if you're in the mood for classic rock. In summer there are live bands on weekends and deejays Tuesday through Thursday. ~ 1313 Sheridan Avenue; 307-587-3554. For belly-up-to-the-bar conversation and drinks, a local favorite is **The Irma**. ~ 1192 Sheridan Avenue; 307-587-4221. Another popular hangout is the **Proud Cut Saloon**. ~ 1227 Sheridan Avenue; 307-527-6905.

BECK LAKE PARK AND RECREATION AREA

PARKS

Recreational development at this Cody city park is an ongoing community project, with many provisions for the handicapped.

The park and recreation area actually encompasses four modest-sized lakes with extensive wetlands, especially adjacent Alkali Lake. Some 80 species of waterfowl and songbirds inhabit the area. Beck Lake is stocked with rainbow trout, but only non-motorized boating is permitted. There are picnic areas and restrooms. ~ From Stampede Avenue, between 8th Street and the Greybull Highway, take 14th Street south into the park; 307-527-7511.

▼▼▼▼▼▼▼▼▼▼
Wapiti Valley

There are many who consider the Yellowstone Highway, which runs west from Cody to Yellowstone National Park, to be among the most scenic roads in America. The 52-mile byway (Route 14/16/20), which follows the canyon of the North Fork of the Shoshone River through the Wapiti Valley to the park's east entrance, passes Buffalo Bill Dam and Reservoir and a circus of vivid rock formations. Shoshone National Forest campgrounds and a profusion of guest ranches, including Colonel Cody's own Pahaska Tepee, provide a wide range of recreational opportunities.

SIGHTS

The Yellowstone Highway tunnels through Rattlesnake Mountain six miles west of downtown Cody and emerges at the **Buffalo Bill Dam**, the first concrete-arch dam ever constructed. It was also the highest dam in the world (325 feet) when completed in 1910, the first project of the new U.S. Bureau of Reclamation. A modern visitors center affords spectacular views of the Shoshone River, 353 feet straight down, rushing toward Cody, and has exhibits that describe how the vast cropland to the east is almost solely dependent upon this project. An eight-year project to raise the dam 25 feet and increase the reservoir's capacity by more than 50 percent was finished in 1992. ~ Yellowstone Highway, Cody; 307-527-6076.

Behind the dam is the five-mile-long **Buffalo Bill Reservoir**, encompassed by 11,500-acre **Buffalo Bill State Park** (see "Parks").

Bison can be viewed from the highway as it proceeds west past the **Trout Creek Buffalo Preserve**, 14 miles out of Cody at the foot of Sheep Mountain.

About 20 miles from Cody, the road enters the community of Wapiti, spread along the highway for about five miles to the south of the towering Absaroka volcanic thrust. This valley takes its name—the Shoshone word for *elk*—from the **Wapiti District Ranger Station**, the first ever built in the United States (in 1903). Located 29 miles from Cody, it has interpretive displays not of elk but of grizzly bears. ~ Yellowstone Highway, Wapiti; 307-527-6921.

The ranger station is just within the boundary of **Shoshone National Forest** (see "Parks" below), the direct result of more political finagling by Buffalo Bill. The colonel's influence led President Benjamin Harrison to proclaim the Yellowstone Park Timberland Reserve in 1891, protecting the timber on public domain; four years later, it became the first parcel of the new U.S. Forest Service. The territory's name was changed to Shoshone National Forest in 1945.

Such odd red-rock formations as the Playground of the Gods, the Chinese Wall, the Laughing Pig and the Holy City add fascination to the second half of the drive from Cody to Yellowstone. About 36 miles from Cody, the **Blackwater Memorial**, standing beside the highway at the mouth of Blackwater Creek, pays homage to 15 firefighters who died combating a 1937 blaze. A memorial trail leads to the burned-over area on Clayton Mountain, six miles south of here.

LODGING

There are no fewer than 15 guest ranches along this route, many of them well worth a long stay. None, however, has the same history attached to it as **Pahaska Tepee Resort**, Buffalo Bill Cody's original 1904 hunting lodge. Located just two miles from the east entrance to Yellowstone, the rough-hewn log lodge, nestled in pines near the North Fork of the Shoshone River, is surrounded by 50 two- to six-room cabins. Rustic decor pervades the cabins, dining room and tavern. There are facilities for horseback riding and fishing in summer, snowmobiling and cross-country skiing in winter. Closed mid-October through December and March through April. ~ 183 Yellowstone Highway, Cody; 307-527-7701, 800-628-7791, fax 307-527-4019. MODERATE.

The classiest of the Wapiti Valley guest ranches may be the **Rimrock Dude Ranch**, almost exactly halfway between Cody and Yellowstone Park. Established in 1927, it lodges up to 35 guests in private log cabins with full baths. Several larger cabins have living rooms with stone fireplaces. Family-style meals are served in the main ranch house, and evening entertainment ranges from rodeo activities to square dancing. A horseback-riding program includes instruction, trail rides and wilderness pack trips; fishing and river rafting are among other activities. Open mid-May through mid-September for all-inclusive full-week packages. ~ 2728 Yellowstone Highway, Wapiti; 307-587-3970. ULTRA-DELUXE.

DINING

Cody residents have no problem driving 40 miles west to the Elephant Head Lodge's **Elk & Ale** restaurant, where they order filet mignon, New York strip and rib-eye steak all marinated in a special secret sauce. There are also home-style beef and seafood plates. Breakfast is offered, too. Closed October to mid-May. ~ 1170 Yellowstone Highway, Wapiti; 307-587-3980. MODERATE TO DELUXE.

Another good dining option here is the **Absaroka Mountain Lodge Restaurant**, which has developed a reputation among anglers as the best place to bring your trout to have it professionally cooked. Steak, salmon, crab, pasta and chicken dishes are also on the menu. Closed October through April. ~ 1231 Yellowstone Highway, Wapiti; 307-587-3963. BUDGET TO MODERATE.

PARKS

BUFFALO BILL STATE PARK 🛶 🏊 🎣 🚤 🏍 Encompassing five-mile-long Buffalo Bill Reservoir, created in 1910 by the Buffalo Bill Dam on the North and South forks of the Shoshone River, this 12,000-acre state park actually has four parcels—two for day use only (Sheep Mountain and Bartlett Lane) and two that welcome overnight campers (North Shore Bay and North Fork). The park is popular among boaters and anglers; *Outside* magazine has rated the reservoir as one of the ten best places for board sailing in the United States. The reservoir is home to brown, rainbow, cutthroat and lake trout (mackinaw) as well as mountain whitefish. Facilities include picnic areas and restrooms. Day-use fee, $3. ~ Take the Yellowstone Highway (Route 14/16/20) west eight miles from Cody to the reservoir. It's nine miles to North Shore Bay and to park headquarters, 14 miles to North Fork and Sheep Mountain. To reach the Bartlett Lane area, take South Fork Road (Route 291) six miles south and west from Cody; continue straight one mile at Bartlett Lane; 307-587-9227.

▲ There are 97 RV/tent units plus six for tents only at two campgrounds (no hookups); $4 per night; 14-day maximum stay. Closed October through April.

SHOSHONE NATIONAL FOREST 🚶 🚴 🏇 🎿 🏕 🎣 🚤 🏍 The nation's first protected forest when it was established in 1891 as the Yellowstone Park Timberland Reserve, Shoshone contains the first U.S. ranger station (at Wapiti). Today, the two and a half million acres of this preserve spread south for 170 miles from the Montana border, along the eastern border of Yellowstone National Park and the east slope of the Wind River Range. Shoshone shares Gannett Peak, Wyoming's highest (13,804 feet), with Bridger-Teton National Forest, and embraces four wilderness areas and part of a fifth. Attractions include two national scenic byways, the Chief Joseph and the Beartooth; two national wild and scenic rivers, Clark's Fork of the Yellowstone and the North Fork of the Shoshone; alpine lakes and streams for fishing. Facilities include picnic areas and restrooms. ~ The Yellowstone Highway (Route 14/16/20), Chief Joseph Scenic Highway (Route 296), Beartooth Highway (Route 212) and South Fork Road (Route 291) all run through Shoshone National Forest; 307-527-6921.

▲ There are 340 RV/tent units plus 201 for tents only in 35 campgrounds (no hookups), including ten campgrounds along the North Fork and ten campgrounds in the Sunlight Basin–Beartooth area; $8 per night; 14-day maximum stay.

Spirit of the Old West

Probably the single most remarkable character the Old West ever produced was William F. "Buffalo Bill" Cody.

Trapper, wrangler, Pony Express rider, Army scout, buffalo hunter, wagonmaster, stagecoach driver, Indian fighter, actor and entrepreneur, Cody more than any other individual was responsible for giving the West the romantic image it held around the world at the turn of the 20th century.

Born in rural Iowa in 1846, Cody was forced at age 11, upon his father's death, to go to work as a mounted messenger. He rode for the Pony Express for 18 months, and after its demise in 1861 served in the Civil War.

In 1867, Cody was hired by the Union Pacific Railroad to hunt buffalo to feed its construction crews. In eight months, he shot an average of 18 bison a day, over 4000 in all. He was bestowed the nickname "Buffalo Bill."

Through his 20s, Cody's frontier savvy—his horsemanship and marksmanship, his courage and stamina, his understanding of the wilderness, his understanding of American Indian life—placed him in high esteem as a scout and guide. The Fifth Cavalry employed him almost continuously in its wars against the Plains Indians. Cody himself took part in 16 of those battles and was awarded a Congressional Medal of Honor for bravery.

Back East, sensationalist reporters and paperback novelists transformed this upstart frontiersman into a folk hero. When Cody was approached to play himself on stage, he proved to be a natural showman who substituted dash and humor for polish and experience. By 1883, Cody had put together his own Buffalo Bill's Wild West Show. For three decades—including ten years in Europe—this stage spectacular promoted the Old West with exhibitions of shooting and roping, a buffalo stampede, a stagecoach holdup, and all manner of cowboy and Indian lore. Stars like riflewoman Annie Oakley and Sitting Bull, the Sioux chief, added to the myth.

Cody reveled in his personal fame—by some estimations, "the Colonel" was the world's best-known personality in 1900—but he used it as a vehicle to bring public attention to his favorite causes. In spite of his role in their decline, Cody championed both the integrity of American Indian heritage and the recovery of the bison population. And he was an outspoken advocate of women's rights: "If a woman can do the same work that a man can do and do it just as well, she should have the same pay," he said.

A founder of the town of Cody in 1895, he held that preservation must go hand in hand with development. To that end, he invested his fortune in town planning, ranching, mining, irrigation and newspaper publishing.

Cody died in 1917 while visiting his sister in Denver.

WASHAKIE WILDERNESS AREA 👤🏇🛶⬛ Steep-sided, flat-topped, 12,000-foot-high mountains and plateaus—with names like Citadel, Fortress, Battlement and Wall—are hallmarks of this 704,000-acre wilderness. Extending from Yellowstone National Park to the Wind River Indian Reservation, it is rich in wildlife and backcountry hiking opportunities. ~ Trails head south into the Washakie from several points along the Yellowstone Highway, including Elk Fork, Blackwater, Fishhawk, Kitty and Eagle creeks. From South Fork Road (Route 291), there are numerous other access points; 307-527-6921.

▲ Primitive only.

Chief Joseph Highway

Much less traveled than the Yellowstone Highway but certainly its scenic equal is the 46-mile Chief Joseph Scenic Highway (Route 296). This road from Cody to the northeast entrance of Yellowstone Park skirts beautiful Sunlight Basin before connecting with the Beartooth Highway southeast of Cooke City, Montana. (In all, the distance from Cody to the northeast entrance is 81 miles.)

It could be argued that Route 296 is not really much of a highway. One seven-mile stretch—over 8071-foot Dead Indian Pass—is as yet unpaved, but the road is well maintained, and the drive as a whole is easily accomplished in most weather conditions.

SIGHTS   The highway begins 17 miles north of Cody, turning west off Route 120 (the principal Cody-Billings road). After crossing the Two Dot Ranch, it winds to the top of Dead Indian Pass. Chief Joseph and his Nez Perce followers evaded the U.S. Army here in 1877 during their flight for freedom; the **Nez Perce (Nee-Me-Poo) National Historic Trail** retraces their escape route down the steep, nearly impassable slope of Clark's Fork Canyon.

From the **Dead Indian Pass Overlook,** travelers have a remarkable view in all directions: South and southwest to Sunlight Basin and the North Absaroka Wilderness Area, north and northwest to the Beartooth Plateau and the Clark's Fork of the Yellowstone River (Wyoming's only nationally designated Wild and Scenic River), east past Heart Mountain to Big Horn Basin.

Sunlight Basin, for many, is the highlight of this trip. The road from Dead Indian Pass descends about 2000 feet to the Sunlight Creek Bridge, suspended nearly a quarter-mile above spectacular **Sunlight Gorge**. The bridge is Wyoming's highest. Forest Road 101, an improved gravel road, follows Sunlight Creek about 15 miles upstream from here, past ranches, a ranger station and Shoshone National Forest campgrounds, to the foot of 11,950-foot Sunlight Peak. This is a region extremely rich in wildlife, including elk, moose, bear, mountain goat and bighorn sheep. In all, there are seven U.S. Forest Service campgrounds in the Sunlight Basin area, 11 maintained hiking trails and a handful of working and guest ranches.

The Chief Joseph Highway continues from the Sunlight Creek Bridge another 26 miles to its intersection with Route 212 (the Beartooth Highway), passing en route another area of dude ranches and a ranger station at **Crandall Creek**. From the junction, Cooke City (see Chapter Two, "Yellowstone National Park") is 14 miles northwest; Red Lodge, Montana, is 50 miles northeast across 10,947-foot **Beartooth Pass**.

LODGING

A dozen rustic cabins in an aspen grove near unsullied Sunlight Creek—that's the **7D Ranch**. The cabins vary in size from one to four bedrooms, but all have wood stoves and private baths. Most of the beef served in the atmospheric dining room is raised right on the ranch. The stables here have 70 horses available for daily rides into the North Absaroka Wilderness; other activities include flyfishing excursions, trap shooting and hiking. Guests are booked on a weekly basis. ~ Sunlight Basin, P.O. Box 100, Cody, WY 82414; 307-587-3997 (summer), 307-587-9885 (winter). ULTRA-DELUXE.

Clark's Fork of the Yellowstone River flows through the heart of the **Hunter Peak Ranch**, dividing its main lodge and a pair of cabins from 120 acres of irrigated pasture. Homesteaded in 1907, the ranch offers no planned activities, but horseback riding and trout fishing are most popular. You can eat with the hosts in the hand-hewn lodge or cook for yourself. ~ Box 1731, Painter Route, Cody, WY 82414; 307-587-3711 (summer), 307-754-5878 (winter). MODERATE.

DINING

There are few places to stop for a bite along the Chief Joseph Highway, but one worthy of note is the **Cary Inn Restaurant**, near the Crandall Creek ranger station. The Cary Inn serves home-style beef and pork dishes, trout, burgers and sandwiches. Closed from December through April. ~ 3946 Crandall Road; 307-527-5510, 307-527-5248 (adjacent store). BUDGET TO MODERATE.

PARKS

NORTH ABSAROKA WILDERNESS AREA 🚶 🐎 🏕️ 🎣 This 350,000-acre wilderness along Yellowstone Park's northeastern boundary defines the rugged eastern flank of the Absaroka Range, with its populations of bighorn sheep, elk, moose and grizzly bear. Numerous trails lead up streams to alpine meadows well above timberline. Rainbow and cutthroat trout fishing are excellent in mountain streams, including the North Fork of the Shoshone River, Crandall Creek and Dead Indian Creek. ~ Several trailheads depart north off the Yellowstone Highway (Route 14/16/20), especially from the Pahaska Tepee area. There are other access points at Sunlight Basin and Crandall Creek, off Route 296; 307-527-6921.

▲ Primitive only.

The North Basin Loop

There are three main highways, and a handful of lesser routes, crossing the Big Horn Basin east of Cody. Two gratifying all-day or multi-day driving loops can be made via these roads: one through the northern part of the basin, one through the southern section.

The 207-mile northern loop trip from Cody on Routes 14A and 14 follows the agriculturally thriving Shoshone River valley to Bighorn Canyon National Recreation Area. It then, climbs through the spectacular canyon country on the west slope of the 13,000-foot Big Horn Mountains and returns to Cody through semiarid grasslands.

SIGHTS

The first quarter of the route traces the northern edge of the Big Horn Basin. Fifteen miles northeast of Cody, a half mile off Route 14A on Road 19, is a memorial to the **Heart Mountain Relocation Center**, where 11,000 Japanese Americans were interned during World War II. "May the injustices of the removal and incarceration of 120,000 persons of Japanese ancestry during World War II, two-thirds of whom were American citizens, never be repeated," reads the plaque, listed on the National Register of Historic Places. An earlier memorial details the layout of the camp. There's a visitors center and an interpretive walkway. Twenty-one camp internees and one Caucasian camp schoolteacher died fighting for the Allies during the war.

The region's hub is the grain and sugar-beet farming community of **Powell**, 24 miles from Cody in the heart of the Shoshone Reclamation Project that owes its existence to water from Buffalo Bill Reservoir. Founded in 1909 and named for early Rocky Mountain river explorer John Wesley Powell, it is the home of **Northwest Community College**, a two-year institution established in the 1950s. ~ 231 West 6th Street. Also visit the **Homesteader Museum**, an impressive collection of early-20th-century Big Horn Basin settlers' memorabilia. Closed Saturday through Monday in summer, Sunday through Thursday in winter. ~ 1st and Clark streets; 307-754-9481. **Elk Basin**, 15 miles north of Powell on Route 295, was one of America's largest oil-producing fields during and immediately after World War I.

Twenty-five miles east of Powell is **Lovell**, a pleasant community that calls itself "The Rose Town of Wyoming." Private gardens and public parks throughout the town boast floral displays that demand a second look—a tribute to former Lovell parks director and community physician Dr. William Horsley, a 12-year director of the American Rose Society who died in 1971.

For travelers, Lovell is most notable as the gateway to the **Bighorn Canyon National Recreation Area**. It took 64 million years of geological artistry for the Bighorn River to sculpt the 2200-foot-deep Bighorn Canyon. It took only a few years of engineering artistry for Montana's 525-foot Yellowtail Dam to fill the canyon in 1967 and create 71-mile-long Bighorn Lake. The result: 250,000 kilowatts of electricity, an important irrigation source for farmers of the eastern Rockies and Great Plains and a new playground for boaters and fishermen. ~ 406-666-2412.

> Eleven thousand Japanese Americans were interned during World War II at the Heart Mountain Relocation Center; 21 died fighting for the Allies.

Begin your exploration of the national recreation area with a stop at the **Bighorn Canyon Visitors Center**, just east of town. The first National Park Service building to employ solar energy as its principal heating source (it opened in 1976), it offers geology, history, recreation and solar-energy displays, a three-dimensional relief map of the area, and a worthwhile short film titled "The Bighorn Canyon Experience." ~ 20 Route 14A East, Lovell; 307-548-2251.

Principal access to the recreation area is via the TransPark Highway (Route 37), which turns north off Route 14A about two and a half miles east of Lovell. **The Marina at Horseshoe Bend**, located where the river emerges from the red-rock canyon to beget the broad southern section of Bighorn Lake, is 14 miles from Lovell; its facilities include boat rentals, a campground, a swimming beach and concessions. During the winter, ice-fishing is popular here. ~ 307-548-7326. In summer, the 15-passenger *Canyon Queen* tour boat offers excursions upstream and down. Admission. ~ 307-548-7858.

The trip downriver is a good way to grasp the geological importance of this canyon, which slices deeply through the ancient Bighorn and Pryor anticlines. More than 500 million years of earth's history, dating back to early Paleozoic times (when shallow seas covered this part of the continent), can be read in these cliffs. Fossils of marine trilobites and of dinosaurs that inhabited tropical marshes or conifer forests have been found here. For road travelers, **Devil Canyon Overlook**, 18 miles north of Lovell in Montana, offers a 1000-foot-deep perspective on the Bighorn Canyon.

The TransPark Highway passes through a portion of the **Pryor Mountain Wild Horse Range**, a 47,000-acre Bureau of Land Management preserve established in 1968, and follows the route of **Bad Pass Trail**. This pathway was employed by American Indians as long as 10,000 years ago and as recently as the early 19th century by Crow Indians and white trappers. Rock cairns and tepee rings are still evident north of Devil Canyon Overlook. The off-road sections of the trail are not open today, even to hikers.

Route 37 ends 27 miles north of Lovell at **Barry's Landing**. In the vicinity are the remains of G. W. Barry's 1903 Cedarvale Dude Ranch at the ghost town of Hillsboro and the 1926 Lockhart Ranch of Western novelist Carolyn Lockhart. North of Barry's Landing, for 35 miles downstream to the Ok-A-Beh area near the Yellowtail Dam, access is strictly by boat. The north end of Bighorn Canyon is reached from Fort Smith, south of Hardin, Montana.

But there's one more section of the national recreation area accessible from Lovell. Nine miles east of the visitors center, Route 14A crosses Bighorn Lake on the Causeway, one mile long. This southern section of the recreation area embraces the **Yellowtail Wildlife Habitat Management Area**. This wetland region at the confluence of the Bighorn and Shoshone rivers attracts waterfowl, raptors, deer, wild turkeys and small predator mammals of many species. ~ 307-527-7125.

About two miles south of the Kane Bridge there's a turnoff to the 1883 **Mason-Lovell Ranch** on the lakeshore. The M-L Ranch, as it's usually called, was built as headquarters for a classic open-range cattle ranch operated by A. L. Mason and H. C. Lovell before the invention of barbed wire changed the West forever. A bunkhouse, blacksmith shop and married employees' cabin still stand.

From the Bighorn Canyon, Route 14A rapidly ascends the west slope of the Big Horn Mountains, climbing from about 3800 feet at the lake to about 9600 at Baldy Pass. About 12 miles from the M-L Ranch, it enters 1.1-million-acre **Bighorn National Forest**, which blankets the Big Horn Mountains from north to south. (For information on facilities, see "Sheridan Area Parks" in Chapter Nine.)

The Big Horn Mountains—as well as Bighorn National Forest, the Bighorn River, the Big Horn Basin, Big Horn County, and so forth—took their name from the bighorn sheep, which thrived in this region in the decades before Anglo settlement. The animal is currently making a comeback in remote alpine areas thanks to an aggressive game-management program.

HIDDEN ►

The national forest is home to one of the most remarkable places in Wyoming: the **Medicine Wheel National Historic Landmark**. Located about 32 miles from Lovell, one-and-a-half miles off Route 14A via a steep, narrow, gravel Forest Service road and a one-and-a-half-mile trail, this ancient site near the summit of the Big Horns (at about 9400 feet) is as much a mystery to modern archaeologists as to the American Indians who consider it sacred ground. From a hub of rocks piled three feet high in a 12-foot circle, 28 spokes radiate to an outer circle of flat, white stones, 75 feet across and 245 feet in circumference. Outside this "Great Wheel," six small cairns stand beside a rock arrow that points toward Meeteetse, 70 miles southwest, where remnants of a similar wheel have been discovered. ~ Forest Road 12; 307-548-6541.

There are many theories about what the Medicine Wheel might have been and about the long-forgotten peoples who may have built it between A.D. 1200 and 1700. Some say it was a monument to a great chief; others suggest its use in vision quests. Perhaps the most intriguing hypothesis is that it was an astronomical observatory along the lines of Stonehenge in England, used as a calendar to determine the summer solstice. Is it divine irony that the Federal Aviation Administration has a state-of-the-art radar facility in a geodesic dome overlooking the site from atop adjacent Medicine Mountain?

On the roof of the Big Horns, between 9000 and 10,000 feet in elevation, are mile after mile of undulating alpine meadows crisscrossed by Forest Service roads. It's ideal country for viewing deer, elk, sheep and other high-country wildlife. Then at Burgess Junction, 106 miles from Cody, Route 14A joins Route 14 for a twisting descent of the Big Horns' east slope to Dayton and Sheridan (49 miles).

To return to Cody via Route 14, turn southwest at this junction. Route 14 from Dayton to Shell is called the **Bighorn Scenic Byway**. For the first 12 miles south, it continues across the meadowlands, past campgrounds and fishing-access roads, to the South Tongue River. Route 14 then crosses 9033-foot **Granite Pass**, goes by the nearby **Antelope Butte Ski Area** (307-655-9530) and turns sharply west as it descends rapidly into **Shell Canyon**.

Millions of years of erosion by Shell Creek have carved this picturesque canyon, whose sedimentary deposits contain some of the earliest-known fossils of ammonites, hard-shelled marine creatures. About halfway through the canyon, the creek flows into a deep chasm through three-billion-year-old granite, out of which plummet **Shell Falls**. Most of the year, about 3600 gallons of water per second roar over these falls, among the highest in Wyoming outside of Yellowstone Park. An interpretive exhibit at the falls overlook describes canyon geology. By the time Shell Creek has reached the hamlet of **Shell**, at about 4200 feet, it has slowed to become a stream colored ruddy by the red sandstone through which it has swept.

About nine miles west of Shell (six miles east of Greybull), the highway passes the **Lower Shell Valley Stone Schoolhouse**, a classic one-room schoolhouse constructed in 1903 of locally quarried sandstone. Listed on the National Register, it is still in use as a rental home. ~ Route 14, Greybull; 307-765-4384.

Greybull, named for a legendary albino bison held sacred by American Indians, was founded in 1905 as a railroad town at the confluence of the Greybull and Bighorn rivers. An important center for the mining of bentonite, a volcanic clay, Greybull is also an outfitting hub for the Big Horn Mountains and the gateway to a geologically intriguing badlands region. A giant allosaurus and 12 large sauropods are among the dinosaurs that have been dug from the clay and bedrock over six decades.

The Greybull Museum displays part of the wealth of fossils, gems and American Indian artifacts uncovered in the area, as well as a variety of pioneer utensils and antiques. Closed Saturday and Sunday. Abbreviated schedule in winter. ~ 325 Greybull Avenue; 307-765-2444. And on the west side of town, the Greybull Airport Museum exhibits dozens of World War II bombers and transport aircraft, including five of the last PB4Y-2 planes used against the Japanese in the South Pacific. Closed Saturday and Sunday in winter. ~ Route 14 West; 307-765-4482.

From Greybull, Route 14 joins with Routes 16 and 20 to cross 53 miles of dry creek and grassland back to Cody.

LODGING   If you stop at the Best Western Kings Inn at any time between late August and early June, you'll get a bargain rate at this two-story motor inn. Rates increase 65 percent during the high tourist season, however. All 48 rooms have coffeemakers and cable TV; the establishment also has an outdoor pool, a restaurant with an American and Mexican menu, and a lounge. ~ 777 East 2nd Street, Powell; 307-754-5117, 800-441-7778, fax 307-754-2198. MODERATE.

Up in the Bighorn Canyon area, the Horseshoe Bend Motel offers 22 cozy rooms, including four efficiency units with refrigerators and microwaves. There's also a swimming pool. ~ 375 East

---

✔ **CHECK THESE OUT—UNIQUE LODGING**

- *Budget to moderate:* Hole up in a log cabin high in the Big Horn Mountains and spend your days fishing at the **Meadowlark Lake Resort.** *page 133*
- *Moderate:* Escape to a rustic cabin at **Pahaska Tepee Resort,** Buffalo Bill's 1904 hunting lodge. *page 117*
- *Moderate to deluxe:* Belly up to the cherrywood bar at **The Irma,** a hotel built in 1902 by Buffalo Bill for his daughter. *page 112*
- *Ultra-deluxe:* Go horseback riding in the daytime, then enjoy evening billiards or square dancing at the **Rimrock Dude Ranch.** *page 117*

Budget: under $50   Moderate: $50–$90   Deluxe: $90–$130   Ultra-deluxe: over $130

Main Street, Lovell; 307-548-2221, 800-548-2850, fax 307-548-2131. BUDGET.

Cattle ranching was never so plush as at **The Hideout at Flitner Ranch**. Guest accommodations are in log cabins outfitted with modern amenities. The main lodge has a hot tub, lounge and a library. Visitors can lend a hand in daily chores, or just relax soaking in the dramatic Big Horns. Ultra-deluxe prices include lodging, meals and use of the horses. Three-night minimum. ~ 3208 Beaver Creek Road, Greybull; 307-765-2080, 800-354-8637, fax 307-765-2681; www.thehideout.com. ULTRA-DELUXE.

The **Yellowstone Motel** has lovely landscaped grounds—including a putting green and a heated outdoor swimming pool—at the foot of the Big Horns. The 35 large rooms (including two family suites) have full baths and cable TV. ~ 247 Greybull Avenue, Greybull; 307-765-4456, fax 307-765-2108. MODERATE.

DINING

Pepe's provides satisfying Mexican food in a dining area done in desert colors and Santa Fe decor. At breakfast you can order *huevos rancheros* and *chilaquiles*; lunch and dinner feature green chile pork, chimichangas, cheese enchiladas and shrimp fajitas. Breakfast only on Sunday. No dinner on Monday. ~ 333 East 2nd Street, Powell; 307-754-4665. BUDGET TO MODERATE.

Seafood is the specialty at the **Big Horn Restaurant**, which provides three generous meals daily. Shrimp dishes, prime rib and a big salad bar draw Wyomingites from miles around. ~ 605 East Main Street, Lovell; 307-548-6811. MODERATE.

Elsewhere, the fare is heavily meat and potatoes. A pleasant exception is **Lisa's**, which adds a creative touch to home cookin' along the Bighorn River. Open for three meals daily in summer, lunch and dinner the rest of the year, the restaurant serves up a great Tex-Mex steak as well as chicken and pasta. There's a lounge and a children's menu. ~ 200 Greybull Avenue, Greybull; 307-765-4765. MODERATE.

SHOPPING

Since 1944, **Probst Western and Outdoor Clothing** has outfitted cowboys, cowgirls and tourists alike with a wide variety of boots, hats, denim, jewelry, saddles and accessories. Closed Sunday. ~ 547 Greybull Avenue, Greybull; 307-765-2171.

NIGHTLIFE

For cappuccino and conversation, stop by the **Parlor News Coffeehouse**. In addition to coffee drinks, there are fruit smoothies, bagels and cookies. Open until 9 p.m. when the college is in session. ~ 135 East 2nd Street, Powell; 307-754-0717.

Those who desire a more potent potable can try one of the local bars in town. There's the tiny **K-Bar Saloon**. ~ 219 East 1st Street, Powell; 307-754-4286. **Peaks** entertains with jukebox-generated tunes and a pool table. ~ 127 South Bent Street, Powell;

307-754-5551. **LaVina's**, adjoining a liquor store of the same name, occasionally has live music. Diversions include a pool table, darts, pinball and a jukebox filled with rock and country singles. ~ 238 South Douglas Street, Powell; 307-754-4713.

PARKS

BIGHORN CANYON NATIONAL RECREATION AREA 🚶 🚴 🐎 🎣
🛶 🎿 🚣 ⛷ 🚤 🛥 🏊 ⛴ Wedged between cliffs nearly one-half mile high, 71-mile-long Bighorn Lake is the centerpiece of this paradise for boating and fishing enthusiasts. The damming of the Bighorn River in 1967 created the lake; the canyon was 64 million years in the making, and its strata reveal 500 million years of geologic history. The Lovell visitors center directs travelers north, up the TransPark Highway, to The Marina at Horseshoe Bend, a camping resort at the south end of the canyon; to Devil Canyon Overlook, which offers a glorious panorama of the gorge; and to Barry's Landing, another camping and boating area. The wetlands of the Yellowtail Wildlife Habitat Management Area and the historic ruins of the 1883 Mason-Lovell Ranch are east of Lovell. The northern (Montana) end of the canyon can be reached only by boat or a roundabout road trip of more than 100 miles. Facilities include picnic areas, restrooms, a visitors center, a marina with boat rentals and lifeguarded swimming beach, concessions and, boat tours (admission). Species of fish in Bighorn Lake include brown, lake and rainbow trout; walleye; sauger; largemouth bass; channel catfish; yellow perch; sunfish; and ling. There is excellent ice fishing in winter. Day-use fee, $5. ~ Take Route 37 north from Lovell to reach the canyon; Route 14A east from Lovell to the Mason-Lovell Ranch; Route 313 south from Hardin, Montana, to Fort Smith and the Yellowtail Dam; 307-548-2251.

▲ There are 137 RV/tent sites plus seven for tents only in three campgrounds (one accessible only by boat) in the southern (Wyoming) section; 126 hookups are available at Horseshoe Bend. Closed Labor Day to Memorial Day.

▼▼▼▼▼▼▼▼▼▼▼▼▼▼▼▼

The South Basin Loop

This 260-mile circuit hits the high points of the southern Big Horn Basin, including the cowboy flavor of Meeteetse, the renowned hot springs at Thermopolis and the Ten Sleep Canyon country east of Worland, before returning to Cody along the Greybull River. This is an important region to those who study the distant past: Its rocks are a treasure trove of fossils and ancient petroglyphs.

SIGHTS

Route 120 southeast from Cody skirts the Oregon Basin and Elk Butte oil fields before climbing the 6000-foot Meeteetse Rim into **Meeteetse**. Settled in the 1880s as a ranching center and given a Crow Indian name that means "meeting place," this town 32 miles southeast of Cody has stubbornly clung to a colorful Old West ambience with century-old architecture including wooden side-walks and hitching rails.

The **Meeteetse Museums** tell the town's history in three sepa-rate buildings. The Hall Museum, in a 1900 Masonic hall, displays frontier artifacts. ~ 942 Mondale Street. The Bank Archives, in a 1901 bank building, contain records and documents. ~ 1033 Park Avenue. The Belden Museum of Western Photography exhibits both historic and modern work. ~ 1947 State Street; 307-868-2423.

From Meeteetse, Route 290 provides access up the Greybull River to the Pitchfork Ranch (established in 1878), Shoshone Na-tional Forest and the Washakie Wilderness Area. The Wood River Road (Forest Road 200) takes you to the **Wood River Valley Ski Touring Park,** one of the largest cross-country areas in northern Wyoming, 22 miles southwest. ~ 307-868-2603.

Though a little hard to find and off the beaten path, the **Legend**   ◄ HIDDEN
Rock State Petroglyph Site is worth a detour. Some of the most impressive prehistoric rock carvings in America illustrate hun-dreds of yards of sandstone cliffs. Archaeologists have identified at least 283 pictures on 92 rock panels, some dating back to the time of Christ. Images range from identifiable animals, birds and humans to strange-looking figures wearing horned headdresses.

To reach the site, turn west off Route 120 on Upper Cotton-wood Creek Road about 32 miles southeast of Meeteetse. Follow this road five miles to the Hamilton Dome junction, continuing west on BLM Road 1305. Turn left after the second cattle guard and left again at a Y intersection, continuing to a locked gate. Park here and walk a half mile downhill to the site, or obtain a key from Hot Springs State Park headquarters in Thermopolis during week-day business hours. ~ Upper Cottonwood Creek Road, Hamilton Dome; 307-864-2176.

You were going to—or coming from—**Hot Springs State Park** anyway. The world's largest single mineral hot spring, is located on the east bank of the Bighorn River at the north edge of the town of Thermopolis, 83 miles from Cody. Big Spring churns out 3.6 million gallons of 127°F water each day; at least 27 different minerals contained in the water have been identified, including large amounts of bicarbonate, sulfate, chloride and sodium. Some of the water is cooled and piped to a state-owned bath house (free) and two water parks (admission) for public use; the balance flows over colorful **Rainbow Terrace**, reminiscent of the thermal features of Yellowstone Park, and into the Bighorn River. Other springs in the park are Black Sulphur Spring, White Sulphur Spring and Ponce de Leon Spring. ~ 220 Park Street off Route 20, Thermopolis; 307-864-2176.

The town of **Thermopolis**, whose name is a combination of the Greek words for *heat* and *city*, was established around the springs after that 1896 government purchase. **Hot Springs Histori-cal Museum** recalls the town's early years with a re-created newspaper office, blacksmith shop, dentist's office and general store, as well as the original back bar from the Hole-in-the-Wall Saloon. An elk hide painted by Chief Washakie himself highlights an impressive collection of American Indian artifacts. Admission. ~ 700 Broadway, Thermopolis; 307-864-5183.

South of Thermopolis, Route 2 follows the Wind River Canyon 32 miles to the small town of Shoshoni. American Indians named the Wind River for the ever-present breeze funneling down the 2000-foot-deep gorge; yet as the river leaves the canyon about four miles above Thermopolis at the **Wedding of the Waters**, its name changes to the Bighorn. Highway signs placed throughout the canyon by the Wyoming Geological Association identify the eras of different rock strata.

Traveling north down the Bighorn River from Thermopolis, Route 20 parallels the Burlington Northern railroad tracks, so important to this region when they were laid in 1914. Coal-mining towns like **Crosby** and **Gebo**, 11 and 15 miles from Thermopolis, respectively, supplied the fuel for the train; the ruins of these ghost towns (abandoned in the 1950s) can be viewed to the west of Route 20.

Worland is 33 miles north of Thermopolis. Founded in 1903 on the west bank of the Bighorn, the entire town was moved two years later, building by building, to the east bank when residents learned that that was where the railroad would be built, making their move in the dead of winter when the river was completely frozen over. Today the town is the hub of a heavily irrigated agricultural district that produces malt barley, alfalfa hay, corn, beans, sugar beets and other crops.

Worland is also an important paleontological area. Remains of eohippus, the prehistoric ancestor of the modern horse, were

GIFT OF THE WATERS

When white pioneers settled the land where the town of Thermopolis now stands, its hot springs belonged to the Wind River Shoshone, who had long acknowledged their healing powers. Chief Washakie insisted, when selling a ten-square-mile portion of the Wind River Reservation to the federal government in 1896, that a portion of the waters be set aside for free public use. In one of its wiser actions, the government donated the springs to Wyoming, which in turn made them the first Wyoming state park. Shoshone tribespeople and Thermopolis residents commemorate the transaction annually, on the first weekend of August during the colorful Gift of the Waters Pageant.

discovered among the badlands of the **Gooseberry Formations** and **Painted Desert**, off Route 431 some 20 miles west of town. Fossil discoveries and geology are featured at the **Washakie Museum of History, Art and Earth Science**, along with historical cowboy and ranch equipment. ~ 1115 Obie Sue Avenue, Worland; 307-347-4102.

Route 20 continues north, down the Bighorn River, from Worland. Route 16 heads due east 26 miles across arid plains to **Ten Sleep**, at the foot of the Big Horn Mountains. The community was built at a creek ford that was, in American Indian parlance, 11 days' (ten sleeps') journey from . . . somewhere. You can learn about this and the 1909 Spring Creek Raid, which climaxed the age of range wars, at the **Ten Sleep Pioneer Museum**. ~ Ten Sleep Public Park, Route 16; no phone. Today Ten Sleep is the gateway to **Ten Sleep Canyon**, which begins about five miles east of town.

The sculpted limestone canyon is the southern of the three highway corridors through the Big Horn Mountains. Designated as the **Cloud Peak Skyway**, a national scenic byway, the route follows Ten Sleep Creek and transits 9666-foot **Powder River Pass** on its 65-mile run to Buffalo. En route, it passes a **Nature Conservancy center**, six miles east of Ten Sleep, and two fish hatcheries —the spring-fed **Wigwam Fish Rearing Station**, near Canyon Creek, and the log-construction **Ten Sleep Fish Hatchery**, on Leigh Creek, both run by the Wyoming Game and Fish Division.

The route's summit offers the nearest highway access to the **Cloud Peak Wilderness**, a 195,000-acre primitive preserve capped by 13,165-foot Cloud Peak, the apex of the Big Horns. Hundreds of pristine mountain lakes speckle the slopes of the jagged peaks, both above and below timberline; they're remnants of the Ice Age glaciers that once covered the entire range. Numerous hiking and horse trails traverse the wilderness. Wreckage of a 1943 U.S. Air Force B-17 crash that killed all ten crew members can still be seen on Bomber Mountain, just south of Cloud Peak.

After the detour up Ten Sleep Canyon, this loop trip heads north from the town of Ten Sleep, following Lower Nowood Road (Route 47) and Cold Springs Road (Route 31) to isolated Hyattville, at the confluence of Paintrock and Medicine Lodge creeks. Amid the rugged gulches of these Big Horn Mountain foothills is the **Medicine Lodge State Archaeological Site**, six miles northeast of Hyattville, one of the most important sites in North America for the study of prehistoric man. ~ Road 268A, Hyattville; 307-469-2234.

◄ HIDDEN

Though the prehistoric petroglyphs and pictographs on Medicine Lodge's red sandstone cliffs have long attracted visitors, it was not until 1969 that the full importance of the site was realized. A state archaeology team, digging through 26 feet of soil and rock, found more than 60 cultural levels spanning 10,000 years of human occupation. A visitors center interprets some of the on-going discoveries. The site offers trails, fishing and camping facilities and is open May through November 4. Nearby is the 12,127-acre **Medicine Lodge Wildlife Habitat Management Area**, ideal winter range for elk and mule deer.

Adventurous travelers can take the **Red Gulch/Alkali National Back Country Byway** north from Hyattville to Route 14 between Shell and Greybull. Interpretive kiosks stand at each end of this 32-mile gravel-and-dirt road, maintained by the BLM. In 1998, an archaeologist unwittingly discovered about 500 dinosaur tracks near—and in—the road. The BLM plans a viewing area and facilities to accompany the tracks, which date back to the Sundance geological era. Other highlights include heavily eroded table rocks, steep canyons, caves, and the red hills of the 230 million-year-old Chugwater Formation. Keep an eye out for wooden mining-claim markers and for rock cairns, placed by American Indians to mark routes and by livestock herders to indicate springs. Two-wheel-drive vehicles with ten-inch clearance can easily manage the road from May into October, although any amount of rainfall creates muddy conditions.

A more direct route from Hyattville is Route 31, which travels 22 miles west to tiny **Manderson** on the Bighorn River. Here you can pick up Route 16/20 again, proceeding north to the town of **Basin**, surrounded by rich irrigated farmlands. Basin's place in Old West history was affirmed in 1909 when the perpetrators of the final raid in the great range wars were convicted of murder here. The National Guard stood by to prevent further violence between the two vying factions: the open-range cattle ranchers and the homesteaders and sheepherders.

West from Basin, Route 30 crosses through the midriff of the Big Horn Basin's grain-producing and livestock-raising belt. It's 46 miles via Burlington and Lower Greybull Road to Route 120, just north of Meeteetse. Complete the loop by turning north on 120 and returning to Cody, a distance of about 24 miles.

LODGING   The **Broken Spoke B&B** lets two rooms above a café of the same name. Accommodations with private baths have queen beds, hardwood floors and Western decor. Breakfast is conveniently served in the café below. ~ 1947 State Street, Meeteetse; 307-868-2362. BUDGET.

To stay in style at Hot Springs State Park, look no further than the **Holiday Inn of the Waters**. This two-story motor inn is within the park itself and offers a hot-spring jacuzzi, private mineral hot baths and a heated freshwater pool and wading pool, as well as a full health club, saunas, a whirlpool and racquetball courts. The deluxe Safari Club restaurant and lounge (so named for their collection of big-game heads) are on premises. The 80 air-conditioned guest rooms are spacious and tastefully decorated. Bicycles and a laundry are available to guests. ~ Park and Pioneer streets, Thermopolis; phone/fax 307-864-3131, 800-465-4329. DELUXE.

You'll get a free continental breakfast with your room at the **Best Western Settlers Inn**, a mile east of downtown Worland on Route 16 toward Ten Sleep Canyon. Inside corridors access all 44 rooms in this modern two-story motor inn; some rooms have refrigerators, all have coffee makers. A coin laundry is available to guests. Children under 12 stay free with adults. ~ 2200 Big Horn Avenue, Worland; 307-347-8201, fax 307-347-9323. MODERATE.

East of Worland near the summit of the Big Horn Mountains, **Meadowlark Lake Resort** offers lodge-style cabins and modern condo units beside a lovely alpine lake at 8500-foot elevation. Three meals daily are served in the restaurant, and the saloon offers a full bar. Best of all, there's trout fishing and boating in the 300-acre lake and mountain biking in the Bighorn National Forest; in winter, there's downhill and nordic skiing, snowmobiling and ice fishing. Equipment rentals are available. The resort also has a convenience store and gas station. ~ Route 16 East, Ten Sleep; 307-366-2424, 800-858-5672. BUDGET TO MODERATE.

DINING

The place to grab a bite in Meeteetse is **Lucille's Cafe**, where home cooking has become something of an art form. You can get everything from a slice of pie and a cup of coffee to a full-on dinner, and locals rave about Lucille's hamburgers and homemade soups. Abbreviated hours from October through April. ~ 1906 State Street, Meeteetse; 307-868-2250. BUDGET.

PumperNicks offers everything from crêpes and stuffed croissants for lunch to steak, chicken and seafood for dinner. An open-air patio adds to an atmosphere that evokes a previous century. ~ 512 Broadway, Thermopolis; 307-864-5151. MODERATE.

▲▲

✔ CHECK THESE OUT—UNIQUE DINING

- *Budget:* Grab a table at **Lucille's Cafe** and find out why locals can't get enough of her burgers and soups. *page 133*
- *Moderate:* Add sizzle to your diet with **Lisa's** Tex-Mex steak when you dine along the Bighorn River. *page 127*
- *Deluxe:* Indulge in "kickass cowboy cuisine" like Rocky Mountain oysters at the **Proud Cut Saloon & Restaurant**. *page 113*
- *Ultra-deluxe:* Choose from 100 wines at **Franca's**, but request no changes in your exquisite prix-fixe, four-course, northern Italian meal. *page 113*

Budget: under $7   Moderate: $7–$12   Deluxe: $12–$20   Ultra-deluxe: over $20

Got a hankering for prime rib? It's on the menu every night of the week at **Tom and Jerry's Steakhouse & Lounge**. The Route 16 restaurant specializes in steak and seafood in a family-dining setting at lunch and dinner. There's also a lounge with a full bar. ~ 1620 Big Horn Avenue, Worland; 307-347-9261. MODERATE TO DELUXE.

SHOPPING   The historic **Meeteetse Mercantile Co.** has been in continuous operation since 1899. This is a true old-time general store, selling everything from groceries and dry goods to clothing, hardware and antiques. Check out the old-time soda fountain, too. ~ 1946 State Street, Meeteetse; 307-868-2561.

In Washakie County, **Center Stage** has antiques, homemade candy and souvenirs. Closed Sunday. ~ 608 Big Horn Avenue, Worland; 307-347-3817.

PARKS   **HOT SPRINGS STATE PARK** 🏃🚲⛵🚤🏊 The park has several springs and terraces, but Big Spring (the largest mineral hot spring on earth) is the one that really matters to most visitors. Twenty-five thousand gallons of water per minute pour from this single 30-foot-wide spring at a temperature of 127°F, year after year. Some of the spring's water, which contains 27 minerals, is cooled in retaining pools to 104°F and piped for public and private use—which is why visitors have made this the most popular park in Wyoming after Yellowstone and Grand Teton. The state bath house is free, but there is admission to the two water parks. A pier north of the park entrance extends into the Bighorn River, where anglers can cast for brown, rainbow and cutthroat trout. Facilities include picnic areas, restrooms and playgrounds. ~ From downtown Thermopolis take Park Street east off Route 20; 307-864-2176.

CLOUD PEAK WILDERNESS AREA 🏃🚶🐎🏕 The highest point of the Big Horns—13,165-foot Cloud Peak—crowns this 195,000-acre preserve, most of it above 10,000 feet in elevation. Jagged peaks, created by Ice Age glaciation, provide dramatic scenery. The region has a rich animal and bird life. Some 150 miles of trails connect more than 250 unsullied alpine lakes, all offering good trout fishing. Lake Solitude, on the west flank of Cloud Peak, is noted for its mackinaw (lake trout). The season is short, however—often only from July through mid-September. ~ There are trailheads off Routes 14 and 16 and many forest roads on all sides of the wilderness. Among the most popular are West Tensleep Lake, 25 miles east of Ten Sleep via Meadowlark Lake, and Hunter Creek, 14 miles west of Buffalo, both off Route 16; 307-672-0751.

▲ Primitive only.

MEDICINE LODGE STATE ARCHAEOLOGICAL SITE 🚶 🚲 🛶

⌐ One of the most important sites in North America for the study of prehistoric man, Medicine Lodge has revealed 10,000 years of civilization in 26 feet of soil and rock. Archaeological digs have been filled in for their preservation, but visitors can still study vivid pictographs and petroglyphs on red sandstone cliffs. Medicine Lodge Creek winds through an important adjacent habitat for elk and mule deer. The site, administered by the state parks division, is open May 1 to November 4. Facilities include picnic areas, restrooms, a visitors center and a playground. ~ Take Route 16/20 north 19 miles from Worland or south 20 miles from Greybull to Manderson. From there, follow Route 31 east 22 miles. Just before reaching Hyattville, turn left on Cold Springs Road and continue four-and-a-half miles, then turn left on Road 52 to the site; 307-469-2234.

▲ There are 25 free units (no hookups); 14-day maximum stay. Prices may change; call ahead for more information.

The streams and lakes of northern Wyoming are renowned for their trout fishing. Fly-fishermen in their waders, thigh-deep in a rushing mountain river, choose hand-tied flies that match the caddis and mayfly hatches to bring in trophy-size rainbow, cutthroat, brown and brook trout. Spin anglers cast their lures for grayling and mountain whitefish. At a lower elevation, trollers drag live bait behind their boats to capture walleye, bass, northern pike, yellow perch and channel catfish from lakes and reservoirs. A pamphlet listing the state's fishing regulations for the current season can be obtained from the Cody regional office of the **Wyoming Game and Fish Division**. ~ 307-527-7125.

▼▼▼▼▼▼▼▼▼▼▼▼▼

Outdoor Adventures

FISHING

The North and South forks of the Shoshone River, west of Cody, have sizable populations of rainbow, brown and cutthroat trout as well as whitefish. Buffalo Bill Reservoir also has lake trout. Fly-fishermen try the wild and scenic Clark's Fork for cutthroat, rainbow and brook trout. In the alpine lakes of the Absaroka and Beartooth ranges, the rare golden trout is a diamond among other species.

The yields of bluegills and crappies in Deaver Reservoir, 16 miles northeast of Powell, will put smiles on the faces of both youngsters and parents.

Bighorn Lake has both cold- and warm-water species: brown, lake and rainbow trout; walleye, sauger, ling, perch, catfish and largemouth bass. It's an angler's grab bag. Streams on the west slope of the Big Horn Mountains, produce brook, brown and rainbow trout, and sometimes mackinaw.

In Cody, a leading outfitter in northwest Wyoming is Tim **Wade's North Fork Anglers**. Guided trips and an extensive supply of retail gear are their specialties. ~ 1438 Sheridan Avenue, Cody; 307-527-7274. **Aune's Absaroka Angler** specializes in fly-fishing trips close to home in the Big Horn Basin. ~ 754 Yellow-stone Avenue, Cody; 307-587-5105. Elsewhere in the region, **Wyoming Wilderness Outfitters** conducts multi-day trips. ~ 1134 Road 14, Powell; 307-754-4320.

BOATING

The region's two principal venues for water sports in this semi-arid land are manmade: Buffalo Bill Reservoir, near Cody, and, Bighorn Lake, near Lovell.

There are several boat launches, but no rentals, at **Buffalo Bill State Park**. ~ Yellowstone Highway, Cody; 307-587-9227. *Outside* magazine considers Buffalo Bill to be one of the ten best places for board sailing in the United States.

Bighorn Lake supports the **Bighorn Canyon National Recreation Area**. ~ Lovell; 307-548-2251. A variety of boats can be rented at **The Marina at Horseshoe Bend**. Boat tours are also offered from The Marina. ~ Route 37, Lovell; 307-548-7230.

RIVER RUNNING

Rafting the Shoshone can mean very different experiences depending on which section of the river you choose. For example, the rapids on the 38-mile stretch of the North Fork that follows Route 14/16/20 from Sleeping Giant campground, near Pahaska Tepee, to Buffalo Bill Reservoir offer excitement but little risk to novice rafters on commercial trips.

Immediately below the Buffalo Bill Dam, a four-mile stretch of the main Shoshone offers severe drops like Iron Curtain that delight experienced kayakers and thrill-seeking rafters. At DeMaris Hot Springs, near Trail Town, the river levels out and quiets down. Most commercial trips put in at DeMaris. Shorter floats through the upper Red Rock Canyon are about four miles long and take about two hours, including transportation time to and from the put-in and take-out. Longer 11-mile floats, continuing through the Lower Canyon, last about four hours.

River Runners rafts the Shoshone River. ~ 1491 Sheridan Avenue; 307-527-7238, 800-535-7238. **Wyoming River Trips** do family-oriented runs on the north and main forks of the Shoshone. ~ 1701 Sheridan Avenue; 307-587-6661.

The Clark's Fork of the Yellowstone is for experts only. No commercial trips are offered.

From Thermopolis, **Wind River Canyon Whitewater** takes river enthusiasts on half-day, full-day and overnight excursions on the Wind River. ~ 210 Suite 5, Route 20 South, Thermopolis; 307-864-9343.

DOWNHILL SKIING

Three small ski hills—one in the Absarokas, two in the Big Horns—offer family recreation without the glitz of major resorts.

Sleeping Giant Ski Area, located 48 miles west of Cody and just four miles from Yellowstone Park's east entrance, has a day lodge, one chairlift and a surface lift. Vertical drop is 500 feet. ~ 349 Yellowstone Highway, Cody; 307-587-4044.

Antelope Butte Ski Area, in Bighorn National Forest, has two chairlifts, one surface lift and 1000 feet of vertical. Located on the west side of 9000-foot Granite Pass, at the head of Shell Canyon, it is open Wednesdays through Sundays, and on holidays, from December through April. There's a shop with full alpine and snowboard rentals. ~ Route 14, Shell; 307-655-9530.

The **Big Horn Ski Area**, 45 miles east of Worland and 41 miles west of Buffalo, also in Bighorn National Forest, has three lifts that service 14 runs on 800 vertical feet of terrain. Overlooking Meadowlark Lake on the west side of Powder River Pass, it also has equipment rentals. Open weekends and holidays from November through April. ~ Route 16, Ten Sleep; 307-366-2600.

Cross-country ski opportunities in the area—especially in Shoshone National Forest—are almost limitless. ~ 307-527-6241. From **Pahaska Tepee Resort**, for instance, some 12 kilometers of groomed track connect with Sleeping Giant Ski Area base facilities and extend into the national forest, where there are another 40 kilometers of marked (but ungroomed) nordic trails. Rentals are available at the resort. ~ 183 Yellowstone Highway, Wapiti; 307-527-7701.

There are more groomed trails in the Sunlight Basin area off Route 296, but without special facilities.

Wood River Valley Ski Touring Park, one of the largest cross-country areas in northern Wyoming, is 22 miles southwest of Meeteetse. There are 25 kilometers of groomed novice and intermediate trails here, as well as a backcountry trail system, a warming hut and a cabin available by reservation. ~ Wood River Road, Meeteetse; 307-868-2603.

CROSS-COUNTRY SKIING

✔ CHECK THESE OUT—UNIQUE OUTDOOR ADVENTURES

- Windsurf the whitecaps at Buffalo Bill Reservoir, rated among the ten best places for board sailing by *Outside* magazine. *page 118*
- Rent a boat from the Horseshoe Bend marina and drop a line for fish from trout to catfish at Bighorn Lake. *page 135*
- Glide over 25 kilometers of groomed cross-country ski trails in the Wood River Valley. *page 137*
- Retrace the footsteps of Bill Cody and Albert I, prince of Monaco, when you hike the Pahaska-Sunlight Trail. *page 140*

In the Big Horn Mountains, the **Willow Park Ski Touring Area**, 45 miles east of Worland near Meadowlark Lake, offers 37 kilometers of groomed trails. ~ Route 16, Ten Sleep; 307-672-0751.

Ski Rentals   Topographical maps, as well as full Nordic equipment rentals, are found at **Sunlight Sports**. ~ 1251 Sheridan Avenue, Cody; 307-587-9517.

OTHER WINTER SPORTS

Two of Wyoming's most popular snowmobiling routes are accessible from Cody. The **Pahaska Tepee** route, with three groomed road miles extending west to Yellowstone National Park's east entrance from Buffalo Bill's original hunting lodge, and the **Sunlight Trail**, incorporating 28 miles of Beartooth Highway at the edge of the Absaroka-Beartooth Wilderness northwest of Cody, get a tremendous amount of winter use.

Skating takes place from December through February at **Homesteader Park** at the east edge of Powell. The ice arena, open days and lit for night skating, has a warming house, skate rentals and concessions. There's no admission charge. ~ Route 14A; 307-754-5106.

GOLF

Cody's **Olive Glenn Golf & Country Club** has been rated one of the top five 18-hole courses in Wyoming. The course has a pro shop with rentals, a driving range and a restaurant. ~ 802 Meadow Lane Drive; 307-587-5551.

The nine-hole **Legion Golf Course** is also highly regarded. ~ North 7th Street, Thermopolis; 307-864-5294. Other courses in the region are in Worland, Powell, Greybull and Basin. As snowmelt allows, the golf courses may open by April 1 and remain playable through October.

TENNIS

Three of Cody's 17 city parks have outdoor tennis courts, including two lighted courts near downtown at **Paul Stock Park**. ~ Beck Avenue and 8th Street. A single, unsurfaced court is at **Glendale Park** (Meadow Lane Avenue and 14th Street) and a lighted double court is at **Highland Manor Park** (Newton Avenue and 24th Street). For information, call the Cody Parks Department 307-527-7511.

RIDING STABLES

Serious riders probably want to book a stay of a week or longer at one of the dozens of guest (or "dude") ranches throughout northern Wyoming. This book recommends only a few. For a more complete listing, contact local visitors bureaus or chambers of commerce, or the **Wyoming Division of Tourism and Travel**. ~ Route 25 at College Drive, Cheyenne; 307-777-7777, 800-225-5996. There are also several books that list guest ranches; a favorite is Gene Kilgore's *Ranch Vacations*, 3rd edition (Santa Fe, New Mexico: John Muir Publications, 1994).

Many of the 23 guest ranches in the Cody area make horses available to day guests for guided trail rides. Perhaps your best bet, just two miles from Yellowstone Park's east entrance, is Buffalo Bill's **Pahaska Tepee Resort**. ~ 183 Yellowstone Highway, Wapiti; 307-527-7701.

Ron Dube's Wilderness Adventure offers deluxe expeditions into the high country of the Absaroka Range, including the Washakie and Teton wilderness areas. ~ P.O. Box 167, Wapiti, WY 82450; 307-527-7815.

PACK TRIPS & LLAMA TREKS

For a complete listing of licensed backcountry outfitters, contact the **Wyoming State Board of Outfitters and Professional Guides**. ~ 1750 Westland Road, Cheyenne; 307-777-5323.

Favorite excursions in Buffalo Bill country are **Rattlesnake Mountain**, a 17-mile climb (mainly through BLM land) to this bluff that overlooks Buffalo Bill Reservoir on the west side of Cody, and side trips off **South Fork Road**, which extends into Shoshone National Forest southwest of Cody.

BIKING

On the west slope of the Big Horn Mountains, there's great biking on Bighorn National Forest roads, especially on Forest Roads 10 and 15—on either side of Route 14A between Medicine Wheel and Burgess Junction.

Bike Rentals   **Olde Faithful Bicycles** offers rentals and repairs of mountain and touring bikes. Three-hour guided mountain-bike tours are also available. Closed Sunday. ~ 1362 Sheridan Avenue, Cody; 307-527-5110. **Larsen's Bicycles** offers repairs and rentals of mountain bikes. ~ 255 East 2nd Street, Powell; 307-754-5481.

The Absaroka and Big Horn ranges provide prime terrain for both day hikers and backcountry adventurers. All distances listed for hiking trails are one way unless otherwise noted.

HIKING

WAPITI VALLEY   West of Cody, off the Yellowstone Highway, numerous long trails (and shorter segments thereof) lead from campgrounds, picnic areas and guest ranches into the adjacent Washakie and North Absaroka wilderness areas.

The strenuous **South Fork Trail** (36 miles) begins at the end of South Fork Road 43 miles southwest of Cody, follows the South Fork of the Shoshone River upstream to its Washakie Wilderness headwaters near Shoshone Pass, at 9800 feet, and then descends to Trail Lake north of Dubois.

The steep and strenuous **Elk Fork Trail** (21 miles) follows Elk Fork Creek upstream from the Elk Fork campground into the Washakie Wilderness Area at Rampart Pass, on the col between 11,869-foot Overlook Mountain and 10,900-foot Ishawooa Cone. On the other side of the pass, **Open Creek Trail** descends 18 miles through the Teton Wilderness Area to the Thorofare Creek ranger station in Yellowstone National Park.

The moderate **Pahaska-Sunlight Trail** (18 miles) is best accomplished from the top down. Arrange a drop-off in the Silvertip Basin at the end of the Sunlight Basin Road off Route 296, about 65 miles northwest of Cody. Descend 3700 feet along the North Fork of the Shoshone River to the Pahaska Tepee Resort on the Yellowstone Highway. Tent one night at Camp Monaco, seven miles downstream, where Buffalo Bill hosted Albert I, prince of Monaco, on Cody's final big-game hunt in 1913.

Consult the rangers at **Shoshone National Forest** for full information on regional trails. ~ P.O. Box 2140, Cody, WY 82414; 307-527-6241.

CHIEF JOSEPH HIGHWAY The **Beartooth Loop National Recreation Trail** (18 miles) begins and ends at Gardner Lake off Route 212, about 85 miles north of Cody between Cooke City and Red Lodge, Montana. The moderately difficult trail passes lakes, meadows and gentle river canyons on the Beartooth Plateau, varying in elevation from about 10,500 feet down to about 9000 feet. This is a Shoshone National Forest trail; expect to share it with motorized vehicles.

NORTH BASIN LOOP **Bucking Mule Falls National Recreation Trail** (11 miles), in the northern Big Horn Mountains, rewards hikers with the sight of Bucking Mule Falls plunging 600 feet into Devil Canyon. The upper trailhead is at the end of Devil Canyon Road (Forest Road 14), off Route 14A east of Medicine Wheel. The well-marked, moderate but often-steep trail descends Bucking Mule Creek, crosses Devil Canyon and then follows Porcupine Creek downstream to Porcupine campground in Bighorn National Forest.

SOUTH BASIN LOOP **Mistymoon Trail** (6.5 miles) leads to a string of beautiful alpine lakes on the western slope of the Cloud Peak Wilderness. Beginning at West Tensleep Lake, eight miles north of Meadowlark Lake off Route 16, the trail climbs steadily about 1200 feet (to above 10,000 feet) to Lakes Helen, Marion and Mistymoon. Ascents of 13,165-foot Cloud Peak often begin here. Backcountry permits are not required, but hikers are asked to fill out registration cards at trailheads.

Equipment Get maps and all the gear you'll need at **Sunlight Sports**. ~ 1251 Sheridan Avenue, Cody; 307-587-9517.

▼▼▼▼▼▼▼▼▼▼▼
Transportation

CAR

Cody is slightly off the beaten track as far as interstate highways go, but it's at a junction of several major U.S. and state highways. To reach Buffalo Bill country, take **Route 14/16/20**, east from Yellowstone; **Route 120** northwest from Thermopolis or south from Red Lodge, Montana; **Route**

16 west off Route 25 at Buffalo; or **Route 14** west off Route 25 near Sheridan.

The distance between Cody and Sheridan is 147 miles; Cody is 79 miles east of Lake Village in Yellowstone National Park. From Cheyenne, the Wyoming state capital, it's 393 miles to Cody.

For road reports, call 800-442-9090 statewide.

Cody's **Yellowstone Regional Airport** has daily service year-round to and from Denver with Continental Express and United Express, and year-round service to and from Salt Lake City with SkyWest (for Delta). ~ 3001 Duggleby Drive, Cody; 307-587-5096.

AIR

Powder River Transportation is the regional line, connecting with national Greyhound routes from Casper and from Billings, Montana. ~ 1452 Sheridan Avenue, Cody; 307-527-7658. The line is based in Gillette.

BUS

Cody's Yellowstone Regional Airport has agents for **Avis Rent A Car** (800-831-2847), **Hertz Rent A Car** (800-654-3131) and **Rent A Wreck** (307-587-4993, 800-452-0396).

CAR RENTALS

In the absence of a public bus system, **Cody Taxi** does yeoman's work. ~ Cody; 307-527-9066.

TAXIS

FIVE

Wind River Country

Credit the farsightedness of a Shoshone Indian chief named Washakie for preserving much of the natural integrity of the Wind River Valley.

In the 1860s, when land grabbing by white settlers was leading other American Indian tribes to counterattack the invaders, Chief Washakie perceived that such a response would be futile. He befriended the newcomers, cooperated with the U.S. government's campaign of "manifest destiny," and was rewarded in 1868 with a huge land grant that is now the 3500-square-mile Wind River Indian Reservation, Wyoming's only reservation and one of the largest in the United States.

The lofty Wind River Range marks the western edge of this fertile valley; its slopes feed the Popo Agie (pronounced po-po'AHZ-sha) and Little Wind rivers. The main Wind River flows southeast from Togwotee Pass, eventually turning north through the magnificent Wind River Canyon and emerging into the Big Horn Basin.

Today, the valley's three main communities are spaced around the edges of the reservation. Riverton, a farming hub, is to the east. Dubois, an old ranching town, is in the far northwest. Lander, a center for outfitters and environmentalists, is just south of the reservation.

From Togwotee Pass above Dubois to historic South Pass on the old Oregon Trail, the Wind River Range marks the Continental Divide for more than 100 miles. A granitic range with numerous 13,000-foot summits, its crags and faces were sculpted by eons of erosion from wind, water and glaciers. Today it provides some of Wyoming's finest backcountry for outdoors enthusiasts. Only a few, unpaved roads lead into these mountains; the higher reaches are vast designated wilderness areas. Gannett Peak, highest in Wyoming at 13,804 feet, is surrounded by the seven largest glaciers in the United States outside of Alaska.

West of the Wind River Range, across the Continental Divide, the upper Green River Valley is renowned as the location of the greatest trading rendezvous of the 1825–1840 "mountain man" era. Jim Bridger, William Sublette, Thomas "Broken

Hand" Fitzpatrick and other colorful characters swapped furs and tall tales with Indians and settlers alike near the banks of Horse Creek for several years in the 1830s. The view of the heavily glaciated Wind River Range is spectacular from here; Pinedale, the regional center, is a fine base for exploring the lakes and roadless wilderness areas of these mountains.

▼▼▼▼▼▼▼▼▼▼▼▼▼▼▼

Riverton-Dubois and the Reservation

When the U.S. government awarded the Wind River Reservation to the Eastern Shoshone tribe, treaty makers said they were honoring Chief Washakie's request that the land be his people's "for as long as the grass shall grow and the rivers shall flow." They considered the chief's friendship a welcome buffer from hostile tribes for westbound pioneers and transcontinental railroad workers. In typical period fashion, though, the promise was compromised more than once. In order to receive his own military protection from Sioux and Arapaho raids, Washakie had to surrender 600,000 acres in the Popo Agie valley, on the south side of the reservation, in 1872. When the Northern Arapaho were subjugated, this tribe was moved onto the southeast portion of the reservation in 1878. (Though no longer enemies, the tribes still maintain separate identities.) Finally, in 1906, the federal government withdrew another half-million-acre tract of farmland north of Riverton, in the heart of the reservation, opening it to homesteaders.

SIGHTS

Riverton today is the largest town in the Wind River Valley with about 9200 people. Initially a farming center, as witnessed by its plethora of grain elevators, Riverton grew rapidly as a service center to the Gas Hills uranium boom of the 1960s and 1970s, 45 miles east. A subsequent price collapse cost the town income and population, so that today Riverton is a community in transition: It has a modern junior-college campus, stylish shops and upscale residential districts, but its commercial strip, extending south along Route 789 toward Lander, is singularly unattractive. A highlight of the town is the **Riverton Museum**, where various artifacts from the community's early-20th-century homesteading era are proudly displayed. Also here are photos of Wyoming rancher Leslie King, the father of former U.S. President Gerald Ford. Closed Sunday and Monday. ~ 700 East Park Avenue, Riverton; 307-856-2665.

Twenty-two miles northeast of Riverton via Route 26 is the small town of **Shoshoni**, a former rail terminus at the foot of the Owl Creek Mountains. Today it is the gateway to **Boysen State Park**, a popular site for water sports on bright, blue, 57-square-mile Boysen Reservoir, and to the spectacular **Wind River Canyon**. The ten-mile-long canyon begins just above the Boysen Dam.

Sheer red-rock cliffs rise to 2500 feet above the green waters of the Wind River; roadside signs describe the one billion years of geological history revealed in their strata. When the river emerges near Thermopolis, its name has changed from the Wind to the Big Horn.

HIDDEN ►

Route 136, which extends east from Riverton to the Gas Hills mining district, also leads to an unusual geological area known as the **Castle Gardens.** Located 40 miles from Riverton at the virtual geographic center of Wyoming, this badland region of sandstone knobs and pinnacles rising as many as 100 feet above the prairie has been designated a state historical monument. It's not the formations themselves that have earned it recognition, but the medieval petroglyphs carved in their sides: warriors and hunters, including their weapons and game, among them.

Most of the remaining Wind River Indian Reservation lies to the west of Riverton. About 3500 American Indians live here. The majority are Shoshones, whose main communities are Fort Washakie and Wind River in the south-central part of the reservation and Crowheart in the northwest. The main Arapaho villages are Ethete, Arapahoe and St. Stephens in the southeast. About three-fourths of the reservation is wild mountain country. Oil and gas leases and livestock ranching, primarily cattle, provide the tribe's main income. During the summer, powwows, rodeos and other public events are held most weekends in reservation communities. For information, phone the **Lander Chamber of Commerce.** ~ 160 North 1st Street, Lander; 307-332-3892.

Fort Washakie, the reservation's largest town, originally was christened Fort Brown when the U.S. Army established itself here in 1872, but the name was changed to honor Chief Washakie in 1879. The post was closed in 1909, but its buildings (many on the national historic register) have been incorporated into tribal offices. Among them is the **Shoshone Tribal Cultural Center,** which exhibits tribal arts and crafts as well as old photographs and documents, and maps for self-guided tours of the reservation. Open by appointment only on weekends. ~ 31 1st Street, Fort Washakie; 307-332-9106. The center also provides information about events on the reservation. Call or write to P.O. Box 1008, Fort Washakie, WY 82514.

The **grave of Chief Washakie,** who died in 1900 (aged somewhere between 96 and 102), is located in the old military cemetery along the Little Wind River directly behind the office compound. He was the first American Indian ever accorded full military honors at burial. Washakie's inscribed granite tomb is the most substantial memorial in this desolate graveyard of plain wooden crosses and occasional stone monuments. The grave of his youngest son, Charles Washakie (1873–1953), is next to the chief's. ~ North Fork Road, Fort Washakie.

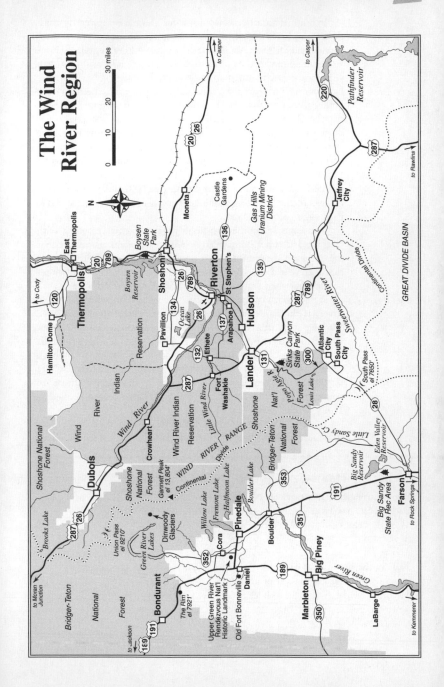

The Wind River Region

In a more remote civilian cemetery about a mile west, a monument marks what is said to be the **grave of Sacajawea**. A Shoshone woman from the Idaho–Montana border region, Sacajawea was kidnapped as a teenager in a tribal raid and sold as a wife to a French-Canadian fur trader, Toussaint Charbonneau. Lewis and Clark hired the couple in 1805 to guide them on their 3000-mile westward trek, Sacajawea carrying her infant son, Baptiste, all the way. Encyclopedias will tell you that Sacajawea was 26 when she died in 1812 at a Missouri River trading post. The Wind River Shoshones maintain, however, that this romantic heroine returned to her tribe and finally succumbed to old age in 1884. The Reverend John Roberts, a reservation missionary, claimed to have identified her remains in 1907; he, of course, officiated at the burial. A monument to an adopted nephew, Bazil, flanks that of Sacajawea.

You may see some Shoshone graves in this cemetery with clothing and other items piled on top; tribe members believe that the deceased should take their personal belongings with them to the next world. In some cases, that even includes their white-painted iron bed frames. ~ South Fork Road, Wind River.

A mile south of the Sacajawea gravesite, in the village of Wind River, is the **Roberts Episcopal Mission**, established as a girls' school and spiritual center for the Shoshone people. John Roberts, who came from his native Wales in 1883, preached here until his death in the 1940s. The original pink school building has been closed, but the church and parish hall remain well attended. Chief Washakie, who urged Roberts to focus his missionary efforts on young people, embraced Christianity here just before he died. ~ Trout Creek Road, Wind River.

Roberts also founded **St. Michael's Mission**, east of Fort Washakie in the village of Ethete, in 1889 as the principal school

✔ CHECK THESE OUT—UNIQUE SIGHTS

- Pay your respects at the graves of Washakie, a great Shoshone chief, and pathfinder Sacajawea on the **Wind River Indian Reservation**. *page 144*
- Marvel at the Popo Agie River in **Sinks Canyon State Park** as it disappears into a limestone cliff and reappears 600 yards downstream. *page 152*
- Wander the dirt streets of **South Pass City**, Wyoming's best-preserved ghost town, near the highest point on the Oregon Trail. *page 153*
- Meditate on the river plain where the **Upper Green River Rendezvous**, the greatest of the mountain men's trade fairs, took place. *page 162*

for Arapaho children. The mission consists mainly of a circle of red stone buildings. But its church, known as Our Father's House, is a low log behind whose altar (a tribal drum) is a picture window through which the Wind River Range is beautifully framed. Note the bishop's chair, made of elkhorn. ~ Ethete Road, Ethete.

The oldest of several missions on the reservation is **St. Stephen's Mission**, three miles south of Riverton. Here, for three years in the 1870s, Jesuit missionaries held mass for Arapaho converts in tents before completing a Victorian convent and other mission buildings. The present church, built in 1928, is brilliantly decorated with Arapaho designs inside and out. A small tepee serves as an altar tabernacle, and a log stump supports the christening font. The church has old photographs and antique beadwork, paintings and other creations on display. There are also a working art studio and a store where contemporary Arapaho arts and crafts are offered for sale. Near the mission are some impressive tribal buildings, including a public school with a tepee-shaped gymnasium roof. Gift shop is closed Thursday, Saturday and Sunday. ~ Route 138, St. Stephen's; 307-856-4330.

Traveling northwest through the Wind River reservation, Route 26 from Riverton meets Route 287 from Lander 16 miles north of Fort Washakie near the Bull Lake irrigation dam. Fourteen miles further is the village of **Crowheart**, named for a nearby mesa.

Flat-topped **Crowheart Butte**, which rises several hundred feet above the Wind River in the heart of the reservation, got its name from a legendary 1866 battle between Chief Washakie's Shoshone tribe and an invading party of Crow. As the story goes, the Crow stole a large number of horses but were tracked down by Shoshone warriors and forced to take refuge atop this butte without food or water. On the third day of the siege, the Crows' leader, Big Robber, taunted Washakie to climb the rock and fight him personally. Over his people's protest, the Shoshone leader did scale the rock; he killed Big Robber and, to underscore his triumph, cut out the Crow's heart and ate it. When asked about the incident in his later years, Washakie said only, "When you are young and full of life, you do strange things."

It's another 30 miles from this community to **Dubois**, an old ranching community of about 1000 people beyond the reservation boundaries. Situated amid foothills on the upper Wind River about halfway between Riverton and Jackson, Dubois has become a center for outdoor recreation (especially fishing and big-game hunting), rockhounding and modern dude ranching. Dubois' **National Bighorn Sheep Interpretive Center** has exhibits on efforts to reintroduce this handsome Rocky Mountain native to its original habitats. The largest wintering herd of these animals is just outside Dubois. Call for hours from mid-November to mid-May. Admission. ~ 907 West Ramshorn Road, Dubois; 307-455-3429.

Next door, the **Dubois Museum** has displays on the natural and cultural history of the region, including the unusual profession of tie-hacking. There are also prehistoric exhibits. Closed Sunday and from October through March. Admission. ~ 909 West Ramshorn Road, Dubois; 307-455-2284.

You'll learn more about tie-hacking 20 miles northwest of Dubois if you stop at the **Tie Hack Memorial.** Tie hackers were loggers who specialized in cutting railroad ties. Between 1914 and the early 1950s, these men split and planed logs from the Wind River forests, then floated them downstream to shipping ports. Some 700,000 ties were cut in 1947, the peak year; but when the railroad industry declined, this business disappeared. ~ Route 26/287, Dubois.

LODGING   The **Hi-Lo Motel** is a well-kept, 23-room ma-and-pa establishment that may be old-fashioned, but has everything the traveler needs, including TVs and phones in every room. They'll even welcome your pet. ~ 414 North Federal Boulevard, Riverton; 307-856-9223. BUDGET.

The single biggest property in the Wind River Country is the **Holiday Inn.** It's a rather bleak-looking place. The 121-room, two-story hotel has a central "fundome," an indoor recreation area with a small swimming pool and fitness center. It also has a restaurant and lounge, a coin laundry and data ports for business travelers in its modest rooms. ~ 900 East Sunset Street, Riverton; 307-856-8100, fax 307-856-0266. MODERATE.

There aren't many places to stay on the Wind River reservation itself. One of the few (open from June through August only) is the **Early Guest Ranch,** which appeals to travelers whose main

---

✔ **CHECK THESE OUT—UNIQUE LODGING**

- *Budget:* Relax in historic lodgepole furniture at the **Twin Pines Lodge & Cabins,** a National Register complex in Dubois. *page 149*
- *Moderate:* Study fine woodwork and beveled glass at the **Blue Spruce Inn,** a craftsman-style bed-and-breakfast home in Lander. *page 155*
- *Moderate:* Step outside your cabin and cast for trout at **The Resort at Louis Lake,** a rustic 1930s retreat at 9000 feet elevation. *page 156*
- *Deluxe:* Join a pack trip to mountain streams and lakes when you stay at the **Flying A Ranch** on the slopes of the Wind River Range. *page 163*

Budget: under $50   Moderate: $50–$90   Deluxe: $90–$130   Ultra-deluxe: over $130

interest is horseback riding. Guests may participate in cowboy work on this 5000-acre cattle ranch. Accommodations are in pleasant though not lavish individual log cabins. ~ 7374 Route 26, Crowheart; 307-455-4055, 800-532-4055, fax 307-455-2414; www.earlyranch.com. DELUXE.

I appreciate the atmosphere at the **Twin Pines Lodge & Cabins** in the heart of Dubois. This two-story log complex—listed on the national historic register—has 17 guest units. Some of them boast original lodgepole furnishings. Twin Pines has TVs and phones. This is a nonsmoking establishment. Open mid-May to mid-November and by reservation. ~ 218 West Ramshorn Street, Dubois; 307-455-2600. BUDGET.

One of the nicer small lodgings in this mountain region is the **Wapiti Ridge Ranch Bed & Breakfast Inn,** situated 18 miles west of Dubois. All 12 of the nonsmoking guest rooms here have private baths, and hearty breakfasts are a given. In winter, guests park their snowmobiles directly outside their doors. ~ 3915 Route 26, Dubois; phone/fax 307-455-2219; e-mail wapitiridgeb-b@ wyoming.com. MODERATE.

Some of the family-oriented ranches in the upper Wind River country offer a roster of activities that may make you feel like you're at summer camp or Club Med. An example is the **Double Bar J Ranch,** situated 20 miles west of Dubois in Shoshone National Forest. Here you can join in horseback riding, mountain biking, pack trips, fishing, skeet shooting, bonfires, horseshoes, volleyball and, in the winter, snowmobiling, cross-country skiing and sleigh rides. Accommodations are in log cabins with contemporary furnishings. Ranch-style breakfasts and dinners are included in the rates. ~ 3609 Route 26, Dubois; 307-455-2681, fax 307-455-3360. ULTRA-DELUXE.

Gotta have that espresso to begin the day? Look no further than **Split Rock Coffee & Bakery**. This popular café also serves midday soups, salads and sandwiches with an organic-food orientation. Closed Sunday. ~ 219 East Main Street, Riverton; 307-856-4334. BUDGET.

DINING

Heartier fare is served at the **Trailhead Family Restaurant** on the southbound commercial strip. Folks flock here for the steak, seafood and chicken dishes, the soups of the day, the salad bar and the homemade cakes and pies. ~ 831 North Federal Boulevard, Riverton; 307-856-7990. BUDGET TO MODERATE.

The Depot, ensconced in a remodeled former train station, is Riverton's best bet for Mexican food. During the warmer months, diners knock back margaritas with their meals on an outdoor patio. ~ 110 South 1st Street East, Riverton; 307-856-2221. MODERATE TO DELUXE.

A historic hotel in the center of town now houses **The Broker Restaurant**. This gracious establishment offers a gourmet experience while welcoming casual diners. Prime rib and seafood are the house specialties; there's also a children's menu. ~ 203 East Main Street, Riverton; 307-856-0555. DELUXE.

Follow the trail of rainbow sprinkles and powdered sugar to **Daylight Donuts & Village Café**, where the sweet treats are made on-site. In addition, you can order full breakfasts, steaks, burgers and other standards. ~ 515 West Ramshorn Street, Dubois; 307-455-2122. BUDGET TO MODERATE.

Serving breakfast staples like eggs, pancakes and grits all day long, the **Cowboy Café** also offers other fare for lunch and dinner. Steaks, deli sandwiches, burgers, seafood and salads number among the items on the extensive menu. ~ 115 East Ramshorn Street, Dubois; 307-455-2595. MODERATE TO DELUXE.

There is a deli at the **Ramshorn Inn** that is open for breakfast and lunch. The fare is the usual—pastries and sandwiches. Closed Sunday. ~ 202 East Ramshorn Street, Dubois; 307-455-2400. BUDGET.

SHOPPING   Perhaps the best prospect for souvenir hunting in the region is **St. Stephen's Mission**, south of Riverton on the Wind River reservation. Native artisans sell their jewelry, beadwork, carvings and other arts and crafts directly to the public through the church-operated store. For more than a century, the Jesuit fathers here have worked with the Arapaho people to preserve their cultural manifestations. Among the most prominent artists today is Bob Spoonhunter, who maintains a working studio here; his work blends modern techniques with traditional motifs. Closed Thursday, Saturday and Sunday. ~ Route 138, St. Stephen's; 307-856-4330.

Bronze sculptures are exhibited at the **R. V. Greeves Art Gallery**. By appointment only. ~ 53 North Fork Road, Fort Washakie; 307-332-3557. Beaded headpieces, necklaces, bolo ties, moccasins and assorted earrings are crafted by Shoshone artisans at the **Warm Valley Arts & Crafts Gift Shop**. By appointment only on Saturday. Closed Sunday. ~ Shoshone Cultural Center, Building 31, Black Coal Street, Fort Washakie; 307-332-9106.

NIGHTLIFE   In Dubois, you'll find a bar featuring karaoke on Friday night at the **Ramshorn Inn**. ~ 202 East Ramshorn Street, Dubois; 307-455-2444. There's rock next door at the **Outlaw Saloon**. ~ 204 West Ramshorn Street, Dubois; 307-455-2387.

PARKS   **BOYSEN STATE PARK**   Water sports of all kinds dominate visitor activities at this popular state park on Boysen Reservoir, a 20-mile-long, manmade lake on the eastern border of the Wind River Indian Reservation north of Shoshoni. The water is delightfully warm in summer, even at the upper end of the lake, where the Boysen Dam marks the mouth of the spectacular Wind River Canyon. There is a marina here, and a swimming beach on the east shore of the lake; fishing is good for brown and rainbow trout, walleye, ling, sauger, smallmouth bass, perch and crappie. Facilities include picnic areas, restrooms, a playground and a small grocery. ~ Access is via any of several entrance roads off Route 20, beginning about 14 miles north of Shoshoni; 307-876-2796.

▲ There are 180 RV/tent sites (no hookups); $4 per night. The park also administers cabins and a trailer park.

SHOSHONE NATIONAL FOREST 🏃 🚲 🐎 🔫 🎣 🛶 🚣 🚤

🚤 🛶 This rugged 2.4-million-acre national forest spans the east side of the Wind River Range as well as all the forest land adjoining the eastern boundary of Yellowstone National Park. Its peaks and remote canyons are home to moose, elk, grizzly bears and a host of other wildlife. Readily accessible facilities include picnic areas and restrooms. Three wilderness areas—the Washakie (see Chapter Four), Fitzpatrick and Popo Agie—are readily accessible from the Wind River Valley; they contain numerous glaciers, hundreds of natural lakes and Wyoming's highest mountains. ~ Numerous forest roads extend north and south of Route 26/287 in the Dubois area; Trail Lake (Forest Road 257) and Brooks Lake (Forest Road 515) are two of the most popular access areas. Route 131 (Sinks Canyon Road) southwest of Lander is the main byway into the southern section of the national forest; 307-527-6241 (Cody headquarters), 307-455-2466 (Dubois), 307-332-5460 (Lander).

> Wind River citizens in the 19th century often complained that Dubois horse rancher George Parker sold more stock than he raised. Parker later became known by another name: Butch Cassidy.

▲ The national forest has 340 RV/tent units, plus 201 for tents only, in 35 campgrounds (no hookups). That includes three campgrounds with 48 RV/tent sites in the Dubois area and four campgrounds with 66 RV/tent sites in the Lander area; $8 per night; 14-day maximum stay.

FITZPATRICK WILDERNESS AREA 🏃 🐎 🎣 🚣 Wyoming's

highest mountains, and the Rockies' greatest remnants of the Ice Ages, are contained within this 198,000-acre wilderness area that begins just four miles south of Dubois. Spectacularly rugged, it crests at 13,804-foot Gannett Peak, highest summit in the state, surrounded by the seven largest glaciers in the conterminous United States. (In all, there are 44 glaciers in the wilderness.) Myriad alpine lakes teem with trout for intrepid anglers. ~ The most popular access from Dubois is via the Torrey Lake Road (Forest

Road 257), which begins four miles southeast of town off Route 26/287; 307-455-2466.

▲ Primitive only.

▼▼▼▼▼▼▼▼▼▼▼▼▼▼▼▼

Lander and South Pass

Lander is the single best base from which to explore the Wind River Country. Though marginally smaller than Riverton, it has a more scenic location (on the Popo Agie River at the foot of the southern Wind River Range), a more historic atmosphere (it is one of the oldest towns in the state, founded as Camp Augur in 1869), and a growing mystique as the spiritual home of environmentalism in Wyoming. Far removed from major interstate highway routes and from the tourism hubbub surrounding Yellowstone and Jackson, it retains the peaceful, amazingly ordinary character of 1950s small-town America. It's a one-story town with a Norman Rockwell main street and neat, shady residential areas of modest turn-of-the-century frame houses.

Immediately outside of Lander are some of Wyoming's most intriguing sights. In Sinks Canyon State Park, the Popo Agie disappears into a canyon wall and reemerges in a crystal pool some distance downstream. South Pass City is a lovingly preserved goldmining boom town near the highest pass on the Oregon Trail. And there are mountains and lakes and forests to thrill even the most jaded backpacker.

SIGHTS

At the north end of town you'll find **Lander Jaycee Park**. Cultural programs are presented here on Wednesday evenings from June through August. ~ Corner of 1st and Main streets, Lander; 307-332-3892.

Lander is also home to the **National Outdoor Leadership Training School**, established here in 1965. College credit is offered to students of wilderness-survival skills, including mountaineering and ski touring. The presence of this school has contributed to Lander becoming the home of the International Climbers' Festival, established in 1994 and now held every July. ~ 288 Main Street, Lander; 307-332-4784.

A half- to full-day's drive around south Fremont County's **Loop Road** is the best way to acquaint yourself with Lander's mountain environs. Head southwest on Route 131 to Sinks Canyon State Park, continue on the gravel Louis Lake Road through Shoshone National Forest, and return to Lander on Route 28, the main northbound highway, after stopping to explore the old mining settlements of South Pass City and Atlantic City.

Sinks Canyon State Park occupies a limestone canyon, located seven miles west of town. Sedimentary cliffs tower above the rushing Popo Agie, whose Shoshone name means "the beginning of the waters." You'll discover why at The Sinks themselves: Midway down the canyon, the Popo Agie simply vanishes, plunging into an underwater cavern near the park's visitor center. Six hundred yards downstream, it re-emerges like a spring at The Rise, a calm, crystal-clear pool where trout can frolic safe from fishermen. (They surface, in fact, for bread thrown by visitors.) The hiking and wildlife viewing are outstanding at this park, especially in spring and early summer when the riverbanks are ablaze with wildflowers. ~ Route 131, Lander; 307-332-6333, 307-332-3077.

Beyond the park's west boundary, pavement gives way to a good gravel road, easily driven in most weather conditions. It switchbacks quickly up the sparsely foliated side of 9000-foot Fossil Hill, affording impressive views back down the Popo Agie valley. Once atop the ridge, you can look forward to a pleasant drive across a forested plateau speckled with small lakes like Frye, Worthen Meadow, Fiddlers and Louis, all accessible by road. Although clear-cut logging has violated some of this Shoshone National Forest timberland, it remains an area exceedingly popular with anglers and campers.

Esther Hobart Morris, appointed justice of the peace in South Pass City in 1870, tried 26 cases as the nation's first female judge.

Beyond Louis Lake, 21 miles from Sinks Canyon Park, the road descends gradually through pine-and-sagebrush country to Route 28. Turn right at this highway to cross the Continental Divide at **South Pass**, at 7650 feet the highest point on the Oregon Trail, and the halfway point of the pioneers' 2000-mile journey from the Missouri River to the West Coast. As the easiest crossing of the Rockies—a wide, easy passage through the southernmost foothills of the Wind River Range, at the headwaters of the Sweetwater River—it has been designated a national historic landmark. Here wagon trains rendezvoused before descending steeply from the high plains into arid basin-and-range terrain that stretched for another thousand miles: If you look closely, you can still see their ruts in this open rangeland.

In June 1867, less than two years before the transcontinental railroad would divert the flow of settlers to its southerly route, a rich vein of gold was discovered near South Pass. As the Carissa Mine went into large-scale operation, hordes of prospectors afflicted with "Sweetwater Fever" flocked to South Pass to search for the hard-rock mother lode from which the vein originated. Thirty more miles of the vein were opened. In less than a year, **South Pass City** grew into a community of more than 2000 people. Its dusty main street, which followed Willow Creek down an open canyon surrounded by barren hills, was lined for half a mile with hotels (5), saloons (13), stores, lawyers' and doctors' offices, brothels, and even a bowling alley.

South Pass City also had a school that was considered one of Wyoming's best, a five-column newspaper, and by 1870 two stage lines connecting it to the nearest Union Pacific Railroad station east of Rock Springs. Its residents included saloon-keeper William H. Bright, who authored the territorial bill that made Wyoming the first to give equal suffrage to women; and Esther Hobart Morris, a woman's rights advocate from Illinois who was appointed the town's justice of the peace in the wake of the bill's passage, and who thus became the first woman to hold public office in the United States. (The intimidation factor of Mrs. Morris's imposing size—six feet tall, 180 pounds—may well have contributed to her success.)

The South Pass gold boom was short-lived. The Carissa vein played out in just five years, and the mother lode was never found. By 1875, South Pass City was virtually a ghost town, many of its 250 buildings having been dismantled and moved to Lander or other locations. Occasional small mining rushes in subsequent decades kept a few hundred people in the area until, in 1966, the community was purchased by the Wyoming 75th Anniversary Commission as a "birthday present" for citizens of the state. Two dozen once-dilapidated buildings were carefully restored; they now comprise **South Pass City State Historic Site**.

As you stroll down South Pass Avenue from the visitors center, just two miles south off Route 28, you'll pass the remains of the school, miners' cabins, a butcher shop and the Carissa Saloon. Pause at the Jim Smith Store, now a mining museum; archaeologists found gold buried in a cast-iron pot behind the stone wall of an adjacent building, where women and children were hidden during Indian attacks. The site curator lives next door in the John & Lida Sherlock House. Across the street are the South Pass Hotel (once the city's finest), the newspaper office, a restaurant and a bank.

Turn north on Washington Street to see the only remaining stamp mill of 20 that once operated in this mining district. The waterwheel-powered mill crushed gold-bearing ore under its half-ton pistons. The South Pass jail and a quarantine hospital are located south of Willow Creek off Price Street. Free from touristy commercialism, South Park City is one of the best-preserved and most picturesque old mining boomtowns in the Rocky Mountain West. Admission. ~ Route 237; 307-332-3684.

But even while South Pass City has gone to the ghosts, it has a gold-rush suburb that has not. **Atlantic City,** four and a half miles northeast on Route 237, an unpaved back road, has never been completely abandoned. Named for the Atlantic Ledge mine (it's on the Atlantic Ocean side of the Continental Divide), it attained a population of about 500 before the gold ran out. But a handful of its modern residents still mine gold and iron ore, while others run a general store, tourist shops and a couple of atmospheric restaurants. A few reclusive craftspeople have established their homes and studios here as well.

You can complete the 70-mile loop tour and return to Lander by picking up the main highway, Route 28, two miles north of Atlantic City. An interesting diversion en route is **Red Canyon**, a brilliant red-rock gulch whose walls of oxidized iron were created 200 million years ago by an ancient sea. Red Canyon Road (Route 235) follows the rim of this "national natural landmark" for about six miles after turning off Route 28 six miles north of the Atlantic City junction.

Wendy Gibson, co-owner of Lander's Pronghorn Lodge, commissioned a life-size bronze sculpture of a bull elk after such an animal kept her company as she lay injured and waiting for help atop a Wind River mountaintop in 1991.

If you're in the mood for more exploring, turn east off Route 28 nine miles south of Lander and cross 50 miles of prairies, the last of them in the valley of the eastward-flowing Sweetwater River, to **Jeffrey City**. The population of this once-booming uranium-mining center has dwindled from 2000 to 700. Wyoming's first uranium mill was built here in 1957; today, however, the community calls itself the "jade capital" of the state.

LODGING

You can't miss the **Pronghorn Lodge**, Lander's largest: There's a bronze sculpture of a bull elk standing right in front of it. The two-story "Budget Host" property has 54 spacious, comfortably furnished rooms, a whirlpool spa, an exercise room, a coin laundry and a conference center. Continental breakfast is included. ~ 150 East Main Street, Lander; 307-332-3940, fax 307-332-2651. BUDGET.

Another good bet is the two-story **Silver Spur Motel**, which has 25 rooms on the quiet, west side of town. In addition to a nightly Western barbecue in summer, the motel has three two-bedroom family units, four efficiency units with microwaves and refrigerators, and a heated pool. ~ 340 North 10th Street, Lander; 307-332-5189, 800-922-7831. BUDGET.

More than a half-dozen bed and breakfasts have sprung up in the Lander area. My favorite is the **Blue Spruce Inn**, a huge brick home surrounded by large evergreen trees. Built in arts-and-crafts style in 1920, it is of architectural interest for its dark oak woodwork and stained and beveled glasswork. There are four bedrooms with varying decor, all with private baths, and separate TV, sitting and recreation rooms. There is also a sunporch for lounging. Children under 12 are not allowed. A full breakfast is served each morning. Smoking is not permitted. ~ 677 South 3rd Street, Lander; phone/fax 307-332-8253, 888-503-3311; www.bluespruce inn.com. MODERATE.

If you're looking for something a bit more rustic, the **Piece of Cake Bed & Breakfast** might suit you. Located a few miles west of town, this log lodge and four adjacent cabins afford spectacular vistas of soaring eagles and the Wind River Range. All six guest units have private baths; the two antique-furnished lodge rooms adjoin a guest living room with a TV and VCR, while the log cabins have refrigerators and microwaves. Children and pets are welcome. Rates include a full breakfast. ~ 2343 Baldwin Creek Road, Lander; 307-332-7608. MODERATE.

Five miles northwest of town, **Edna's Bed & Breakfast** offers two upstairs bedrooms with shared bath in the main house of a working cattle ranch. Children are welcome but the owners of the home, which was built in 1889, do not permit smoking. Rates include a full "country-style" breakfast. ~ 53 North Fork Road, Lander; 307-332-3175. BUDGET.

HIDDEN ►   Outdoor recreationists will love **The Resort at Louis Lake**. This rustic log resort is located at 9000 feet elevation in Shoshone National Forest, 28 miles south of Lander. Five one-room cabins with wood stoves, built in the 1930s and renovated, share a central bathhouse. A pair of two-bedroom cabins have full baths and modern kitchens. On the premises is the Louis Lake Outdoor Center, which houses outfitters and offers outdoor equipment rentals. A fishing pier and boat dock extend into the pine-shrouded alpine lake. ~ 1811 Louis Lake (off Route 131), Lander; 307-332-5549, 888-422-2246; www.4acabin.com. BUDGET TO DELUXE.

DINING   The Wind River Country's only microbrewery is located in **The Ranch Restaurant**, which serves dishes from hamburgers to prime rib. The spacious dining room is decorated in a Western style. ~ 148 Main Street, Lander; 307-332-7388. MODERATE TO DELUXE.

If you'd like, you can have breakfast for all three meals at the **Showboat Diner**. Or choose seafood, burgers, sandwiches, steaks and mouth-watering pies, all served in a nautical-themed dining

✔ **CHECK THESE OUT—UNIQUE DINING**

- *Budget:* Join locals for an early-morning dose of caffeine at **Split Rock Coffee & Bakery**, which also has an array of lunchables. *page 149*
- *Moderate to deluxe:* Knock back a margarita or two in a remodeled train station while you enjoy a Mexican meal at **The Depot** in Riverton. *page 149*
- *Moderate to deluxe:* Savor gourmet cuisine by the light of an oil lantern at the **Atlantic City Mercantile**, in an 1893 adobe building. *page 157*
- *Deluxe:* Reserve a table at **Miner's Delight Inn**, set in a 1904 log hotel, for a six-course, prix-fixe meal. *page 157*

Budget: under $7   Moderate: $7–$12   Deluxe: $12–$20   Ultra-deluxe: over $20

room. ~ 173 Main Street, Lander; 307-332-2710. BUDGET TO
DELUXE.

For the best salad bar in town, try **The Hitching Rack**, another
steak-and-seafood restaurant designed with family dining in mind.
There are good nightly pasta and chicken dishes and weekend
prime rib here, and the wine list is decent. Closed Sunday. ~ Route
287 South, Lander; 307-332-4322. MODERATE TO DELUXE.

The Breadboard specializes in deli-style sandwiches, made
with fresh bread, baked here daily. Homemade soups are also popular, as are smoothies. ~ 1350 Main Street, Lander; 307-332-
6090. BUDGET.

For something completely different, try the **Big Noi Restaurant**. The Thai food may not rival the best you've ever tried, but
it is unquestionably the best Thai food in town. Steaks and seafood share the menu. ~ 8125 Route 789 North, Lander; 307-332-
3102. MODERATE.

Improbable though it may seem, some of the Lander area's
finest dining takes place in the near–ghost town of Atlantic City,
some 20 miles south of Lander. **Atlantic City Mercantile** serves
diners in the authentic mining-camp setting of an 1893 adobe-
brick building, complete with low ceilings and oil lanterns. Lunches
and dinners feature rib-eye steaks smoke-grilled over aspen em-
bers. Ask about the seven-course, family-style Basque dinners,
served summer Wednesday nights (by reservation only). Closed
Monday through Wednesday in winter. ~ Off of Route 28, Atlantic City; 307-332-5143. MODERATE TO DELUXE.

The nearby **Miner's Delight Inn**, ensconced in the two-story
log Carpenter Hotel (built in 1904), features lavish six-course,
fixed-price dinners Friday and Saturday, and Thursday in summer
by appointment only. The well-publicized inn enjoys an international reputation, though many frontier gourmands contend that
it no longer measures up to the competition. ~ 290 Atlantic City
Road, Atlantic City; 307-332-0248. DELUXE.

The small farming town of Hudson, ten miles east of Lander
on Route 789, takes great community pride in its **Club El Toro**.
This long-established steakhouse is owned by a family of Eastern
European descent, the Viniches, whose patriarch is a leading poli-
tician in the state. The homemade ravioli and the cabbage rolls
are wonderful. Dinner only. Closed alternating Mondays. ~ 132
South Main Street, Hudson; 307-332-4627. MODERATE TO ULTRA-
DELUXE.

Perhaps the most interesting stop is **Eagle Bronze**, a large foundry   **SHOPPING**
that casts and produces bronze statues and monuments for artists
and other clients all over the world. Visitors who join guided
tours (offered at 10 a.m. Tuesdays and Thursdays from September

through April; at 9:30 a.m. and 12:30 p.m. on weekdays from May through August; and other times by reservation) see demonstrations of the traditional lost-wax casting process. A small gallery has bronzes for sale. The foundry is located two miles from downtown in the South Lander Industrial Park off Route 28. Admission. ~ 130 Poppy Street, Lander; 307-332-5436.

A number of Western artists make their homes in the Lander area and show their work in studios and galleries here. Worth visiting is **Bar-Bar-A's Art Gallery**, which exhibits oils, acrylics, watercolors and photographs by local artists. ~ 555 West Main Street, Lander; 307-332-7798.

The bronco-riding cowboy depicted on Wyoming license plates is Lander rancher Stub Farlow (1886–1953), seated atop a horse named Deadman. A Denver artist based his design on a photo of Farlow.

American Indian jewelry and beadwork can be found in the **A & P Pawn Shop**. Closed Sunday. ~ 220 Main Street, Lander; 307-332-7043.

For books in Lander, you have two choices. **The Booke Shoppe** offers books on a variety of subjects, with an emphasis on Western and American Indian history and fiction and natural history. ~ 160 North 2nd Street, Lander; 307-332-6221. **Cabin Fever Books** carries new books, but also has a used-book section where you can trade in old volumes. Closed weekends. ~ 163 South 5th Street, Lander; 307-332-9580.

NIGHTLIFE A handful of Lander nightspots offer dancing on weekends. Among them is the **Lander Bar**, located in the historic (1907) Lander Hotel; it features live music on Friday or Saturday, plus live acoustic music Sunday evenings. Locals feed on burgers and pizzas from the adjoining Gannett Grill. ~ 126 Main Street, Lander; 307-332-7009.

For rock, the **One Shot Lounge** is a good bet. ~ 695 Main Street, Lander; 307-332-2692.

PARKS **SINKS CANYON STATE PARK** 🏃 🏊 ☕ The Popo Agie River disappears into an underwater cave (The Sinks) in a limestone canyon, emerging 600 yards downstream in a clear pool (The Rise). There are two interpretive nature trails here, and trout fishing is excellent, although The Rise itself is closed to anglers. You'll find a visitors center, picnic areas and restrooms; handicapped accessible. ~ From Lander, take Route 131 seven miles west; 307-332-6333, 307-332-3077.

▲ The state park's Sawmill Campground has 5 RV/tent sites (no hookups); $4 per night. In the adjacent national forest's Popo Agie Campground, there are 25 RV/tent sites (no hookups); $4 per night. Both are closed October through April; 14-day maximum stay.

POPO AGIE WILDERNESS AREA 🚶 🐎 🛶 Permanent snowfields cloak the rooftop of this 102,000-acre wilderness, which boasts 20 mountains over 12,000 feet in elevation. Resting on the eastern flank of the Continental Divide, west of Lander, this rugged, roadless wilderness contains more than 100 lakes and is rich in historical lore from the days of the "mountain men." ~ From Lander, the most direct access is via Forest Road 300 at Worthen Meadow Reservoir, 20 miles west of town off the Louis Lake Road; 307-332-5460.

▲ Primitive only.

The west slope of the Wind River Range is a region of solemn grandeur, of snow-capped mountains and rolling rangeland. Drained by the Green River, which gives life to the intermontane prairies between the Wind Rivers and the slightly lower (11,000-foot) Wyoming Range to the west, this 7000-foot plateau is one of the state's least known yet most unforgettable districts.

Pinedale and the Upper Green River

Route 191, which connects Jackson and Rock Springs, and Route 189, which extends south to Kemmerer and Evanston, are the sole highways running through the region. And the only community of size is Pinedale, a town of barely 1200 people, whose economy is pegged to outfitting hunting and fishing expeditions into the Bridger Wilderness Area, Wyoming's largest.

Yet these prairies were well known to the "mountain men." It's no accident that the political entity enveloping this magnificence, Sublette County, was named for one of these early-19th-century trappers, nor that the Bridger Wilderness, which defines much of its eastern boundary, was christened for another. Even before that, the Shoshone Indians considered the wildlife-rich banks of the Green River to be their tribal hunting ground.

The Green, indeed, sets the tone here. Flowing from its headwaters in the Dinwoody Glaciers on the Continental Divide, it weaves its way south between the ranges and ultimately joins the Colorado River, which continues to the Gulf of California. (This is, in fact, the northernmost reach of the Colorado's drainage. To the east, the Wind and Sweetwater flow into the Missouri and Mississippi rivers and on to the Atlantic, while to the north and west, the Snake River and its tributaries proceed to the Pacific.)

Approaching the Green River region from South Pass, Route 28 retraces the Oregon Trail route as it descends Pacific Creek some 34 miles to Farson, a quiet junction town on Sandy Creek. A few miles north of here is the **Big Sandy State Recreation Area**, an unlikely water-sports destination on a large desert reservoir.

Turn north here on Route 191. The next hour's drive doesn't yield much in terms of traditional sightseeing stops, but if you like

SIGHTS

mountain panoramas, this one is hard to top. As you draw slowly closer to the alpine heart of the Wind River Mountains, you'll see the full breadth of this lofty range, with nothing standing between you and the summits but cattle, sheep and occasional antelope on the brown prairies.

Shortly after you cross the New Fork of the Green River, 43 miles north of Farson, you return to a pocket of civilization at the small town of **Boulder**, notable for its efforts to perpetuate the tradition of the pine-log cabin in new construction. Twelve miles further is **Pinedale**, which appears as a typical Old West ranching town with false-front buildings lining the wide highway through downtown.

Pick up a brochure describing the town's historic district from the **Pinedale Area Chamber of Commerce**. Closed weekends. ~ East Pine Street, Pinedale; 307-367-2242. Then wander over to the **Museum of the Mountain Man**, where artifacts and photographs will teach you not only about these early fur traders, but also about regional Indian culture and the early settlement of this part of Wyoming. Open daily May through September and by appointment the rest of the year. Admission. ~ Fremont Lake Road, Pinedale; 307-367-4101.

Fremont Lake Road continues past the museum about three miles to **Fremont Lake**, the largest of a dozen or more Pinedale-area lakes that owe their origins to glaciers of the distant past. Fremont is ten miles long and a mile and a half wide, framed at its far end by the steep summits of the Wind River Range. On the lakeshore are a lodge and marina where boat trips can be booked to the Fremont Creek campground at the lake's north end. Another campground, halfway up the east shore, is accessible by road.

Other sizable lakes within 25 miles' drive of Pinedale include Boulder, Burnt, Halfmoon, Willow and New Fork lakes. But for travelers willing to put a good half-day into probing the slopes of Wyoming's highest mountains in **Bridger-Teton National Forest**, a jaunt north from Pinedale on Route 352 (which branches north off Route 191 six miles west of town) is recommended.

The road passes through the tiny community of Cora, crosses a sagebrush plain and drops into the upper Green River valley, whose banks are home to numerous ranches. After 25 miles, the pavement turns to gravel at a colony of summer homes, and you are in the national forest. You'll pass several campgrounds and historical markers, as well as the **Kendall Warm Springs**, which have a constant, year-round temperature of 84.4°F. These springs are home to the Kendall dace, a unique species of fish that is two inches long when fully grown. During breeding season, males are purple, females green.

HIDDEN ▶

The road ends 45 miles from Pinedale at the **Green River Lakes**, at about 8000 feet elevation. There's a formal campground

The Green River Rendezvous

Out on the cottonwood flats where Horse Creek joins the Green River, about 14 miles west of Pinedale, a small stone memorial near old Fort Bonneville recalls the site of the Upper Green River Rendezvous. Beyond that, you'll have to use your imagination: There's little else to indicate that here, in the 1830s, some of the most significant events in the history of the early American West took place.

Rendez-vous is a French word that means "meeting" or "appointment" . . . or, more literally, "pay yourselves back." The rendezvous were means by which the mountain men could reward themselves. These wilderness-hardened trappers and traders spent far more time mingling with native tribes and tackling the challenges of nature than consorting with each other. So once each summer, from 1825 through 1840, they convened somewhere in their northern Rocky Mountain realm. The upper Green River area was a favorite; six of the last eight rendezvous were held in this area.

The rendezvous were ostensibly trade fairs. Indian tribes from throughout the West were invited to join the trappers in trading hides and furs for guns and horses or other desirable items. In the late 1830s, supply caravans from St. Louis made the rendezvous an essential stop. But the rendezvous were principally an opportunity for a good party. Participants drank, danced, gambled, tested their strength and skill in various contests and swapped the tallest of tall tales.

Jim Bridger, the most famous of all the mountain men, missed no more than two of these legendary gatherings. David Jackson, Jedediah Smith, Thomas "Broken Hand" Fitzpatrick, Jeremiah "Liver Eatin'" Johnston, Nathaniel Wyeth (of the famous Wyeth family of painters) and many others were regular attendees. Many travelers from the East didn't know what to make of them. When Bridger and friends performed an impromptu dance for a quartet of missionary wives in 1838, for instance, one of them wrote: "No pen can describe the horrible scene they presented. Could not imagine that white men, brought up in a civilized land, can appear to so much imitate the devil."

The best-documented rendezvous was the 1833 affair, the first on the upper Green River. Washington Irving described it at length in his 1837 book, *The Adventures of Captain Bonneville*, based upon Benjamin Bonneville's own journal. After the 1840 rendezvous, the sponsoring American Fur Company closed them down: The fur trade was waning, and increasing travel through the region served a growing trade function in its own right.

Today's best tribute to the 1830s rendezvous is the modern Green River Rendezvous in nearby Pinedale. For more than 50 years, many of the original mountain-man activities—black-powder shooting, tomahawk throwing, storytelling—have taken place there for a full weekend each July.

and picnic area on the beautiful lower lake, its eastern flank dominated by striking, 11,670-foot Square Top Mountain. Trails lead from here into the Bridger Wilderness and the upper lake.

Routes 191 and 189 join near **Daniel**, a little village that has kept its Old West charm intact. It is located in a broad cottonwood valley where Horse Creek enters the Green River. About a mile east of the community on Route 191, keep an eye out for the **Father De Smet Monument**. This little shrine, dedicated in 1925 near the Daniel Cemetery, commemorates the site where Belgian Father Pierre-Jean de Smet (1801–1873) celebrated Wyoming's first Roman Catholic Mass (known as "La Prairie de la Messe") on July 5, 1840.

A couple of miles west of Daniel on Route 354, another historical marker recalls **Old Fort Bonneville**. Its establishment in 1832 by the Rocky Mountain Fur Company—whose principals were mountain men Jedediah Smith, David Jackson and William Sublette—was largely responsible for a half-dozen trading rendezvous being held near this site through 1840. Although their actual location may have varied geographically by a few miles from year to year (a sign acknowledging the **Upper Green River Rendezvous National Historic Landmark** is sited at the Cora junction on Route 187 west of Pinedale), these rendezvous were an important part of the pioneer history of the American West. (See "The Green River Rendezvous" in this chapter.)

At Daniel Junction, travelers decide whether to turn north or south on Route 189. North leads 65 miles to Jackson over a low, pine-shrouded divide called The Rim (7921 feet) and down the Hoback valley through **Bondurant**, a small summer-cottage and ranching community.

South takes you 92 miles down the Green River valley, through rangeland, badlands and alkali flats, to Kemmerer. The primary settlements along this route are the twin towns of **Big Piney** and **Marbleton**, which have a joint population of about 1400. Their economy is based on ranching and, since the mid-1950s, rich oil and natural-gas deposits.

LODGING   A pleasant older property in downtown Pinedale is the **Sun Dance Motel**. Its 18 rooms, including a trio of two-bedroom units, are simple but lovingly maintained. They also rent out a cabin. Closed November through April. ~ 148 East Pine Street, Pinedale; 307-367-4336, 800-833-9178. MODERATE.

If you're seeking something more upscale, try the **Best Western Pinedale Inn**. A two-story motel with 59 rooms off interior corridors, it also offers a hot tub, an exercise room, a heated indoor pool and spa. Some of the rooms have refrigerators and microwaves; all have TVs, but none have telephones. Continental breakfast is included. ~ 850 West Pine Street, Pinedale; 307-367-6869, 800-528-1234, fax 307-367-6897. MODERATE.

Window on the Winds is a pleasant bed-and-breakfast home, a big log house in the country with four nonsmoking guest rooms. Children and pets are welcome, and there's a hot tub, but you may have to share a bath. Guests also share a television and phone in the common parlor. A full breakfast is served. ~ 10151 Route 191, Pinedale; 307-367-2600, 888-367-1345, fax 307-367-2395; www.cruising-america.com. MODERATE.

Ranch accommodations outnumber motels in the Pinedale area. Many are geared toward fishing, including the **Flying A Ranch** on the slopes of the Wind River Range. Trout anglers can cast their flies right at the ranch. The ranch offers unlimited horseback riding, and guests can join guided hiking or horseback trips to mountain streams and lakes. Accommodations are in luxuriously appointed log cabins with private baths, separate living rooms, porches, and fireplaces or woodburning stoves. Closed mid-October to mid-June. ~ 771 Flying A Ranch Road, Pinedale, WY 82941; 307-367-2385, 800-678-6543, fax 605-330-8731; www.flyinga.com. DELUXE.

Half Moon Lake Resort, situated lakeside ten miles north of Pinedale, has three cabins (they expect to have seven by the end of 1999). Unlike many of the area's guest ranches, the lodge accepts overnight and weekend guests and does not require a minimum stay. Boat rentals are available. Other activities at this year-round resort include horseback riding, mountain biking and hiking. Closed November to Memorial Day. ~ P.O. Box 983, Pinedale, WY 82941; 307-367-6373, fax 307-367-6538; www.halfmoon lake.com. ~ MODERATE TO ULTRA-DELUXE.

On the Route 189 corridor, your best lodging prospect is the **Marbleton Inn,** a 34-room motel with TV and phone in each room, a restaurant and lounge adjoining. ~ 405 Winkelman Street, Marbleton; 307-276-5231, fax 307-276-5233. BUDGET.

DINING

Although dining options are limited in Pinedale, the little town has one of the best restaurants in Wyoming in **McGregor's Pub**. Prime rib is the specialty, and there is an unusually broad selection of seafood, all served in the warm, contemporary Western atmosphere of a renovated turn-of-the-century hotel. Seating is available on the large outdoor patio in the summer. No lunch on Saturday or Sunday. ~ 21 North Franklin Avenue, Pinedale; 307-367-4443. MODERATE TO DELUXE.

For inexpensive eats, try **Calamity Jane's,** a down-home café serving hamburgers, french fries, pizza and burritos. ~ 30 West Pine Street, Pinedale; 307-367-2469. BUDGET.

NIGHTLIFE

There's live country music in Pinedale on weekends at the Stockman's Bar. ~ 16 North Maybell Avenue, Pinedale; 307-367-4562.

PARKS

BIG SANDY STATE RECREATION AREA

Water sports are the *raison d'être* for this recreation area on Big Sandy Reservoir, created by a dam on Big Sandy Creek, a Green River tributary. The 3130-acre desert park entirely surrounds the vaguely heart-shaped lake. Facilities include picnic areas and pit toilets; bring your own drinking water. Closed mid-October to Memorial Day. ~ Eight miles north of Farson on Route 191, then two miles east on Big Sandy Reservoir Road; 307-537-5675.

▲ There are 12 RV/tent sites (no hookups); no charge; 14-day maximum stay.

BRIDGER-TETON NATIONAL FOREST

This 3.4-million-acre forest encompasses the entire western slope of the Wind River Range, as well as the Wyoming and Salt ranges to the west. Because this side of the Wind Rivers receives more rainfall than the east, streams and lakes—rich in trout and other fish—are everywhere in its pine, spruce and fir forests. Most of this range has been set aside as the roadless Bridger Wilderness (see below). There are picnic areas and restrooms. ~ Route 189/191 north of Daniel transits the national forest en route to Jackson. Other principal access routes in this region are Fremont Lake Road northeast of Pinedale, Route 350 west of Big Piney, Route 352 north of Pinedale, Route 353 east of Boulder and Route 354 west of Daniel; 307-367-4326.

▲ Ten Forest Service campgrounds in the upper Green River area have a total of 198 RV/tent sites (no hookups), many of them on lakeshores; $4 to $7 per night; 10- to 16-day maximum stay. None is open longer than June through September.

BRIDGER WILDERNESS AREA The largest federally designated wilderness area in Wyoming, the 428,000-acre Bridger extends for 90 miles down the spine of the Wind River Range, on the west side of the Continental Divide. It includes 16 of the state's 17 highest summits (capped by 13,804-foot Gannett Peak, which it shares with the Fitzpatrick Wilderness). Some 1300 lakes are connected by more than 600 miles of hiking trails. ~ The most direct access is from Pinedale. Take Fremont Lake Road into Forest Road 134, which ends at a campground and trailhead at the edge of the Bridger Wilderness 13 miles northeast of town. Another popular access is from Green River Lakes at the end of Route 352 north of Pinedale; 307-367-4326.

▲ Primitive only.

▼▼▼▼▼▼▼▼▼▼▼▼▼▼▼
Outdoor Adventures

FISHING

Trout are by far the most common sport fish in almost all Wyoming lakes, river and streams. Rainbow trout are the favorite stocked variety; others include brown, brook, cutthroat and lake trout (mackinaw). A few fishing areas boast rarer trout species, such as the golden trout found in the Popo Agie River near Lander and the splake found in nearby Louis Lake.

Apart from the Wind, the Green and tributary rivers, the myriad lakes of the Wind River Range offer superb cold-water angling opportunities. Fremont and Half Moon lakes, just northeast of Pinedale, are famous for trout and grayling.

Warm-water anglers are directed to Ocean Lake, a state wildlife management unit 15 miles northwest of Riverton off Route 134. There is excellent walleye, bass and crappie fishing, as well as winter ling, in this nine-and-a-half-square-mile public reservoir.

You can buy fishing supplies and Wyoming state fishing licenses in Lander at **The Good Place**. Closed Sunday. ~ 155 Main Street; 307-332-3158. There's also **Rocky Mountain Dubbing**, the region's largest fly-fishing specialty shop, located in the South Lander Industrial Park. Closed Sunday. ~ Route 287 South; 307-332-2989.

For guided trips, in Dubois contact the **Great Outdoor Adventure Company**. ~ P.O. Box 1150, Dubois, WY 82513; 307-455-3344. **Outfitters of the Wyoming Wilderness** conducts one- to ten-day expeditions from June through September into the Washakie, Fitzpatrick and Bridger-Teton wildernesses. ~ P.O. Box 695, Dubois, WY 82513; 307-455-2725. For float-fishing trips on the Snake, Green and New Fork rivers and in Yellowstone National Park, contact **John Henry Lee Outfitters**. Closed October through May. ~ P.O. Box 8368, Jackson, WY 83002; 307-733-9441, 800-352-2576.

BOATING

Boating and other water sports are very popular in Boysen Reservoir (Boysen State Park) near Shoshoni and Big Sandy Reservoir (Big Sandy State Recreation Area) north of Farson.

In Shoshone National Forest, favored places include Brooks Lake, north of Dubois; Torrey, Ring and Trail lakes, south of Dubois; and Fiddlers and Louis lakes, west of Lander. In the Pinedale area, Fremont, Half Moon, Willow and New Fork lakes all welcome boaters.

CANOEING & KAYAKING

Apart from the area's slow-moving rivers, one of the most popular runs is the two-mile stretch of Roaring Fork Creek between Worthen Meadow Reservoir and Frye Lake, west of Sinks Canyon in Shoshone National Forest west of Lander.

RIVER RUNNING

From Memorial Day through Labor Day, **Wind River Canyon Whitewater** offers rafting trips through the magnificent Wind River Canyon, beginning just below the Boysen Dam north of Shoshoni. Flyfishing trips for rainbow trout are also available. ~ 210 Route 20 South, Suite 5, Thermopolis; 307-864-9343.

CLIMBING

There are endless climbing opportunities in the Wind River Range. Hardcore rock climbers, however, prefer to challenge the limestone walls of Wild Iris and Sinks Canyon, both just west of Lander. The latter is particularly popular in winter, when its south-facing cliff walls gather heat. In addition, Lander has an indoor climbing gym at the **Gravity Club**. ~ 2nd and Garfield streets.

For equipment and information, visit **Wild Iris Mountain Sports**. ~ 333 Main Street, Lander; 307-332-4541. The shop is a major sponsor of the International Climbers' Festival, held in Lander each July.

CROSS-COUNTRY SKIING

The three wilderness areas of the Wind River Range—the Bridger, Fitzpatrick and Popo Agie—offer unrivaled opportunities for backcountry skiing on hundreds of miles of trails, where motorized vehicles are prohibited. Skiers who like to stay a little closer to civilization enjoy the trails of Sinks Canyon State Park, near Lander, and the Bridger-Teton National Forest roads above Pinedale. **Ski Rentals** A good place to find Nordic skis for rent is **Freewheel Ski & Cycle**. ~ 258 Main Street, Lander; 307-332-6616.

OTHER WINTER SPORTS

Wyoming's **Continental Divide Snowmobile Trail** runs 300 miles from Lander north via Pinedale to Togwotee Pass, just east of Grand Teton National Park. As no motorized vehicles are allowed in the wilderness areas, the trail actually crosses the Divide near Louis Lake (north of South Pass), follows the west side of the Wind River Range, then crosses back to the east at Union Pass west of Dubois.

There are extensive networks of branch trails in the Lander and Dubois areas.

Trail users must purchase permits, for sale at various locations in towns along the route. You can pick up permits at **Cowboy Polaris**. ~ 618 South 1st Street, Dubois; 307-455-3464. **Big J's Rentals** offers guided snowmobile tours as well as rentals. ~ 641 West Pine Street, Pinedale; 307-367-2833. In Atlantic City, **A.C.E.** rents snowmobiles out of Atlantic City Mercantile. ~ 100 East Main Street, Atlantic City; 307-332-9290.

In February, the Continental Divide Trail is route for the **International Rocky Mountain Stage Stop Sled Dog Race**. Mushers begin and end in Jackson, turning around in Lander. Amateurs can try their hand behind a dog sled by booking a trip with **Geyser Creek Adventures**, which offers full-day and overnight trips in the Brooks Lake and Togwotee Pass areas. ~ P.O. Box 846, Dubois, WY 82513, 307-455-2702, 800-531-6874. **Dog Sled Tours by Washakie Outfitting** mushes throughout Shoshone National Forest. Half-day, full-day or overnight excursions are available. ~ P.O. Box 1054, Dubois, WY 82513; 307-455-2616, 800-249-0662.

Lander has an outdoor community ice rink for hardy winter skaters at the City Park, located at 405 Fremont Street. Contact the **Lander Chamber of Commerce** for more information. ~ 160 North 1st Street; 307-332-3892, 800-433-0662.

GOLF

There are two 18-hole, par-72 courses in the Wind River Country. The public **Lander Golf & Country Club** is scenic and challenging. ~ 1 Golf Course Drive, Capital Hill, Lander; 307-332-4653. The **Riverton Country Club**, private but open to the public for a modest fee, is notorious for its proliferation of sand and water traps. ~ 4275 Country Club Road, Riverton; 307-856-4779.

In addition, there are a pair of nine-hole courses in the region. The **Antelope Hills Golf Course** has an impressive layout in the foothills of the Wind River Range. ~ Route 287, Dubois; 307-455-2888. The **Rendezvous Meadows Golf Club** is nestled near the west slope of the same mountains. ~ 55 Clubhouse Road, Pinedale; 307-367-4252.

RIDING STABLES

A great way to explore the backcountry wilderness of the Wind River Range is by horseback. Among outfitters offering tours are Jim and Mary Allen's **Diamond Four Ranch**, specializing in multinight pack trips. ~ P.O. Box 243, Lander, WY 82520; 307-332-2995. In Riverton, try **Strathkay Wranglers Adventures** for a working ranch experience. ~ 189 Young Road; 307-856-2194. In Pinedale, **Bridger Wilderness Outfitters** rents horses for half- or full-day excursions. They also facilitate pack trips, gear drops, and other wilderness trips. ~ P.O. Box 561, Pinedale, WY 82941; 307-367-2268; www.bwo.com.

Rent horses or embark on a guided ride from June through October with **Outfitters of the Wyoming Wilderness**. ~ P.O. Box 695, Dubois, WY 82513; 307-455-2725.

✔ **CHECK THESE OUT—UNIQUE OUTDOOR ADVENTURES**

- Raft down the ten-mile-long Wind River Canyon, its half-mile-high cliffs towering above the green waters of the Wind River. *page 165*
- Try your hand at mushing a team of sled dogs through the snow of forested Togwotee Pass near Dubois. *page 166*
- Retrace the Oregon Trail near South Pass by horseback, passing by pioneer grave markers and abandoned settlers' cabins. *page 168*
- Hike the Clear Creek Trail from the Green River Lakes north of Pinedale, through a massive boulder to a natural bridge. *page 169*

PACK TRIPS & LLAMA TREKS

Dozens of outfitters throughout the region offer trips ranging from overnight to weeks. Among them are those listed under "Riding Stables," above. In addition, **Western Encounters** has a calendar of week-long rides on various historic trails (Pony Express, Oregon Trail, etc.) scheduled from late May until mid-September, as well as two early-season cattle drives. ~ 24 Birchfield Lane, Lander; 307-332-5434, 800-572-1230. **Old West Outfitters**, based at the Two Bar A Ranch south of Lander, recreates Oregon Trail wagon trips twice each in July and August. ~ 47 Iiams Road, Lander; 307-332-2701. Participants in any of these trips should expect to pay $150–$200 per person, per day. **Rocky Mountain Horseback Adventures** conducts one- to five-day pack trips for serious trout fishing in alpine lakes along the Continental Divide, and also recreates Oregon Trail trips from May through September. ~ P.O. Box 592, Lander, WY 82520; 307-332-9149, 800-408-9149.

If you don't mind walking, but are pleased to have a beast of burden carry your load, llama trekking may be just the thing for you. The **Lander Llama Company** offers trips of three to ten days into the backcountry lakes of the Wind River and Absaroka ranges between June and September, at rates that start around $150 per person, per day. In May, several Red Desert trips are planned. ~ 2024 Mortimore Lane, Lander; 307-332-5624, 800-582-5262; e-mail woodruff@wyoming.com.

BIKING

Hundreds of miles of forest roads and trails climb far into the Wind River Range, while BLM roads crisscross the central Wyoming prairies. Maps are available from bike shops throughout the region.

Popular cycling areas include South Pass, with fairly gentle roads and outstanding scenery; the Louis Lake Road, a rolling Shoshone National Forest grade with plenty of lakes and shady wooded areas; the Union Pass region northwest of Dubois; and the upper Green River valley north of Pinedale.

For mountain-bike rentals, consult **Freewheel Ski & Cycle**. ~ 258 Main Street, Lander; 307-332-6616. Rentals are also available at **Bob's Bike Corral**, which rents, sells and services mountain bikes; helmets are supplied with rentals. In summer, guided bike rides can be arranged. Closed Sunday and Monday from May through September; call for winter hours. ~ 8 Stalnaker Street, Dubois; 307-455-3193.

HIKING

Hundreds of miles of wilderness trails in the Wind River Range have given the mountains a reputation for the finest hiking in Wyoming. All distances listed here are one way unless otherwise noted.

DUBOIS AREA One of the longest and most challenging treks into the Shoshone National Forest's Fitzpatrick Wilderness is the well-marked **Glacier Trail** (25.4 miles), which begins at Trail Lake, 12 miles south of Dubois via gravel County Road 257. Cresting numerous high ridges, passing back and forth between meadows and forests and by numerous cold alpine lakes, it climaxes at the Dinwoody Glacier, high on the slope of Wyoming's tallest mountain, Gannett Peak.

A good all-day hike is the **Frontier Creek Trail** (9 miles), which follows an Absaroka Mountain stream up a sheltered canyon through the Washakie Wilderness. The gradual 1500-foot climb begins at the Shoshone National Forest's Double Cabin Guard Station, reached via Horse Creek Road and Forest Road 285, about 22 miles north of Dubois.

LANDER AREA A spectacular short hike is the **Popo Agie Falls Trail** (1.5 miles), a moderate climb through a forested canyon to a series of roaring waterfalls that plunge as much as 60 feet. The trail begins at the Bruce Picnic Area, one miles above Sinks Canyon State Park, eight miles west of Lander. In spring and early summer, the banks of the Popo Agie are cloaked with wildflowers. Bear in mind that you'll be sharing this trail—narrow and rocky in some spots—with horses and mountain bikes.

Main access trails to high country of the Popo Agie Wilderness include the **Middle Fork Trail** (6 miles), which also starts near the upper end of Popo Agie Canyon, and the easier **Sheep Bridge Trail** (3 miles), from Worthen Meadow Reservoir on Louis Lake Road. The two trails converge and climb into the wilderness, where various paths fork off to places like Ice Lakes (12 miles), Sweetwater Gap (16 miles) and the magnificent Cirque of the Towers (22 miles).

PINEDALE AREA The **Horseshoe Lake Trail** (7.5 miles) is among the most popular of several routes that climb (first rapidly, then gently) into the moist, forested meadows of the Bridger Wilderness on the western slope of the Wind River Range. From Pinedale, travel 12 miles south to Route 353 east of Boulder, then turn north on County Road 125 (Boulder Lake Road). This road extends about nine miles to the trailhead at the Boulder Lake campground.

From the Green River Lakes, 45 miles north of Pinedale via Route 352, the **Clear Creek Trail** (4 miles) ascends to a natural bridge formed when Clear Creek burrowed under a massive rock and slowly eroded it away. An unmaintained trail continues an additional two miles to little Clear Lake, on the flank of Square Top Mountain.

Other major trailheads for the Bridger Wilderness are at the ends of Fremont Lake Road and Willow Creek Road north of Pinedale. Both offer entry to a network of more than a dozen interconnecting trails that span the full 60-mile length of the wilderness.

Transportation

Although there is no interstate highway access, several U.S. and state routes crisscross the Wind River country.

CAR

All of the U.S. highways run in a roughly northwesterly direction. **Route 20** (Casper–Cody) passes through Shoshoni and the Wind River Canyon. **Route 26** (Casper–Jackson) is the main artery up the Wind River valley, through Riverton and Dubois. **Route 189** (Evanston–Jackson) follows the Green River through Big Piney. **Route 191** (Rock Springs–Jackson) runs through Pinedale en route. **Route 287** (Laramie–Yellowstone) passes through Lander and Dubois.

The most important state highways in this region are **Route 28**, which links Lander with Route 191 at Farson (south of Pinedale), and **Route 789**, the direct road between Lander and Riverton.

To get to Lander from the state capital of Cheyenne, take **Route 80**, the interstate highway, 149 miles west to Rawlins, then **Route 287** northwest another 125 miles up the valley of the Sweetwater River.

For road reports, call 307-856-9966 in Riverton or 888-996-7623 in Lander.

AIR

United Express flies into the **Riverton Regional Airport.** ~ 4800 Airport Road, Riverton; 307-856-1307, 800-241-6522. There are also smaller private airports at Dubois, Lander, Pinedale and Marbleton.

BUS

Powder River Transportation serves the main towns of the region from Shoshoni. ~ 107 West 2nd Street; 307-876-2561. **Wind River Transportation Authority** provides service throughout Fremont County (Riverton, Lander, Shoshoni, Rock Springs) as well as on-demand airport shuttles. ~ 2554 Airport Drive, Riverton; 800-439-7118.

CAR RENTALS

Rental agencies at Riverton Regional Airport include **Avis Rent A Car** (800-331-1212) and **Hertz Rent A Car** (800-654-3131). Rentals are also available in Lander from the **Fremont Motor Company.** ~ 555 East Main Street; 307-332-4355.

SIX

Southwestern Wyoming

Ever since the first pioneers traversed this arid region in their covered wagons, southwestern Wyoming has been an area that people have passed through but have rarely paused to explore. Although American Indians lived in the valley of the Green River as many as 8000 years ago, there has been little to entice anyone to stay for long. The Oregon and Mormon trails, the Overland Stage and the Pony Express all made fast work of this corner of Wyoming in the 1840s and 1850s. The Union Pacific cut its transcontinental rail route across these windblown plains in the late 1860s, spawning a coal industry that helped to bring the first sizable rush of settlers. Today, interstate Route 80 more or less follows the Overland Stage and Union Pacific routes as it connects Cheyenne with Salt Lake City. But some cowboys say driving across Wyoming on Route 80 is more than a hassle: "It's a career."

Fewer people live in all of southwestern Wyoming than in greater Cheyenne. These hardy residents will admit that winters here are brutally cold, summers are as dry as dust, and the wind never stops. But the same folks will urge you to stop for a closer look, to discover some of the least-visited historic sites and natural areas in the state.

Nearly 35,000 people, or about half the total population of the three-county region, live in the twin mining cities of Rock Springs and Green River, a 90-minute freeway drive east of the Utah border. East from here, however, there's a lot of desolation. The highway crosses the bleak desert of the Great Divide Basin—once a waterless five-day trip for pioneers—before reestablishing contact with civilization at Rawlins, a 108-mile drive from Rock Springs.

South of Rock Springs and Green River is the spectacular Flaming Gorge National Recreation Area, a mecca for water-sports lovers of all persuasions. West, en route to Salt Lake, is Fort Bridger, a state historic site that once was the second leading outfitting stop on the Overland Trail, and the historic railroad town of Evanston. Northwest is Kemmerer, where entrepreneur J.C. Penney got his start amidst a rugged landscape that features Fossil Butte National Monument and, beyond that, the lovely if isolated Star Valley.

Rock Springs and Green River

Coal, oil, natural gas and trona—the ore from which soda ash is extracted—are the cornerstones to the economic success of southwestern Wyoming's metropolitan center, such as it is. But emptiness surrounds the cities of Rock Springs and Green River. Some of it, including the Great Divide Basin, is as desolate as you're likely to find on this continent. Other areas, like the Flaming Gorge of the Green River, are consumed in desert beauty.

SIGHTS

For travelers approaching southwestern Wyoming from Rawlins and the east, the **Great Divide Basin** is a forbidding introduction. This arid region is unique in that any water that falls here drains to neither the Atlantic nor Pacific oceans, but only into the lowest parts of the basin itself. If even a modest amount of rain fell each year, the basin would fill with water to form an inland sea larger than the Great Salt Lake. But most of what little precipitation does fall from occasional passing clouds evaporates before reaching the ground.

Hot and barren though this trek may be, it was favored by many early travelers because it avoided a steep climb over the Rocky Mountain crest. The rise across this 6600- to 7500-foot plateau is virtually unnoticeable. Except for the occasional railroad siding and the village of **Wamsutter** (240 people), there are no settlements or inhabited ranches for 50 miles north or south of the interstate. For that matter, there are no roads except for a handful of Jeep tracks leading to remote oil and gas wells.

Wildlife biologists, however, are fascinated with the basin's ecosystem, particularly in the **Red Desert** region northwest of Wamsutter. Teeming with life despite its sterile appearance, the desert is a major pronghorn antelope range and home to one of the largest remaining herds of wild horses (about 5000 of them) in the United States. Rabbits and prairie dogs are prey for coyotes, bobcats and occasional mountain lions. Hawks and eagles circle in the air, while the sage grouse scurries along close to the ground. Elk and mule deer are commonly found in the Antelope Hills on the northern edge of the Great Divide Basin and near

HIDDEN ►

the **Killpecker Dune Field** to its west.

This area of shifting dunes, known to locals as "The Sands," features wind-contoured cornices that rise as much as 150 feet above the surrounding landscape. Running intermittently for more than 100 miles from the Seminoe Mountains (north of Rawlins) to just east of the tiny oasis town of Eden (north of Rock Springs), it is especially remarkable in its western half, where strong, funneled winds have sculpted the largest dunes. Seasonal waterholes (where blowing sand traps snowbanks) and grassy meadows between the dunes attract much wildlife. Adventurers can also find

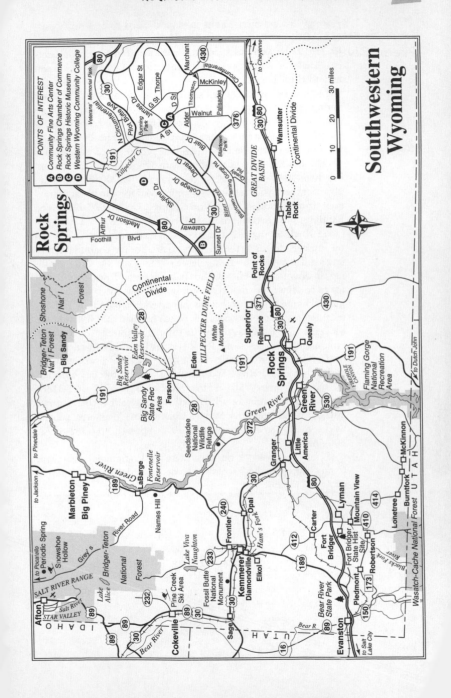

Rock Springs

POINTS OF INTEREST
Ⓐ Community Fine Arts Center
Ⓑ Rock Springs Chamber of Commerce
Ⓒ Rock Springs Historic Museum
Ⓓ Western Wyoming Community College

Southwestern Wyoming

petroglyphs and pictographs in several canyons and rocky out-crops near the dunes, especially at White Mountain, just east of Route 191 between Rock Springs and Eden. Elsewhere, archaeol-ogists have uncovered a pair of prehistoric sites littered with bison and antelope bones.

At **Point of Rocks,** a rail siding about 25 miles east of Rock Springs, you'll find the remains of an old Overland Stage station; rail travelers to South Pass City once made connections at this sandstone house. A little further west, a spur road heads nine miles north to **Superior,** a mining town that produced 23 million tons of coal in the four decades ending with World War II. Population has dwindled from an international colony of 3000 to fewer than 200, but the town's residents still mine coal for a living and draw their drinking water from hillside springs. The town's abandoned buildings now make an impressive movie set.

HIDDEN ▶

In **Rock Springs** itself, coal has at least partly given way to oil and natural gas as the economic base. But the coalmining her-itage still is evident in the opulence of the stone and brick build-ings in downtown's Historic Business District. (Townspeople will try to convince you that the notorious outlaw Butch Cassidy got his nickname here when he was employed as a butcher.) The dis-trict focuses on the old city hall, which fulfilled that function for 88 years after its construction in 1894. The spired Romanesque building now serves as the **Rock Springs Historic Museum,** with displays that represent the city's history and the diverse nation-alities that called Rock Springs home. Closed Sunday through Tuesday in winter. ~ 201 B Street, Rock Springs; 307-362-3138. For a map describing a self-guided walking tour of the historic district, contact the **Rock Springs Chamber of Commerce.** Closed weekends. ~ 1897 Dewar Drive, Rock Springs; 307-362-3771, 800-463-8637.

Elsewhere in Rock Springs, there's a **Community Fine Arts Center,** started by high school students in the 1930s, that features

✔ CHECK THESE OUT—UNIQUE SIGHTS

- Track a herd of 5000 wild horses and explore ancient sites in the 100-mile-long **Killpecker Dune Field** on the Great Divide Basin. *page 172*
- Cruise 91 miles down a reservoir in **Flaming Gorge National Recreation Area,** so named for the vivid colors of its cliffs. *page 175*
- Picture yourself as a pioneer at an 1840s trading post when you join living-history programs at **Fort Bridger State Historic Site.** *page 182*
- Hike to a quarry at **Fossil Butte National Monument,** where more marine fossils have been found than anywhere else in America. *page 187*

more than 450 original works by such notable artists as Norman Rockwell and Grandma Moses. Closed Sunday and alternating Fridays and Saturdays. ~ Rock Springs Library, 400 C Street, Rock Springs; 307-362-6212. And you can see one of the nation's finest dinosaur displays (ten full-size replica skeletons, plus numerous other fossils) at the natural-history museum of the hillside **Western Wyoming Community College.** ~ 2500 College Drive, Rock Springs; 307-382-1600.

Green River, 15 miles west, has a different economic history from other towns of the region. Granted, it, too, once provided fuel for the Union Pacific's coal-powered locomotives. But it got its start as a timber town in anticipation of the railroad's arrival: "Tie hacks," cut on the slopes of the Wind River Range north of Pinedale, were floated downriver and shaped into rail ties at mills here.

Today, Green River has become the "Trona Capital of the World." Five plants process this naturally occurring sodium bicarbonate into soda ash, an industrial chemical used in baking soda, detergents and glass products. Two-thirds of the world's commercial supply of trona comes from the briny bed of ancient Lake Goshuite, which once covered the plain north and west of here.

The **Sweetwater County Museum** has numerous displays, including an impressive exhibit of historical photographs, recalling the history of the Green River area. ~ 80 West Flaming Gorge Way, Green River; 307-872-6411. Here you'll also learn about John Wesley Powell, a one-armed Army major and professor who in 1869 led the first expedition down the Green and Colorado rivers and through the Grand Canyon. A historical marker on **Expedition Island**, a riverine park adjacent to a wetland nature reserve south of downtown, denotes the point from which Powell and his party departed.

The very first section of river that Powell charted is today contained within **Flaming Gorge National Recreation Area**, which extends south 91 miles along the Green River into Utah. Established by Congress in 1968, the beautiful preserve beckons sportsmen and nature lovers to explore serpentine Flaming Gorge Reservoir, created by a hydroelectric dam built in 1964.

Part of its 375 miles of shoreline is composed of cliffs that may rise more than 1500 feet above the water . . . such as at **Firehole Canyon**, whose bright-orange chimneys and pinnacles reflect in the lake's blue water above the confluence of the Black's Fork River with the Green. Throughout the Flaming Gorge, you'll discover similar scenes of living color. Geologists and photographers love the rock formations, sculpted by centuries of wind and water erosion, and the wedding-cake strata, a legacy of millions of years of accumulated sediment from a great freshwater sea that once blanketed this part of North America.

Although most of the reservoir is in Wyoming, the dam and park headquarters are in Utah. Devote a day to explore Flaming Gorge by car, on a 143-mile loop drive that follows several U.S. and state highways around its circumference. Head south on Route 191, which branches off Route 80 five miles west of Rock Springs. Thirteen miles down this road, you'll want to detour onto paved Flaming Gorge Road (County Road 33), which runs ten miles west to Firehole Canyon. Otherwise, unless you choose to bounce through sagebrush-covered hills on gravel roads, you'll cross 40 more miles of desert before entering Utah.

About nine miles beyond the border, just south of the town of Dutch John, you'll find the recreation area headquarters at the **Flaming Gorge Dam Visitor Center**. Exhibits here describe geology, natural history and recreation, as well as the dam's function. Guided tours of the 502-foot hydro dam and generating station are offered daily during the spring and summer, and on weekends in winter. ~ Route 191, Dutch John, Utah; 435-885-3135.

But the best way to explore Flaming Gorge is from the water. You can rent a boat either at the Cedar Springs Marina, near the dam; the Lucerne Valley Marina, near the town of Manila; or the Buckboard Marina, 25 miles south of Green River, back in Wyoming. (Manila is only 36 road miles from Dutch John via Route 44 at Greendale Junction.) En route are numerous intriguing driving loops and scenic diversions, including the Sheep Creek Geological Loop. Get more information from the **Flaming Gorge Ranger District**. ~ Ashley National Forest, P.O. Box 279, Manila, UT 84046; 435-784-3445.

Route 44 becomes Route 530 upon crossing the Wyoming state line as you return north toward Green River. Numerous gravel roads along the shoreline lead to boating access points for anglers, who find fishing in this reservoir to be among the best in the western United States. Each year, it seems, new records are set here, like a 26-pound rainbow trout or a 51-pound mackinaw (lake trout). Other water sports, especially waterskiing, are also popular.

Other Green River–area attractions pale when compared to the Flaming Gorge. Twenty-nine miles west of the city, on Route 30 at the Black's Fork River, is the **Granger Stage Station**. This sandstone structure served both the Overland Stage and the Pony Express around 1860, when such travelers as Mark Twain and Horace Greeley passed through. Beginning 23 miles northwest and stretching another 35 miles up the Green River, nearly to the Fontenelle Dam, is the **Seedskadee National Wildlife Refuge**. This serene, 25,000-acre wetland refuge is a spring and fall staging area for flocks of birds migrating between subarctic and subtropical areas. More than 170 avian species have been sighted here, and many types of ducks make it a breeding ground. Its name comes from a Crow Indian word meaning "prairie hen." ~ Route 372, Green River; 307-875-2187.

The nicest of a number of inexpensively priced motels is the **Springs Motel**, a lovingly maintained, 23-room property with all standard amenities. ~ 1525 9th Street, Rock Springs; 307-362-6683. BUDGET.

Top of the line is **The Inn at Rock Springs**, an ultramodern 149-unit hotel with a sports pub, room service and the best exercise facilities in town, including an indoor swimming pool and whirlpool spa. Adjoining the lobby, a veritable museum of Wild West decor, are a popular restaurant and lounge. Guest rooms are recently remodeled, spacious and stylish; most have balconies or patios. Children under 17 stay free with parents. ~ 2518 Foothill Boulevard, Rock Springs; 307-362-9600, 800-442-9692, fax 307-362-8846. MODERATE.

In a similar price range is the 114-room **Holiday Inn**, which has an indoor heated swimming pool and a jacuzzi open 24 hours. The four-story hotel has its own restaurant and lounge, as well as a guest laundry. Units with kitchens are available. ~ 1675 Sunset Drive, Rock Springs; 307-382-9200, fax 307-362-1064. MODERATE.

A good choice among the many low-priced motels is the **Western Motel**, a slightly larger, two-story place with refrigerators in most of its 32 rooms. ~ 890 West Flaming Gorge Way, Green River; 307-875-2840, fax 307-875-2843. BUDGET.

The **Little America Hotel** is the showplace motor inn of the Great Divide Basin and was one of the world's first motels. All alone in one of the West's most godforsaken locations, 20 miles west of Green River, Little America was built in 1932 by a local

---

✔ CHECK THESE OUT—UNIQUE LODGING

- *Budget:* Relax in a reconditioned, 1940s log cabin at the **Corral Motel**, a charming bargain in the Star Valley. *page 191*
- *Budget to moderate:* Drink in views of Flaming Gorge Reservoir from your 1930s log-cabin perch at **Red Canyon Lodge**. *page 178*
- *Moderate:* Ogle the Eastlake-style antiques that adorn the **Pine Gables Bed & Breakfast**, in a historic 1883 mansion in Evanston. *page 183*
- *Moderate to deluxe:* Take an extra lap of the pool to honor the rancher who in 1932 built the **Little America Hotel** as a desert way station. *page 177*

Budget: under $50   Moderate: $50–$90   Deluxe: $90–$130   Ultra-deluxe: over $130

rancher who envisioned it as a way station for travelers stranded by blizzards. Hotelier Earl Holding, who bought the motor inn in the 1960s, upscaled the facilities and made this the flagship of a luxury lodging chain. On hot desert days you can cool off in the outdoor swimming pool, surrounded by neat lawns and evergreen trees. The 140 guest rooms are spacious and well lit, with earth-tone decor. ~ Route 80 Exit 68, Little America; 307-875-2400, 800-634-2401; fax 307-872-2666; www.lamerica.com/wyoming.html. MODERATE TO DELUXE.

If you're planning an overnight on Flaming Gorge Reservoir, the cream of the crop is the **Red Canyon Lodge**. Rustic two-room log cabins built in the 1930s sit on the canyon rim overlooking the deep-blue lake, while the main lodge offers several more modern luxury cabins with covered porches and kitchenettes. Some of the older cabins share a central bathhouse, but the newer units all have private baths. There's a good steak-and-trout restaurant here as well. ~ Route 44, Flaming Gorge National Recreation Area, Utah; 435-889-3759, fax 435-889-5106; www.redcanyonlodge.com. BUDGET TO MODERATE.

DINING

The scent of hickory-smoked ribs lures diners to **Pam's Bar-B-Cue**. The fare at this no-frills establishment also includes barbecued chicken and beef brisket. Closed Sunday. ~ 2506 Foothill Boulevard, Rock Springs; 307-362-1043. BUDGET.

Among the half-dozen Chinese restaurants in the area—all of which also serve American dishes—the **Sands Café**, specializing in Cantonese, Szechuan and Mandarin dishes, offers the widest selection and most exotic decor. ~ 1549 9th Street, Rock Springs; 307-362-5633. MODERATE.

Mexican food is also easy to find. If you like it spicy, you'll be pleased at the **Santa Fe Trail**, located just off the interstate in the American Family Inn. This cafe features tacos, burritos, some American Indian specialties, and juicy steaks. ~ 1635 Elk Street, Rock Springs; 307-362-5427. BUDGET.

Situated in a former garage, **Bitter Creek Brewing** presents a menu of typical pub grub: burgers, pizzas and fried calamari along with a few steak and pasta entrées. Not so typical is the list

DIAMONDS AREN'T FOREVER

In 1876, two wily miners scammed gem seekers of $500,000 at Table Rock, east of Rock Springs. Potential buyers were blindfolded and taken to a mesa salted with diamonds and other rocks from Holland. Among those bilked: Horace Greeley, Louis Tiffany and the Rothschilds.

of made-on-the-premises beers such as Sweetwater Wheat, Coal Porter and a stout simply named Bob. A skylight and high ceilings create an airy atmosphere that draws a lively crowd. ~ 604 Broadway, Rock Springs; 307-362-4782. MODERATE TO DELUXE.

At **Rocky Mountain Noodle**, classics like shrimp scampi, veal parmesan and fettuccine alfredo share the menu with less traditional preparations such as Chicken Cordon Bleu (penne with chicken in a dijon mustard cream sauce) and Italian Cowboy Pasta (breaded steak served with gnocchi). Photographs of Italy on the walls and two fireplaces make this a comfortable place to dine. Closed Sunday. ~ 1679 Sunset Drive, Rock Springs; 307-382-7076. MODERATE.

Fine dining is the order of business at **The Greens of White Mountain**. Cajun-seasoned duck, blackened catfish and gumbo highlight the offerings. In the summer, you can opt for a table out on the patio. Closed Monday and Tuesday. Dinner only in winter. ~ 1501 Club House Drive, Rock Springs; 307-362-3950. DELUXE TO ULTRA-DELUXE.

For a fancy night out, locals choose from a handful of possibilities. One of the best, located at the Flaming Gorge exit from Route 80 west of Rock Springs, is **Ted's Supper Club**. It specializes in steak (some say the best in the state) and shellfish in a relatively elegant atmosphere: candlelight, white tablecloths and heavy chairs. ~ 9 Purple Sage Road, Rock Springs; 307-362-7323. MODERATE TO DELUXE.

Another favorite in the same neck of the woods is **The Log Inn**, which recreates a rustic Old West ambience. Steaks and seafood make up the majority of the menu; specialties include barbecued ribs and deep-fried lobster. ~ 12 Purple Sage Road, Rock Springs; 307-362-7166. MODERATE TO DELUXE.

On the south side of Green River off Uinta Drive is **Don Pedro's Mexican Restaurant**. Authentic south-of-the-border cuisine includes *chalupas*, chimichangas and chicken *mole*. ~ 520 Wilkes Drive, Green River; 307-875-7324. MODERATE.

SHOPPING

Southwestern Wyoming's largest modern shopping center is the **White Mountain Mall**. Here you can get anything and everything you may have forgotten before leaving home. ~ 2441 Foothill Boulevard, Rock Springs; 307-382-9680.

In the downtown historic districts of both Rock Springs (South Main and North Front streets) and Green River (Flaming Gorge Way), you'll find a diverse assortment of shops selling everything from antiques and Western art to gifts and clothing. One such place worth tarrying awhile is the **Green River Merc**, one of the oldest stores in the state. Closed Sunday. ~ 79 North 1st Street East, Green River; 307-875-2126.

NIGHTLIFE   Both Rock Springs and Green River have big, tough bar scenes that cater to well-paid oil riggers and mineworkers who don't have many other places to spend their earnings. Prostitution, drugs and gambling are wide-open secrets out here.

The lounges of better hotels and restaurants in Rock Springs offer some upbeat entertainment. **Killpeppers**, for instance, has a Top-40 dancefloor. Live bands occasionally play. Cover for live bands. ~ 1030 Dewar Drive, Rock Springs; 307-382-8012. **Mr. C's**, in the Holiday Inn, sometimes presents live lounge acts. ~ 1675 Sunset Drive, Rock Springs; 307-382-9200. And the **Outlaw Inn**, the town's Best Western entry, has a popular saloon on the property. ~ 1630 Elk Street, Rock Springs; 307-362-6623.

Check out the saloons along Railroad Avenue in Green River for raunchy nightlife. **The Brewery** is one such place with its pool tables and lonesome cowboys. ~ 50 West Railroad Avenue, Green River; 307-875-5255. **Ponderosa Bar & Lounge** has the occasional drunken brawl. ~ 41 East Railroad Avenue, Green River; 307-875-4614. The **Embassy Bar** has pool tables, sad country songs playing on the jukebox, and seating in dark corners. ~ 77 East Railroad Avenue, Green River; 307-875-5552.

PARKS   **FLAMING GORGE NATIONAL RECREATION AREA** 🚶 🚴 🐎
🏕 🏊 🎣 🛶 🚤 ⛴ ⛵ Most recreational facilities, and the most spectacular scenery, of 91-mile-long Flaming Gorge Reservoir lie on the Utah side of the state line. Most of the shoreline on the Wyoming side is flat, brown, rocky and less than impressive, with the exception of Firehole Canyon; here, a ten-mile paved road winds through colorful desert geology on its way to the lakeshore. There are boat ramps at Upper Marsh Creek on the east shore and Squaw Hollow on the west shore. The only full-service marina (with boat rentals) on the Wyoming side of the state line is Buckboard Marina on the west shore. Mountain biking is a popular fall and spring sport in the backcountry. Swimming is permitted at Firehole Canyon, and fishing is superb year-round for mackinaw, rainbow and brown trout, smallmouth bass and kokanee salmon. (You'll need a license from either Wyoming or Utah, plus a special use stamp, to allow you to fish in both states.) Facilities include picnic areas and restrooms; groceries at Buckboard Marina. Day-use fee, $2. ~ To reach Firehole Canyon, turn west on a paved road 13 miles south of Rock Springs off Route 191. To reach Buckboard Crossing, drive 25 miles south of Green River on Route 530. From either highway, dozens of primitive dirt roads lead to virtually every cove along the shoreline.

▲ Of the 19 campgrounds in this national recreation area, only two are in Wyoming: 40 RV/tent sites at Firehole Canyon (closed October through April) and 68 RV/tent sites at Buckboard

Crossing (closed mid-September to mid-May). None have hookups; $5 to $18 per night; 14-day maximum stay.

SEEDSKADEE NATIONAL WILDLIFE REFUGE 🚶 🚲 🐎 🛶
🛶 This 25,000-acre expanse along the Green River north of Route 25 is one of the best birdwatching areas in Wyoming. More than 170 species of birds, including sandhill cranes, Canada geese and many species of ducks, rest here on their fall migration and breed here in the spring. The river attracts an astonishing variety of wildlife, from golden eagles to deer, antelope and even moose, making it a popular area for rafting and canoeing. Fishing is good for rainbow trout. Restrooms are available. ~ Take Route 372 north from Green River for 27 miles and turn northeast on the marked road to the refuge headquarters; 305-875-2187.

Wyoming's southwesternmost corner has traditionally been a place that people pass through, rather than spend time in. The Oregon and Mormon trails, the Overland Stage and Pony Express routes may have paused at Fort Bridger, but they kept going. It wasn't until the Union Pacific extended its route westward at the end of the 1860s that solid communities began to form.

Evanston and Fort Bridger

SIGHTS

Evanston was founded with the iron horse in 1868; within three years, the railroad had established its roundhouse and machine shops here, giving the settlement permanence. Many of the town's brick turn-of-the-century buildings, among them a Gothic-style Union Pacific station and a handsome Carnegie Library, have been restored as part of the town's **Depot Square Park** project at 10th and Front streets. The library today houses the local chamber of commerce and the **Uinta County Historical Museum**, where early ranching and mining paraphernalia are on display. The museum also has a fascinating collection of Chinese artifacts, including a dragon that once was paraded through the streets of Evanston on the lunar new year. Open weekdays and by appointment. ~ 36 10th Street, Evanston; 307-783-0370.

Nearby is a reconstructed joss house—a traditional Chinese place of worship—which replaced a very elaborate structure that burned down in the 1920s. In its early years, Evanston was home to a large number of Chinese rail workers and coal miners, most of whom lived in a shantytown beside the tracks. Modern Evanston's 11,000 citizens still celebrate the Chinese New Year each February.

The Bear River, which flows northward through Evanston (it later makes a horseshoe turn in Idaho and runs south into the Great Salt Lake), provides a venue for Evanston's primary recreational attractions. A riverfront greenbelt, known as the **B.E.A.R.**

Parkway, runs through a section of town, and **Bear River State Park**, the newest in the Wyoming system, is just east of town off Route 80. Many Wyomingites, however, know Evanston principally for its horseracing track. At **Wyoming Downs**, eight miles north, thoroughbred and quarterhorse races are held on weekends from Memorial Day to Labor Day; parimutuel off-track betting is offered year-round. ~ Route 89, Evanston.

On Labor Day weekend, a three-day mountain men's rendezvous takes place at Fort Bridger State Historic Site.

Before Evanston was founded, another settlement called Bear River City, ten miles south, was the rail workers' staging point. This rough-and-ready community gained notoriety on November 21, 1868, when a disagreement between rail laborers and a gang of confidence racketeers erupted into a riot of classic Western-movie proportions. By the time soldiers from Fort Bridger arrived to put down the disorder, the railroad men had established the upper hand.

There's not much left today of Bear River City, which was essentially a tent town. But east from here, off Route 150, you can retrace the path of the original transcontinental railroad bed along **HIDDEN ►** **Piedmont Road** (County Road 173). Passing Sulphur Creek Reservoir, this 22-mile graded road skirts a severe rock cut—the product of hand labor—that separates the Bear and Green river drainages. Keep an eye on the road surface for original hand-hewn railroad ties, as well as for ruts left by the Mormon Trail and Pony Express Route, which preceded the rail line's construction. Near the all-but-a-ghost-town of Piedmont, you'll pass several beehive-shaped charcoal kilns, built in 1869 to supply fuel for Mormon iron-ore smelters in the Salt Lake Valley. Piedmont Road joins Route 80 at the Leroy Road interchange, nine miles west of Fort Bridger.

Fort Bridger State Historic Site, located 32 miles east of Evanston and 55 miles west of Green River, is this region's most important attraction. Famed mountain man Jim Bridger and his partner, Louis Vasquez, built the original fort on the Black's Fork of the Green River in 1842 and opened it as a fur-trading post the following year. But as the Shoshone fur trade fell off, the post grew in importance as a supply point for westward-bound pioneers. Of forts along the Overland Trail, only Fort Laramie was a busier outfitting center.

Jim Bridger supported the Mormons who paused at his post on their way west; legend has it that he originally pointed Brigham Young to the Salt Lake Valley in 1847. But in 1853, the Mormons built their own post, Fort Supply, 12 miles southwest of Fort Bridger on Black's Fork, and began aggressively competing for business. Before long, a Mormon force drove Bridger and Vasquez from their bastion and took over the rival fort. The occupation didn't last long, however: In 1857, in what has become known as the Mormon War, U.S. President James Buchanan sent in troops to face down Young, who had refused to give federal political and social institutions priority over Mormon beliefs, such as polygamy. As the army approached the Mormons set forts Bridger and Supply on fire and fled.

Fort Supply was devastated, but Fort Bridger was salvageable. The army leased the site from Bridger and Vasquez and rebuilt it as a military base. It subsequently served as an Overland Stage and Pony Express station in the 1860s, a supply center for rail workers and South Pass gold seekers, and a deterrent to marauding Indians who may have wanted to attack either group. The army pulled out in 1890, and Fort Bridger became a private home until the State of Wyoming purchased the site in the late 1920s.

It wasn't until 1964 that a serious restoration was undertaken. Today, more than a dozen of the old fort buildings are scattered across parklike grounds. A museum (open weekends only in April and October; open daily May through September) displays artifacts from the fort's various occupants and visitors, and Bridger's trading post has been rebuilt on its original foundation. Through the summer, docents present interpretive living-history demonstrations. Picnic tables are set beneath shade trees around the grounds, located about a mile south of the highway on the banks of Groshon Creek. Admission. ~ Business Loop 80, Fort Bridger; 307-782-3842.

Fort Bridger is the most northwesterly of several small towns in the Bridger Valley, an agricultural area along the Black's Fork for more than a century. The largest community in the area is **Lyman**, with about 2000 people. Southeast about 25 miles, near the ranching settlement of **Lonetree** on the Henry's Fork, a roadside plaque marks the site of the first of 16 fur-trade rendezvous, held in this area in 1825.

The best bet for a quality, low-cost motel in Evanston is the **Prairie Inn**. This one-story establishment offers a complimentary continental breakfast to guests in its 31 spacious rooms, which offer all standard amenities. ~ 264 Bear River Drive, Evanston; 307-789-2920. BUDGET.

LODGING

A dozen or so motel-style accommodations cluster around the interstate exits in Evanston. A contrast is the **Pine Gables Bed & Breakfast**, framed by tall pine trees in a quiet residential area. The six nonsmoking guest rooms, all with private baths, are in a historic 1883 mansion furnished with Eastlake-style antiques. Rooms have TVs and phones. ~ 1049 Center Street, Evanston; 307-789-2069, 800-789-2069; www.cruising-america.com/pine gables. MODERATE.

The best of those motel properties is the **Dunmar Inn**, Evanston's entry in the Best Western group. Its 166 luxurious rooms are spread across ten acres of beautifully landscaped grounds in a single story. Motel facilities include a large swimming pool and weight/exercise room, and the restaurant and lounge are rated among Evanston's best. There's also a gift shop here. Kitchen units are available. Children under 12 stay free with parents. ~ 1601 Harrison Drive, Evanston; 307-789-3770, 800-654-6509, fax 307-789-3758. MODERATE.

The only lodging in the Fort Bridger area is the pleasant if ordinary **Wagon Wheel Motel**. The 36 guest rooms have standard amenities, from showers to bolted-down televisions. A dining room and lounge are located at the motel. ~ 270 North Main Street, Fort Bridger; 307-782-6361, 888-228-5475, fax 307-782-3545. BUDGET.

DINING   Start your morning with breakfast and an espresso at the **Main Street Deli**. This downtown institution also serves good home-made soups, sandwiches and lunch specials at midday. Closed weekends. ~ 1025 Main Street, Evanston; 307-789-1599. BUDGET.

It's nothing fancy, but if you crave Chinese, visit **Dragon Wall Restaurant**. Sweet-and-sour pork, Hunan beef, won ton soup and potstickers are some of the favorites here. There is a buffet at both lunch and dinner. ~ 140 Front Street, Evanston; 307-789-7788. BUDGET TO MODERATE.

There are lots of families enjoying the all-American food at the aptly named **Lotty's Family Restaurant**. À la carte entrées include roast beef, breaded veal, steak and shrimp scampi. Or you can partake in the all-you-can-eat buffet offered at lunch and dinner. ~ 1925 Harrison Drive, Evanston; 307-789-9660. BUDGET TO MODERATE.

The area's best dining experience is in its best hotel. So popular is the **Legal Tender**, in the Dunmar Inn, that Utahns often

---

✔ CHECK THESE OUT—UNIQUE DINING

- *Budget:* Wear your bib when you dive into the chicken and ribs flamed over an open-pit fire at **Pam's Bar-B-Cue** in Rock Springs. *page 178*
- *Budget to moderate:* Learn more about the Star Valley—straight from the locals—as you fill up on homestyle cooking at the **Elkhorn Family Restaurant**. *page 191*
- *Moderate to deluxe:* Keep an eye out for anglers bringing in their catch when you dine at the **Lake Viva Naughton Marina** north of Kemmerer. *page 189*
- *Moderate to deluxe:* Cut into what some claim is Wyoming's best steak dinner at **Ted's Supper Club**, west of Rock Springs. *page 179*

Budget: under $7   Moderate: $7–$12   Deluxe: $12–$20   Ultra-deluxe: over $20

make the drive across the border just to eat here. The fare is Continental, and steaks are consistently good. There's a big salad bar, and children are welcomed. ~ 1601 Harrison Drive, Evanston; 307-789-3770. MODERATE TO DELUXE.

At **Bridger Trading Post**, look at American Indian beadwork, hand-made brass lamps, antelope-horn vials and other old-fashioned treasures that you may not see for sale anywhere else. While you browse, modern-day mountain men can tell you about black-powder shooting and similar events held at recreated rendezvous around the state each summer. Closed November through March. ~ Fort Bridger State Historic Site, Fort Bridger; 307-782-3842.

SHOPPING

The downstairs lounge at the **Legal Tender** in the Dunmar Inn has music most nights. The Legal Tender covers its bases by offering disco dancing for a different crowd in its upstairs lounge. ~ 1601 Harrison Drive, Evanston; 307-789-3770.

NIGHTLIFE

BEAR RIVER STATE PARK 🏃 🚲 🏇 🚣 Undoubtedly the best rest area along Route 80, this park has trails along a marshy stretch of the Bear River, which it shares with protected herds of elk and bison. There are also opportunities for fishing and bird-watching. A large state tourist information center is located here; other facilities include a sheltered picnic area and restrooms. ~ Exit 6 Route 80, on the east edge of Evanston; 307-789-6547.

PARKS

WASATCH-CACHE NATIONAL FOREST 🏃 🚲 🏇 🚣 ⛵ 🎣 ⛵ ⛵ 🚤 🚣 Only about 70 square miles of this 1.3-million-acre national forest extends into Uinta County from Utah. Most of the roads leading south from Evanston and the Bridger Valley end at campgrounds and trailheads from which backcountry lovers can climb into the High Uinta Wilderness. The only forest site of special note in Wyoming is Meeks Cabin Reservoir, near the headwaters of Black's Fork of the Green River. Day-use fee, $3. ~ From Evanston, take Route 150 south up the Bear River 27 miles (four miles into Utah) to enter the national forest. For Meeks Cabin Reservoir, take County Road 271 south up Black's Fork, off Route 410 west of Robertson; 307-789-3194.

▲ In the northeastern section of the national forest, administered from Wyoming, are 11 campgrounds with 246 RV/tent sites and four for tents only (at Little Lyman Lake); closed September through May; $8 to $12 per night; 14-day maximum stay.

Like many other towns in Wyoming's Green and Bear river valleys, Kemmerer grew around coal. But the area has become better known for other things. In the wake of a turn-of-the-century mining boom, for instance, a young James

▼▼▼▼▼▼▼▼▼▼▼▼▼▼▼▼▼▼
Kemmerer and Fossil Butte

Cash Penney opened a retail outlet (the Golden Rule store) that would grow to become the nationwide JCPenney chain. At about the same time, on a big white ridge just west of Kemmerer, geologists were uncovering a remarkable collection of prehistoric marine fossils that led to the creation of Fossil Butte National Monument. Today, manmade lakes and traces of pioneer trails draw everyone from fishermen to amateur historians.

SIGHTS

Located 50 miles north of Evanston and 71 miles west of Green River, **Kemmerer** and its adjoining community of Diamondville are quiet towns amid the badlands of Ham's Fork of the Green River. Most of the 4500 residents still depend upon coal for their livelihoods: A huge open-pit coal mine—once the world's largest, and still Wyoming's longest continuously operating mine—is just six miles south of Kemmerer, off Route 189 at Elkol. Two-thirds of the fossil fuel extracted there is burned at the adjacent Naughton Power Plant to produce 710 megawatts of electricity for Utah Power & Light.

The first mine here opened in 1894, and the town was incorporated in 1896. Six years later, James Penney opened the Golden Rule dry-goods store. So quickly did he establish a reputation for quality and honesty that he expanded his young empire to 34 stores within ten years; in 1913, the chain's name was changed to J.C. Penney. Penney nearly recouped his initial $500 investment on the first day the Golden Rule was open: His sales on April 14, 1902, came to $466.59. In its first year, the store grossed $29,000. That wood-frame structure has long since burned down, but the current **JCPenney Mother Store**, built in 1928, remains a thriving business. Closed Sunday. ~ 722 J.C. Penney Drive, Kemmerer; 307-877-3164.

True merchandising-trivia addicts can also visit the **J.C. Penney Homestead**, a six-room cottage where Penney and his family lived between 1903 and 1909. Moved from its original location and provided with period furnishings and family keepsakes, it is open for guided tours daily in summer, by appointment in winter. ~ 107 J.C. Penney Drive, Kemmerer; 307-877-4501.

The Penney home is across the street from **Herschler Triangle Park**, where the local chamber of commerce and visitor center shares its headquarters with a gift shop and small museum of local history. (Locals joke that Kemmerer is too small for a town square, so it has a town triangle instead.) Museum closed Sunday in summer, and Saturday in winter. ~ 800 Pine Avenue, Kemmerer; 307-877-9761.

Visitors more serious about learning the whys and wherefores of this part of Wyoming head for the **Fossil Country Frontier Museum**, four blocks north. Here, in a former church, you'll find exhibits on local mining and archaeology, as well as art and pioneer lore. A display of various types of barbed wire from the late

19th century, and a moonshine still and vat from the Prohibition era, when Kemmerer was a national center for bootlegging, are especially interesting. Closed Sunday. ~ 400 Pine Avenue, Kemmerer; 307-877-6551.

The foremost area attraction is **Fossil Butte National Monument.** Located 14 miles west of Kemmerer on Route 30, the huge, flat-topped butte is a sedimentary remnant of a large lake, 50 miles long and 20 miles wide, that covered this area 50 million years ago. Today the butte harbors billions of aquatic fossils in its layers of limestone, mudstone and volcanic ash: turtles, stingrays, five-foot garfish, bowfins, paddlefish, enormous schools of herring and other lake inhabitants. Paleontologists also have found leaves and seeds from palms, cypresses and other trees that once took root in this land; and mammals such as North America's oldest bat, a 13-foot crocodile, catlike horses and prehistoric tapirs.

Some of the thousands of fossils discovered here are on display at the visitors center, which also offers films and an artist's rendering of how the area around ancient Fossil Lake may have appeared. In addition, two loop trails, 1.5 and 2.5 miles long, go to an abandoned fossil quarry (active from the 1890s to the 1970s) and an area of geological interest where the strata of the Wasatch and Green River formations can be clearly seen. The marine fossils are found in the steep, buff-to-white Green River Formation, here about 300 feet thick; the skeletal remains of land animals are mainly in the horizontal, brightly colored (red, purple, yellow and gray) Wasatch Formation, which underlies the other.

The national monument, which covers about 13 square miles, was established in 1972 and is administered by the National Park Service. Admission. ~ P.O. Box 592, Kemmerer, WY 83101; 307-877-4455; www.nps.gov/fobu.

While the collection of fossils is forbidden within the national monument itself, fossickers have options in the immediate vicin-

◆◆

THE BEAUTY AND THE BEEF

The adage that "crime doesn't pay" certainly was true in the case of Anne Richey, the only woman ever convicted of cattle rustling in Wyoming. Richey was said to have been a beautiful and cultured woman who was wealthy enough not to require the additional income rustling might bring. She had a ranch near Fossil Station, west of Kemmerer. Accused of rustling in 1919, Richey was shot by a masked rider while en route to her trial in Kemmerer. After she recovered, she stood trial and was convicted, but was freed on bond to allow her to wind up her ranch business before going to prison. But someone poisoned her while she was at the ranch, and she died. Her murderer was never discovered.

ity. Very near Fossil Butte, for instance, are the privately owned **Ulrich's Fossil Quarries** where, for $55, you can hunt for fossils on a guided tour and keep all you find. Advance reservations are required. ~ Route 30 West, Fossil Station; 307-877-6466. Ask at the chamber of commerce about other fossil quarries, or visit **Tynsky's Fossil Fish Center**, next door to the JCPenney Mother Store. They carry rocks, fossils, books and jewelry. ~ 716 J.C. Penney Drive, Kemmerer; 307-877-6885.

Gravesites along the Oregon Trail in the Kemmerer vicinity are reminders that many migrants confronted their own fossilization when they undertook the dangerous westward journey. One such site is the **Nancy's Hill Grave**, overlooking Ham's Fork near Viva Naughton Reservoir, north of Kemmerer off Route 233. This pioneer woman was buried along the Sublette Cutoff, which bypassed Fort Bridger between South Pass and Fort Hall, Idaho, and trimmed time to the Oregon Country by several days.

Another memorial to those hardy travelers is **Names Hill**, called by some "the calendar of the West." Hundreds of passersby, among them Jim Bridger, carved their names or initials into this soft sandstone bluff. It's located on the west side of Route 189 five miles south of LaBarge, near the head of Fontenelle Reservoir. A few miles further south is the site of the **Old Mormon Ferry**, constructed by the Brigham Young–led Mormons in 1847 to help Utah-bound emigrants get across the Green River.

Sublette's Cutoff crossed Ham's Fork, site of the 1834 fur-trade rendezvous, just north of present-day Kemmerer, passing Fossil Butte and rejoining the main Oregon Trail near modern **Cokeville**. This small town was built in 1874 when the Oregon Short Line Railroad was extended to link Montpelier, Idaho, with Green River, Wyoming. Today it is a trade center for the Bear River Valley. Despite its name, it was never a coal town. The railroad mistakenly switched its name with that of another, much smaller community.

LODGING The **Energy Inn**, located where Routes 30 and 189 join south of Diamondville, is the area's best accommodation. The two-story motel has 42 modest rooms with cable TV and king-size beds; 11 rooms have kitchens with refrigerators. ~ 360 Route 30 North, Diamondville; phone/fax 307-877-6901. BUDGET.

A "ma-and-pa" alternative is the Fossil Butte Motel, with 13 well-kept units on the low-key "strip" between Diamondville and Kemmerer. All have standard lodging amenities. ~ 1424 Central Avenue, Kemmerer; 307-877-3996. BUDGET.

DINING Luigi's is the district's best restaurant, with an excellent menu of steaks, seafood and Italian cuisine in historic downtown Diamondville. Try the rack of lamb or risotto. Closed Sunday through Tues-

day. ~ 807 Susie Avenue, Diamondville; 307-877-6221. MODER-
ATE TO DELUXE.

Kemmerer's **Busy B Cafe**, just a block south of the Triangle,
draws a steady clientele for its hearty breakfasts and homemade
soups. They also have daily dinner specials. ~ 919 Pine Avenue,
Kemmerer; 307-877-6820. BUDGET.

Fifteen miles north of Kemmerer, the restaurant at **Lake Viva**   ◄ *HIDDEN*
Naughton Marina is a great getaway for breakfast, hamburger
lunches, and steak or seafood dinners. It's part of a lake resort
with an adjoining campground, popular among local fishermen.
Closed weekdays in winter. ~ Route 233, Frontier; 307-877-9669.
MODERATE TO DELUXE.

When in Kemmerer, of course, you mustn't miss a visit to the   **SHOPPING**
JCPenney Mother Store, even if its stock doesn't vary a great deal
from other Penney's stores around North America. Closed Sunday.
~ 722 J.C. Penney Drive, Kemmerer; 307-877-3164. A better place
to seek out regional souvenirs is the **Fossil Country Frontier Museum**, whose gift shop includes a good selection of work from
local artists and craftspeople. ~ 400 Pine Avenue, Kemmerer; 307-
877-6551.

You can find locally quarried and prepared fossils at several
galleries in the area. **Ulrich's Fossil Gallery**, which opened in 1947,
is the most widely acclaimed. ~ Route 30 West, Fossil Station;
307-877-6466. **Tynsky's Fossil Fish Center** is in downtown Kemmerer. ~ 716 J.C. Penney Drive, Kemmerer; 307-877-6885.

FOSSIL BUTTE NATIONAL MONUMENT 🏃 🚴 🎣 Fossil Butte   **PARKS**
is a broad, flat-topped ridge that rises to an elevation of 8084
feet, some 1500 feet above the surrounding Twin Creek Valley.
Ruggedly impressive, it has been identified by scientists as the single most important site in North America for studying the evolution of fresh-water fishes. As the remnant core of a lake that
covered this area 50 million years ago, Fossil Butte has yielded
billions of aquatic fossils, as well as those of mammals and plants
of the time. Many are displayed at the visitors center. Guided
hikes are offered in summer. The park has several hiking trails,
a picnic area and restrooms. There are no campgrounds. Groceries
and restaurants are in Kemmerer and Diamondville. ~ From Kemmerer, take Route 30 west 14 miles; 307-877-4455.

▼▼▼▼▼▼▼▼▼▼

This lush stovepipe of west central Wyoming, framed
on west and east by the Idaho border and high moun-   **The Star Valley**
tains, on the north by the Snake River and on the south
by coal-rich badlands, prides itself on its nickname: the "Little
Switzerland of America."

Colonized in the 1870s by Mormons from Utah who gave the area its reputation for dairy farming, the Star Valley slopes gently upward from the Salt River (a northward-flowing Snake tributary) to Idaho's Caribou Mountains, on its west, and the rugged, 11,000-foot heights of the Salt River and Wyoming ranges, on its east. Neat-as-a-pin family farms raise dairy cattle that have made the Star Valley Wyoming's leader in milk production. The area's cheese is widely known.

SIGHTS

Afton, with an intensely Mormon population of about 1400, is the largest community in the valley. The principal attraction is an arch of more than 3000 elk antlers—claimed to be the world's largest such arch—that spans Washington Street, the town's main street. The **Daughters of the Utah Pioneers Museum** recounts the valley's Mormon history. Open weekday afternoons from mid-June to mid-August, and by appointment. ~ 46 East 5th Street, Afton; 307-886-3004. Here also is the **CallAir Museum**, a tribute to the Star Valley's aviation industry. Most visitors are surprised to learn that some of the world's finest aerobatic aircraft are manufactured in this valley by Aviat Aircraft; keep an eye on the sky and you may be lucky to see a test flight in progress. Closed in winter. ~ Afton Airport, Route 89, Afton; 307-886-9881.

HIDDEN ►

Five miles east of Afton in Bridger-Teton National Forest is the unique **Periodic Spring**, a natural cold-water geyser. Also known as Intermittent Spring, this is the largest of only three known fluctuating springs in the world. American Indians once traveled here from far away to bathe in "the spring that breathes," as they called it. From mid-August to mid-May, the spring gushes for 18 minutes from a crack in a perpendicular cliff, cascading a half-mile over moss-covered rocks down to Swift Creek. Then, as reliably as Old Faithful, it turns off entirely for a similar period of time. During the summer when snowmelt is at its peak, the flow fluctuates but does not entirely stop. To get there, head east on 2nd Avenue from downtown Afton, continuing into the national forest on gravel Swift Creek Canyon Road (Forest Road 10211). It's a three-quarter-mile hike from the end of the road.

Scientists theorize that the intermittent flow of Periodic Spring is caused by a natural siphon from an underground lake.

The village of Thayne, 15 miles north of Afton, is the location of the **Star Valley Cheese Factory**. Most of this excellent cheese is distributed to markets in several western states, but you can get free samples of mozzarella, provolone and ricotta when you join one of the public tours. ~ Route 89, Thayne; 307-883-2446.

Alpine, located at the north end of the valley where the Salt and Grey's rivers empty into the Snake, is a road junction notable as a recreational gateway to adjacent Palisades Reservoir. While nearly all of this lake is across the border in Idaho, it is an attractive destination for anglers coming from Jackson, just 35 miles northeast of here.

One of Wyoming's most charming lodgings is the **Corral Motel,**   **LODGING** a group of 15 small log cabins built in the 1940s but kept in superb condition. Four of the cabins have two bedrooms, and two have kitchens (but no utensils). On the groomed grounds are picnic tables with grills and a swing set. Closed November through mid-April. ~ 161 Washington Street, Afton; 307-886-5424, fax 307-886-5464. BUDGET.

A more traditional motel, the **Mountain Inn,** is a mile and a half south of Afton on the town's nine-hole golf course. The 20 rooms are spacious and comfortable; motel facilities include a heated swimming pool, whirlpool, sauna and playground. A restaurant is nearby. ~ Route 89 South, Afton; 307-886-3156, 800-682-5356. MODERATE.

At the top end of the Star Valley is the **Alpen Haus,** a three-story motor inn built in Swiss chalet style. Many of the 45 large rooms have balconies, and some have minibars or refrigerators. Aside from an excellent restaurant and lounge, the inn has a coin laundry, whirlpool, playground and gift shop; there are also trails for summer horseback riding (stables on site) and winter cross-country skiing. ~ Routes 89 and 26, Alpine; 307-654-7545, 800-343-6755, fax 307-654-7546; www.alpenhaus.com. MODERATE TO DELUXE.

Good, all-American homestyle cooking for breakfast, lunch and   **DINING** dinner is the specialty of the **Elkhorn Family Restaurant.** A few Mexican dishes are also served in this cozy local café. Closed Sunday. ~ 465 Washington Street, Afton; 307-886-3080. BUDGET TO MODERATE.

Star Valley residents love **Dad's Bar & Steakhouse,** even   ◄ HIDDEN though it's open only Friday and Saturday. The menu is heavy on steaks and prime rib, with halibut and chicken, too. ~ Main Street, Thayne; 307-883-2300. MODERATE.

Up on the Snake River, **Bette's Coffee Shop** is known for its hearty breakfasts and burgers. Bette's is open for breakfast, lunch and dinner. ~ 117510 Route 89, Alpine; 307-654-7536. BUDGET.

The best souvenir shopping in the valley is in Thayne. Check out   **SHOPPING** the **Star Valley Gift & Rock Shop** for a variety of handicrafts as well as Indian artifacts, jewelry and geological oddities. Closed Sunday in the winter. ~ Route 89, Thayne; 307-883-2028. Off on a side road is the **Warfield Fossil Studio and Preparatory Shop,** where fossils excavated near Fossil Butte are readied for purchase. Closed weekends. ~ 2072 Muddy String Road, Thayne; 307-883-2445.

PARKS

BRIDGER-TETON NATIONAL FOREST 🧍 🚴 🐴 ⛷ 🚣 🏕 🏊

🛶🦆🚤🚤⛷ The Grey's River and Kemmerer ranger districts of this huge (3.4-million-acre) national forest are bisected by the lovely Grey's River. This stream forms a long, wooded gorge between the Salt River Range on its west, crowned by 10,759-foot Mount Wagner, and the Wyoming Range on its east, with 11,363-foot Wyoming Peak at its summit. Numerous backcountry roads and trails crisscross the forest, giving access to many small lakes. A favorite is Lake Alice, south of Afton. Facilities include picnic areas and restrooms. ~ The best access route is the Grey's River Road (Forest Road 10138), a gravel road that runs for more than 100 miles from Alpine southeast to LaBarge. Numerous shorter forest roads extend east off Route 89 through the Star Valley; 307-886-3166.

▲ In this section of the national forest, there are 14 campgrounds with 206 RV/tent sites and 20 for RVs only (at the Hoffman Campground near Alpine); closed mid-September through May; no charge to $18 per night (most $5 or $6); 10- to 16-day maximum stay.

▼▼▼▼▼▼▼▼▼▼▼▼▼▼

Outdoor Adventures

FISHING

By far the most common sport fish in the rivers and lakes of southwestern Wyoming are trout. Rainbow trout are the favorite stocked variety; others include brown, brook and cutthroat. A few reservoirs may have bass, catfish and/or walleye.

Flaming Gorge Reservoir is the most renowned locale in the region. Record fish caught here are indicative of truly world-class angling: lake trout (51 pounds), brown trout (33 pounds), rainbow trout (26 pounds), channel catfish (18 pounds), kokanee salmon (5½ pounds) and smallmouth bass (4½ pounds), for instance.

Two other popular reservoirs are Fontenelle and Viva Naughton. **Fontenelle Reservoir**, 35 miles northeast of Kemmerer on Route 189, is a 15-mile-long, mile-and-a-half-wide lake created by a dam on the Green River. **Lake Viva Naughton**, on the Ham's Fork, is much smaller—only about three miles long—but like Fontenelle it yields many large trout. Viva Naughton in particular is well known for its winter ice-fishing tournaments.

All of the region's rivers offer good fishing, especially the **Salt River** through the Star Valley. Cutthroat and brown trout tend to prefer its lower (northern) reaches in the late spring and summer, its cooler upper stretches in the late summer and fall.

For further information, contact the **Wyoming Fish and Game Commission** in any of the following towns: Rock Springs, 307-382-5658; Green River, 307-875-3223, 800-843-8096; Evanston, 307-789-3285; Kemmerer, 307-877-3278; Afton, 307-886-3717.

The principal boat launch and rental location is **Buckboard Marina**, on the western shore of Flaming Gorge Reservoir 25 miles south of Green River. ~ Route 530, Green River; 307-875-6927. There are also boat launches at Fontenelle and Viva Naughton reservoirs, as well as at Woodruff Narrows Reservoir north of Evanston via Route 89. Waterskiing is popular at all of these lakes.

BOATING & WATER-SKIING

The best places for canoeing or kayaking are the Green River through Seedskadee National Wildlife Refuge, northwest of the town of Green River, and the Salt River through the Star Valley. The myriad inlets of Flaming Gorge Reservoir are beautiful, especially at the south end.

CANOEING & KAYAKING

For instruction in the Snake and Salt River areas, contact the **Snake River Kayak & Canoe School**. ~ 155 West Gill Street, Jackson; 307-733-3127.

Trips of varying degrees of difficulty are offered on both the Snake and Salt rivers. You can paddle hard through whitewater, or enjoy a relaxing float through beautiful countryside. **Barker-Ewing River Trips** offers half-day, full-day and overnight trips on the Snake River. ~ 45 West Broadway, Jackson; 307-733-1000. There is also **Mad River Boat Trips** for whitewater or float trips down the Snake. ~ 1060 South Route 89, Jackson; 307-733-6203.

RIVER RUNNING

For whitewater addicts, there are far bigger challenges in Dinosaur National Monument, on the Colorado–Utah border southeast of Flaming Gorge. The Green River, from the Gates of Ladore to its confluence with the Yampa River, is one of North America's best-known rafting adventures. One of the best of many outfitters running this stretch of river is **Nichols Expeditions**. Because they have a limited number of whitewater runs on the Salmon River each summer, it's important to make reservations early. ~ 497 North Main Street, Moab, Utah; 435-259-3999.

There are two small alpine ski resorts in southwestern Wyoming. The **Pine Creek Ski Area**, six miles east of Cokeville, is a family-oriented area in Pine Creek Canyon with one chair lift and one rope tow servicing 14 runs over a 1200-foot vertical drop. ~ Pine Creek Road (Route 232), Cokeville; 307-279-3201. Star Valley beginners are satisfied with the **Snowshoe Hollow Ski Area**, where a rope tow serves a 200-foot drop. ~ Swift Creek Canyon Road, Afton; 307-886-9831. Both are open weekends and holidays from mid-December through March.

DOWNHILL SKIING

Groomed trails in Wasatch-Cache and Bridger-Teton national forests serve nordic skiers from the Evanston, Kemmerer and Star Valley regions.

CROSS-COUNTRY SKIING

The **Lilly Lake Nordic Ski Association** maintains 30 miles of track on 340 acres along the north slope of the Uinta Mountains in Wasatch-Cache. The Evanston Parks and Recreation District has details on skiing here and at Bear River State Park, just east of Evanston.

Kemmerer opens its town golf course, by the Ham's Fork River, to winter skiers; some prefer the frozen river bed of **Seedskadee National Wildlife Refuge**. For information, contact the Kemmerer/Diamondville Chamber of Commerce. ~ 800 Pine Avenue, Kemmerer; 307-877-9761, 307-875-2187 (refuge).

In the Star Valley, a system of trails extends more than 50 miles between Afton and Alpine. The southernmost segment is especially popular: the Bridger-Teton's **Fish Creek Ski Trail** is a four-mile intermediate-level loop to the summit of Salt River Pass, 14 miles south of Afton. Shorter tracks include Afton's **Valli Vu Ski Trail** (a golf course in summer) and Alpine's **Alpen Haus Ski Trail** (used by horses when the snow is gone). Your best source of information is the Bridger-Teton Grey's River Ranger District office. ~ 125 Washington Street, Afton; 307-886-3166.

WINTER SPORTS

Snowmobiling is all the rage in southwestern Wyoming in winter. The favored playground is the Wyoming Range, which offers 365 miles of trail (144 miles of it groomed weekly) between Kemmerer and Alpine. Eighty-four miles are on a single track between Afton and Alpine, primarily down the Grey's River Road through the heart of Bridger-Teton National Forest. Contact the district ranger's office for further details. ~ 125 Washington Street, Afton; 307-886-3166. Or call the snowmobile trail report. ~ 800-225-5996.

For rentals in the Star Valley, visit **TJ's Sports**. ~ 204 Grays River Road, Alpine; 307-654-7815. Or check with **Star Valley Ski-Doo**. ~ Route 89, Thayne; 307-883-2714.

As for other winter sports, a season of dogsled racing is highlighted by the International Rocky Mountain Stage Stop Sled Dog Race, which begins and ends in Jackson but runs through Alpine, Afton and Kemmerer, the first week of February each year. Also, the Star Valley is home to one of America's most unique sports: cutter, or chariot, racing. (See "The Unique Sport of Cutter Racing" in this chapter.)

GOLF

Rock Springs' **White Mountain Golf Course** is the region's best 18-hole course. ~ 1820 Yellowstone Road; 307-352-1415. Another 18 holes are open to the public at the **Rolling Green Country Club**. ~ Route 374 West, Green River; 307-875-6200.

Throughout the region are several public nine-hole courses. Evanston linksters play at the **Purple Sage Golf Course**. Closed October through March. ~ Route 89; 307-789-2383. The municipal **Kemmerer Field Club Golf Course** is set beside the Ham's Fork River. ~ Route 189, Kemmerer; 307-877-6954. The Star Valley converts its **Valli Vu Golf Club** into a cross-country ski area in winter. ~ Route 89, Afton; 307-886-3338.

There are indoor tennis courts, available by reservation, at the **Rock Springs Recreation Center**. ~ 3900 Sweetwater Drive, Rock Springs; 307-352-1440. Other towns throughout the region have outdoor courts in city parks.

TENNIS

Full and half-day trail rides are offered by numerous outfitters in the region from late spring through October. In Rock Springs, try the **Sweetwater Gap Ranch**. They will rent you a horse by the hour or the day for a guided tour through the Wind River foothills. ~ P.O. Box 26, Rock Springs, WY 82902; 307-362-2798. In the Star Valley, a favorite is **Haderlie Outfitters**, which works out of the Tincup Mountain Guest Ranch just across the state border in Idaho. Guides will take you across Rocky Mountain terrain by the hour, the day or overnight. ~ P.O. Box 175, Freedom, WY 83120; 800-253-2368.

RIDING STABLES

Any of the outfitters recommended under "Riding Stables" also can arrange longer expeditions of one night to two weeks. For those seeking a more unique experience, here are a couple of options:

PACK TRIPS

Preston Ranches place adventurers on cattle drives of up to five days long, as cowboys move livestock between open range and valley meadows. ~ P.O. Box 162, Bedford, WY 83112; 307-883-2742.

Peterson's Wagons West offers summer covered-wagon treks of two, four and six days, mainly along the back roads of Bridger-Teton National Forest surrounding Jackson Hole. Participants ride

---

✔ CHECK THESE OUT—UNIQUE OUTDOOR ADVENTURES

- Keep your fingers crossed that a 50-pound lake trout will take your line when you go fishing in Flaming Gorge Reservoir. *page 192*
- Paddle a canoe through Seedskadee National Wildlife Refuge, where 170 species of migratory birds and waterfowl are seen each year. *page 193*
- Shout for your favorite cutter-racing team as pairs of horses pull tiny chariots down an icy quarter-mile Star Valley track. *page 197*
- Hike three-quarters of a mile to Periodic Spring, east of Afton, to see the world's largest natural cold-water geyser. *page 198*

by day, and enjoy dutch-oven meals and campfire entertainment by night. Closed September through May. ~ P.O. Box 1156, Afton, WY 83110; 307-886-9693, 800-447-4711.

BIKING   Mountain biking has not swept southwestern Wyoming the way it has other parts of the Rockies. Although the mountains, the prairies and even the Great Divide Basin desert have plenty of easy-riding back roads and trails, bicycle rentals are a rarity.

Evanston's **B.E.A.R. Parkway,** a paved riverside track that leads several miles to Bear River State Park, is one of the best biking options in the region. The back roads of the Star Valley are also good; the graded, upcountry **Grey's River Road** between Afton and Alpine is recommended.

HIKING   Whereas the windswept wastelands of the Red Desert and Great Divide Basin don't offer much to any but the most intrepid hikers, good hikes can be found in several other places. All distances listed for hiking trails are one way unless otherwise noted.

ROCK SPRINGS AND GREEN RIVER   There aren't any formal trails of note in the Wyoming portion of Flaming Gorge National Recreation Area, but in Utah there are several. Most popular is the **Canyon Rim Trail** (2.5 miles), an easy walk on mostly flat terrain from the Greendale Overlook near the Red Canyon visitors center. More challenging is the **Hideout-Carter Creek Trail** (10 miles), a steep path that descends to the lake with many overlooks; its trailhead is on Route 44, four miles west of the Red Canyon turnoff. The **Little Hole Trail** (7 miles) is a national recreation trail that follows the Green River from the Flaming Gorge Dam gauging station.

EVANSTON AND FORT BRIDGER   Wasatch-Cache National Forest has numerous trails. The most arduous may be the **Bear River-Smith's Fork Trail** (31 miles), which extends west to east, much of it above 10,000 feet elevation, from the Trailhead Campground near State Line Reservoir (south of Robertson) along the north slope of the Uinta Mountains to Route 150, 32 miles from Evanston.

KEMMERER AND FOSSIL BUTTE   Fossil Butte National Monument has two outstanding short hiking trails. The **Fossil Lake Trail** (1.5 miles roundtrip), a loop from the picnic area, has trailside exhibits that compare modern natural history to the prehistoric flora and fauna of 50-million-year-old Fossil Lake, as unveiled in exposed rock faces. The **Quarry Trail** (2.5 miles roundtrip), a loop from a parking area off Route 300 on the southeast side of the monument, climbs Fossil Butte to an abandoned cabin and fossil quarry worked from the late 1800s to the 1970s. Interpretive signs provide information on the plants, animals and geology of the area.

The Unique Sport
of Cutter Racing

What began seven decades ago in the Star Valley, as a one-upmanship contest, between dairymen trying to keep warm while waiting to deliver their containers at the creamery, has evolved into one of the most exciting and unusual sports in North America.

Cutter racing—or chariot racing, as it is often called—has become much more than a challenge between two-horse sleighs. It now boasts hundreds of racing teams in seven western states, and its world championships draw thousands of spectators.

Thayne, with a population of fewer than 300, is regarded as the birthplace of the sport. In the cold winters of the 1920s, dairymen hauled their milk to the local creamery on sleighs (cutters). Short sprints to the head of the unloading line led to heady challenges: "I'll bet my milk check that my horses are faster than yours." At some point, a Mormon bishop challenged a local rancher to a race down Thayne's iced-over main street, and the townspeople responded so enthusiastically that they added cutter racing to their winter carnival schedule.

Wheels eventually replaced runners as the milk-delivery cutters were replaced by custom-made racing chariots. In 1948, second-generation racers organized the All American Cutter Racing Association in Thayne and began a competitive circuit that held regular winter meetings in Thayne, Afton and Jackson, and across the border in Driggs, Idaho. In 1964, a World Cutter and Chariot Racing Association was organized in Pocatello, Idaho. Today, the top teams from 26 member associations vie for the World Cup title each March.

According to Bill Clay, president of the All American Cutter Racing Association, it takes two to three months to train cutter horses. The steeds begin by simply walking the light chariot up and down a track. After about a month, the driver (called a captain) urges them into a trot. Once they're at full speed, the horses will cover the quarter-mile-long straight track in less than 30 seconds. The world record, set in 1992, is 21.64 seconds.

Except when Mother Nature is subjecting western Wyoming to a severe blizzard, cutter races are held most Saturday afternoons from late November to early March in Afton, Thayne or Jackson. Highlights of the season are the Shriners Invitational in Jackson, in mid-February, with proceeds benefitting the Shriners Hospital in Salt Lake City, and the state championship meet. The top four teams from this race qualify for the world finals.

THE STAR VALLEY Bridger-Teton National Forest above the Star Valley offers probably the greatest variety of hikes in southwestern Wyoming. The **Lake Alice Trail** (1.5 miles) extends to the largest natural lake (three miles long) in this part of Wyoming. Formed by an ancient landslide, its pristine beauty is preserved by the exclusion of all motorized vehicles. The trailhead is at the Hobble Creek Campground on Forest Road 10070, about 32 miles northeast of Cokeville. The **Periodic Spring Trail** follows Swift Creek for three-quarters of a mile from the trailhead at the end of Swift Creek Canyon Road (Forest Road 10211). (See "Star Valley Sights.") Other than foot traffic, only mountain bikes are permitted on this trail. The **Lake Barstow Trail** (1.5 miles), by contrast, is open to all motorized trail vehicles; beginning at the end of Forest Road 10043 off Grey's River Road, 40 miles southeast of Alpine, it follows North Three Forks Creek to a tiny lake popular among anglers.

▼▼▼▼▼▼▼▼▼▼▼▼

Transportation

CAR

Route 80 is the main artery of southwestern Wyoming. This interstate freeway extends west from Cheyenne through Rock Springs, Green River and Evanston en route to Salt Lake City.

Other main highways are:

Route 191, which runs north from Rock Springs to Pinedale and Jackson, south past the Flaming Gorge into Utah.

Route 189, which links Evanston with Kemmerer, Big Piney and Jackson.

Route 89, which meanders across state borders from Evanston through Cokeville and the Star Valley to Jackson.

Route 30, which branches off Route 80 near Little America and proceeds west through Kemmerer and Cokeville into Idaho.

For road and travel information in Rock Springs, Green River and Evanston, call 888-996-7623.

AIR

The **Sweetwater County Airport** is 15 miles east of Rock Springs off Route 80. ~ Airport Road; 307-352-6880. Commuter service via United Express (800-241-6522) is available from here to Denver.

BUS

Greyhound Bus Lines operates several buses a day in both directions on Route 80. Greyhound has a major depot in Rock Springs. ~ 1655 Sunset Boulevard; 307-362-2931, 800-231-2222. **Powder River Transportation** also provides regional transportation from a station in Green River. ~ 1420 Uinta Drive; 307-875-4228.

TRAIN

Since the discontinuation of Amtrak's east–west "Pioneer" in May 1997, passenger service is no longer available through southern Wyoming.

The Rock Springs Municipal Airport has desks for **Avis Rent A Car** (800-331-1212) and **Hertz Rent A Car** (800-654-3131).

CAR RENTALS

Rock Springs and Green River are linked by a bus service known as STAR (Sweetwater Transit Authority Resources). In Rock Springs, call 307-382-7827. In Green River, call 307-875-7827.

PUBLIC TRANSIT

City Cab is the sole taxi company in Rock Springs. ~ 307-382-1100.

TAXIS

SEVEN

Southeastern Wyoming

When you think of the Wild West as depicted by television and the movies, think of southeastern Wyoming.

First traversed by nomadic Plains Indian tribes hunting buffalo and pronghorn antelope, and later by white fur trappers, intrepid pioneers and a handful of U.S. Army troops, the region did not come into its own until the advent of the Union Pacific Railroad in the late 1860s. The main Oregon Trail had bypassed this corner, opting instead to follow the North Platte River to the north; and until the Overland Stage Route was established across these precincts about 1860, there was little reason to sink roots.

The railroad changed everything. Almost overnight, towns like Cheyenne, Laramie and Rawlins burst into being with populations in the thousands. Many of the newcomers were speculators looking to make a fast buck in retail or real estate and vanish as quickly as they had materialized. Others were professional gamblers and gunmen who preyed upon the financially innovative.

Those who came to stay were mostly hardworking citizens looking to find a place they could call home. They were shopkeepers and restaurateurs, doctors and pastors, tradesmen and cowboys who worked the prairie spreads surrounding these towns. When a criminal element grew to a point where it became intolerable, and local law-enforcement officials seemed unable to handle the problem themselves, these citizens formed vigilante committees and dealt with the outlaws in their own way. Thus did southeastern Wyoming become a peaceful place to live.

Some of the West's most famous—or infamous—names are associated with this part of the state. The notorious Butch Cassidy served his only jail time—18 months for horse theft—at the Territorial Prison in Laramie, and made the isolated Little Snake River Valley one of his favorite hideaways. Midwesterner Bill Nye came to Laramie to start a newspaper (it's still published today) and became one of the best-known satirists of the early American West. Harvard-educated Owen Wister fell in love with the small town of Medicine Bow and made it the focus of his great romantic cowboy novel, *The Virginian*.

Today Wyoming's "population belt," such as it is, is here in the southeast. Cheyenne, the state capital and largest city with 50,000 people, sits just ten miles north of the Colorado border at a crossroads of interstate highways. Surrounded by lush grasslands, it retains a cowboy flair best seen for ten days in late July, when Frontier Days—the world's largest professional rodeo—consumes the city.

Laramie, an exuberant university town of 27,000, is a 45-minute drive west of Cheyenne across the low, gentle Laramie Mountains. It's another hour and a half on the freeway to Rawlins, a ranching center of 9400 at the edge of the Great Divide Basin. Between these cities, Medicine Bow National Forest cloaks the craggy peaks of the Medicine Bow Mountains, traversed by the Snowy Range Scenic Byway. Here are ice-cold alpine lakes; forests of pine and aspen; meadows ablaze with wildflowers. The North Platte and Laramie rivers have their headwaters here, and the hot-springs resort community of Saratoga lies along the North Platte on the mountains' flank.

▼▼▼▼▼▼▼▼▼▼ Cheyenne Area

Cheyenne, named for the Plains Indian tribe, was a Union Pacific town that actually *preceded* the railroad. When rail laborers laying the tracks from the east arrived here in November 1867, they found a thriving community on Crow Creek: A company surveyor had established a camp at the intersection of trails between several military camps in the region. Beginning in July of that year, 4000 people had established residence at the junction in anticipation of the railroad's arrival. They were not only shopkeepers and cowboys, gamblers and professional gunmen, but also real-estate salesman and speculators whose presence guaranteed that land prices would soar. There was always a dollar to be made, and liquor was as cheap as life itself, or so some would have it. The town at the end of the tracks quickly became known as "Hell on Wheels."

The U.S. Army established Fort Russell (now Fort Warren) at Cheyenne that same year to protect rail workers and pioneer residents from bands of hostile Indians, and cattle ranchers made the new town their headquarters for shipping the livestock that foraged in the surrounding grasslands. With the arrival of the railroad, Cheyenne boomed as a supply and transportation center. It was only natural that it be named territorial capital when the Wyoming Territory was created in 1869, and state capital in 1890. As a legislative center, it attracted visitors from all over Wyoming as well as other parts of the United States.

Today, located at the crossroads of two major interstate freeways and of the Union Pacific and Burlington Northern railroads, Cheyenne is the retail and banking center for all of Wyoming and neighboring western Nebraska. Livestock ranching has continued to imbue the area with a strong cowboy flavor, but fossil fuels (oil and coal) and timber production also help support the economy.

SIGHTS   The 50-foot-diameter gold-leaf dome that tops the **Wyoming State Capitol,** the tallest building in Cheyenne, is visible for miles across the plains. Built in 1887 to resemble the U.S. Capitol building in Washington, D.C., Wyoming's capitol is a sandstone structure of neoclassical style with Corinthian features. Its most remarkable features are huge Tiffany stained-glass ceilings, floodlit from above, set into the interior of the capitol dome as well as the chambers of the House of Representatives and Senate. Both chambers boast large murals that depict episodes from Wyoming history. Free guided tours, offered weekdays year-round from 8:30 a.m. to 4:30 p.m., begin in the rotunda, which is adorned by full-size mounts of a bison and elk. ~ Capitol Avenue between 24th and 25th streets, Cheyenne; 307-777-7220.

The capitol's most striking artworks are those outside the building. On the west side is "The Spirit of Wyoming," sculptor Ed Fraughton's dramatic bronze rendition of the state's trademark, a bucking bronco and rider. On the opposite side of the building stands a horseless but slightly larger-than-life bronze statue of Esther Hobart Morris, who became the first woman public office-holder in the United States when she was elected justice of the peace in South Pass City in 1870. A year before her election, Wyoming's territorial legislature had passed the first law in the country prohibiting discrimination on the basis of sex and granting women the right to vote.

Wyoming also elected the first woman governor in the United States: Nellie Tayloe Ross, chosen for office in 1924 to complete the last two years of her deceased husband's term. Although she was not reelected, probably because she supported Prohibition and opposed prizefighting, Ross was considered effective in improving public education and reducing the state debt. In 1933, she was appointed the first woman director of the U.S. Mint, a post she kept for 20 years. Wyoming, ironically, has not elected another woman governor since Ross.

The official state nickname is "The Equality State," and the state motto is "Equal rights." Well, almost equal: About one out of four state legislators is female.

The nearby **Wyoming State Museum**'s permanent historical collection chronicles the Old West in its vast array of artifacts and clothing from native Indian tribes, early trappers, pioneers, ranchers, cowboys and soldiers. You'll also find prehistoric objects uncovered by archaeologists and a variety of items showing Wyoming's 20th-century evolution through the decades: domestic and industrial, economic and political. The museum incorporates the Wyoming State Art Gallery, with works by state and regional artists, the state archives and a gift shop. Closed Sunday and Monday. ~ 24th Street and Central Avenue, Cheyenne; 307-777-7022.

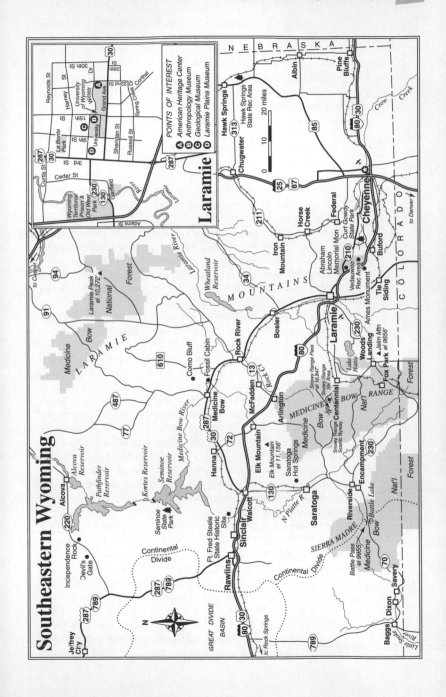

Southeastern Wyoming

Laramie

POINTS OF INTEREST

- **Ⓐ** American Heritage Center
- **Ⓑ** Anthropology Museum
- **Ⓒ** Geological Museum
- **Ⓓ** Laramie Plains Museum

NEBRASKA

COLORADO

to Denver

to Casper

GREAT DIVIDE BASIN

SIERRA MADRE

Continental Divide

Continental Divide

N

A short walk southeast is the **Historic Governors' Mansion State Historic Site**, a huge, redundantly named Georgian-style manor that for 72 years served as the home of Wyoming's first families. Built in 1904 and occupied the following year, it was in continual use through 1976. Today you can view a videotape on the mansion's interior design and the people who lived here, Nellie Ross among them. Then take a free, self-guided tour of its various rooms, furnished and decorated in styles representing the decades when the mansion was in use. (The present Governors' Mansion, which is not open to the public, fronts on Frontier Park.) Closed Sunday and Monday. ~ 300 East 21st Street, Cheyenne; 307-777-7878.

The most interesting museum in town is the **Cheyenne Frontier Days Old West Museum**, next to the rodeo grounds, which presents a century of memorabilia from the Frontier Days celebration: In effect, the museum is a history of the sport of rodeo. There's also a collection of more than 150 horsedrawn vehicles, including buckboards, covered wagons, stagecoaches and carriages, some of which are used in the annual Frontier Days Parade; and a display of American Indian and cowboy artifacts similar to the one in the Wyoming State Museum. A small gallery of Western art is the location of the Western Art Show during Frontier Days. There's also a nice gift shop. Admission. ~ North Carey Avenue at Frontier Park, Cheyenne; 307-778-7290.

Across Carey Street from the Frontier Park rodeo grounds, **Lions Park** surrounds peaceful Sloans Lake. Its broad, green lawns are perfect for picnicking. The park's best feature is the **Botanical Garden**: In addition to native trees and plants of Wyoming, it has solar greenhouses that simulate desert and tropical rainforest environments, and vegetable gardens grown as part of local rehabilitation programs for handicapped persons and disturbed youths. A miniature zoo boasts bison and elk, and there also are bike paths, a miniature golf course, a children's playground, restrooms and a public swimming pool. The lake is used for boating, fishing and ice skating. ~ North Carey Avenue at 8th Avenue, Cheyenne; 307-637-6458.

At **Holliday Park**, in the heart of downtown, you may be stunned by the size of the world's largest steam locomotive, on permanent display here. Old Number 4004, better known as "Big Boy," did the work of two normal steam engines in the days before modern diesel engines were developed. The Union Pacific built the locomotive in 1941 for the run across the Rockies to Ogden, Utah, and retired it to Holliday Park 15 years later. "Big Boy" could carry 28 tons of fuel and 25,000 gallons of water. Holliday Park also boasts tennis, horseshoes, canoeing and picnicking. ~ Morris Avenue and 19th Street, Cheyenne; 307-637-6401.

Aside from state government, Cheyenne's major employer is the **F. E. Warren Air Force Base**, where the federal government keeps intercontinental ballistic missiles at the ready. Established in 1867 as Fort D.A. Russell, it was later renamed after Francis E. Warren, Wyoming's first governor and later a U.S. senator for 37 years. Assigned to the Air Force in 1947, it became a National Historic Landmark district in 1969, and many multi-story brick structures still loom over its tree-lined streets. Free guided tours —conducted at 9 a.m. the first and third Fridays of the month between April and September or by appointment—take in a small museum that traces the fort's history. Closed weekends. ~ Randall Avenue at Route 25, Cheyenne; 307-773-3381.

You won't hear shots fired today at the military installation. You *will* hear—and see—them fired during the months of June and July at **Old Town Square**. That's where the Cheyenne Gunslingers stage almost-daily Old West shootouts (6 p.m. Monday through Friday, noon Saturday). The adjacent **Cheyenne Area Convention and Visitors Bureau** offices are the best place around to get information on sights (ask for a pamphlet describing a self-guided tour of the downtown historic district) and lodging. ~ 309 West Lincolnway, Cheyenne; 307-778-3133, 800-426-5009; e-mail info@cheyenne.org.

There are plenty of places around the city to experience native wildlife. One of the best introductions is the **Wildlife Visitors Center**, administered by the Wyoming Game & Fish Department. Inside are photographs and stuffed specimens of many of the state's 600-plus mammal, bird, reptile and fish species; outside is a living backyard habitat area. Open daily in summer, weekdays the rest of the year. ~ 5400 Bishop Boulevard at Route 25 and Central Avenue, Cheyenne; 307-777-4541.

▲▲

✔ CHECK THESE OUT—UNIQUE SIGHTS

- Tour the neoclassical **Wyoming State Capitol** in Cheyenne and marvel at the Tiffany stained-glass ceiling within its gold-leaf dome. *page 202*
- Go for a stagecoach ride in Laramie's **Wyoming Territorial Prison & Old West Park**, where a 19th-century ambience lives on in a recreated frontier village. *page 215*
- Drive the **Snowy Range Scenic Byway** over a 10,847-foot pass to Saratoga, whose hot springs are the equal of Baden-Baden. *page 220*
- Wander the dinosaur graveyard of **Como Bluff**, a true Jurassic park, and drop in at the Bedrock-style "world's oldest building." *page 227*

There's a greater entertainment factor at the **Terry Bison Ranch**, where guests can ride horses or join a horsedrawn wagon tour past a herd of buffaloes living on this 27,500-acre spread. This old working ranch, seven miles south of Cheyenne off Route 25, Exit 2, also offers Friday and Saturday night chuckwagon dinners (featuring roast buffalo, of course) with live Western music. Admission. ~ 51 Route 25 Service Road East, Cheyenne; 307-634-4171, 800-319-4171.

Tom Horn, a "livestock detective," was hanged in Cheyenne in 1903 for the murder of a young Nate Champion.

Five miles east of Cheyenne, the **Wyoming Hereford Ranch** invites visitors to tour its 60,000 acres and see a major Western cattle operation at work. The ranch, established in 1883, has many historic farm structures. ~ Campstool Road, Cheyenne; 307-634-1905.

If you head east 40 miles across the grasslands from Cheyenne, the small town of **Pine Bluffs**, set hard against the Nebraska border, is worth a visit for the history it preserves. Drovers on the old Texas Cattle Trail used to stop here at Lodgepole Creek to water their livestock, and in the 1870s and 1880s, the young rail town of Pine Bluffs was the largest cattle-shipping point in the world: 600,000 head of cattle were herded through this crossroads in 1871 alone. The **Texas Trail Museum and Park**, open May through September, displays many items from that era; its transportation exhibit beside the railroad track is particularly well done. ~ 3rd and Market streets, Pine Bluffs; 307-245-3713.

Long before white men tread this ground, Plains Indians made their homes in the Pine Bluffs area. Arrowheads and other artifacts from a civilization that thrived here 8000 years ago have been exposed at an archaeological dig just outside of the town; they are displayed daily, June through August, at the **University of Wyoming Archaeological Lab and Visitors Center**. ~ 2nd and Elm streets, Pine Bluffs; 307-245-9372. Check here for tours of the dig site, which is adjacent to the **Pine Bluffs Information Center and Rest Area**. The center, just off the freeway on the south side of town, also displays ancient artifacts and reproduced paintings at its replica tepee village. A series of nature trails extends uphill from here. ~ 904 Parsons Street, Pine Bluffs; 307-245-3695.

West of Cheyenne, two routes of equal (48-mile) distance traverse the Laramie mountains to the university town of Laramie. Travelers in a hurry—which means most of them—take Route 80, the interstate freeway, also known as the Lincoln Highway. The alternative track across the mountains is Route 210, better known as the **Happy Jack Road.** Named for lumberjack Jack Hollingworth, who built the first path for hauling timber from the hills in the 1880s, it is slower and more picturesque than Route 80.

Climbing from the grasslands of eastern Wyoming into the rocky foothills of the Laramie Range, the road passes **Curt Gowdy**

State Park 24 miles west of Cheyenne. Named for a Wyoming native who achieved national fame as a sports broadcaster, it encompasses two small lakes surrounded by rocky, timbered bluffs. ~ 1351 Hynds Lodge Road; 307-632-7946. Above the state park, the Happy Jack Road winds through a rugged section of Medicine Bow National Forest before joining Route 80 at its 8640-foot summit, 12 miles east of Laramie.

Cheyenne's motel strip is Lincolnway. No fewer than 22 lodgings line this artery from the 2800 block West to the 3800 block East.   **LODGING**

One of the best, in a lower price range, is the **Fleetwood Motel**. The two-story motel has 21 rooms with basic amenities, plus a heated outdoor swimming pool. ~ 3800 East Lincolnway, Cheyenne; 307-638-8908, 800-634-7763. BUDGET.

A cautious step up in size and luxury is the **Lincoln Court**. This 65-room motel has moderately sized rooms (some with refrigerators) in the original building and smaller but more modern units in a newer wing. There are indoor and outdoor pools as well

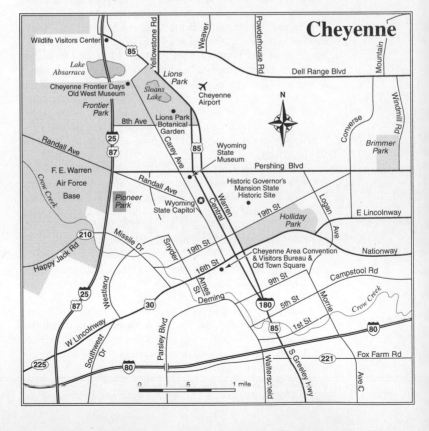

as a children's playground and coin laundry; guests get privileges at a nearby fitness center. A restaurant is adjacent. ~ 1720 West Lincolnway, Cheyenne; 307-638-3302, 800-221-0125, fax 307-638-7921. MODERATE.

If having a kitchen is important to you, your best bet may be the **Round-Up Motel**. All but 5 of the 36 rooms here are efficiency units with stoves, refrigerators and microwaves. Otherwise, these are basic rooms, with TVs, phones and not much else. ~ 403 South Greeley Highway, Cheyenne; 307-634-7741. BUDGET.

Cheyenne's finest accommodations are at the **Little America Hotel & Resort**, located at the crossroads of Routes 25 and 80. The sprawling 188-room, 80-acre complex boasts such facilities as a nine-hole golf course, Olympic-size swimming pool and jogging track. The spacious rooms feature contemporary furnishings and warm color schemes. Room service is available from the coffee shop; the resort also has a fine-dining restaurant and a lounge with live entertainment. ~ 2800 West Lincolnway, Cheyenne; 307-775-8400, 800-445-6945, fax 307-775-8425; www.lamerica.com. DELUXE.

The only refurbished historic hotel in Cheyenne, and one of the few in the state, is the **Plains Hotel**. The lobby of this 1911 inn is full of Old West atmosphere, while 40 of the 140 accommodations are oversized guest rooms that feature such amenities as marble bathrooms and queen-size beds. Adjacent to the dining room is a bar that once was the soul of Wyoming politics: More major decisions were made here, it is said, than in the capitol building. The location is convenient for strolling downtown and the capitol district. ~ 1600 Central Avenue, Cheyenne; 307-638-3311. BUDGET.

One of the nicest of Cheyenne's numerous bed and breakfasts is the **Rainsford Inn**, a stately, three-story Victorian listed on the National Register of Historic Places. It's located in the quiet, residential Rainsford Historic District near downtown, on what was known in Cheyenne's early days as "Cattle Baron Row." The five suites are individually furnished with antiques and small televisions; some have whirlpool baths. Common areas feature a piano, sun porch and guest laundry. ~ 219 East 18th Street, Cheyenne; 307-638-2337, fax 307-634-4506; e-mail tobeds@sisna.com. DELUXE.

Midway between Cheyenne and Laramie, just west of the entrance to Curt Gowdy State Park, is **A. Drummond's Ranch Bed and Breakfast**. The location of this two-story ranch house on a 120-acre plot is ideal for outdoor recreation lovers. There are four nonsmoking guest rooms and a carriage house loft with a private entrance, a fireplace and a steam sauna. Some rooms have private outdoor hot tubs with unobstructed mountain views, but you may have to share a bathroom. An indoor arena offers facilities for stabling horses and boarding pets. A full breakfast is served; advance bookings are essential. ~ 399 Happy Jack Road, Cheyenne; phone/fax 307-634-6042; e-mail adrummond@juno.com. MODERATE TO ULTRA-DELUXE.

If you're determined to overnight in Pine Bluffs, you can rest your head at the **Gator's Travelyn Motel**. The 31 rooms in this family-operated lodging have TVs and phones, and your pet is welcome as well. ~ 515 West 7th Street, Pine Bluffs; 307-245-3226. MODERATE.

DINING

Some argue that Cheyenne's most popular restaurant is in its oldest building. That would be **Lexie's Café**, housed in a 19th-century brick building in the downtown core. Lexie's serves hearty, ranch-style breakfasts such as steak and eggs, and the biggest, juiciest hamburgers in town at lunchtime. Dinner offers steak, seafood and chicken dishes. No dinner Monday; closed Sunday. ~ 216 East 17th Street, Cheyenne; 307-638-8712. MODERATE.

A casual, family-style spot is the **Owl Inn**, which has been in continual operation since 1935. It's open for three meals daily, serving all-American fare—steak, potatoes and apple pie—that seems to please everyone. There are special menus for children. ~ 3919 Central Avenue, Cheyenne; 307-638-8578. MODERATE.

International cuisine in Cheyenne generally means Mexican food, in which several restaurants around town excel. Among the best eateries is **Los Amigos Restaurant**, where authentic south-of-the-border dishes surpass the standard piñatas-and-serapes ambience. Closed Sunday. ~ 620 Central Avenue, Cheyenne; 307-638-8591. BUDGET.

The **Victorian Rose**, in the historic Plains Hotel, is an enjoyable place with an old-fashioned feel. Its varied menu features pastas and daily specials, as well as prime rib, trout and steaks. The restaurant is open 24 hours on Friday and Saturday. ~ 1600 Central Avenue, Cheyenne; 307-637-8701. BUDGET TO MODERATE.

◆◆

A HOME WHERE THE BUFFALO COMB

Early telegraph-line crews in the Cheyenne area encountered a unique problem: Resident bison liked to use the poles as scratching posts, and the animals' strength was such that it only took a few hours of scratching before a pole could be rubbed right out of the ground. An innovative line boss proposed that spikes be pounded into the lower sections of each pole. Local legend maintains this improvement was so popular with the buffaloes, they formed waiting lines at every telegraph pole.

You won't have any problem satisfying your hunger at **Sanford's Grub & Pub**, where Cajun crawfish and barbecued ribs are all-you-can-eat, depending on the day. If you're not up to the challenge, the menu features do-able portions of steak, burgers and chicken. Sports memorabilia galore decorate this convivial restaurant, which boasts 55 beers on tap and 102 bottled brews. ~ 115 East 17th Street, Cheyenne; 307-634-3381. BUDGET TO DELUXE.

Two fine dinner houses at the Best Western Hitching Post Inn cater to a wide range of guests. **The Cheyenne Cattle Company** is the city's best steakhouse; the smoke-free restaurant also has a big salad bar, a luncheon buffet, and evening entertainment. MODERATE. The **Carriage Court** is a more intimate, gourmet establishment that caters to couples, with Continental cuisine and tableside flambé service. ~ 1700 West Lincolnway, Cheyenne; 307-638-3301. DELUXE.

Outside of a couple of hotel restaurants, the best fine dining in Cheyenne is at **Poor Richard's**, whose early American ambience would make Ben Franklin proud. The gourmet menu boasts prime rib and seafood specialties and an excellent salad bar. But don't be fooled by the fine atmosphere, for this restaurant welcomes children and other casual diners. A Saturday brunch is served, and a patio is open to dining in warmer weather. ~ 2233 East Lincolnway, Cheyenne; 307-635-5114. MODERATE TO DELUXE.

South of town a few miles, **Senator's** is a year-round steakhouse at the Terry Bison Ranch—open even when the summer chuckwagon dinners are not being served. Buffalo and beefsteak are the specialties served in the rustic pine dining room. Lunch and dinner are served daily from Memorial Day to Labor Day, limited

THE "DADDY OF 'EM ALL"

Frontier Days, probably the world's largest professional rodeo, increases Cheyenne's population to more than 300,000 during the last week of July. Riding the wave of popularity following the 1897 introduction of Buffalo Bill's Wild West Show, the first Frontier Days attracted 15,000 spectators to watch bronco riding, steer roping, horse racing, reenactments of a stagecoach robbery and a skirmish between Indians and cavalrymen. One of the original rodeo champions was the infamous Tom Horn, later hanged as an assassin. Rodeo remains at the heart of this ten-day celebration. But there's more: parades showcasing several dozen horsedrawn vehicles, nightly concerts by country-western stars, Indian dancing at tepee villages, precision flying shows, squaredancing and shootouts, chili cookoffs and free pancake breakfasts.

hours during the rest of the year. ~ 51 Route 25 Service Road East, Cheyenne; 307-634-4994. MODERATE.

East of Cheyenne on the Route 80 corridor, your best bet is the **Total Wild Horse Cafe**. Always open, the family restaurant focuses on home-style cooking. ~ 600 Parsons Street, Pine Bluffs; 307-245-9365. MODERATE.

SHOPPING

If it's Levi's, Tony Lamas or Stetsons you have in mind, you're in luck in downtown Cheyenne, where one of the largest selections of Western wear in the state can be found at **Wrangler**. ~ 1518 Capitol Avenue, Cheyenne; 307-634-3048.

Wyoming's largest modern shopping center is the **Frontier Mall**, where more than 90 stores cluster around Sears and JC Penney. ~ 1400 Dell Range Boulevard, Cheyenne; 307-638-2290.

NIGHTLIFE

For highbrow culture, many Cheyenne residents set their sights on the university towns of Laramie and Fort Collins, Colorado, both about 45 minutes' drive away . . . or, better yet, on Denver, less than two hours' drive south. But this state capital is not devoid of sophistication. The performance hall at the **Cheyenne Civic Center** hosts frequent concerts throughout the year by well-known performing artists on tour. ~ 510 West 20th Street, Cheyenne; 307-637-6363. Some of the visitors may be backed by the **Cheyenne Symphony Orchestra**, which also presents six regular concerts during a September-to-May season. ~ 307-778-8561.

As far as stage productions go, the **Cheyenne Little Theatre** offers dramas and musicals performed by local actors year-round. ~ 2706 East Pershing Boulevard, Cheyenne; 307-638-6543. In summer, the troupe moves to the historic **Atlas Theatre** for a July–August series of comic melodramas, a big hit among the tourist audience. ~ 211 West Lincolnway, Cheyenne; 307-635-0199.

The Cheyenne club scene is heavily oriented toward country-and-western. You can two-step late into the night at the **Cheyenne Club**, a great big barnlike dance hall right downtown featuring live bands and C&W dance lessons some evenings. ~ 1617 Capitol Avenue, Cheyenne; 307-635-7777. An even bigger C&W club with live music is the **Cowboy South**. ~ 312 South Greeley Highway, Cheyenne; 307-637-3800.

PARKS

CURT GOWDY STATE PARK Named for the Wyoming-born sportscaster, this 1635-acre park in the foothills of the Laramie Mountains encompasses meadows, rolling pine-shaded hills and rugged granite rock formations surrounding two reservoirs that provide Cheyenne's water supply. Unpaved roads almost completely encircle both lakes, providing access to 18 camping and picnic areas along the shores. Powerboats dominate large Granite Lake, while anglers in hand-launched skiffs use the smaller Crystal Lake. Fishing is good for rainbow trout, mackinaw and kokanee salmon. The park is crowded on weekends but practically deserted during the week. Facilities include picnic areas, restrooms, a nature trail (used in winter by skiers), an archery range, an amphitheater and two group shelters. Day-use fee, $5. ~ The park entrance road begins 24 miles west of Cheyenne and 26 miles east of Laramie off Route 210 (Happy Jack Road); 307-632-7946.

▲ There are 280 RV/tent sites (no hookups); $9 per night per vehicle; 14-day maximum stay.

Laramie Area

Laramie is one of numerous places in southeastern Wyoming (along with Laramie County, the Laramie Mountains, Laramie Peak, the Laramie River and Fort Laramie) named after Jacques La Remy, a French trapper believed to have been the first European ever to set foot in eastern Wyoming. He vanished in 1820; most historians believe he either went to live among the Arapaho people or died at their hands.

Like Cheyenne, Laramie got its start as a rough-and-ready railroad town. But Laramie's future was aimed in a different direction in 1886 with the establishment of the University of Wyoming as the state's only four-year, land-grant college. Today the UW is the center of life in Laramie: Its 10,000 students make up the core of the city, and many other residents work at the university or have dependent retail businesses.

Cheyenne is in Laramie County, but the city of Laramie, 48 miles west, is in Albany County. The two cities are separated by the low Laramie Mountains, covered in ponderosa forest and studded with granite formations large and small. Two paved routes cross the mountains between the two cities. The slower Happy Jack Road was described in "Cheyenne Area," above. If you're like most travelers, you'll take the Route 80 freeway from Cheyenne, which whisks you over the mountains and down into Laramie in about 45 minutes. But several diversions along the interstate may lead you to spend more time en route than you had planned.

SIGHTS   The first of them is the **Vedauwoo Recreation Area**, 31 miles west of Cheyenne and 17 miles southeast of Laramie in Medicine Bow National Forest. This ice-age legacy is reached by a dirt road a short distance north of the freeway. Balanced rocks and myriad other weird granite formations sprout from the earth everywhere you look. The major attraction is an area of sheer cliffs, overhanging in many spots, which rock climbers consider one of the great technical climbs in Wyoming. On most summer days and any weekend when the weather is sunny you can watch as dozens of climbers inch their ways up the crags, clinging to rock faces with fingers and toes. The name Vedauwoo, incidentally, comes from an Arapaho Indian word meaning "earth-borne spirits." Picnicking and camping are permitted here from May to October, and climbing is allowed any time of the day or night, weather permitting. The campsites are usually occupied by climbers, who need no permits to test their skills here. ~ Route 80 Exit 329, Laramie; 307-745-8971 or 307-745-2300.

Reached from the same Route 80 exit as Vedauwoo but two miles south of the freeway is the **Ames Monument**, a state historic site. The 60-foot pyramid, which stands alone on a ridge, was built in 1882 to immortalize Oakes and Oliver Ames, brothers who helped finance and promote the Union Pacific Railroad's transcontinental venture. Their portraits in stone, now badly eroded and apparently used for target practice from time to time, are mounted high on opposite sides of the pyramid. When the monument was built, the community of Sherman, a train inspection point, was located here at the highest point on the rail route. After the Ames brothers were disgraced in a government scandal, the tracks were rerouted to bypass the monument and Sherman became a ghost town. ~ Ames Road, Laramie; 307-777-6323 or 307-632-7946.

Today the highest point on transcontinental Route 80 is 8640-foot Sherman Hill, just ten miles southeast of Laramie. At the hill's summit, just above an information center and rest area where the Happy Jack Road rejoins the freeway, the **Abraham Lincoln Memorial Monument** overlooks Laramie by 1500 feet. The 42-foot-tall bronze bust, mounted on a granite pedestal, was the work of Robert Russin, Wyoming's leading sculptor; when it was unveiled in 1959, it commemorated the former president's 150th birthday. From New York and Chicago to San Francisco, Route 80 follows the original Lincoln Highway. It opened in 1912, three years behind schedule (it had been planned for the centennial of Lincoln's 1809 birth).

Laramie, established in 1868 on the Union Pacific tracks, was always a law-abiding town. The presence of the army's Fort Sanders, a few miles south, may have helped, but city fathers wasted no time playing their hand when they felt the federal authorities weren't doing their job. A vigilante posse of 500 drove most of the criminal element out of town in 1869; those reluctant to leave were invited to "necktie parties." Laramie garnered bigger national headlines in March 1870, when it sat the nation's first women jurors, and in November 1871, when "Grandma" Louiza Swain became the first woman to vote in a general election.

One of Laramie's most notable early citizens was Edward W. "Bill" Nye, who in 1881 founded the town newspaper that continues to be published daily today. The *Laramie Boomerang* was, in fact, named for Nye's favorite mule. But this quirky man, who arrived in Laramie with only 35 cents in his pocket, did well for himself. During the seven years he lived in Laramie, Nye was justice of the peace, federal commissioner and postmaster, as well as the editor/publisher of the *Boomerang*. He left Wyoming for big-city journalism and became a noted humorist, lecturer and writer on the early West.

You'll learn a few tidbits about Nye at the **Laramie Plains Museum**, the elegant late-Victorian mansion of Edward Ivinson. The pioneer banker and his wife, Jane, built the manse at a cost of $40,000 in 1892, the year Ivinson ran unsuccessfully for governor. Apparently, he had hoped to turn his estate into a permanent governor's mansion. Instead it became an Episcopal girls' school after his death. When that closed, local citizens raised $74,000 to buy the home and prevent its being razed in favor of a supermarket.

Now on the National Register of Historic Places, this museum-née-mansion has been lavishly restored with antique furniture, turn-of-the-century kitchen appliances and handmade toys. Everywhere are historical photos and documents from Laramie's early days. The meticulous interior woodwork is worth the price of admission. Among the colorful gardens of the mansion's meticulously landscaped grounds are a carriage house, a cowboy line cabin and a one-room frontier schoolhouse. Guided tours are offered daily in summer; call for hours the rest of the year. Admission. ~ 603 Ivinson Avenue, Laramie; 307-742-4448.

The Ivinson mansion is just one museum, however; on the 780-acre **University of Wyoming** campus in the heart of the city, there are four. You still can see the university's original granite building, known as Old Main; most of the buildings that surround Prexy's Pasture, the campus quadrangle, are made of native limestone. ~ Ivinson Avenue and 14th Street, Laramie; 307-766-1121.

The campus has two highlights. One is the **Geological Museum**, which you'll recognize immediately by the full-scale copper model of *Tyrannosaurus rex* that stands outside. Exhibits attend two billion years of geological history through the display of rocks, minerals and fossils, and include a rare full skeleton of an *apatosaurus*—a brontosaurus-type creature that roamed Wyoming's prehistoric swamps. There are also specimens of the state's jade and uranium, and core samples from oil probes. ~ East wing, S. H. Knight Building, Laramie; 307-766-4218.

The other main UW attraction is the **American Heritage Center**, housed in the Centennial Complex designed by Antoine Predock. Paramount in the Heritage Center collection are great works of art of the Old West, including Alfred Jacob Miller's "The Rendezvous Near Green River." Miller was the only trained artist who ever attended a mountain-man rendezvous; this painting is valued at $750,000. Works by George Catlin, Frederic Remington, Thomas Moran and William Henry Jackson are among others presented here. There's a section of film memorabilia from Hollywood oaters, such as Hopalong Cassidy's six-shooters and a saddle presented to silent-movie star Tim McCoy by Shoshone Indians in 1918. And there are exhibits on the evolution of Wyoming industry and environment, as well as thousands of historical manuscripts, maps and photos and more than 50,000 rare books. Closed Sunday. ~ 22nd Street and Willett Drive, Laramie; 307-766-4114.

Also in the Centennial Complex is the **University Art Museum**, whose collection includes paintings and sculptures, artifacts and prints from many different cultures and historical periods: more than 6000 items in all. The museum specializes not only in American art, but also in foreign artists who influenced the work of later Americans. Closed Sunday. ~ 22nd Street and Willett Drive, Laramie; 307-766-6622.

The university also has an **Anthropology Museum** with collections that chronicle the cultures of Northern Plains tribes and other North American Indians. Closed weekends. ~ Anthropology (Old Law) Building; 307-766-5136. And the campus also boasts a botany conservatory (307-766-6487).

For most visitors to Laramie, however, the city's biggest attraction is **Wyoming Territorial Prison & Old West Park.** A Western-heritage theme park that opened in 1994, it is built around the original Territorial Prison (1872–1901) and includes a recreated Frontier Town, the National U.S. Marshals Museum and a dinner theater.

The only time Butch Cassidy is known to have spent behind bars was the 18 months he served here for stealing horses early in his outlaw career. Legend has it that in Laramie he learned the finer points of train robbery and met many of the men who later would ride with his Wild Bunch. The prison was considered progressive in its day because it was the first one in the West to separate women inmates from the male prison population. Guided tours take you through restored cell blocks, the dining area and the chapel, but much of what visitors see today is a restoration.

A number of original pioneer buildings have been moved to **Frontier Town** from different parts of the state—among them a mercantile, a print shop, a doctor's office and a saloon where there's ongoing entertainment. Men and women in period dress demonstrate historic crafts and trades; in the streets you might even run into Calamity Jane, portrayed here by her real-life great-grandniece. The Marshals Museum chronicles 200 years of law enforcement, while the Horse Barn Dinner Theatre presents Western musicals that demand the participation of audience members as they dine. Activities for children include stagecoach rides, puppet shows and a petting corral. Open daily from mid-June to mid-August; and weekends from Memorial Day weekend through

September. Admission. ~ 975 Snowy Range Road at Route 80; 307-745-6161, 800-845-2287; www.wyoprisonpark.org.

Unfortunately, the Wyoming & Colorado Scenic Railroad, which once ran daily throughout the summer from the Old West Park into the Snowy Range on a five-and-a-half-hour, 108-mile excursion, has closed down. One hopes this premier attraction will someday be reinstated.

LODGING   Most motels in Laramie are found on the west side of town along 3rd Street (Route 287) or around the Snowy Range Road exit from Route 80, close by Wyoming Territorial Prison & Old West Park.

One of the larger motels along the 3rd Street corridor is the **First Inn Gold**. The 80 rooms in this two-story property vary from small traditional units to modern suites with queen-size beds and microwave ovens. The Inn has a heated outdoor swimming pool, a hot tub, laundry facilities, a Mexican restaurant and a lounge; best of all for families, kids stay free and pets are welcome. ~ 421 Boswell Street, Laramie; 307-742-3721, 800-642-4212, fax 307-742-5473. MODERATE.

Out near the Territorial Prison/Park is the **Camelot Motel**, a neat-and-clean if modest place. Its 33 rooms have all standard amenities, plus a coin laundry, and there's a 24-hour coffee shop just down the street. ~ 523 Adams Street, Laramie; 307-721-8860, 800-659-7915. MODERATE.

That coffee shop is at the **Best Western Foster's Country Inn**, one of the largest motor inns in town with 112 units. The guest rooms in this two-story, white brick building have a clean, new feeling and furnishings so familiar you may feel that you've been

---

✔ CHECK THESE OUT—UNIQUE LODGING

- *Budget:* Pay tribute to novelist Owen Wister at **The Virginian Hotel**, which retains the spirit of his era. *page 230*
- *Moderate:* Bed down in a 1912 home that once served as both a fraternity and a sorority—**Annie Moore's Guest House**. *page 217*
- *Deluxe:* Relax in the turn-of-the-century ambience of the **Rainsford Inn**, a three-story Victorian located on what was known as "Cattle Baron Row." *page 208*
- *Ultra-deluxe:* Saddle up at the **Two Bars Seven Ranch** south of Laramie: The working cattle range offers unlimited riding, though you may be asked to assist with chores. *page 217*

Budget: under $50   Moderate: $50–$90   Deluxe: $90–$130   Ultra-deluxe: over $130

here before. Besides the restaurant and lounge, Foster's has a heated indoor swimming pool and whirlpool bath. Children under 12 stay free with parents. The moderate prices creep into the deluxe range during Frontier Days. ~ 1561 Snowy Range Road at Route 80, Laramie; 307-742-8371, 800-526-5145, fax 307-742-0884. MODERATE.

Well away from the motel strips is the **University Inn**, an older-style motel that faces the University of Wyoming campus. This is a great place for longer stays as all 37 rooms have refrigerators and microwaves. Six of the units are two-bedroom suites. ~ 1720 Grand Avenue, Laramie; 307-721-8855, fax 307-742-5919. MODERATE.

The largest of several bed and breakfasts in the same university district is **Annie Moore's Guest House**. The three guest rooms in this 1912 residence, a former fraternity and sorority house (though not, to the students' chagrin, at the same time), are bright, cheerful and accented with period antiques. Baths are shared; smoking is not permitted. A continental breakfast is included in the rates. ~ 819 University Avenue, Laramie; 307-721-4177. MODERATE.

For the ultimate Western experience, head south from Laramie 27 miles on Route 287 to the **Two Bars Seven Ranch** on the Wyoming–Colorado border. Up to 20 guests stay in the lodge complex between May and November, assisting on horseback with cattle-ranching chores, dining family-style at a single table and relaxing in the evenings around a fireplace. The big attraction is unlimited horseback riding (including instruction), but if you don't want to ride you may get a break on rates. All meals and activities are included. Minimum stay is three days; weekly is preferred. ~ P.O. Box 67, Tie Siding, WY 82084; phone/fax 307-742-6072; www.twobarssevenranch.com. ULTRA-DELUXE.

DINING

Primarily a bar, the **3rd Street Bar & Grill** attracts an upscale clientele that comes for its subdued atmosphere. But the gourmet pub fare is worth a visit; highlights include a portobello mushroom sandwich with a Thai peanut sauce, crudité served with a creamy artichoke/heart of palm dip, brie with almonds and crab-stuffed mushrooms. There's also a host of salads like chicken with mandarin oranges and pineapple. Closed Sunday. ~ 216 East Grand Avenue, Laramie; 307-742-5522. MODERATE.

The elegant **Overland Restaurant** sits beside the railroad tracks in Laramie's downtown historic district. Although three meals a day are served here, the specialties are wild game (tenderloin of red deer) and trout (pan-fried almandine), offered evenings with an award-winning wine list that features 57 cabernets alone. Everything is made from scratch. In the morning, try a malted waffle or a relleño omelet; at midday, a quiche, salad or sandwich such as a maple-mustard chicken breast. A patio is open for summer dining. ~ 100 Ivinson Avenue, Laramie; 307-721-2800. MODERATE.

Corona Village's menu features standard combination meals as well as Guadalajaran specialties such as *pollo en mole* (chicken in a chile-chocolate sauce), *carne asada* (charcoal-broiled steak) and *chile verde* (pork in a tomatillo sauce). You can also get fish tacos, not to mention the best margaritas in town. ~ First Gold Inn, 421 Boswell Street, Laramie; 307-721-0167. MODERATE.

Nearby is **Cafe Ole**, which has been dishing up Mexican and American food—chile rellenos, chimichangas, fajitas, steaks, burgers and chicken—for two decades. There's a children's menu (peanut butter and jelly sandwiches and the like), making this eatery popular with families. ~ 519 Boswell Drive, Laramie; 307-742-8383. MODERATE.

Vegetarians find an oasis at **Jeffrey's Bistro**, where a good selection of meatless dishes is always available. Other natural-foods plates, such as Siamese chicken and pasta primavera, appeal to students and travelers alike. The desserts are locally famous. Closed Sunday. ~ 123 Ivinson Avenue, Laramie; 307-742-7046. MODERATE.

Vitale's Italian Cowboy boasts one of just three wood-burning ovens in the state and they put it to good use. Cheese bread fresh from the oven is popular, as are the Sicilian-style and thin-crust pizzas. Lasagna, pasta, seafood, Italian sausage and steak entrées fill out the menu. Closed Sunday. ~ 2127 East Grand Avenue, Laramie; 307-755-1500. MODERATE.

Across the street from the University of Wyoming is **The Library**, possibly the only domed microbrewery in the world. Filled with bookshelves and other antique furnishings (so there's no need to lie to Mom about where you've been), The Library is noted for its generous portions and fine service. A lunch menu, served all

✔ **CHECK THESE OUT—UNIQUE DINING**

- *Budget to moderate:* Catch the mood of ceiling and floor paintings and a 40-foot jade bar at the **Old Dip Bar & Diner** in Medicine Bow. *page 230*
- *Moderate:* Find a good book at **The Library** in Laramie, then enjoy it with a steak and a beer in an unusual domed microbrewery. *page 218*
- *Moderate to deluxe:* Enjoy the early-American atmosphere of **Poor Richard's** in Cheyenne; Ben Franklin never had a salad bar this good. *page 210*
- *Deluxe:* Round up the whole family for three-pound "dream steaks" and Rocky Mountain oysters at **The Old Corral**. *page 225*

Budget: under $7   Moderate: $7–$12   Deluxe: $12–$20   Ultra-deluxe: over $20

day, features burgers and other sandwiches, salads and pizza; evening dining includes steaks, seafood, chicken dishes and pastas. ~ 1622 Grand Avenue, Laramie; 307-742-0500. MODERATE.

For an espresso drink or herbal tea any time of day, the place to head is the **Coal Creek Coffee Company**. This popular downtown gathering place also serves "organic" light meals such as soups, salads, whole-grain sandwiches and breakfast breads. It's open early 'til late. ~ 110 Grand Avenue, Laramie; 307-745-7737. BUDGET.

SHOPPING

The most interesting place to shop in Laramie is the small downtown historic district along Ivinson and Grand avenues, and along intersecting 2nd and 3rd streets. Here you'll find art galleries, antique shops, bookstores and much more.

NIGHTLIFE

Performing-arts programs and concerts of all kinds, from symphonic to jazz to touring popular artists, are held year-round on the **University of Wyoming** campus. Theater and concert seasons begin in October and run into May, and a summer music festival is launched in June. ~ University Avenue, Laramie; 307-766-1121.

Among student hangouts in the university area, one of the most popular is **The Library**. The domed microbrewery produces six different microbeers, which can be consumed right here amidst the brewing vessels. The 10,000-square-foot building is also noted for its collection of single-malt scotches and its sports-bar ambience. ~ 1622 Grand Avenue, Laramie; 307-742-0500.

The **Buckhorn Bar** is a popular student watering hole downtown. ~ 114 Ivinson Avenue, Laramie; 307-742-3554. Pool, darts, Foosball and other youthful distractions entertain a mostly college crowd at **Sins Saloon**. There are occasionally live bands when school is in session. Closed Sunday. Cover for live music. ~ 334 South Fillmore Street, Laramie; 307-745-9859.

A live blues band plays Friday nights at the **Fireside Lounge**. There's a dancefloor and outdoor patio seating when the weather's nice. Cover for live music. ~ 201 East Custer Street, Laramie; 307-745-0890.

For a bit of quietude with your martini, visit **3rd Street Bar & Grill**, a classy joint that also offers a light café menu with a gourmet touch. Closed Sunday. ~ 216 East Grand Avenue, Laramie; 307-742-5522.

PARKS

VEDAUWOO RECREATION AREA 🚶 🚲 The primary appeal of this nook in Medicine Bow National Forest is its rocky landscape. Strange and ancient sandstone formations have created a weird geology here. Not surprisingly, it's a hit among rock climbers, who you'll see here in precarious positions throughout the summer and weekends year-round. Facilities are limited to picnic areas and restrooms. ~ Located 17 miles southeast of Laramie at Exit 329 off Route 80; 307-745-8971 or 307-745-2300.

▲ There are 28 RV/tent sites (no hookups); closed November through April; $10 per night; 14-day maximum stay.

Saratoga and the Snowy Range

West of Laramie, the recreation-rich Medicine Bow National Forest embraces two short but rugged ranges of mountains. The Medicine Bow Mountains, better known as the Snowy Range, rise to more than 12,000 feet before dropping into the valley of the headwaters of the North Platte River. Located here is Saratoga, a hot-springs resort town of 2000 people that is the main population center of the region. West of Saratoga, the topography rises again to the Sierra Madre, which surpass 11,000 feet in elevation.

SIGHTS

The most traveled path for exploring the Snowy Range is Route 130, which runs west from Laramie to Saratoga, a distance of 79 miles, via 10,847-foot Snowy Range Pass. Formally known as the **Snowy Range Scenic Byway**, this paved highway rises to a higher elevation than any other major route in Wyoming. This being so, it's got a limited open season: Memorial Day weekend until the autumn's first major snowfall, usually sometime in October. Visitors centers on the eastern and western boundaries of Medicine Bow National Forest give information about the drive.

At the foot of the Snowy Range, 30 miles west of Laramie, is the old mining town of **Centennial**. The community has put on an Old West face for tourists, who have returned the favor by injecting new life into its restaurants and saloons, overnight cabins and gift shops. It was named in honor of the United States' 100th birthday when a quartz-rock gold mine was discovered nearby in 1876. Prospectors came from all directions to work four mines on a supposed mother lode, but their source soon disappeared, and the "Lost Centennial Lode" became a Wyoming legend.

Today Centennial is an outdoor recreational hub. Its little **Nici Self Museum** is worth a stop: Housed in a turn-of-the-century train depot, it exhibits items that illustrate the town's diverse mining, ranching, logging and railroading history. The museum is open from July 4 to Labor Day or by appointment; call for hours. ~ Route 130, Centennial; 307-742-7158.

Centennial is busy in the winter, too, as the gateway to the **Snowy Range Ski Area**, just four miles west of town. Wyoming's best outside of the Jackson Hole region has four lifts and 25 runs, and is open mid-November to mid-April, snow permitting. ~ Route 130, Centennial; 307-745-5750, 800-462-7669.

Snow usually does come early and stay late—that's why they call these mountains the Snowy Range. Route 130 rises almost imperceptibly across the grasslands from Laramie to Centennial, but west of the mining town the change is much more dramatic. Following tumbling Libby Creek into the highlands, 130 soon climbs to an alpine tundra region where a chain of crystal lakes fill glacial pockets. Their waters mirror the granite crags of 12,013-foot Medicine Bow Peak, so close you'll think you can throw a stone and pierce the snow that clings year-round to the north-facing slopes. At Snowy Range Pass, the **Libby Flats Observatory** offers a glorious panorama of the surrounding mountains, lakes and forests from a viewing platform. On the west side of the pass, the Sugarloaf Recreation Area encompasses pristine Lake Marie and Mirror Lake, both of which are surrounded by meadows ablaze with wildflowers in early summer. Keep your eyes peeled here for elk and mule deer, and perhaps—if you're lucky—a black bear or mountain lion.

Route 130 descends from the Snowy Range and crosses the uppermost section of the North Platte River, one of America's premier trout streams, eight miles from the isolated hot-springs resort community of **Saratoga**. When the town's developers came to the area in 1878, they envisioned it as a Western version of upstate New York's famed Saratoga Springs health spa, but it never really caught on. Perhaps they failed to take into account the distance from population centers.

Today, **Saratoga Hot Springs** are open to the public for free. They include a large swimming pool, a smaller hot pool and several small, muddy 114°F springs along the bank of Spring Creek. Hydrologists claim the clear, odorless water has a medicinal value equivalent to that of Germany's famous hot springs. ~ East Walnut Avenue, Saratoga; 307-326-8855.

The **Saratoga Museum** is located in the 1917 Union Pacific depot. It contains prehistoric American Indian artifacts, a replica of a homestead's interior, a blacksmith shop, a sheep wagon, a geology display and a research library of family histories, photographs and diaries. Open daily from Memorial Day weekend to Labor Day, by appointment other times. Admission. ~ 104 Constitution Avenue, Saratoga; 307-326-5511.

Two and a half miles north of town, then one and a half miles east on a dirt road, is the **Saratoga National Fish Hatchery**, established in 1915. The fingerlings and mature trout it raises are used to stock lakes and streams all over the nation. It's no accident that the headwaters of the North Platte River, which extends 64 miles south from here to its source in Colorado, is a nationally designated blue-ribbon trout fishery. The public is welcome to visit the hatchery. ~ County Road 207, Saratoga; 307-326-5662.

An alternative drive between Laramie and Saratoga is Route 230, also known as the **Rivers Road**. A longer, 105-mile trip, it finds a lower pass through the Snowy Range near the headwaters of the Laramie River and dives into Colorado's North Park for 18 miles. En route, it passes through several picturesque mountain villages. **Woods Landing**, 27 miles southwest of Laramie at the foot of 9656-foot Jelm Mountain, is notable as the home of the University of Wyoming's **Jelm Observatory**, one of the world's largest infra-red telescopes. The community of **Fox Park**, located about 11 miles beyond Woods Landing on a short side road, was for a long time the terminus of the now-defunct Wyoming & Colorado Scenic Railroad.

On the west side of the Snowy Range, 19 miles south of Saratoga and a mile south of the River Road on Route 70, is the interesting small town of **Encampment**. Named to acknowledge an area where Indian tribes once gathered during prolonged big-game hunts, the community was founded in 1897 when copper ore was discovered in the adjacent Sierra Madre range. During the subsequent decade, until the vein was exhausted, the town's population exceeded 5000 —more than ten times what it is today. Encampment had the largest smelter in the region, and a 16-mile-long tramway carried ore over the crest of the Sierra Madre from mines farther west.

Thomas Edison was fishing on Battle Lake, west of Encampment, in 1878 when he came up with the idea for a filament for the incandescent electric lamp.

A section of the tramway is among items now exhibited at the **Grand Encampment Museum**, three blocks south of the town's post office. Its highlight is a village of 14 ghost-town buildings, among them a homesteader's cabin, a saloon, a blacksmith shop, a newspaper office, an early forest-service lookout and a two-story outhouse. You'll also find prehistoric Indian artifacts, minerals, ranch equipment, horsedrawn vehicles, 19th-century apparel and rare historic photographs. Open daily, Memorial Day weekend to Labor Day, and weekends in September and October. ~ 817 Barnett Street; 307-327-5308 or 307-327-5310.

Today ranching and wood products support the economy of Encampment, which celebrates the latter industry with a timber carnival each June. Ruins of old copper mines can be found to the west in the **Sierra Madre**, which constitute part of Medicine Bow National Forest.

Route 70, also known as the Battle Highway, crosses the range at 9955-foot Battle Pass on the Continental Divide. (Like the Snowy Range Scenic Byway, this is closed in winter.) The ghost towns of Battle and Rambler are on either side of the pass, and on the west side of the Divide you'll also find enchanting little **Battle Lake**. Local legend maintains that, in 1878, inventor Thomas Edison was fishing here when he conceived the idea of a filament for the incandescent light bulb he was then developing. Looking at the frayed end of his bamboo fly rod, he intuited that carbonized bamboo might serve his purpose.

On the west side of the Sierra Madre in the valley of the **Little** ◄ *HIDDEN*
Snake River, a Yampa River tributary, is one of Wyoming's most
remote yet historic districts. Route 70 passes through Savery,
Dixon and Baggs, which also are accessible via Route 789 from
Rawlins (77 miles north of Baggs) or Craig, Colorado (41 miles
south). The valley's isolation made it a popular rendezvous point
for outlaws in the late 19th century: Butch Cassidy and his Wild
Bunch even made **Baggs** its favorite place to celebrate after lucrative holdups. A cabin that Cassidy built still stands here on the
old Main Street; it's called the Gaddis-Mathews House. **Dixon** is
known for the amateur rodeo it holds each June, while **Savery** is
the home of the **Little Snake River Valley Museum,** which displays
pioneer memorabilia in an old schoolhouse. Beside the museum
is a two-story log blockhouse built in the 1870s by mountain man
Jim Baker. Open Wednesday from Memorial Day through October. ~ Route 70; 307-383-7262.

Whether powdered with snow during winter or aspen-shaded in   **LODGING**
summer, the cabins at **Rainbow Valley Resort** are a relaxing getaway. All accommodations have full kitchens, refrigerators and
outdoor gas grills. The nearby national forest affords plenty of
opportunities for fishing, cross-country skiing, hiking and bird-
watching. Two-night minimum in winter; three-night minimum
in summer. ~ P.O. Box 135, Centennial, WY 82055; 307-745-
0368; www.rainbowvalleyresort.com. MODERATE TO DELUXE.

One of the most delightful places to stay in this part of Wyoming is the **Snowy Mountain Lodge,** located six miles west of Centennial. Built in 1927 as a summer study center for University of
Wyoming science students, it is now open year-round. There are
seven large cabins complete with full kitchens, private baths and
gas fireplaces; two mid-size ones with private baths and refrigerators; and four small cabins that share a bathhouse. The main
lodge has a fireplace, a full-service restaurant, cocktail lounge and
dancefloor. Your pet is welcome, too. In winter, you can rent
cross-country skis. ~ 3474 Route 130 (Snowy Range Road), Centennial; 307-742-7669. BUDGET TO DELUXE.

In the same neck of the woods is the **Brooklyn Lodge Bed &**
Breakfast. Built in the early 20th century by cohorts of Buffalo
Bill Cody, this pine lodge at 10,200 feet elevation offers alpine
serenity. There are but two nonsmoking rooms, each with a king-
size bed and a private sitting area; the bathroom is shared. In the
evening, guests gather around a huge stone fireplace. A full breakfast is served each morning and fresh-baked goodies are made
every afternoon. The highway to the lodge is closed from October
to Memorial Day weekend so winter access is by snowmobile or

cross-country skis only. ~ P.O. Box 292 (Route 130 West), Centennial, WY 82055; 307-742-6916. DELUXE.

The friendly innkeepers at **Far Out West Bed & Breakfast and Gathering Place** rent five individually decorated guest rooms and one three-room cottage. If fishing's your game, Far Out provides a fish-cleaning area complete with grills and smokers to prepare your catch. A filling country breakfast is served in the main house at your leisure. Beach towels are available if guests want to visit the nearby natural hot springs. ~ 304 North 2nd Street, Saratoga; 307-326-5869, fax 307-326-9864; www.cruising-america.com/farout.html. DELUXE.

The region's best-known historic structure is **Hotel Wolf** in Saratoga, a National Register property built in 1893 for just $6000. The large brick building has a trio of gables above its renowned dining room and lounge. The nine simple guest rooms are decorated with a few turn-of-the-century antiques. Request the "penthouse suite" behind the gables. ~ 101 East Bridge Street, Saratoga; 307-326-5525. BUDGET TO MODERATE.

If only modern lodging will do, the **Hacienda Motel** has you covered. This well-kept, two-story inn has 32 air-conditioned rooms with entrances off interior hallways. They include three efficiency units with refrigerators (but no utensils). Coffee's on the house. ~ Route 130 South, Saratoga; 307-326-5751. MODERATE.

A fine guest ranch, 16 miles southeast of Saratoga on a North Platte tributary, is the **Brush Creek Ranch.** The historic ranch was homesteaded in the 1880s and purchased in the early 1900s by heirs to the Schlitz Breweries fortune, who built a luxuriously rustic red-roofed, white-and-blue lodge on a ridge overlooking meadows and creek. Guests stay in private cabins with wood-paneled interiors and simple furnishings. Brush Creek is a working cattle ranch, and guests may participate in ranch chores if they wish. Activities include horseback riding, fishing, snowmobiling and cross-country skiing. Three-night minimum. ~ Brush Creek Road (Star Route Box 10), Saratoga; 307-327-5241, 800-726-2499. ULTRA-DELUXE.

Substantial, family-style meals are provided when you stay in one of twelve cabins at **Medicine Bow Lodge and Guest Ranch**. Fresh air, babbling streams and proximity to outdoor activities are big draws. Amenities include a hot tub, a sauna, a workout facility, and horse and snowmobile rentals. ~ Route 130, Saratoga; 307-326-5439, 800-409-5439; www.medbowlodge.com. ULTRA-DELUXE.

Vacher's Bighorn Lodge is a small motel with just 12 units (two have kitchenettes). Carpeted rooms, which have either one or two double beds, are individually decorated with cute touches such as elk wallpaper. There's a hot tub on the premises. ~ 508 McCaffrey Street, Encampment; 307-327-5110. BUDGET.

The Old Corral has been a Centennial institution for over half a century. Open for three meals daily much of the year, and for dinner Wednesday through Sunday in winter, it offers everything from burgers and fried chicken to Rocky Mountain oysters. Many folks come especially for the three-pound "dream steaks" that feed a whole family. ~ Route 130, Centennial; 307-745-5918. DELUXE.

The **Hotel Wolf Restaurant** draws raves from visitors. The casual yet highly regarded dining room serves more prime rib than any other menu item, though its steaks and seafood are also superb. Diners enjoy the salad bar and homemade desserts. An old-fashioned but elegant pub adjoins. ~ 101 East Bridge Street, Saratoga; 307-326-5525. DELUXE TO ULTRA-DELUXE.

If you don't mind getting your fingers greasy, **Bubba's Bar-B-Que Restaurant** may be the place for you. Its Texas-style chicken and pork combination platters come with all the fixin's. Plan on pie for dessert. ~ 119 North River Street, Saratoga; 307-326-5427. MODERATE.

A longtime Encampment favorite is the **Sierra Madre Cookhouse**, which serves up steak dinners and pizza. In the evening it shares clientele with the Pine Lodge Bar next door. Open Friday and Saturday nights and Sunday morning. ~ 520 McCaffrey Street, Encampment; 307-327-5203. MODERATE TO DELUXE.

DINING

The **Blackhawk Gallery** specializes in regional artwork, pottery and jewelry. Closed Saturday and Sunday from mid-October through April. ~ 100 North 1st Street, Saratoga; 307-326-5063. For gifts, try the **Fishpaw Trading Company**, near the Hotel Wolf. Closed Sunday from October through May. ~ 120 East Bridge Street, Saratoga; 307-326-5000.

Buggie Bear Station carries handmade, one-of-a-kind items including painted T-shirts, wool blankets, candles and home decorations. Closed Sunday from October to mid-May. ~ 106 East Bridge Street, Saratoga; 307-326-9663.

SHOPPING

MEDICINE BOW NATIONAL FOREST 🚶🚴🏇⛷️🏛️🛶🚤🎣 There are three divisions to this 1.1-million-acre national forest. The largest sections envelop the Medicine Bow Mountains (the Snowy Range) and the Sierra Madre on either side of Saratoga; the others are atop the Laramie Mountains east of Laramie and southeast of Casper. Unpaved roads provide access to most areas of the forest, but four small, roadless wilderness areas are accessible by trail only: Platte River and Savage Run, in the Snowy Range, and Encampment River and Huston Park, in the Sierra Madre. There's plenty of wildlife and superb trout fishing even in winter, when ice fishing is popular. Facilities include picnic areas and restrooms; groceries and restaurants are in several towns. ~ Three major highways—Route 210 (Happy Jack Road) between

PARKS

Cheyenne and Laramie, Route 130 (Snowy Range Scenic Byway) between Laramie and Saratoga (closed December through April), and Route 70 (Battle Highway) between Encampment and Savery (closed seasonally)—all cut through the national forest. The most direct access to the northern section is via Routes 91 and 94 southwest from Douglas; 307-358-4690.

▲ As a whole, the national forest has 38 campgrounds with 684 RV/tent sites (no hookups), the vast majority in the Snowy Range; $10 per night; 14-day maximum stay. Campsites may open as early as May 1 or as late as July 15 and may close as early as September 10 or as late as November 1.

▼▼▼▼▼▼▼▼▼▼▼▼▼▼▼▼▼▼

Medicine Bow and Rawlins

There are really two ways to get from Laramie to Rawlins. The standard 98-mile drive on the Route 80 freeway follows the old Overland Trail stagecoach and covered-wagon route across the high plains, around the north shoulder of Elk Mountain and into the valley of the North Platte River. But for those with a little more time and adventuresome spirit, the original Lincoln Highway—Route 30/287 through Medicine Bow—offers an alternative only 16 miles longer.

Medicine Bow's fame derives from its role in Owen Wister's 1902 book *The Virginian*, acclaimed by some as the "first great Western novel." The small town has retained an air of rawhide and six-guns even to this day. Rawlins, the largest community between Laramie and Rock Springs, has stepped beyond that; built on the Union Pacific line like so many other southern Wyoming towns, it is now a livestock-ranching center noted for its Old Frontier Prison. Between Medicine Bow and Rawlins are settlements like Hanna and Sinclair that built their economies on coal and oil.

SIGHTS

The old Lincoln Highway northwest from Laramie follows the Laramie River as far as tiny Bosler, then leaves the river as it crosses wide-open ranchland to Rock River, 39 miles from Laramie. This village along the Union Pacific tracks is of note solely for its intriguing little **Rock River Museum**, whose collection includes native rocks, dinosaur fossils and a safe that once was robbed by Butch Cassidy . . . or so the curator claims. ~ Route 30/287, Rock River.

One might disbelieve the Cassidy tale, but not the oversized fossils. Eleven miles further northwest, and just seven miles east of Medicine Bow, the highway passes the **Fossil Cabin**, built entirely of dinosaur bones. (It likes to call itself "the world's oldest building.") Sadly, it is not open to the public. ~ Route 30/287, Medicine Bow; 307-379-2383.

The bones come from **Como Bluff**, a couple of miles east of here. This ridge, on the south side of Rock Creek, is one of the world's great treasure troves of dinosaur skeletons. Since the first discovery was made here in 1877, Como Bluff has provided natural-history museums around the world with thousands of near-perfect bones to reconstruct brontosaurus, tyrannosaurus, triceratops and many other species. Eighty previously unknown vertebrate species have been uncovered at this site, now a National Natural Landmark. ~ County Road 610 (Marshall Road).

> Owen Wister's seminal Western novel, *The Virginian*, was set in Medicine Bow, Wyoming.

The name **Medicine Bow** is attributed to Plains Indians, probably Cheyennes, who found some of the best plant materials for their bows and arrows along the banks of this river. They called it "good medicine." Today this town of about 400 people has two sites of particular interest to tourists. **The Virginian Hotel**, built in 1911 after the publication of Owen Wister's novel and named in its honor, was once the largest and most sophisticated hotel along the rail route between Denver and Salt Lake City. ~ Main Street, Medicine Bow; 307-379-2377.

Across the street, the **Medicine Bow Museum** exhibits historical items such as old blacksmith tools and branding irons in a 1913 Union Pacific depot. On the grounds are a cabin where Wister lived in the 1890s, a restored caboose and a picnic area. Closed Labor Day to Memorial Day. ~ Main Street, Medicine Bow; 307-379-2383.

Also still standing, one block south of the main street, is the **general store**, where Wister spent his first night in Medicine Bow in 1885, there having been no room at the inn. Although he first described Medicine Bow as a "wretched husk of squalor," he later adopted it as his home and set large parts of *The Virginian* there. The book later was adapted for two stage plays, three movies (one starring a young Gary Cooper) and a 1960s television series.

Legend holds that the book's most timeless line was one that Wister overheard as he observed a high-stakes poker game in a saloon. "Why, you son of a bitch!" exclaimed one player when a deputy sheriff named James Davis displayed a winning hand. A stoic Davis responded: "When you call me that, smile."

The boom-and-bust coal town of **Hanna** is about 20 miles west of Medicine Bow. Founded as a fuel depot by the Union Pacific in 1889, it weathered two coalmining disasters (in 1903 and 1908), was revitalized in the 1970s but withered again in the '80s. More than 1000 people continue to live in the town, whose highlights are a pair of monuments that honor fallen miners. Route 30/287 rejoins interstate Route 80 at Walcott, some 36 miles west of Medicine Bow and 21 miles east of Rawlins.

The first half-hour of driving the **Overland Trail** route from Laramie is rather mundane. As the highway creases the northern edge of the Snowy Range, however, scenery becomes more impressive. At **Arlington**, 40 miles from Laramie on Rock Creek, buildings still stand from the 1860s: a homestead cabin and a log structure variously used as a general store, a blacksmith shop, a dance hall/saloon and a schoolhouse. Now part of the Pitcher Co. Ranch, they can be toured by appointment in summer and fall. ~ Wagon Hound Road, Arlington; 307-378-2333.

Just west is the town of **Elk Mountain**, which sits at the foot of a namesake 11,156-foot upthrust noted for its abundance of elk, mule deer and other wild game. Known to early pioneers as "The Crossing"—here was where they forded the Medicine Bow River—it has a restored 19th-century hotel and an adjacent dance hall that are on the National Register of Historic Places.

After picking up Route 30/287 at tiny Walcott, Route 80 crosses the North Platte River six miles further west at **Fort Fred Steele State Historic Site**. Here you'll find the remains of an army fort built in 1868 to protect the newly completed transcontinental railroad from Indian attacks. It was abandoned in 1886. Much of the abandoned fort was destroyed by fire in 1976, but an interpretive center is open May to mid-September, and the site offers a pleasant stretch of riverbank along the North Platte. ~ 307-320-3013.

Nine miles on, the interstate skirts **Sinclair**, once known as the "Wonder Town of Wyoming." Dubbed Parco when it was built in 1922 as a showpiece company town for Wyoming's first oil firm, the Producers Oil and Refining Co., its name was changed in 1943 when Sinclair Oil bought the town lock, stock and barrel. Remnants of the graceful Spanish mission–style architecture that set it apart from other communities in the region can still be seen. Sinclair was designed for 1500 residents but never reached that size; current population is about 500. Its modern refinery, which processes 54,000 barrels of crude oil a day, is visible for many miles around.

From Sinclair, a paved road runs north 34 miles to **Seminoe State Park** headquarters, just south of the Seminoe Dam. The

THE GENTLEMAN ROBBER

The best-known inmate of Rawlins' Frontier Prison was Bill Carlisle, the "gentleman robber." In three Union Pacific train robberies, he refused to take money from women. Some said he used the money to buy gifts for children. Pardoned in 1936, he became a motel owner in Laramie and published a book, *The Lone Bandit*.

17,000-acre recreation area encompasses Seminoe Reservoir, created in 1939 by the 295-foot concrete-arch dam just above the confluence of the Medicine Bow and North Platte rivers. Stretching 20 miles south and 15 miles east from the dam, the lake is surrounded not only by acres of sagebrush but also by a desolate area of giant white sand dunes. The lake is renowned for its fishing and other water sports; and perhaps because hunting isn't permitted in the park, wildlife abounds, including pronghorn antelope, bighorn sheep, elk and sage grouse. The name "Seminoe," incidentally, is a bastardization of the name of an early French trapper: Basil Cimineau Lejeunesse. ~ County Road 351 (Seminoe Dam Road); 307-320-3013.

Rawlins, six miles west of Sinclair, was founded in 1868 as the Union Pacific tracks were laid. Within two years, it had become an important junction for miners heading for the goldfields at South Pass. Through the 1870s, it had a well-deserved reputation as a town where outlaws had the upper hand over the law. But when the notorious "Big Nose" George Parrott was lynched and skinned by a vigilante committee of some of the town's established citizens in 1881, two dozen other known outlaws left town the next day. Today Rawlins is a sheep and cattle-ranching center, as well as a rail-shipment point for coal, oil, uranium and other mineral resources.

Rawlins' most provocative attraction is the **Wyoming Frontier Prison**, which replaced Laramie's Territorial Prison in 1901. The medieval-looking Frontier Prison was used for 80 years before a new penitentiary was opened south of town; the new state prison continues to be Rawlins' largest employer. One-hour guided tours of the Frontier Prison usher visitors through forbidding sandstone walls into austere cell blocks where graffiti drawn by inmates is still visible. You're also taken to the main dining area, exercise areas, an infirmary and an isolation dungeon. Unlike Laramie's Territorial Prison, this prison gives the impression that it was lived in until just yesterday: an impression preserved partly because it is used as a motion-picture location. But it didn't have indoor plumbing until 1951, and there was no hot water before 1978.

The ultimate eerie sight on the tour is the gas chamber, where five prisoners were executed. Prior to its installation in 1936, nine other men were hanged here. Photographs and prison artifacts are exhibited in the entry lobby. Open Memorial Day weekend through Labor Day and by appointment. Admission. ~ 5th Street at Walnut Street, Rawlins; 307-324-4422.

More conventional historic artifacts are displayed at the **Carbon County Museum**, including prehistoric Indian basketry and pottery, frontier firearms, pioneer quilts and embroidery, large stained-glass windows and photographs of 19th-century Rawlins. A collection of vehicles include a traditional herder's sheepwagon of a type said to have originated in Rawlins, as well as a 1920 hook-and-ladder firetruck. Open daily May through September; Monday, Wednesday and Saturday afternoons the rest of the year. ~ 9th and Walnut streets, Rawlins; 307-328-2740.

The **Rawlins-Carbon County Chamber of Commerce** produces an excellent 30-page brochure describing the city's downtown historic district, available on request. ~ 519 West Cedar Street, Rawlins; 307-324-4111, 800-228-3547; e-mail rcccoc@ trib.com.

LODGING

For historic flavor, you can't beat **The Virginian Hotel** in Medicine Bow. Built in 1911 and named in honor of Wister's novel, it was once the most important lodging on the track connecting Denver with Salt Lake City. Its two dozen second-story rooms have been restored with a bath in each one; toilets (down the hall) are shared. Another eight modern rooms with private baths are in a motel extension. If you want to splurge, you can reserve the four-room Owen Wister Suite for $75. The hotel also has a popular restaurant and lounge. ~ Lincoln Highway, Medicine Bow; 307-379-2377. BUDGET.

The **Bit O' Country Bed & Breakfast** is housed in a 1903 Queen Anne mansion. Two guest rooms have private baths and are furnished with antiques. A wraparound porch is great for relaxing and watching the world go by. In the evening, there are fresh-baked cookies. ~ 221 West Spruce Street, Rawlins; 307-328-2111, 888-328-2111; www.bbonline.com/wy/country. MODERATE.

For inexpensive accommodations, go and check out the **Rawlins Motel**, an older, one-story place with 25 homey units. Four are two-bedroom suites with refrigerators and microwave ovens. The rooms all have cable television, and the motel welcomes pets. ~ 905 West Spruce Street, Rawlins; 307-324-3456. BUDGET.

The most upscale spot in town is the **Best Western Cottontree Inn**, with a king- or queen-size bed in every one of its 122 rooms. Guests can enjoy a heated indoor swimming pool, hot tub and sauna, or take advantage of free privileges at a nearby health club. In the morning, coffee and a copy of *USA Today* are complimentary. A lounge and dining room also cater to guests. ~ 2300 West Spruce Street, Rawlins; 307-324-2737, 800-662-6886, fax 307-324-5011. MODERATE.

DINING

You might think twice about patronizing an establishment that calls itself the **Old Dip Bar & Diner**, but this Old Dip is the real thing. Named in honor of the diplodocus dinosaur, whose skeleton was first discovered nearby, it features a 40-foot jade bar cut from a four-and-a-half-ton boulder found near Rock Springs. The owner, an artist, uses the Old Dip as a vehicle for his work: paintings on ceiling, floor, walls and tables, and carved replicas of

Indian apparel. The food isn't nearly so creative, but it satisfies as standard American fare. Closed Sunday. ~ 202 Lincoln Highway, Medicine Bow; 307-379-2312. BUDGET TO MODERATE.

If you're sticking to Route 80 on your way from Laramie to Rawlins, and you find yourself hungry about halfway between, a good place to pull off the freeway is at the **Elk Mountain Trading Co. & Wild Wonder Cafe**. This classic general store offers great burgers and sandwiches, and you can't go wrong with the chili. ~ 205 Bridge Street, Elk Mountain; 307-348-7478. BUDGET.

For something more elaborate, you'll have to wait 'til Rawlins and **The Aspen House**. This turn-of-the-century manor is something of an anomaly on the arid high plains: It serves Singaporean cuisine, a blend of Chinese and Malay. But don't fret if you're not an Asian food fan. There's also a fine classic American menu of steaks, seafood, poultry and pasta, including some dishes prepared in the Cajun blackened style. Closed Sunday. ~ 318 5th Street, Rawlins; 307-324-4787. MODERATE.

The Pantry is the closest thing to a steakhouse in Rawlins. There are rib-eye, New York strip and tenderloin entrées on the menu, but you'll also find baked herb chicken, vegetarian stir fry, shrimp and salmon. Closed Sunday. ~ 221 West Cedar Street, Rawlins; 307-324-7860. MODERATE TO DELUXE.

SEMINOE STATE PARK 🚶 🛶 ⛺ 🚤 🛥️ 🚣 This remote, sprawling reservoir, with 180 miles of shoreline, is surrounded by huge white sand dunes and sagebrush country teeming with pronghorn. It is known for fine birdwatching as well as boating to wild backcountry shores. Fishing is excellent for brown, rainbow and cutthroat trout as well as walleye. Facilities include picnic areas, restrooms and a playground. Closed mid-October through April. ~ The entrance is located 34 miles north of Sinclair on paved Seminoe Road; 307-328-0115.

▲ Three campgrounds have 94 RV/tent sites (no hookups); $4 per night; 14-day maximum stay.

PARKS

▼▼▼▼▼▼▼▼▼▼▼▼▼▼
Outdoor Adventures

FISHING

The best fishing in this part of the state is along the **North Platte River**, two sections of which are rated "blue ribbon" trout fisheries by the U.S. Forest Service. These are the uppermost 64 miles of the river, between the Colorado border and the town of Saratoga; and the "Miracle Mile" (actually about four miles) between Pathfinder and Kortes reservoirs, eight miles north of the Seminoe Dam. Cast a fly here for rainbow, brook, brown or cutthroat trout.

In fact, trout are ubiquitous throughout the lakes, rivers and streams of southeastern Wyoming. Besides the North Platte and its various tributaries, you'll do well in the Laramie and Medicine Bow rivers as well. The small lakes of the Snowy Range are rife with hungry trout. Don't overlook the two small reservoirs at Curt Gowdy State Park; Lake Hattie Reservoir and neighboring lakes west of Laramie; or Saratoga Lake, just outside of Saratoga. And in big Seminoe Reservoir, you'll catch walleye pike as well. The season generally runs from mid-June through October.

Fishing access areas are well posted everywhere, especially along the North Platte. If you prefer a guide, Saratoga has two fine outfitters. **Hack's Tackle and Outfitters** provide half- and full-day trips with a full-service shop for bait and tackle. ~ 407 North 1st Street; 307-326-9823. The other is **Great Rocky Mountain Outfitters**, which offers similar excursions for rainbow, brown and cutthroat trout. ~ 216 East Walnut Street; 307-326-8750, 800-326-5390.

WATER SPORTS

Unquestionably the best place in the region for water sports of any kind is **Seminoe State Park**, which surrounds sprawling, 20-mile-long Seminoe Reservoir. There are boat ramps and a variety of facilities. Little Saratoga Lake, and Granite Springs Reservoir at Curt Gowdy State Park, are other reasonable options.

RIVER RUNNING

The Laramie and North Platte both offer excellent opportunities for river sports. The North Platte, in particular, has some superb whitewater through the **Platte River Wilderness** just above the Colorado border off Route 230. To run these rapids, contact **Rocky Mountain Adventures**. ~ P.O. Box 1989, Fort Collins, CO 80522; 970-493-4005, 800-858-6808. Or try **Platte Valley Outfitters**. ~ 307-326-5750.

For a more sedate outing, take a scenic float. The terrain along the Platte varies from alpine canyon to high desert. **Great Rocky Mountain Outfitters** offers customized half- and full-day excursions. ~ 216 East Walnut Street, Saratoga; 307-326-8750, 800-326-5390. Half-day floats are also available from **Medicine**

✔ **CHECK THESE OUT—UNIQUE OUTDOOR ADVENTURES**

- Cast your fly on the rippling waters of the North Platte River, which boasts blue-ribbon trout fishing south and north of Saratoga. *page 231*
- Launch your boat at sprawling Seminoe Reservoir and waterski past sand dunes, where you may spot pronghorn or sage hen. *page 232*
- Test your strength and courage rock climbing on the sheer granite cliffs of the Vedauwoo Recreation Area. *page 233*
- Practice your backcountry telemarking while cross-country skiing on the Libby Creek Trail in the Snowy Range west of Laramie. *page 233*

Bow Drifters. ~ P.O. Box 1642, Saratoga, WY 82331; 307-326-8002.

Many climbers will tell you that the best challenge in Wyoming is the **Vedauwoo Recreation Area,** 17 miles southeast of Laramie in Medicine Bow National Forest. From sheer cliffs to balanced rocks and oddly shaped granite formations, this is the place to come with ropes and pitons. It's open day and night, May to October. ~ Route 80 Exit 329, Laramie; 307-745-8971.

CLIMBING

The **Snowy Range Ski Area,** 32 miles west of Laramie and just four miles outside of Centennial, is Wyoming's best ski area outside of the Jackson Hole region. The area has one triple chairlift and three double cha]irs serving 25 runs on a 1000-foot vertical drop. There's also a snowboard park. A café and lounge are at the resort; rentals and instruction are also available here. Closed mid-April to mid-November. ~ Route 130, Centennial; 307-745-5750, 800-462-7669.

DOWNHILL SKIING

As might be expected from Laramie's large student population, cross-country skiing is a very popular winter sport, both to the east and west. The Medicine Bow Nordic Association maintains the extensive **Tie City/Happy Jack** network of trails 15 miles east of Laramie on the Happy Jack Road; they are groomed regularly for skating and set-track skiing.

CROSS-COUNTRY SKIING

From the **Snowy Range Ski Area,** 35 miles west, nordic skiers can connect to the Corner Mountain, Little Laramie and Libby Creek trail loops. Libby Creek is regarded as a difficult trail and provides backcountry telemark skiing.

Beginners enjoy the **Chimney Park** trail system on Route 230 southwest of Laramie, seven miles above Woods Landing. More challenging tracks begin at the Brush Creek Ranger Station on the west side of the Snowy Range via Route 130, and from the end of snowplowed Route 230 west of Encampment.

Ski Rentals In Laramie, **Fine Edge** rents downhill and cross-country skis, as well as snowboards. ~ 1660-E North 4th Street; 307-745-4499. **Cross Country Connection** at the Snowy Range Ski Area specializes in Nordic equipment. ~ Route 130; 307-745-5750.

For snowmobilers, the **Snowy Range** offers 186 miles of groomed trails and 129 miles of ungroomed but signed trails. Another 30 miles are groomed and 66 miles ungroomed in the **Sierra Madre.** The season generally runs from November through April; snow depths can exceed 12 feet.

WINTER SPORTS

Ice skaters will be pleased to find that the pond in Cheyenne's **Lions Park** is maintained as a skating rink in winter.

Text continued on page 236.

The Sport of Rodeo

The writhing bull bursts from its pen the moment the gate is yanked open, bucking and spinning, lunging and kicking, as if under some voodoo sorcerer's spell. Its muscled neck jerks in one direction, its rump strains the other way, and for a long moment it leaves its feet entirely and twists like a demonic contortionist into a one-ton pretzel.

Clinging by a single hand to a plaited rope around the bull's girth, stirrups locked into its thick sides, the cowboy is out for the ride of his life. Eight seconds is an eternity when you're atop a creature this massive, with horns like plowshares and hooves like blacksmith's anvils, especially when the bull is as angry as a yellowjacket in an abandoned outhouse.

Some people might say bull riders are the craziest of all cowboys, putting their lives on the line, week after week, for what more often than not is a meager paycheck.

"It's a dangerous sport, no doubt one of the most dangerous you can do," six-time world all-around champion Ty Murray told me in 1997. "But if it wasn't, guys probably wouldn't do it, and people certainly wouldn't come watch it."

And watch it they do. It's estimated that a quarter-million people come to Cheyenne for its Frontier Days celebration, featuring the world's largest professional rodeo, in late July each year. Throughout Wyoming, there are rodeos all summer long. Full weekends are devoted to the sport, with parades, barbecues, street dances and country entertainment complementing the main event.

Rodeo evolved in the late 19th century from cowboys' desire to see who was the best calf roper, bronc rider or steer wrestler. Prize money and silver belt buckles were awarded to the winners, who often reinvested their earnings into next year's circuit. Losers usually gained nothing but broken bones.

A rodeo has six principal events: saddle bronc riding, bareback bronc riding, bull riding, steer wrestling, calf roping (team and individual) and women's barrel racing. Scoring is based on difficulty (stronger, more temperamental animals earn the riders higher points) and, in the latter three events, speed. Thus, while skill and courage are essential ingredients, winners also take the luck of the draw in being matched with higher-scoring livestock.

Rides on bucking broncos last but eight seconds: horses are released from chutes (fenced-in enclosures) with riders already aboard. With saddle broncs, cowboys dig in with stirrups and hold onto a thick rope rein; with bareback broncs, there are no stirrups and no reins, only a pair of tightly cinched straps to which the rider clings. The horses buck wildly to throw their passengers off; cowboys who succeed in staying aboard do so with a rhythmic rocking motion. A pickup man rides alongside the bucking horse when the eight-second clock has sounded, and the rider slides off to safety.

Bull riding is considerably more dangerous. Riders must attempt to remain on the back of a 2000-pound bull for eight full seconds while clenching a single thick rope wrapped around its chest. The bull jumps, kicks and rams the wall to throw its rider, then it may turn and attack with its horns or hooves. Some riders have died, and many have been seriously injured. As fallen bull riders attempt to escape their foes, they put their faith in foolish-looking but daring rodeo clowns who risk their lives to lure bulls away from the cowboys until they can be recaptured.

In steer wrestling (also known as bulldogging) a cowboy must leap from his horse onto the back of a full-grown steer, grab his horns, and wrestle him to the ground with his feet and head facing the same direction. This involves a two-man team: a mounted "hazer" forces the steer to run straight ahead while the "dogger" gets into position for his leap. A good team can take down a 700-pound steer, running at 25 miles per hour, in less than seven seconds.

Team calf roping, perhaps the truest test of a cowboy's skill, is the most highly contested of all events. Riding trained horses, two riders lasso a young heifer (which may weigh 250 to 300 pounds)—one by the neck, one by the hind legs. They quickly leap from their horses and tie it (as if for branding); if the calf cannot free itself within six seconds, the time stands and an "untie man" frees the animal.

Barrel racing is a speed and agility event. Competing women ride their horses in a set pattern around a triangular course of three barrels spaced 100 feet apart. Penalty seconds are added to times for any barrels that are knocked over.

GOLF   Public golf courses are numerous throughout the region and are generally open from April through October. Visitors are welcome to play the flat, full-service course at the **Warren Golf Club**. ~ Randall Avenue at Route 25, Cheyenne; 307-773-3556. And Laramie has its public, flat **Jacoby Park Golf Course**. ~ North 30th Street; 307-745-3111.

Nine-hole public courses in the region include **Kinghams Prairie View Golf Course** ~ 3601 Windmill Road, Cheyenne, 307-637-6420; **Little America Golf Course** ~ 3800 West Lincolnway, Cheyenne, 307-775-8400; the **Saratoga Inn Golf Course** ~ Pic Pike Road, Saratoga, 307-326-5261; and the **Sinclair Golf Course** ~ Seminoe Road, Sinclair, 307-324-3918.

TENNIS   Tennis is played from October through May at Cheyenne's **Frontier Tennis Center** on four indoor courts. Fee. ~ Frontier Park, Hynds Street and 8th Avenue; 307-778-7280. In summer, racqueteers take to the courts in various city parks: **Brimmer Park** (Pershing and Windmill streets), **Holliday Park** (17th and Morrie avenues); **Jaycee Park** (Dillon and Foyer streets); **Martin Luther King Park** (17th Avenue and Ames Street); and **Pioneer Park** (Talbot Court and Cribbon Street).

RIDING STABLES   The trails of Medicine Bow National Forest—in the Laramie, Medicine Bow (Snowy) and Sierra Madre ranges—offer wonderful opportunities for horseback riding. Guest ranches are the best places to find yourself a mount; check the "Lodging" listings above. In Cheyenne, the **Terry Trading Post** conducts guided trips and will rent you a horse by the hour. ~ Route 25 Exit 2; 307-634-4171.

PACK TRIPS   Numerous outfitters take small groups into the mountains on trips ranging from a single day to a week or longer. In Cheyenne, contact **High Mountain Horseback Adventures** for multi-day trips. ~ 3803 Route 80 South Service Road; 307-632-4087. In Laramie, call on **Horseshoe Pack Trips**. ~ P.O. Box 1441, Laramie, WY 82070; 307-745-8362. **Round Oak Trails** offers overnight to three-day trips into Medicine Bow National Forest from Memorial Day to Labor Day. ~ Box 7096, Laramie, WY 82070; 307-755-1855.

BIKING   An extensive network of forest roads and four-wheel-drive trails makes the portion of Medicine Bow National Forest west of Laramie and south of the Snowy Range Scenic Byway a mountain bikers' paradise. The Continental Divide Trail northwest from Battle Mountain, in the Sierra Madre near Encampment, is another favorite spot. Bikes are not allowed in wilderness areas, of course, but they can go anywhere else that rubber treads will take them.

For the slightly less adventurous, the **Cheyenne Greenway** offers a flat, paved nine-mile path for moderate exercise. Maps are available; call 307-637-6285. There are also bike paths at Holliday and Lions parks in Cheyenne. **The Bicycle Station**, located on the Greenway path, provides rentals, sales and repairs. ~ 307-634-4268.

Medicine Bow National Forest offers superb hiking, especially in the Snowy and Sierra Madre ranges. All distances listed here are one way unless otherwise noted.

HIKING

LARAMIE AREA Easily accessible is the **Headquarters National Recreation Trail** (6 miles), which runs around Pole Mountain from the Summit Rest Area east of Laramie. The high-use **Vedauwoo Glen Trail** is short (.6 mile) but steep.

SARATOGA AND THE SNOWY RANGE In the Snowy Range west of Laramie, the **Medicine Bow Peak Trail** (6 miles) ascends 1600 feet from the trailhead at Lake Marie to the 12,013-foot summit of the highest mountain in the area. The **Lost Lake Trail** (3.2 miles) branches off midway up the mountain and leads across open meadows to another alpine lake.

From Encampment, you can take Route 230 southeast 23 miles to Forest Road 492, which leads another two miles to the trailhead of the **Platte River Trail** (6.5 miles) within the Platte River Wilderness. The track descends steeply, then follows the river north to a campground off BLM Road 3423.

MEDICINE BOW AND RAWLINS The **Rock Creek National Recreation Trail** (7 miles) begins near Arlington, just off Route 80, and climbs a steep-sided canyon through a historic mining district at the foot of Lookout Mountain.

▼▼▼▼▼▼▼▼▼▼

Transportation

Interstate **Route 80** is the dominant route through this part of Wyoming, connecting Cheyenne, Laramie and Rawlins en route to Rock Springs and Salt Lake City. **Route 25** intersects Route 80 at Cheyenne; south is Denver, north is Casper.

CAR

Another important road is **Route 287**; from Fort Collins, Colorado, it transits Laramie and Medicine Bow, briefly joins Route 80, then breaks northwesterly at Rawlins en route to Yellowstone National Park.

Cheyenne Airport is served by United Express (307-635-6623) commuter flights from Denver. There's also a charter service, Sky Harbor (307-634-1117), here. Laramie, Rawlins and Saratoga have smaller airports that handle noncommercial flights.

AIR

BUS   Greyhound Bus Lines operates several buses a day in both directions on Route 80. ~ 1503 Capitol Avenue, Cheyenne; 307-634-7744. Located at the same station, **Powder River Transportation** provides transportation to Casper and northern Wyoming destinations. ~ 307-635-1327.

Greyhound also stops in Laramie at 4700 Bluebird Lane, 307-742-5188; and in Rawlins at 11th and Spruce streets, 307-324-4196.

CAR RENTALS   Agencies operating from Cheyenne Airport include **Avis Rent A Car** (800-331-1212), **Dollar Rent A Car** (800-800-4000), **Enterprise Rent A Car** (800-325-8007) and **Hertz Rent A Car** (800-654-3131).

PUBLIC TRANSIT   The state capital's citywide bus service is **Cheyenne Transit**. Call for routes and information. ~ 307-637-6253.

The **Cheyenne Street Railway**, a mid-May through September trolley service, offers two-hour historic tours of major attractions to city visitors. Tours depart twice daily (more frequently in July) from the intersection of Lincolnway and Capitol Avenue. Purchase tickets from the Cheyenne Area Convention and Visitors Bureau. ~ 309 West Lincolnway; 307-778-3133, 800-426-5009.

TAXIS   All of the major towns of the region have taxi service. In Cheyenne, contact **The Taxi/Yellow Cab**. ~ 307-635-5555. In Rawlins, try **City Cab**. ~ 307-328-1039.

EIGHT

The North Platte Valley

The North Platte River is all but synonymous with the Oregon Trail. This granddaddy of all emigrant trails followed the Platte from central Nebraska through eastern Wyoming, then picked up its tributary Sweetwater River for the final miles to South Pass on the Continental Divide. Three hundred fifty thousand pioneers traveled the Oregon Trail—more than on all other routes combined—between the first organized wagon-train expedition in 1842 and the completion of the first transcontinental railroad in 1869.

Wagon trains found it easy to navigate the flood plain of the wide, shallow Platte across the prairies. By contrast, Colorado's mountains could not be scaled by wagons loaded with household goods; farther south, hostile Apaches and the parched Southwest desert made skirting the south end of the Rockies unthinkable.

Today reminders of this pivotal era in American history are legion throughout east-central Wyoming. There are the mid-route oases of Fort Laramie (now a meticulously restored national historic site), Fort Fetterman and Fort Caspar. There are "graffiti walls" at Register and Independence rocks, and wagon ruts permanently chiseled into riverside rock. Most of all, there are the towns that would not be here—places like Torrington, Douglas and Casper—had not these westward-bound settlers first paved the way for the ranchers and homesteaders, loggers and oilmen, who followed.

The Oregon Trail saw three major migrations, all beginning within a few years of one another and overlapping. The first wagon trains were organized by land developers, whose exaggerated tales of rich farmland for the taking in Oregon's Willamette Valley enticed families by the thousands away from the poverty of northeastern industrial cities. Around the same time, the Mormons, then a newly formed religious group on the run from intolerance and frequent mob violence in the Midwest, sought a place to built a "new Zion" in the unexplored West. They followed the Oregon Trail as far as South Pass, then turned southwesterly to reach their promised land on the shores of the Great Salt Lake.

Within three years after the Oregon Trail was opened, gold was discovered in northern California, swelling the traffic along the wagon route with thousands of would-be prospectors hoping to get rich. In April 1849, when news of the first California gold discoveries reached the East, 20,000 people set out on the Oregon Trail in a single month—more than the total number who had gone west up to that time.

Many people headed west alone on horseback, with nothing but what could be carried behind their saddles. A covered wagon, needed to carry a family and basic household goods, was expensive. To buy a wagon, a team of horses, mules or oxen, and food and supplies for the 2000-mile journey cost about $1200. This was more than an average American family earned in a year.

The greatest significance of the route from Fort Laramie to South Pass was that all major emigrant trails came together here. The Oregon Trail had many branches and spur routes, but they converged along this 250-mile stretch. This was even a part of the 1860-61 Pony Express route and the original Overland Stage Route.

At Independence Rock and other Oregon Trail landmarks, modern travelers find crosses and bright wildflowers on the graves of pioneers who did not survive the rugged six-month trip. About 20,000 people—one every 18 who traveled the Oregon Trail—died along the way. Although traditional Hollywood Westerns would have us believe that the greatest hazard the pioneers faced was hostile Indians, the truth is that Indian violence was rare until the 1860s. The biggest killer on the Oregon Trail was cholera, from drinking water that had been inadvertently polluted by earlier travelers.

The old Oregon Trail remains a major traffic route through the West. A section is paralleled by Route 25, the interstate freeway, which connects Casper with Cheyenne (to the south) and Sheridan (to the north). Route 26 follows the North Platte downstream from north of Wheatland past Fort Laramie, while Route 220 southwest of Casper is the main route past Independence Rock toward South Pass. More than 350,000 vacationers each summer—as many pioneers as traveled the original Oregon Trail in its entire history—follow these routes between the Midwestern states and Yellowstone National Park.

▼▼▼▼▼▼▼▼▼▼▼▼▼▼

Fort Laramie Area

The lowermost section of Wyoming's North Platte River Valley has always been a rich agricultural area. The earliest American Indian inhabitants grew crops in the river valley and hunted in the uplands nearby. They were driven out by nomadic Plains tribes, who themselves were displaced as first traders, then settlers moved in.

Fort Laramie, the most important outpost on the entire Oregon Trail, was built on the banks of the North Platte in 1834 and remained active until 1890. Now fully restored and administered by the National Park Service, it is the focus of any traveler's visit to this part of Wyoming. In the surrounding area are several other sites of historical interest, as well as two of Wyoming's finest state parks for water sports and such friendly farming towns as Torrington and Wheatland.

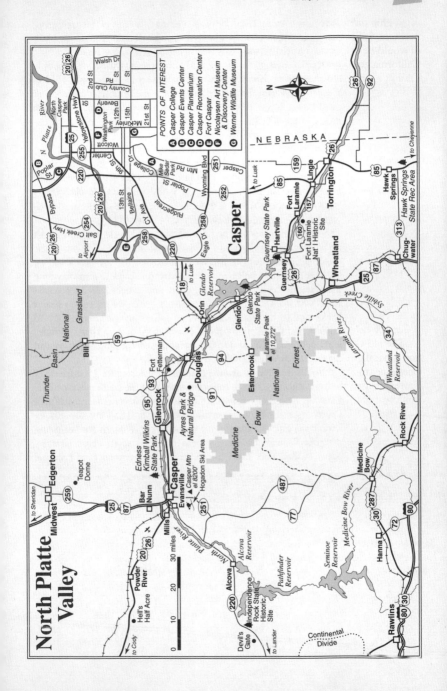

North Platte Valley

POINTS OF INTEREST

Ⓐ Casper College
Ⓑ Casper Events Center
Ⓒ Casper Planetarium
Ⓓ Casper Recreation Center
Ⓔ Fort Caspar
Ⓕ Nicolaysen Art Museum & Discovery Center
Ⓖ Werner Wildlife Museum

Casper

NEBRASKA

SIGHTS

Travelers coming from Nebraska enter this region at **Torrington**, just eight miles west of the state border and on the north bank of the North Platte. Now the heart of a farming region known for its sugar beets, potatoes and corn, this town of 5700 people also has a long history as a livestock ranching center. Its **Homesteaders Museum**, housed (like so many community museums) in an old train depot, displays historical items mainly dating from the area's 1880–1930 homesteading era. Outstanding are its black-and-white photographs; the collection also includes a furnished settler's shack. ~ 495 Main Street; 307-532-5612.

HIDDEN ►

A busy agricultural district extends south of the Platte along Horse Creek past villages like Huntley, Veteran and Yoder. A half hour's drive south of Torrington you'll find the **Hawk Springs State Recreation Area**, a quiet spot for water sports and bird-watching. ~ Route 85, LaGrange; 307-836-2334.

A half-mile west of the farming town of Lingle, ten miles west of Torrington, the **Grattan Massacre Monument** recalls a tragic episode in the history of the West. In August 1854, a Sioux Indian killed a cow that belonged to a Mormon wagon train traveling the Oregon Trail. Lt. John Grattan and a detail of 28 soldiers were sent from Fort Laramie to investigate. When an argument broke out at the Sioux camp, one of Grattan's soldiers shot and killed Chief Conquering Bear. The Sioux—among them a young warrior named Crazy Horse—retaliated by killing Grattan and his entire command. ~ Route 157, Lingle.

You'll find **Fort Laramie National Historic Site** 23 miles west of Torrington and three miles southwest of the small town of Fort Laramie, near the point where the Laramie River enters the North Platte. Established as a small stockade in 1834 by the Rocky Mountain Fur Company and named Fort William for founding member William Sublette, it was replaced seven years later by adobe-walled Fort John. In 1849, it was renamed Fort Laramie

✔ CHECK THESE OUT—UNIQUE SIGHTS

- Relive the 19th century at **Fort Laramie National Historic Site**, a trading post-turned-army garrison on the North Platte River. *page 242*
- Tip your hat to the ten-foot jackalope, a mythical half-rabbit, half-antelope creature, at Douglas' **Centennial Jackalope Square**. *page 248*
- Wonder at nature's power when you view **Ayres Natural Bridge**, a 150-foot-wide sandstone cliff with a stream running beneath it. *page 248*
- Peruse the face of **Independence Rock** for the names of more than 5000 Oregon Trail travelers who carved their signatures on this huge granite dome. *page 257*

after it was purchased (for $4000) and garrisoned by the federal government to protect westbound migrants. It subsequently was a major player in opening the way for the transcontinental railroad, subduing the Plains Indians and developing the open-range cattle industry. The fort remained in Army hands until it was decommissioned in 1890, a final chapter in the closing of the frontier.

When Fort Laramie was shut down, its 67 buildings and surrounding land were sold at public auction. The site remained deserted until 1937, when the Wyoming Legislature purchased the fort and turned it over to the U.S. government, which put it under National Park Service control the following year. Of 22 original structures that remained, eight have been restored and furnished to recapture some of the fort's 19th-century flavor. Among them are "Old Bedlam," which served both as bachelor officers' quarters and the post commander's office; the surgeon's quarters, and the sutler's (provisioner's) store.

A visitors center and museum, located in the 1884 commissary, displays articles illustrating the military, Indian and civilian history of the fort and surrounding plains. Here also are historic photos and a scale model of Fort Laramie in its heyday. You can enjoy an audiovisual presentation here or join a ranger-conducted tour. From June through the middle of August, Park Service personnel don period costumes and re-enact frontier life; the highlight of the season is the Fourth of July celebration. Admission. ~ Route 160, Fort Laramie; 307-837-2221.

Three miles above Fort Laramie, an old **iron Army bridge** spans the North Platte River. One of the first of its kind west of the Missouri River, it was built in 1875 at a cost of $15,000, quite a sum in those days.

The small town of **Guernsey** is 13 miles west of Fort Laramie on Route 26 near the mouth of the Platte River Canyon. Two important historical sites are just south of the town via Wyoming Avenue. It's only a mile to the **Oregon Trail Ruts National Historic Landmark**, where you can get a vivid picture of how many covered wagons passed this way a century and a half ago. Ruts as deep as six feet, created by thousands of heavy wagon wheels and the hooves of oxen, have been worn into an outcropping of soft sandstone just above the banks of the North Platte. Beside the ruts, which extend for several hundred yards, are footpaths used by those who walked alongside the wagons. Interpretive signs are placed along self-guiding trails. This may be the single best remaining vestige of the old Oregon Trail. ~ South Wyoming Avenue, Guernsey.

Another two miles southeast from here is **Register Cliff State Historic Site**, where thousands of pioneers etched their names in the lower reaches of a 150-foot-high sandstone bluff. A day's trek (11 miles) from Fort Laramie, this chalky formation enticed travelers, who camped overnight at its base to carve their names—as well as their cities of departure and intention, and the dates of their visit—into its soft rock. As time passed, it came to be regarded as a sort of giant guest book or hotel register. Most of the inscriptions date from the 1840s and 1850s. A trail along the base of the cliff makes the etchings easy to view. ~ South Guernsey Road, Guernsey.

In fact, soft limestone is found throughout the North Platte Valley around Guernsey. This has proven useful not only for building homes and tools: The first commercially developed deposit of moss agate (for export to Germany) came from this area in the late 1800s. Shortly thereafter, copper was discovered in the area; the village of **Hartville**, six miles north on Route 270, was built near the mines in 1884. This picturesque community has several buildings surviving from that era, including a stone jail and a couple of saloons-cum-restaurants.

HIDDEN ►

Guernsey State Park is three miles northwest of the town of Guernsey on a winding, S-shaped reservoir of the same name. Beautiful Guernsey Reservoir is surrounded by bluffs that shield its waters from wind and keep it a tranquil haven for water sports. Campgrounds and picnic sites are nestled in canyons and on sandy beaches. The park also features several handsome stone-and-timber structures built in the 1930s by the Civilian Conservation Corps; one of them is now the visitors center and museum with exhibits that focus on the area's American Indian and Oregon Trail history as well as its geology and wildlife. The park (admission) is open year-round; the museum is closed from October through April. ~ Route 317, Guernsey; 307-836-2334, 307-836-2900 (museum).

Fifteen miles west of Guernsey, the old Oregon Trail route joins Route 25 in a sagebrush landscape and leaves you with a choice of whether to turn south or north.

South of this junction 13 miles is **Wheatland**, a modest and aptly named town that owes its origin to the Carey Act. This legislation, written by Wyoming Senator Joseph M. Carey and passed by Congress in 1894, offered up to one million acres of federal land to any state that could irrigate and farm it within ten years. Homesteaders poured into the area, built a system of dams and canals, and in no time transformed the valley of the North Platte into productive farmland. Today irrigated wheat remains the region's primary crop. You can learn more about the homesteading era at the town's **Laramie Peak Museum**. Closed October through April. ~ 1601 16th Street North, Wheatland; 307-322-2322.

Load up on maps and brochures at the **Platte County Chamber of Commerce**, which serves Wheatland, Glendo and Guernsey. Closed Saturday and Sunday from Labor Day to Memorial Day; closed Sunday from Memorial Day through Labor Day. ~

65 16th Street, Wheatland; 307-322-2322; e-mail services@platte chamber.com.

For recreation lovers, Wheatland is a gateway to a section of Medicine Bow National Forest crowned by 10,272-foot **Laramie Peak**, the first of the Rocky Mountains that could be seen by westbound pioneers as they trekked up the valley of the North Platte. There's a popular hiking trail to the summit.

Twenty-eight miles southwest of Wheatland, en route to Laramie, is the **Sybille Wildlife Research and Education Center** administered by the Wyoming Game & Fish Department. Learn about native wildlife at the visitors center. Also here are research pens for big game (depending on the weather, you may or may not catch a glimpse of the animals) and a nature trail beside Sybille Creek. Tours can be arranged with advance notice. Closed mid-September through April. ~ 2362 Route 34, Wheatland; 307-322-2784.

◄ *HIDDEN*

North of the Route 26 junction, you can exit Route 25 at tiny Glendo, once a stage stop on the early Overland Trail, and drive southeast five miles to **Glendo State Park** headquarters. Covering 35 square miles and virtually surrounding Glendo Reservoir, the park offers clear waters, sandy beaches and pine-forested campgrounds to outdoors enthusiasts. A full-service marina is one attraction; others are abundant wildlife and sand dunes that rise on the east side of the reservoir. ~ Glendo Park Road, Glendo; 307-735-4433.

Just a few miles in from the Nebraska state line is the **King's Inn**, where you'll get bang for your buck. The two-story motor inn has 52 rooms, an indoor swimming pool and jacuzzi, a full-service restaurant and cocktail lounge, even room service. Guest rooms have cable TV and, for traveling businesspeople, data ports for computers. ~ 1555 Main Street, Torrington; 307-532-4011, 888-532-4011, fax 307-532-7202. MODERATE.

LODGING

▸▸▸

✔ CHECK THESE OUT—UNIQUE LODGING

- *Budget:* Save your money for tracking down the elusive jackalope in Douglas by checking into **The Chieftain**. *page 250*
- *Moderate:* Seize some pioneer spirit when you walk from your room at **The Bunkhouse Motel** through the nearby Oregon Trail Ruts. *page 246*
- *Moderate:* Relax in a clawfoot bathtub at an old railroad inn, the **Hotel Higgins,** without the disturbance of phones or TVs. *page 250*
- *Ultra-deluxe:* Help the hands with sheep- and cattle-tending chores, then relax with a game of volleyball at the **Cheyenne River Ranch**. *page 250*

Budget: under $50   Moderate: $50–$90   Deluxe: $90–$130   Ultra-deluxe: over $130

The rustic Old West decor of **The Bunkhouse Motel** will remind you that the Oregon Trail Ruts are about two miles away. All 31 rooms have cable television, and some have refrigerators. ~ 350 West Whalen Street, Guernsey; 307-836-2356, fax 307-836-2328. MODERATE.

A fenced-off pool and spa are the centerpieces of the two-story **Best Western Torchlite Motor Inn**. All 50 modern rooms boast two queen beds and have refrigerators and data ports; there's free coffee in the lobby anytime, and a restaurant is open for lunch and dinner. In the family spirit, your pet is welcome here. ~ 1809 North 16th Street, Wheatland; 307-322-4070, 800-662-3968, fax 307-322-4072. MODERATE.

DINING

Eight miles east of Torrington, virtually on the state line, is the **Little Moon Lake Supper Club**. Farm families out for a special evening swear by its steaks and seafood. A screened-in patio makes outdoor dining a treat. Dinner only. Closed Sunday. ~ Route 26; 307-532-5750. MODERATE TO DELUXE.

Vimbo's Restaurant is a family dining establishment in Wheatland that offers three square meals every day. Although associated with Vimbo's Motel, it draws a heavily local clientele for its varied American menu, especially steaks, and its casual cocktail lounge. ~ 203 16th Street, Wheatland; 307-322-3725. MODERATE TO DELUXE.

PARKS

HAWK SPRINGS STATE RECREATION AREA 🏊 🎣 ⛵ 🚤 🛶 A prairie oasis, Hawk Springs is an off-the-beaten-path destination for boating, fishing and picnicking beneath shady cottonwood trees. Great blue herons and a variety of migratory waterfowl delight bird watchers. There are picnic areas and pit toilets. Day-use fee, $2 to $3 per vehicle. ~ From Torrington, take Route 85 south 23 miles; two miles past the junction of Route 313, turn east for three miles on County Road 186; 307-836-2334.

▲ There are 24 RV/tent sites (no hookups), available year-round; $4 per night; 14-day maximum stay.

GUERNSEY STATE PARK 🏃 🚴 🏇 🚣 🎣 ⛵ 🚤 🏊 This Platte River reservoir, nestled among sheltering cliffs, has sandy beaches and scenic side canyons. A collection of historic CCC buildings from the Depression era houses a museum (307-836-2900) of natural history and American Indian and pioneer artifacts. There is a full marina, plus picnic areas and restrooms. The reservoir is drained after July 4th weekend, until July 31. Day-use fee, $2 to $3 per vehicle. ~ From Guernsey, take Route 26 west one mile, then Route 317 north three miles; 307-836-2334.

▲ There are 142 RV/tent sites (no hookups), available year-round; $4 per night; 14-day maximum stay.

GLENDO STATE PARK 🏕️ 🚴 ⛵ ⛴️ 🎣 🛶 🚤 🏊 ⛷️ This reservoir on the Platte River is one of Wyoming's prettiest, with sandy beaches and crystal-clear water. High rock bluffs surround the lake, protecting it from wind. It is a popular recreational site for all water sports. Facilities include picnic areas, restrooms, a playground and a full-service marina (307-735-4216) with boat and fishing-gear rentals available. Day-use fee, $3 per vehicle. ~ Park headquarters are five miles east of the town of Glendo, on Glendo Park Road off Route 25; 307-735-4433.

🔺 There are seven campgrounds with 165 RV/tent sites (no hookups), available year-round; $4 per night; 14-day maximum stay.

▼▼▼▼▼▼▼▼▼

Douglas Area

Mention Douglas to the average Wyomingite, and he or she will think of one thing: the state fair. For nearly 100 years, since 1905, this small (5500 people), centrally located town has hosted one of Wyoming's preeminent events each August. The Wyoming State Fair and Rodeo is renowned for its livestock expositions, its arts-and-crafts displays and the three days of professional rodeo that conclude its run, as well as its authentic old-time county fair atmosphere.

But there's more to Douglas, and to the surrounding area, than the fair itself. Don't miss Fort Fetterman, a historic army post preserved by the state; Ayres Natural Bridge, a sandstone cliff through which flows a mountain stream; or Thunder Basin National Grassland, a regenerated dustbowl where pronghorn antelope now graze side-by-side with sheep and cattle.

SIGHTS

Situated 60 miles north of Wheatland (and 50 east of Casper) via the interstate, **Douglas** is another Wyoming town that grew up near a historic fort on the banks of the North Platte River. Although Fort Fetterman, 11 miles northwest, pre-dated the town by nearly 20 years, railroad executives preferred this site when they laid out Douglas in 1886. Initially a cattle-shipping center, that industry was soon eclipsed by agriculture, which remains paramount today.

Any time of year, the main attraction in Douglas is the State Fairgrounds, which spread across 113 acres at the west end of town. Here is located the excellent **Wyoming Pioneer Memorial Museum**. Its extensive collection of American Indian and frontier artifacts include a full-size tepee, pioneer clothing and weaponry, and a relocated one-room schoolhouse and old-time saloon. Open daily except Sunday from Memorial Day weekend to Labor Day; weekdays the rest of the year. ~ 400 West Center Street, Douglas; 307-358-9288.

Perhaps most unforgettably to Wyoming visitors, Douglas is said to be the original home of the jackalope. Throughout the state, you will be confronted by this fanciful hybrid: a jackrabbit with antlers. If you haven't seen a dozen (on postcards, at least) by the time you get to Douglas, you haven't been looking. Taxidermists have helped to perpetuate the hoax. In the heart of Douglas, stop by **Centennial Jackalope Square** to see a ten-foot replica of Wyoming's favorite animal, the "jackalope." ~ 3rd and Center streets. If you're here in late June, you can join the festivities during Jackalope Days.

Speaking of the elusive creature, you can pick up free jackalope hunting licenses and pins at the **Douglas Chamber of Commerce**, along with maps and brochures of the town. Closed Saturday and Sunday. ~ 121 Brownfield Road, Douglas; 307-358-2950; www.chalkbuttes.com/jackalope.

Fort Fetterman State Historic Site was established in 1867 as a cavalry outpost where the Bozeman Trail departed from the Oregon Trail, on a plateau above the confluence of LaPrele Creek with the North Platte. Although the fort was an important supply point, soldiers in the post–Civil War era considered it a "hell hole" for its harsh winters, hostile Indians and windswept isolation. Many of them deserted. When the entire Army abandoned the fort in 1882, it persisted for another four or five years as a civilian trade center known as Fetterman City. So rambunctious was this short-lived town that author Owen Wister used it as a model for his Gomorrah–like community of Drybone in *The Virginian*.

Today only two buildings have been properly restored. A log-construction officers' quarters contains exhibits that depict the fort's history as a military installation and as Fetterman City, and an ordnance warehouse built of adobe offers displays about American Indians, trail transportation and ranch history. There's a self-guided trail around the grounds, which include a picnic area. Closed from Labor Day to Memorial Day. Admission. ~ Route 93, Douglas; 307-358-2864 (summer) or 307-684-7629.

Douglas is a gateway to the northern section of Medicine Bow National Forest. One particularly beautiful spot, 38 miles southwest via Route 91 (Cold Springs Road), is **LaBonte Canyon**. Remarkable for its steep granite walls wooded with aspen and pine trees, the canyon is home to a sizable population of deer, elk and bighorn sheep. ~ Forest Road 658 via County Road 16.

HIDDEN ►

Another geologically intriguing spot (although not in the national forest) is **Ayres Natural Bridge**, one of the world's few arches with water flowing beneath it. LaPrele Creek has eroded its way through a massive sandstone wall, leaving a passageway 30 feet high and 50 feet wide. The rest of the 150-foot-wide cliff is intact. To get there, take Route 25 west 12 miles from Douglas, then follow signs south five miles. The county park at the bridge, open April through October, offers picnic facilities and overnight camping (no hookups) at no charge. No pets allowed. Bring your own water. ~ Natural Bridge Road; 307-358-3532.

Continue 14 miles past the Natural Bridge turnoff to **Glenrock**, another former Overland Stage and Pony Express stop once known as Deer Creek Station. Now a town of 2200 people, its heyday came with the oil-and-gas boom of the early 20th century. The downtown historic district still has several 1880s buildings. The **Rock in the Glen**, east of town, has the names of many Oregon Trail pioneers inscribed in it, and the small **Glenrock Paleontological Museum** displays parts of the first triceratops skeleton discovered in this part of the state. Closed Sunday year-round; closed Monday and Wednesday between Labor Day and Memorial Day. ~ 125 Mustang Trail, Glenrock; 307-436-2667.

The south bank of the North Platte slopes upward from Glenrock and Douglas into the Laramie Mountains, but beyond the north bank are seemingly endless, sagebrush-riddled prairies. This country is rich with oil, natural gas and coal. In its heart is the **Thunder Basin National Grassland.** Covering more than 572,000 acres nestled among patches of privately owned land in five Wyoming counties, this former dust bowl is a model for the regeneration of infertile land. At the turn of the 20th century, homesteaders from the East depleted the semiarid grassland's thin soil when they employed farming methods better suited to more humid climates. The land had been abandoned for decades when the federal government designated it as grazing land for sheep and cattle. Immense herds of pronghorn antelope also live here, along with mule deer, elk, coyotes, sage grouse, wild turkeys and golden eagles. Needless to say, perhaps, hunters love it. Getting a map from the Douglas Ranger District headquarters is advisable; call for details. ~ Route 59; 307-358-4690.

The Bozeman and Texas trails crossed part of Thunder Basin, but the infamous Cheyenne-Deadwood Stage Road skirted the grassland to the east. That took it directly through Hat Creek Station, about ten miles north of **Lusk,** a prairie town of 1500 people located an hour's drive east of Douglas via Route 18 and 20. The stage road (white posts still mark its route) began taking passengers between the railhead at Cheyenne and the Black Hills goldfields of South Dakota in 1876, ten years before Lusk was founded. The coaches' cargoes became such regular targets for daring outlaws that the stage line hired famed gunfighter Wild Bill Hickok to ride shotgun on the stage. No one challenged Hickok's aim nor his nerve. But he had made only a few runs before he was mortally wounded, shot in the back while playing poker in Deadwood.

Lusk became a ranching and farming center when the railroad arrived in 1886. Oil discoveries in 1918 swelled its population to

10,000, but the boom was short-lived. Later exploitation of Silver Cliff west of the town (it's actually red) can be seen in the shafts sunken into the rock; three generations of miners sought silver and uranium ores here.

Lusk keeps memorabilia of its past, and especially of the Cheyenne-Deadwood Road, in the **Stagecoach Museum**. The star of its fine collection is an original Concord stagecoach whose sister vehicle is in the Smithsonian Institution in Washington, D.C. There's also a reconstructed pioneer home and relics from pioneer and Indian days. Open daily in July and August; weekday afternoons in May–June and September–October; other times by appointment. Admission. ~ 322 South Main Street, Lusk; 307-334-3444.

The big annual event is the **Legend of Rawhide Pageant**, a historical recreation of the killing of an Indian princess by a westbound emigrant. Some 15 covered wagons and 200 volunteers, all of them clad in mid-19th-century garb, take part in this mid-July pageant. Why "Rawhide"? That's what the ill-fated settler had by the time the Sioux were done skinning him.

HIDDEN ►

Amateur paleontologists may want to head north from Lusk 30 miles to the **Lance Creek Fossil Area**, a 558-square-mile national natural landmark where 51 new species of prehistoric animals— mammals, birds, reptiles, amphibians and fish—have been unearthed. The discoveries have included the first horned dinosaurs (triceratops) and the first Cretaceous mammals. ~ Routes 270 and 272, Lance Creek.

LODGING

A good place to stay in Douglas is **The Chieftain**, whose 21 rooms all have coffeemakers and free in-room movies. Some of the larger chambers also have refrigerators. ~ 815 East Richards Street, Douglas; 307-358-2673. BUDGET.

For historic flavor, you can't beat the **Hotel Higgins**. Built on the rail line in 1916, it has been refurbished with period antiques as a bed-and-breakfast hotel. The eight guest rooms have brass beds, armoires and so much old-fashioned charm that they provide the perfect antidote to a long day on the interstate. Every room has its own bath, but you'll have to request a phone, cable TV or air-conditioning if you need them. Breakfast is served in The Paisley Shawl, one of Wyoming's few truly great restaurants. ~ 416 West Birch Street, Glenrock; 307-436-9212, 800-458-0144, fax 307-436-9213; e-mail bdoll@trib.com. MODERATE.

HIDDEN ►

At the **Cheyenne River Ranch** in the heart of Thunder Basin National Grassland, guests can assist with tending sheep and cattle and performing other chores. The four rooms at this ranch lack phones and TVs, although some have radios; the main house has a phone and TV. Visitors have access to an above-ground swimming pool, a lighted volleyball court and a guest laundry. To get there, drive north from Douglas 35 miles on Route 59, then another six miles north on County Road 40. Closed November through April. ~ 1031 Steinle Road, Bill; 307-358-2380, fax 307-358-5796; www.cruising-america.com/riverranch. ULTRA-DELUXE.

Your best bet for lodging in Lusk is the **IMA Covered Wagon Motel**. There's plenty to do here: indoors, a heated swimming pool, sauna, whirlpool and exercise room; outdoors, basketball and shuffleboard courts and a children's playground. The 51 rooms have queen- and king-size beds and cable TV. There's also a coin laundry. ~ 730 South Main Street, Lusk; phone/fax 307-334-2836; www.wyoming.com/lazykllamas.com. MODERATE.

DINING

Chutes Wyoming Eatery serves three meals daily in a casual atmosphere with Western charm. There's a cocktail lounge here, as well, and children have a menu of their own. ~ 1450 River Bend Drive, Douglas; 307-358-9790. MODERATE TO DELUXE.

Some folks make the two-and-a-half-hour drive from Cheyenne just to dine at **The Paisley Shawl** located in Glenrock's Hotel Higgins. Rated by *Bon Appetit* as one of the ten best in U.S. historic hotels, it offers a contemporary Continental menu (prime rib, veal scaloppini, shrimp al pesto, lamb chops with honey mustard) amid elegant, early-20th-century decor. Five-course, prix-fixe dinners are always available, and there are different ethnic specials each Friday. The Paisley Shawl has its own dessert chef and an extensive wine list. ~ 416 West Birch Street, Glenrock; 307-436-9212. MODERATE TO DELUXE.

In Lusk, try the **Fireside Inn**, a traditional family-style restaurant open for breakfast, lunch and dinner. Hamburgers, steaks and crab legs are some of the dinner options. The homemade soups and pastries are especially good. ~ 904 South Main Street, Lusk; 307-334-3477. BUDGET TO DELUXE.

✔ **CHECK THESE OUT—UNIQUE DINING**

- *Budget:* Enjoy the peoplewatching with your homestyle breakfast or soup-and-sandwich lunch at **Jacquie's Garden Creek Cafe**. *page 259*
- *Moderate to deluxe:* Create your own pasta when you dine at **Bosco's**, an Italian hideaway that also invents dishes for you. *page 259*
- *Moderate to deluxe:* Start the morning with a Cajun omelette at the **Cottage Café**, then return for steak Jack Daniels at lunchtime. *page 259*
- *Moderate to ultra-deluxe:* Indulge in views of Casper Mountain and Continental-tinged cuisine at **Armor's Silver Fox Restaurant**. *page 260*

Budget: under $7   Moderate: $7–$12   Deluxe: $12–$20   Ultra-deluxe: over $20

▼▼▼▼▼▼▼▼▼
Casper Area

If you were to travel the entire Oregon Trail from start to finish today, the largest city you'd visit between Missouri and Boise, Idaho, would be Casper. With a population of about 50,000, Casper is the commercial center for a huge area where oil drilling is the main business and pronghorn antelope outnumber humans.

The town got its start as the last Oregon Trail crossing of the North Platte River. Near the modern downtown core in 1847, resourceful Mormon travelers established a toll ferry to assist emigrants making the crossing here. In 1859, a bridge was built and a military and trading post (later named Fort Caspar) constructed nearby. The town that emerged initially thrived as a railroad terminus. But when oil was discovered in 1889, and the first well was tapped in the Salt Creek Field 40 miles north of town, Casper found its true calling.

By 1915, oil wildcatters had turned Casper into a boom town the like of 19th-century gold-rush communities. With the advent of World War I, land prices went through the roof with the construction of several of the world's largest refineries. An estimated half-million dollars of oil stocks were traded every day in Casper hotel lobbies.

With the good came the bad: In 1925, the Teapot Dome deal, in which Secretary of the Interior Albert Fall helped bring down the Harding Administration by secretly leasing a naval oil reserve, mushroomed into the biggest corruption scandal to rock the U.S. presidency until Watergate. And in 1929, the stock market crash put an end to the Roaring Twenties and the oilfield speculation.

But oil has continued to flow through Casper, along with additional mineral wealth: coal, natural gas, uranium and bentonite. Light manufacturing supports the town's role as a regional center.

Despite its commercial orientation, alpine beauty can be found just outside of the city on the forested slopes of Mount Casper. Eagles nest in nearby canyons, and wetlands along the banks of the Platte River teem with bird and animal life. Meanwhile, two-thirds of the world's population of pronghorn antelope live in the grasslands that stretch out in every direction.

Pronghorn are not true antelope but the sole living species of a family of animals that had no relatives in Asia or Africa. Pronghorns were hunted to near-extinction during the pioneer migration and railroad era of the late 1800s and were among the first animals to be legally protected as endangered species. Today, they number more than 500,000 and are no longer on the endangered list. In fact, herds of wild pronghorn antelope are one of the Casper area's most interesting and frequent sights.

SIGHTS

Your orientation to this Platte River city should begin at the **Fort Caspar Museum.** (A post office error was responsible for the spelling variation.) Built in 1859 by trader Louis Guinard beside the bridge he constructed over the North Platte River, it soon became a stagecoach stop, Pony Express station and telegraph office. When the Army purchased the redoubt as a cavalry post, it was dubbed the Platte Bridge Station until 1865, when it was renamed for Lieutenant Caspar Collings, killed by Red Cloud's Sioux while trying to reach a supply train. Two years later, the fort was abandoned.

Pronghorn antelope can run as fast as 60 miles per hour for short distances.

In 1936, the Works Progress Administration undertook to rebuild some of the fort's original structures. The trading post, commissary store, stage station, barracks, officers' quarters and blacksmith shop can be explored today, along with an interpretive center with exhibits on regional history. Since this was also the site of the 1847 Mormon ferry crossing, there's a reconstructed ferry on the grounds. Fort buildings are closed mid-September to mid-May. Museum is closed Saturday from mid-September to mid-May. ~ 4001 Fort Caspar Road, Casper; 307-235-8462.

Perhaps the most notable attraction in the city of Casper is the **Nicolaysen Art Museum & Discovery Center**, which features Wyoming's finest collection of contemporary art in a renovated power plant. Besides changing displays of regional and national works, its permanent collection includes fine American Indian art and hundreds of drawings by German-American illustrator Carl Link. The adjoining Discovery Center is geared toward children, and has self-guided art-making stations for people of all ages. On the third floor, the **Wyoming Science Adventure Center** (closed Sunday and Monday; 307-261-6130) offers hands-on fun for budding scientists. Closed Monday. Admission. ~ 400 East Collins Drive, Casper; 307-235-5247.

On the campus of the two-year Casper College is the **Tate Natural Science and Mineralology Museum**, whose emphasis is on paleontology: here you'll find a laboratory where fossils are prepared, as well as the fossilized bones of birds, reptiles and fish more than 50 million years old. There are also lots of rock and gem specimens, meteorites among them, if that's your fancy. Closed Sunday except by appointment. ~ 125 College Drive, Casper; 307-268-2447.

The **Werner Wildlife Museum** may be interesting if you enjoy looking at the stuffed and mounted carcasses of mammals and birds native to Wyoming and elsewhere in North America. Highlights are a pronghorn diorama and a room of hunting trophies from other parts of the world. Closed Saturday and Sunday from mid-September to mid-May; closed Sunday mid-May to mid-September. ~ 405 East 15th Street, Casper; 307-235-2108.

From June through August, the **Casper Planetarium** offers science lovers a chance to study the heavens in comfort at its hour-long programs. Admission. ~ 904 North Poplar Street, Casper; 307-577-0310.

But a better place from which to view the stars any time of year—or to enjoy forested slopes and abundant wildlife—is **Casper Mountain**, just south of the city. Plan a half-day loop drive to properly see the attractions of this 8200-foot mountain. Wildlife is so ample and habitats are of such diversity on the slopes of this most northwesterly point of the Laramie Mountains that the state Game & Fish Department has posted signs with a binoculars symbol to mark the best viewing areas.

Following Casper Mountain Road (Route 251) south from Wyoming Boulevard near the Casper College campus, you enter a mixed ponderosa pine and aspen forest in the area of **Rotary Park** and **Garden Creek Falls**; keep an eye out for deer, elk, beavers and even black bears. The road continues to **Lookout Point**, near the summit of the mountain, for a grand view of the city, the prairie and the river only about ten miles from downtown. Farther along the same route, short unpaved side roads lead to **Casper Mountain Park**, with its Braille Nature Trail, and the dense, dark lodgepole pine forest of **Crimson Dawn Park**. There's also a local ski hill, **Hogadon Ski Area**, and plenty of all-season trails nearby. The pavement ends in a valley between Casper Mountain and Muddy Mountain, where **Circle Drive**, a hard-packed gravel road, leads west through sage and juniper country filled with flowers and songbirds, then joins paved Route 487. To return to Casper via Jackson Canyon, turn right (northeast) on Route 220. For information, call 307-473-3400.

If the city of Casper were in the middle of a clock face, Casper Mountain would be at 6 o'clock. At 3 o'clock, about eight miles east via route 25, is **Edness Kimball Wilkins State Park**, a day-use facility on the Oregon Trail. Located at a cottonwood-shaded bend on the south bank of the North Platte River, the park offers a sandy beach for swimming, several picnic areas and playgrounds, and a network of walking paths that allow nature lovers to observe the bird life of this riparian community. ~ Route 20/26/87 East; 307-577-5150. From the same exit off Route 25, a short drive south on Hat Six Road (Route 253) leads to several marked wildlife-viewing areas on the sagebrush prairie where pronghorn antelope, sage grouse and prairie dogs are abundant.

Westbound Route 25 does a 90-degree turn north at Casper. Within a half-hour after setting out in the direction of Sheridan, travelers will find themselves in the middle of the extensive Salt Creek Oil Field. Its heart is the twin communities of **Midwest** and **Edgerton** (combined population under 500). Some 600 million barrels of oil are pumped from the earth here each year, more than a century after the field's discovery. The notorious **Teapot Dome** naval oil reserve is about ten miles southeast of Midwest.

The Teapot Dome Scandal

Prior to Watergate, the most disgraceful political scandal in American history was that of Teapot Dome.

A low, broad hill about 30 miles north of Casper, Teapot Dome is in the heart of the Salt Creek Oil Field, whose underground wealth had turned Casper into a boom town by 1915. As the United States was pulled into the First World War, President Woodrow Wilson designated the Teapot Dome field— seven miles long and a couple of miles wide—as a naval oil reserve.

With the war a recent memory, President Warren Harding transferred jurisdiction over the Teapot Dome reserve from the U.S. Navy to the Department of the Interior in May 1921, not long after his inauguration. Eleven months later, interior secretary Albert Fall secretly leased exclusive rights to the oil field to his longtime associate Harry Sinclair, owner of the Mammoth Crude Oil Co. Fall did not offer the lease to competitive public bidding, as was required by law. What's more, soon after the lease, he received a payment of more than $200,000 from a source "associated with" Sinclair.

Apparently satisfied with the Teapot Dome lease, the interior secretary then pulled off a similar deal in Southern California. For a $100,000 "loan" from Edward Doheny of the Pan American Petroleum Co., Fall secretly leased portions of the Elk Hills and Buena Vista Hills fields.

When Congress got wind of possible corruption in 1922, Senator Thomas J. Walsh, a respected Montana Democrat, was appointed to head a subcommittee investigation. Walsh broke the scandal in late June 1923, when Harding was in Alaska on a transcontinental tour. Congress directed the president to cancel the leases; a discomfited Harding was stunned by what he called "betrayals." Five weeks later, in a state of exhaustion, the president died in San Francisco.

Harding was not personally involved in the scandal, except through his political naïveté. His Cabinet selections included many unqualified patrons and friends, all of whom he ingenuously trusted. Vice President Calvin Coolidge, never a part of Harding's "inner circle," succeeded him.

In 1927, the Supreme Court handed down its verdicts in the case. Fall took the fall; he was convicted of accepting a bribe in the Elk Hills lease and was imprisoned for several years. Other appointees in his department received lesser penalties; at least one of them committed suicide. The leases were declared fraudulent and illegal, and supervision of Teapot Dome was returned to the Navy. Although he had signed all the leases, Secretary of the Navy Edward Denby was cleared of any criminal charges.

Sinclair and Doheny also were acquitted of charges of bribery and criminal conspiracy. As attested by the green brontosaurus signs that still mean gasoline throughout Wyoming, Sinclair went on to great success.

If you head west from Casper at 10 o'clock, you'll be on Route 20/26 toward Shoshoni, Riverton and Cody. The village of **Powder River**, 37 miles west of Casper, is notable only as the site of a Sheepherders' Rodeo in mid-July each year. But drive another five or ten minutes west from the community and you'll be skirting **Hell's Half Acre**. In fact, this unique and colorful geological depression comprises 320 acres of severe badlands: distorted rock spires, deep caverns, crevices and large pits eroded over time by wind and water. It was once called the Devil's Kitchen because ancient coal deposits continually smoldered, releasing noxious fumes. American Indians used the badlands to trap buffalo: many weapons and other artifacts have been found here. A roadside observation post is open from May through November.

Most travelers take the 8 o'clock road west from Casper, continuing their trek along the old Oregon Trail. This is the two-lane, blacktop Route 220, which eventually joins Route 287 between Rawlins and Lander, 72 miles from Casper.

HIDDEN ►   Ten miles from the city along this route is the **Jackson Canyon Eagle Sanctuary**. The cliffs on either side of this creek, flowing from the western flank of Casper Mountain, are inhabited by bald eagles during the winter months and golden eagles year-round; both species range for up to 100 miles and may be spotted anywhere in the area. ~ County Road 310.

Nearby, a side road (County Road 308) crosses the North Platte at **Bessemer Bend**, whose rich flood-plain soil sustains thick shrubbery that provides habitat for a myriad of wildlife, including deer, antelope, raccoons and songbirds. This is also a stopover point for migrating waterfowl, which sweep through by the millions in the spring and fall. At the end of the road, four and a half miles from Route 220, the **Dan Speas Fish Rearing Station** is open for public visits at no charge. The nearby Goose Egg Spring helps fish grow more rapidly here than at other hatcheries; about

THE LYNCHING OF "CATTLE KATE"

The only woman known to have been lynched in Wyoming was Ella Watson, known as "Cattle Kate" because of her skill with livestock. She and her common-law husband, Jim Averill, ran a saloon in the town of Bothwell (since submerged by Pathfinder Reservoir) in 1889. When stray calves wandered by her nearby homestead, as they often seemed to do, Watson would confer on them her brand, eventually doubling the size of her herd. Area ranchers pointedly suggested that the pair would do well to leave town, but they balked at the idea. The next thing anyone knew, they were found strung up by their necks from a scrub pine tree.

a million fish, mostly trout, are raised each year to stock Wyoming waterways. ~ County Road 308; 307-473-8890.

It's a half-hour drive from Casper to **Alcova Reservoir**, the lowermost of four reservoirs created as part of the Kendrick Reclamation Project on the North Platte River. Benefitting 60,000 acres of otherwise unusable farmland, and also providing hydroelectric power to a wide area, the project includes Seminoe, Kortes and Pathfinder reservoirs above Alcova, as well as the Fremont Canyon Power Plant. The small town of **Alcova**, beside the 700-foot-long dam on the lake's northeastern shore, is a focus for recreation lovers who come here to boat, fish, waterski, sail and windsurf. **Fremont Canyon**, southwest of Alcova via County Road 407 (Kortes Road), has high, red rock walls that rise 500 feet above the North Platte and attract rock climbers from all over.

At the head of Fremont Canyon is the **Pathfinder Dam**, considered a marvel of engineering when it was completed in 1909. (It is listed on the National Register of Historic Places.) An interpretive museum tells its story. ~ Pathfinder Road (Country Road 409); 307-261-5628, 307-235-9325. The north end of Pathfinder Reservoir, where it is joined by the Sweetwater River, is enveloped by **Pathfinder National Wildlife Refuge**, a 16,800-acre sanctuary for such migratory waterfowl as Canada geese and white pelicans. ~ Buzzard Road (County Road 410).

Beyond Pathfinder, a 50-mile drive southwest of Casper, is the highlight of this part of the state: **Independence Rock State Historic Site**. The huge granite dome, bulging 193 feet up from the surrounding grasslands and covering 27 acres, was one of the most familiar landmarks on the Oregon Trail. Travelers camped here beside the Sweetwater River on their way west; more than 5000 of them carved their names on the rock, though only a few dozen are visible from the footpath that leads around its massive base. Most inscriptions are high on the dome, so you have to climb to see them. Look carefully and you may spot the signature of explorer John C. Frémont or Jesuit missionary Father Jean Pierre de Smet.

Besides being a marker for pioneers to gauge their progress across the featureless high plains, Independence Rock became one of the first "tourist traps" in the Rockies: As early as 1855, Mormon entrepreneurs established a business here, charging pioneers $5 each to inscribe their names on this "Register of the Desert" and thus "insure their immortality." Its name, incidentally, was given on July 4, 1830, by a party of fur trappers led by William Sublette. A picnic area is in the north side of the Rock. ~ Route 220; 307-577-5150.

Seven miles farther along Route 220 stands another Oregon Trail landmark, the **Devil's Gate**. Its 330 foot high cliffs flank the Sweetwater River where it knifes through the Rattlesnake Mountains for about 500 yards. Although the original Oregon Trail ran through here, it was later rerouted because of the danger of Indian ambush from the top of the cliffs. The Gate stands near the original ranch house of the Tom Sun Ranch, one of the first cattle ranches in Wyoming, which has operated continuously since 1872.

LODGING   With more than two dozen motels and motor inns, Casper dominates the lodging market in central Wyoming. Competition keeps room rates remarkably low, even in the classiest accommodation in town. That would be the six-story **Radisson Hotel Casper**, whose 229 spacious guest rooms focus around a lofty atrium. Some of the rooms have honor bars, coffeemakers or even whirlpool baths. Within the hotel are an indoor swimming pool, jacuzzi and exercise room, a gift shop, beauty salon, an arcade, two restaurants and a cocktail lounge. ~ 800 North Poplar Street, Casper; 307-266-6000, 800-333-3333, fax 307-473-1010; www. radisson.com. MODERATE.

Casper's largest hotel is the four-story **Parkway Plaza**, a 349-unit hotel with an adjoining convention center. Its rooms vary widely from small older chambers awaiting remodeling right up to luxury suites. Like the Hilton, it has two restaurants and a lounge, and all the rooms have data ports. There's also an outdoor pool and picnic area, and a guest laundry; a jacuzzi sauna and workout station are located indoors. Nonsmokers have a wing of their own. ~ 123 West East Street, Casper; 307-235-1777, 800-270-7829, fax 307-235-8068. MODERATE.

The Radisson, Parkway Plaza and other large motor inns cluster around Exit 188 on Route 25. Smaller, independently owned motels—nearly all of them with rates in the budget range—line the East Yellowstone Highway (Route 20/26) through downtown. Typical of the breed is the **Sage and Sand Motel**. The 34 nearly contemporary, blandly decorated guest rooms have double beds; a few have kitchenettes. Don't look for a pool here, though. ~ 901 West Yellowstone Highway, Casper; 307-237-2088, 800-449-5943. BUDGET.

Another pleasant motel is the **Kelly Inn**, where children up to the age of 16 can stay free when traveling with their parents. Located across the street from the Radisson, this 103-room inn has a whirlpool, sauna and guest laundry, and the coffee pot is always on in the lobby. Continental breakfast. ~ 821 North Poplar Street, Casper; 307-266-2400, 800-635-3559, fax 307-266-1146. BUDGET TO MODERATE.

The **Ivy House Inn Bed & Breakfast** offers three individually decorated rooms with wood floors and shared bath on the main floor. Guests have access to the kitchenette and may soak away in the enclosed outdoor hot tub. Family pets include three cats, which inhabit the second floor, and a dog. Full breakfast provided.

~ 815 South Ash Street, Casper; 307-265-0974; e-mail ivyinn@ trib.com. BUDGET.

It's ironic, perhaps, that in the heart of cowboy and oil country, two of Casper's finest restaurants serve Italian cuisine. With linen tablecloths and candlelight, **Anthony's** is an intimate eatery ideal for diving into a big plate of ravioli or fettuccine and washing it down with a glass of fine Chianti. Seafood, veal and chicken also appear on the menu. Closed Sunday and Monday. ~ 621 Southeast Wyoming Boulevard, Casper; 307-237-9688. MODERATE TO DELUXE.

DINING

Casper's other favorite Italian *ristorante*, **Bosco's**, is also intimate and a little harder to find. The menu features a wide selection of dishes, from spaghettini with white clam sauce to shrimp scampi and veal scaloppine Marsala. Diners are invited to design their own fettuccine from a selection of fresh vegetables, meat and fish. The atmosphere is traditional right down to the red checkerboard tablecloths. No lunch on Saturday; closed Sunday and Monday. ~ 847 East A Street, Casper; 307-265-9658. MODERATE TO DELUXE.

> Casper was named for Lieutenant Caspar Collings, killed in an Indian conflict, but the post office got the spelling confused.

The other popular ethnic food here is, not surprisingly, Mexican. **La Costa Mexican Restaurant** serves fajitas, tacos, flautas, deep-fried *sobitos*, carne asada and sweet *sopapillas*. ~ 400 West F Street, Casper; 307-266-4288. BUDGET TO MODERATE.

Casper's premier steakhouse is **Bum Steer Steakhouse**, where you can count on great ribeyes as well as prime rib, barbecued ribs or deep-fried shrimp. This restaurant does a nice job with children's meals. No lunch on Monday or Saturday. Closed Sunday. ~ 739 North Center Street, Casper; 307-234-4531. MODERATE TO ULTRA-DELUXE.

The **Cottage Café** is more "nouvelle" than you might expect in Casper: light breakfasts, lunches and dinners promise an interesting variety of flavors and ingredients. Their signature tequila-lime chicken soup is a prime example. Breakfast yields Cajun omelettes and fresh strawberry blintzes; chicken breast with gorgonzola and sun-dried tomatoes, along with steak Jack Daniels, are lunch and dinner options. The cottage atmosphere is charming. No breakfast on Monday; no dinner Sunday through Thursday. ~ 116 South Lincoln Street, Casper; 307-234-1157. MODERATE TO DELUXE.

For a homestyle breakfast or a soup-and-sandwich lunch, look no further than **Jacquie's Garden Creek Cafe** in the heart of downtown Casper. The local atmosphere makes this a great place for people-watching. Closed Sunday. ~ 251 South Center Street, Casper; 307-265-9018. BUDGET.

If you're looking for top-end dining, there are a couple of places to consider. **Armor's Silver Fox Restaurant** serves a varied menu with Continental flair in a romantic atmosphere. The menu features Cajun entrées and veal specialties as well as the usual steak, chicken and seafood fare. Big picture windows offer a view to Casper Mountain. No lunch Monday or Saturday. Closed Sunday. ~ 3422 South Energy Lane, Casper; 307-235-3000. MODERATE TO ULTRA-DELUXE.

SHOPPING   Your best shopping bet in Casper may be Western wear. **Lou Taubert Ranch Outfitters** is a complete cowboy department store with nine floors of Western fashions for men, women and children, as well as gifts, artwork, saddles, specialty foods and more than 10,000 pairs of cowboy boots in stock. ~ 125 East 2nd Street, Casper; 307-234-2500.

The main shopping district is around McKinley and A streets, with numerous antique shops and art galleries. Of particular interest is the **West Wind Gallery**, operated by the Casper Artists' Guild, which focuses on contemporary work by regional, national and international artists. Closed Sunday and Monday. ~ 1040 West 15th Street, Casper; 307-265-2655.

For a vast selection of antiques along with regional artwork, visit **Carriage House Antiques Gallery**. Closed Sunday. ~ 520 South Ash Street, Casper; 307-266-2987.

Wood N' Glass Shack carries stained-glass gift items. Closed Friday, Sunday and Monday. ~ 382 West Collins Street, Casper; 307-472-5488.

NIGHTLIFE   The drama scene is surprisingly active in this city. Casper College's 450-seat **Gertrude Krampert Theatre** offers a year-round schedule of student performances: three plays and a musical during the academic year, plus a summer season of musicals and comedies. ~ College Drive, Casper; 307-268-2365, box office 307-268-2500. The **Stage III Community Theatre** has a season that runs from September through June. ~ Sunrise Shopping Center, 4080 South Poplar Street, Casper; 307-234-0946.

There's also a broad spectrum of musical groups. Two of note: The **Wyoming Symphony Orchestra** performs most Saturday evenings in the Natrona County High School auditorium. ~ 930 South Elm Street, Casper; 307-266-1478.

Other performances, including road shows, concerts and sports competitions (from basketball and rodeo to ice shows), are presented at the **Casper Events Center**, which seats as many as 9700 people. ~ 1 Events Drive, Casper; box office 307-577-3030, 800-442-2256.

For more information about cultural and seasonal events, contact the **Casper Area Chamber of Commerce**. Closed Saturday and

Sunday from Labor Day to Memorial Day. ~ 500 North Center Street, Casper; 307-234-5362, 800-852-1889, fax 307-265-2643; www.casperets.com.

The bar scene in Casper varies from small neighborhood bars and biker roadhouses to cocktail lounges in hotels and motor inns. One noteworthy nightspot is the **Beacon Club**, which features live country-and-western bands and a young, lively crowd. Cover. ~ 4100 West Yellowstone Highway, Casper; 307-577-1503. **Club Dance West** is an all-ages spot with country and rock music and a variety of games. Cover. ~ 225 North Wolcott Street, Casper; 307-234-8811.

Rack-Em Up Billiards has nine full-sized, one snooker and two coin-operated tables for your entertainment. If you'd rather sink some quarters instead of balls, there are pinball machines, video games and a jukebox. ~ 128 South Center Street, Casper; 307-235-6574.

EDNESS KIMBALL WILKINS STATE PARK   **PARKS**
The cottonwood-lined banks of the North Platte River form the setting for this 319-acre day-use park designed for picnicking, fishing and birdwatching. Deer are frequently seen in the park. A walking trail that follows the river makes this a beautiful rest spot off Route 25. Swimming is permitted in beach areas, and fishing is good for catfish and a variety of trout. There are restrooms, a picnic area and a playground. Day-use fee, $3 per vehicle. ~ Located off Route 20/26/87, six miles east of Casper. Take Exit 182 north off Route 25 and turn east after crossing the railroad tracks; 307-577-5150.

MEDICINE BOW NATIONAL FOREST   Encompassing much of the Laramie Mountains southeast of Casper, the northern division of this 1.1 million-acre national forest is accessible by mostly unpaved roads. Fishing and wildlife watching are excellent, and there are numerous hiking trails. Facilities include picnic areas and restrooms. ~ The most direct access to this section is via Routes 91 and 94 southwest from Douglas; 307-358-4690.

▲ The northern sector of the national forest has just four campgrounds, all some 35 miles south from Douglas; they include only 33 RV/tent sites (no hookups); free to $5 per night; 14-day maximum stay. Closed November through April.

Outdoor Adventures

FISHING

All along the North Platte the fishing is excellent for a variety of species, including trout (rainbow in particular, but also brown and cutthroat), walleye and catfish. In Hawk Springs Reservoir, you can also angle for largemouth and smallmouth bass. Grayrocks Reservoir, 16 miles northeast of Wheatland, is the only place in Wyoming to catch tiger muskelunge, a hard-fighting fish more common in the Midwest; there are also a variety of panfish on which the muskie feeds. Glendo and Guernsey reservoirs are excellent for walleye and catfish, while Alcova and Pathfinder reservoirs are considered better for trout (as well as walleye).

Platte River Fly Shop arranges fishing trips; the shop also conducts float trips on the North Platte River from mid-March to mid-November. ~ 5033 Alcova Route, Box 3, Casper, WY 82604; 307-237-5997. **Wyoming's Choice** offers full-day trips along the Platte River and at Alcova and Pathfinder reservoirs. ~ 513 North Lennox Street, Casper; 307-234-3870.

BOATING & WATER-SKIING

Boating is excellent at reservoirs throughout central Wyoming, and there's waterskiing on the large reservoirs: Guernsey, Glendo and Alcova.

Several full-service marinas offer boat rentals, fuel, fishing gear and a variety of snack foods and other supplies. They include the **Glendo State Park Marina** (307-735-4216) and the **Alcova Lakeside Marina** (307-472-6666).

SAILING & WIND-SURFING

Alcova and Pathfinder reservoirs are favored for their reliable winds. Glendo also is a favorite of windsurfers. Guernsey Reservoir is too sheltered to propel a sail with much speed.

CANOEING

The North Platte and its component reservoirs are excellent for canoeing, especially along its lower portion near Torrington and through Casper beside the Platte River Parkway.

CLIMBING

Between Alcova and Pathfinder reservoirs, just east of the Pathfinder Dam, **Fremont Canyon** is a favorite of climbers. The red-rock walls here rise 500 feet above the North Platte. ~ County Road 407 (Kortes Road).

DOWNHILL SKIING

The region's only downhill ski slopes are at the **Hogadon Ski Area**, 11 miles south of Casper on Casper Mountain. Sixty acres and 18 groomed runs are served by two chairlifts and a poma lift. Although the vertical drop is only 600 feet, the area, with a peak elevation of 8000 feet, remains open from November through March. Snowboarders are welcome. There's a cafeteria at the foot of the slopes, as well as a rental shop. ~ Route 252; 307-235-8499, 307-235-8369 (snow conditions).

CROSS-COUNTRY SKIING

Just as it is for downhill skiing, Casper Mountain is the region's best place for nordic pursuits. **Beartrap Meadow Park** and **Casper Mountain Park** have an interconnected 15-mile system of groomed trails. Some of them are lit for night skiing. Use permits can be purchased at several locations, including **Mountain Sports,** which also provides ski rentals. ~ 543 South Center Street, Casper; 307-266-1136.

Casper Municipal Golf Course has three nine-hole greens (two par-35s and one par-36) with a clubhouse, restaurant and pro shop. Closed November through February. ~ 2120 Allendale Boulevard; 307-234-1037. Two private courses offer exchanges with club members in other cities: **Casper Country Club** (307-237-1078) is an 18-hole course with a driving range. Closed mid-October through April. **Paradise Valley Country Club** (307-237-3673) has 18 holes and a driving range. Closed mid-October through April.

    Torrington Municipal Golf Course features a driving range and an 18-hole course. Closed November through April. ~ Corner of West 15th Street and Golf Course Road; 307-532-3868. The nine-hole **Wheatland Golf Club** has a driving range. ~ 1253 Cole Street, Wheatland; 307-322-3675. Douglas has the **Douglas Community Golf Course,** an 18-hole green with a driving and chipping range. Closed mid-October through March. ~ Route 59; 307-358-5099. The **Glenrock Golf Course** offers nine holes. Closed mid-October to mid-April. ~ 911 West Grove Street; 307-436-5560.

Casper has 39 city parks, many of them with tennis courts (closed October through March). Among them are **Highland Park** (4th and Beverly streets), **Huber Park** (3031 East 5th Street), **Mike Sedar Park** (25th Street and College Drive), **Paradise Valley Park** (31 Begonia Street) or **Washington Park** (12th and McKinley streets). For information, contact the **Casper Recreation Center.** ~ 1801 East 4th Street; 307-235-8383.

✔ **CHECK THESE OUT—UNIQUE OUTDOOR ADVENTURES**

- Launch your boat at Guernsey State Park and revel in the safe haven of a beautiful reservoir kept calm by surrounding bluffs. *page 262*
- Take advantage of the prairie winds when you go windsurfing at Alcova Reservoir, one of a series of North Platte lakes. *page 262*
- Glide beneath the stars when you go cross-country skiing on Casper Mountain, where some trails are lit for night runs. *page 262*
- Hike to the summit of 10,272-foot Laramie Peak, where a marvelous view of the plains awaits at the end of a steep, 5.5-mile trail. *page 264*

RIDING STABLES

There may not be a lot of choices here, but what is offered is unique. **Historic Trails Expeditions** offers horseback and wagon-train trips of four hours to six days along such 19th-century routes as taken by the Oregon Trail and the Pony Express. Departing from Fort Caspar, riders travel in the actual ruts of the old trails; many of them pause at Independence Rock and go as far as South Pass, crossing into what was then the Oregon Territory. Float trips and cattle drives are other options. Unless weather prohibits, trips begin daily from May through September. ~ P.O. Box 428, Mills, WY 82644; 307-266-4868, fax 307-234-0871.

BIKING

The region's single best place to set out on two wheels is Casper's **Platte River Parkway**. Currently running four miles along the North Platte, this paved "work in progress" will eventually be extended to 11.5 miles, connecting numerous parks en route. To purchase a bike, visit **Dr. Spokes Cyclery**, whose antique bicycle and pedal-car display captures attention. ~ 240 Center Street, Casper; 307-265-7740.

The town of Douglas has its own **River Path**, offering another two and a half miles of riverfront exercise.

For something a little more arduous, head for the mountain-biking trails on **Casper Mountain**. There's a real diversity of terrain here, from open prairie to alpine forests and canyons.

Bike Rentals   Rentals are available from **Eagle Creek Recreation Rental**. ~ 2239 Route 220, Alcova; 307-473-2832.

HIKING

All distances listed for hiking trails are one way unless otherwise noted.

FORT LARAMIE AREA   The **Laramie Peak Trail** (5.5 miles) in Medicine Bow National Forest begins at the Friend Creek Campground, most easily reached through Esterbrook by Forest Roads 653 (Braae Road) and 671. While the ascent of this highest sum-

THE DARING YOUNG MEN OF THE PONY EXPRESS

From April 1860 until the transcontinental telegraph line was completed in October 1861, the Pony Express was the fastest way to get mail from the eastern United States to the West Coast. At its 157 way stations, no more than about 15 miles apart, daring young riders changed to fresh horses or passed their mailbags to another rider; by means of this relay system, the mail reached California from Missouri in about ten days. As a brash 15-year-old, "Buffalo Bill" Cody made the longest ride in its history. Without a rest, he covered 322 round-trip miles between Red Butte (near Fort Caspar) and Rocky Ridge (north of Rock Springs), drawing double duty because his replacement rider had been killed; he made it back to Red Butte on schedule.

mit in the Laramie Range (10,272 feet) is steep, and requires a 2500-foot elevation gain, climbers are rewarded with spectacular panoramas in all directions.

DOUGLAS AREA The **LaBonte Creek Trail** (2 miles) extends down scenic LaBonte Canyon. Many deer, elk and other wildlife live between the canyon's steep walls, heavily wooded with aspens and conifers. The trail begins at the Curtis Gulch Campground, 38 miles southwest of Douglas via Cold Springs Road (Route 91), Country Road 16 and Forest Road 658.

CASPER AREA The **Braille Nature Trail** (.3 mile) is one for everyone—even the blind. Leaving from Skunk Hollow in Casper Mountain Park, the self-guided nature trail has 37 stations with interpretive plaques—written both in English and in Braille— explaining adjacent flora and geology. Safety ropes line the loop trail to provide guidance for the sightless.

▼▼▼▼▼▼▼▼▼▼
Transportation

CAR

Route 25, the main artery of this region, is a north–south interstate freeway running from Route 90 near Sheridan all the south to El Paso, Texas. Via this route, Casper is 147 miles from Sheridan, 50 miles from Douglas and 178 miles from Cheyenne.

If it's your desire to follow the Oregon Trail as nearly as possible, you'll enter Wyoming from Nebraska on **Route 26** at Torrington and proceed 56 miles past Fort Laramie to Route 25, 13 miles north of Wheatland. Continue on Route 25 to Casper, then turn southwest at **Route 220**, which passes Independence Rock and joins Route 287 (toward South Pass) north of Rawlins.

AIR

United Express (800-241-6522) and Sky West (307-234-0607), Delta's commuter carrier, serve Casper's **Natrona County International Airport**. Why international? There are connecting flights from Canada. ~ 307-472-6688.

BUS

Powder River/Coach USA services Casper and connects the city to the transcontinental Greyhound route at Cheyenne and Billings. ~ 123 West E Street, Suite 1159, Casper; 307-266-1904.

CAR RENTALS

Car-rental agencies located at the Casper airport include **Avis Rent A Car** (800-331-1212), **Budget Rent A Car** (800-527-0700), **Enterprise Rent A Car** (800-325-8007) and **Hertz Rent A Car** (800-654-3131).

PUBLIC TRANSIT

City bus services are provided by the **Casper Area Transportation Coalition** (CATC). Call for route and schedule information. ~ 307-265-1313.

TAXIS

Service is provided by **R.C. Cab**. ~ 307-235-5203.

NINE

Northeastern Wyoming

Dramatic natural features like Devils Tower and the Big Horn Mountains are what many visitors remember most about Wyoming's northeastern quadrant. But what really sets the region apart are its open grasslands.

This is cowboy-and-Indian country, the land that fostered the legends of Butch Cassidy, Crazy Horse and Sitting Bull. Cassidy's Hole-in-the-Wall hideout is as remote as it ever was. Memories of Crazy Horse and Sitting Bull, whose proud Sioux warriors once rode the Powder River plains, live on at battlefield sites north and south of Sheridan. Throughout the region, guest ranches inspire horsemanship and campfire cooking.

People have lived in this region for at least 10,000 years, white man for not much more than the last 150. The arrival of the horse around A.D. 1700 brought revolutionary change, as it gave the Lakota Sioux greater opportunity to hunt bison, win battles and dominate the area from the Black Hills to the Big Horn Basin. The threat of Indian hostility against pioneers in the Big Horn region kept this part of the Wyoming territory largely unsettled by whites until the 1880s. Then, army campaigns opened up more livestock range for cattlemen and sheepherders, who were moving north from the rail corridor in southern Wyoming.

Crow, Sioux and Cheyenne considered the Powder River Basin to be a sort of heaven on earth. Extending from the east slope of the Big Horn Mountains to the Black Hills, it had everything they could want: abundant shelter, mild winters, grass for their ponies and plenty of big game for their own sustenance.

It's no wonder that the tribes made their final stand here. The bloody Indian Wars of 1863–68 followed the blazing of the Bozeman Trail from southern Wyoming to the Montana goldfields; after treaties were signed, a Black Hills gold rush brought more whites to the region and another conflict erupted. This one culminated (in 1876) in the infamous Battle of Little Bighorn and "Custer's Last Stand," just north of Sheridan in southern Montana. Chiefs Red Cloud, Sitting Bull and Crazy Horse achieved their fame in these wars. After the uprisings were quelled and the American Indians were removed to reservations, the region quieted down for a few years . . . until the range wars.

East of the Powder River, life was relatively sedate. Gillette was little more than a rail stop for livestock ranchers until the 1950s, when oil and uranium were discovered and coal rediscovered. Now it's the fastest growing city in Wyoming, having more than tripled in population (to 21,000-plus) since 1970.

Not far east is Devils Tower National Monument, at the edge of the Black Hills. Rising a quarter-mile straight up from surrounding pine forests (like a pillar that signals starships!), it was proclaimed America's first national monument by President Theodore Roosevelt in 1906. Remember Steven Spielberg's movie, *Close Encounters of the Third Kind*? This was the place. . . .

Sheridan Area

Other towns may have taken off their chaps and spurs in favor of white shirts and ties, but Sheridan isn't one of them. Established on the Bozeman Trail in 1882 (and named for Civil War General Phillip Sheridan), this town at the foot of the Big Horns became the center of a thriving cattle-ranching district. Today, with a population of 15,000, its cowboy heritage still shines through any contemporary veneer; even sportsjacket-clad businessmen wear hats and boots. Ranching— cattle, sheep and the hay to feed them—remains the key to the local economy, along with coalmining and timber cutting.

SIGHTS

Sheridan's downtown **Main Street District** has more original late-19th- and early-20th-century buildings than any other community in Wyoming. Highlights of the designated National Historic District include a neon bucking horse; a full wall mural (at Main and Loucks streets); and a variety of quaint, canopied retail stores, including Western outfitters and antique galleries. Obtain a walking-tour map from the **Sheridan County Chamber of Commerce**. ~ Exit 23 off Route 90, Sheridan; 307-672-2485.

Among the city's notable buildings is the **Sheridan Inn**, once considered the finest hotel between Chicago and San Francisco. Built for the coming of the Burlington Railroad in 1893, it has hosted the likes of Will Rogers, Ernest Hemingway and three U.S. presidents; "Buffalo Bill" Cody often used its grounds to audition acts for his Wild West Show. Its unique design, with dormer windows extending from every room on the second and third floors, earned the inn recognition from *Ripley's Believe It or Not!* as "the house of 69 gables." Despite being a national historic landmark, it was scheduled for demolition in the 1960s until an area rancher purchased and restored it. Today it has a luncheon restaurant, a saloon and a small museum. Guided tours are offered at a small admission charge, applied for continuing renovation. Call for hours. ~ 856 Broadway, Sheridan; 307-674-5440.

The **Trail End State Historic Site**, a beautiful brick hilltop mansion and carriage house adjacent to Kendrick Park, was the home of John B. Kendrick, a pioneer cattle rancher who became a Wyoming governor and U.S. senator. Kendrick built the three-story, Flemish-style home between 1908 and 1913 at a cost of $165,000. Beautifully carved and burnished woodwork highlights the period decor, which includes original furnishings. The three-and-a-half-acre grounds are planted with several hundred trees and shrubs indigenous to Wyoming, as well as with many non-native species. Closed mid-December through March. Admission. ~ 400 Clarendon Avenue, Sheridan; 307-674-4589.

Also well worth a visit is the **Bradford Brinton Memorial**, comprising the Quarter Circle A Ranch, 12 miles south of Sheridan via Routes 87 and 335. Brinton, an Illinois native, bought the ranch house (built in 1892 by two Scottish brothers) in 1923. Here, in the shadow of the Big Horns, he raised cattle and horses. He expanded the ranch house to 20 rooms and filled it with his vast collection of Western art (including originals by Charles Russell, Frederic Remington and John James Audubon) and rare books (by Robert Louis Stevenson, Samuel Johnson and others). When Brinton died in 1936, his sister created the Bradford Brinton Memorial to preserve his collection. After she died in 1960, the institution was opened to the public as a museum. The memorial, which is on the National Register of Historic Places, is open mid-May through Labor Day. An adjacent gallery displays Indian artifacts and contemporary art. Admission. ~ 239 Brinton Road, Big Horn; 307-672-3173.

Nearby is the **Bozeman Trail Museum**, lodged in a blacksmith shop that served a stagecoach line when it was built in 1879. Within the museum, aside from more than 100 area livestock brands burnt into the ceiling, you'll see a potpourri of such pioneer artifacts as old cameras (and the photographs they took), antique dental equipment and musical instruments, household appliances, and blacksmithing and farming implements. Open summer weekends, the museum arranges town walking tours each Sunday afternoon. ~ Johnson Street, Big Horn; no phone.

The smaller communities in the Big Horn foothills are of interest both for history and for natural beauty. **Ranchester** and **Dayton**, twin ranching communities, 15 and 20 miles northwest of Sheridan, are gateways to the recreational opportunities of the northern Big Horn Mountains.

From Dayton, Route 14 weaves uphill for 25 miles on the **Bighorn Scenic Byway** to Burgess Junction, where the route sends separate forks through **Bighorn National Forest** to Lovell (Route 14A, via Medicine Wheel National Historic Landmark) and Greybull (Route 14, via Shell Canyon; see Chapter Four). ~ 307-672-0751. A roadside lookout southwest of Dayton offers a striking panorama of the Tongue River country as well as a geological phe-

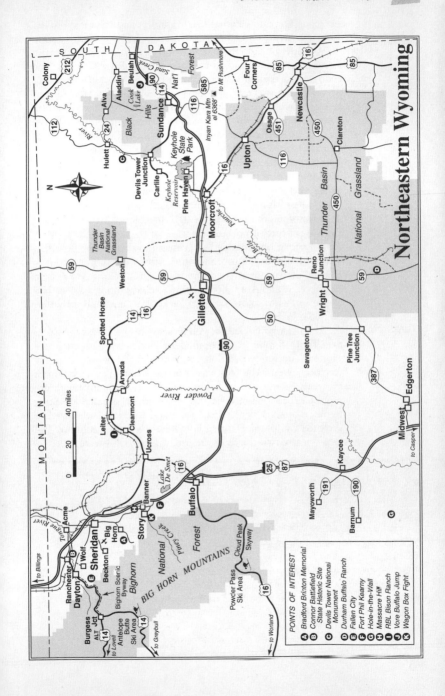

Northeastern Wyoming

SOUTH DAKOTA

MONTANA

Colony
212

Aladdin
Alva
Beulah
90
14
Sundance
116
585 Inyan Kara Mtn el 6368'▲ to Mt Rushmore
Four Corners
85
16
85
Newcastle
451
450
Osage
Clareton
116
Upton
Black Hills
Nat'l Forest
Keyhole State Park
Pine Haven
Keyhole Reservoir
Carlile
Devils Tower Junction
Hulett
24
112
River
Belle Fourche

Moorcroft
16

Thunder Basin National Grassland
450

Weston
59
59
Spotted Horse
14
16
Gillette
90
50
Reno Junction
Wright
59
59
Savageton
Pine Tree Junction
387
Edgerton
Midwest
to Casper

Arvada
Powder River
Leiter
Clearmont
Ucross
Banner
Lake De Smet
16
Buffalo
25
87
Kaycee
191
190
Barnum
Mayoworth

MONTANA

to Billings
Ranchester
Dayton
Wolf
Acme
Sheridan
Beckton
Big Horn
Story
Banner
Burgess Jct
ALT 14
Antelope Butte Ski Area
14
Bighorn Scenic Byway
to Lovell
to Greybull
BIG HORN MOUNTAINS
Big Horn National Forest
Piney Creek
Cloud Peak Skyway
Powder Pass Ski Area
16
to Worland

Tongue River
Goose Creek

N

40 miles
0   20   40

POINTS OF INTEREST

Ⓐ Bradford Brinton Memorial
Ⓑ Connor Battlefield State Historic Site
Ⓒ Devils Tower National Monument
Ⓓ Durham Buffalo Ranch
Ⓔ Fallen City
Ⓕ Fort Phil Kearny
Ⓖ Hole-in-the-Wall
Ⓗ Massacre Hill
Ⓘ RBL Bison Ranch
Ⓙ Vore Buffalo Jump
Ⓚ Wagon Box Fight

nomenon known as **Fallen City**: boulders and columns, broken from a towering cliff, that give the appearance of ancient ruins.

A worthwhile short side trip from Dayton follows Tongue Canyon Road off Route 14 up the **Tongue River Canyon**. The road extends only three and a half miles southwest before ending at a trailhead at the foot of the seven-mile-long canyon. Also in this area, within Bighorn National Forest, is the **Tongue River Cave**, an undeveloped favorite of experienced spelunkers. Crazy Horse requested a reservation in the Tongue River area after his surrender in 1877, but he was murdered at Fort Robinson, Nebraska, before it could be established.

Reminders of the Indian Wars of the 1860s are still evident at several sites within a half-hour's drive of modern Sheridan. On the south side of Ranchester, **Connor Battlefield State Historic Site** commemorates the 1865 Battle of Tongue River. General Patrick Connor set forth from Fort Laramie at the head of the Powder River Expedition, intended to protect travelers on the Bozeman Trail and to punish Sioux and other tribes for attacks on whites. Here on the Tongue River, Connor's 400 troops surprised a camp of Cheyenne and Arapaho, killing 65 and capturing 1000 horses at a loss of eight soldiers. ~ City Park, off Route 14, Ranchester; 307-684-7629.

HIDDEN ►

About a year later, **Fort Phil Kearny** was built near the Bozeman Trail, 18 miles south of modern Sheridan. It had one of the shortest, and surely the bloodiest, histories of any outpost in the American West. The fort was constructed, in open violation of the treaty between the U.S. government and the Sioux, in an unprotected location in the heart of the Sioux's best buffalo-hunting territory. Sioux leaders Red Cloud and Crazy Horse vowed to drive the whites out. During Fort Kearny's first six months, 164 men—nearly two-thirds of the original garrison—were killed.

✔ **CHECK THESE OUT—UNIQUE SIGHTS**

- Wander the turn-of-the-century streets of downtown Sheridan's **Main Street District**, the best preserved of any in Wyoming. *page 267*
- Examine more than 10,000 artifacts at Buffalo's **Jim Gatchell Memorial Museum of the West**, once a pharmacist's private collection. *page 276*
- Get down and dirty when you tour a **coal mine** near Gillette, the self-proclaimed "energy capital of the nation." *page 280*
- Join science students studying the **Vore Buffalo Jump**, where 20,000 bison were killed by American Indians before the arrival of whites. *page 285*

About half of the men were victims of Fetterman's Fight on December 21, 1866. A stone monument on **Massacre Hill**, three miles north of the fort overlooking Route 87, marks the spot where Captain William Fetterman and 80 troops were annihilated by some 2000 Sioux and Cheyenne warriors. In direct defiance of his commanding officer's orders, Fetterman had pursued the warriors after rescuing a wagon train from attack and had ridden directly into a classic ambush.

Reinforcements were sent after a heroic 236-mile journey by civilian scout John "Portugee" Phillips, who reached Fort Laramie on horseback on Christmas Eve, after four nights' travel through one of the worst blizzards of the century. Six dozen new breech-loading rifles came along with the additional troops.

The breechloading Springfield came in handy the following summer, in what has come to be known as the **Wagon Box Fight**. On August 2, 1867, 26 soldiers were guarding six civilian wood-cutters when they were attacked by some 1500 Sioux. Building a circular redoubt from the woodcutters' wagons and boxes, the troops held off wave after wave of Sioux assailants and caused many casualties by the sheer volume of fire from their new rifles. The location is marked by a monument just south of Story, on a dirt road off Route 195, four and a half miles northwest of Fort Kearny.

Though Red Cloud and Crazy Horse lost that battle, they won the war when, a year later, the U.S. government decided to vacate the Powder River Basin and the Bozeman Trail. As soon as the garrison evacuated in August 1868, Fort Kearny was burned to the ground. No original structures remain to be seen today at this state historic site, but a modern museum and visitors center have exhibits and video programs describing the life and times of Fort Kearny, and offer information for self-guided tours of the fort grounds, battle sites and Bozeman Trail. A replica cabin serves as a living-history display. Closed Monday and Tuesday from April to mid-May and from October through November; open only by appointment from December through March. Admission. ~ Route 193, Story; 307-684-7629.

On the prairies east of Sheridan about 45 miles is the RBL **Bison Ranch**, where you'll be encouraged to hand-feed 2000-pound buffalo (from a tour bus window). The restaurant here serves buffalo meat and the gift shop has every kind of kitsch imaginable, from buffalo-foot lamps to buffalo-tooth necklaces. Closed November through April. Admission. ~ 4355 Route 14/16 East, Clearmont; 307-758-4387.

A good choice in Sheridan for economy-minded visitors is the friendly **Rocktrim Motel**. The 18 wood-paneled guest rooms aren't particularly modern, but they're air-conditioned and spa-

LODGING

cious, and some have coffeemakers, mini-refrigerators and microwaves. Four full kitchenettes and non-smoking rooms are available. ~ 449 Coffeen Avenue, Sheridan; 307-672-2464. BUDGET.

Just off Route 90 at the south end of town is the intriguing **Mill Inn**, listed on the National Historic Register. Occupying a former flour mill, the grain elevator still stands next door. It's been entirely altered, of course, and has become a pleasant motel with 45 standard rooms. There's no pool here, but there is an exercise room, and continental breakfast is included in the room rate. ~ 2161 Coffeen Avenue, Sheridan; 307-672-6401. MODERATE.

Top of the line in Sheridan is the five-story **Holiday Inn**, also at the south end. Within its "HoliDome" indoor recreation center are a swimming pool, sauna, hot tub and workout room, not to mention a putting green, racquetball court and game room. The 212 rooms are pretty much standard issue. Hotel facilities include a restaurant, coffee shop, lounge, gift shop and coin laundry. Children under 19 accompanied by their parents stay for free. ~ 1809 Sugarland Drive, Sheridan; 307-672-8931, 800-465-4329, fax 307-672-6388. DELUXE.

Downtown is the **Best Western Sheridan Center**, whose 138 guest rooms are contained in four separate buildings (two of them connected by a skybridge) on three facing corners at Main and 2nd. All rooms feature coffeemakers and king- or queen-size beds. On site are a coffee shop, a dining room and an adjoining lounge. The inn has both indoor and outdoor pools and a hot tub. ~ 612 North Main Street, Sheridan; 307-674-7421, 800-528-1234, fax 307-672-3018. MODERATE.

The granddaddy of all dude ranches is **Eatons' Ranch**, 18 miles west of Sheridan in the Big Horn foothills via Route 331. When the three Eaton brothers earned more money by taking in visitors

---

✔ CHECK THESE OUT—UNIQUE LODGING

- *Budget:* Tempt fate at the **Z Bar Motel**: Take a bite from an apple growing in parklike grounds that surround this log-cabin community. *page 278*
- *Moderate:* Sow your wild oats when you stay at the **Mill Inn**, a converted former flour mill with its grain elevator intact. *page 272*
- *Deluxe:* Relax in the solar-powered log lodge of **Spahn's Big Horn Mountain Bed & Breakfast** after a full day of hiking and wildlife viewing. *page 273*
- *Ultra-deluxe:* Ride a horse to your heart's delight across the 7000 acres that surround **Eatons' Ranch**, the world's first (1904) dude ranch. *page 272*

Budget: under $50   Moderate: $50–$90   Deluxe: $90–$130   Ultra-deluxe: over $130

on their North Dakota hay ranch than they did by selling grain, they relocated in 1904 to this site because it offered better riding country. Today the ranch is still in the hands of the Eaton family. It's grown a lot, though: it now can host up to 125 guests in 51 rustic cabins, most with twin beds, all with private baths. The emphasis at Eatons' is on horses: after guests are fitted with saddles, they ride under the supervision of wranglers until they're ready to ride unescorted and then have free rein throughout the ranch's 7000-acre spread. There's also fishing, hiking, swimming in a heated outdoor pool and weekly square dances. Meals are served in a huge dining room. Three-night minimum. Closed October through May. ~ 270 Eaton Ranch Road, Wolf; 307-655-9285, 800-210-1049, fax 307-655-9269; www.eatonsranch.com. ULTRA-DELUXE.

Considerably more sedate is **Spahn's Big Horn Mountain Bed & Breakfast**, not far from the Bradford Brinton Memorial. From the front porch of this four-story log home on the Big Horn slope you can gaze across 100 miles of Powder River country. Binoculars are served with the country breakfast. There are two rooms with Victorian antiques in the solar-powered lodge, and two outlying cabins, one with its own wood stove and kitchen. All have private bathrooms. Hiking, cross-country skiing and wildlife watching are the activities of choice. ~ P.O. Box 579, Big Horn, WY 82833; 307-674-8150; www.bighorn-wyoming.com. DELUXE.

◄ HIDDEN

In Sheridan it's not hard to find a place to eat that maintains the atmosphere of northern Wyoming during the days of Buffalo Bill. Certainly, the **Sheridan Inn**, where Cody once auditioned Wild West Show acts, is one. Healthy, creative meals are served daily in the pleasant if nondescript restaurant; the Buffalo Bill Saloon is adjacent. Call for hours. ~ 856 Broadway, Sheridan; 307-674-5440. DELUXE TO ULTRA-DELUXE.

DINING

Generous portions of cowboy home cookin' are what you'll get at **The Silver Spur**. This is just a good ol' family café—but the breakfasts and lunches (no dinners) are tasty and filling. Closed Sunday. ~ 832 North Main Street, Sheridan; 307-672-2749. BUDGET.

The cozy **Ciao Bistro** offers a distinctly different choice. Though located right in the heart of the historic district, this restaurant has more in common with big-city nouvelle cafés than with The Mint Bar, Sheridan's landmark watering hole, across the street. The owner, a Seattle implant, tosses organic salads, pastas, vegetarian dishes, Mediterranean-influenced entrées, and breads and desserts baked on-site. The bistro also has a selection of 65 wines from around the world and a full espresso bar. ~ 120 North Main Street, Sheridan; 307-672-2838. DELUXE TO ULTRA-DELUXE.

A Korean restaurant in cowboy country is an oxymoron, to be sure. But **Kim's Family Restaurant** holds its own. In addition to traditional Korean cuisine, the menu features excellent sushi and tempura dinners, making this good-sized eatery an obligatory stop for Japanese tour groups traveling between Yellowstone National Park and Mount Rushmore. American-style breakfasts and lunches are also available. ~ 2004 North Main Street, Sheridan; 307-672-0357. BUDGET TO MODERATE.

If you venture south to the sites around Story, you may want to maintain the historic mood by eating in the **Lodore Supper Club**. Housed in a 1919 dance hall, this lively restaurant specializes in American cuisine, featuring prime rib and seafood. The adjoining Tack Room bar has a big dancefloor. ~ 6 North Piney Road, Story; 307-683-2924. MODERATE.

SHOPPING   The truest "cowboy store" you're ever likely to find is **King's Saddlery and Ropes** in historic downtown Sheridan. All manner of ranch gear is sold here along with gift items for curious visitors. By some estimates, 80 percent of all rodeo cowboys buy their ropes from King's. If you wish, you can take a look at 150 years' worth of Old West equipment, including more than 500 antique saddles and early leather-working tools, in saddlemaker-owner Don King's personal museum. Closed Sunday. ~ 184 North Main Street, Sheridan; 307-672-2702.

If you're looking to get outfitted for a week at a dude ranch, check out **Dan's Western Wear**, which has been serving the city since 1919. This is the place to find your Levi's jeans, Tony Lama boots and Stetson hat, as well as American Indian turquoise and other jewelry. Closed Sunday from September through May. ~ 226 North Main Street, Sheridan; 307-672-9378. If the gear here is too traditional for you, head down the street to the **Custom Cowboy Shop** where you can buy one-of-a-kind designs or have your own conceptions tailor-made. Closed Sunday from September through May. ~ 350 North Main Street, Sheridan; 307-672-7733.

For regional art in Sheridan, visit the **Foothills Gallery** to see Connie Robinson's watercolors and Gene Stewart's oil paintings. Closed Sunday and Monday January through May. Closed Sunday June through December. ~ 134 North Main Street; 307-672-2068. Prints of works by Charles Russell and Frederic Remington and etchings by Hans Kleiber are for sale at the **Hangin' Tree Gallery**. Closed Sunday. ~ 160 North Main Street; 307-674-9869. Hit the **Best Out West Mall** for antiques and gifts. Closed Sunday. ~ 109 North Main Street; 307-674-5003.

A superb collection of Western history and literature by Wyoming and other Western authors can be found at **The Book Shop**. Ask about occasional poetry readings. Closed Sunday. ~ 117 North Main Street, Sheridan; 307-672-6505.

Sheridan is home to one of the great playhouses in the Rockies, **NIGHTLIFE**
the **WYO Theater**. Built in 1923 as a vaudeville and silent-movie
theater called The Lotus (it opened with Lionel Barrymore in *Enemies of Women*), it was fully renovated in art-deco style in 1989
and now stages resident and touring professional productions of
all kinds. Hero-and-villain melodramas and musical revues are
among the variety of shows. Performance days
vary. Call for a current schedule. ~ 42 North Main
Street, Sheridan; 307-672-9083, box office 307-
672-9084.

> In Sheridan's early days,
> there was no postal
> service. Mail was
> dumped into a
> cracker box. Patrons
> helped themselves.

When the cowboys aren't wrestling bulls or roping calves, you may find them during the afternoon
at the **Buffalo Bill Saloon**, sipping on a Wyoming Slug,
a powerful mix of champagne and whiskey. ~ Sheridan
Inn, 856 Broadway, Sheridan; 307-674-5440.

At night, they may be knocking back a Black Dog Ale
at **The Mint Bar**. A Sheridan landmark, The Mint is worth a visit
if only to check out its collection of Old West memorabilia. Closed
Sunday. ~ 151 North Main Street, Sheridan; 307-674-9696.

Carousers not into the country-and-western scene prefer the
Beaver Creek Saloon, a spacious watering hole with pool tables
and live rock bands on most weekends. The building was Sheridan's original town hall. ~ 112 North Main Street, Sheridan; 307-
674-8181.

Sports lovers gather at **The Pony Bar & Grill**, whose satellite
system shows games and events on a big-screen television and
eight smaller TVs. Closed Sunday from March through August.
~ 3 South Gould Street, Sheridan; 307-674-7000.

On Friday and Saturday (more in summer), locals dance the
night away at the **Tack Room**, a bar adjoining the Lodore Supper
Club. Live bands play country-and-western and rock. ~ 6 North
Piney Road, Story; 307-683-2924.

BIGHORN NATIONAL FOREST **PARKS**

The Big Horn Mountains rise rapidly on both the east
and west to a central plateau of alpine meadows and pine forests
at 9000-to-10,000–foot elevation. The entire region—over 1.1
million acres from the Montana border south to the headwaters
of the Powder River—belongs to the national forest. Summer trout
fishing, backpacking, biking and horseback riding; winter skiing
and snowmobiling; year-round wildlife watching (especially for
its herds of elk, deer and bighorn sheep) are popular pursuits.
Highlights of the forest include the Cloud Peak Wilderness Area
and Medicine Wheel National Historic Landmark (see Chapter
Four). You'll find picnic areas and restrooms; there is a resort
complex at Meadowlark Lake and a general store with gas at Burgess Junction. ~ Routes 14 (to Greybull) and 14A (to Lovell) cross

the Big Horns from Dayton, north of Sheridan. Route 16 (to Worland) crosses the range from Buffalo, south of Sheridan. All three access the national forest; 307-672-0751.

▲ There are 415 RV/tent sites at 33 campgrounds; no charge to $10 per night (most $8 to $9); 7- to 30-day maximum stay (most 14 days). Eight campgrounds can be reserved (877-444-6777). Most campgrounds are open from May through October; higher-altitude sites may be open only from June to mid-September.

▼▼▼▼▼▼▼▼▼▼
Buffalo Area

The town of Buffalo, 35 miles south of Sheridan, is inextricably linked with the era of the range wars. The most famous of them was the 1892 Johnson County War. Wealthy cattle barons, fearing that homesteaders and sheep ranchers were rustling their livestock, sent two dozen hired guns from Texas to eliminate 70 "troublemakers." Two sheepmen were gunned down at the KC Ranch; but as the vigilantes moved in on the county seat of Buffalo, that city sent 200 citizens of its own to the cattlemen's TA Ranch headquarters. After a major shoot-out, and with the support of the U.S. cavalry, the Buffalo group made almost 50 arrests—but no one was ever convicted.

Today Buffalo is a quiet town, even though after Sheridan it is the major eastern gateway to the Big Horns and a key transportation hub for the entire region. The Cloud Peak Skyway (Route 16) through the Powder River Pass and Ten Sleep Canyon has its eastern terminus here (see Chapter Four). Two interstate highways, Route 25 (south to Casper, Cheyenne, Denver and Albuquerque) and Route 90 (north and west to Sheridan, Billings and Seattle; east to Gillette, Chicago and Boston), come together at Buffalo.

SIGHTS

Downtown Buffalo's **Main Street Historic District**, built along a crooked old trail that forded Clear Creek, has buildings that have stood since 1884, the year the town was incorporated. Among them is the neoclassical **Johnson County Courthouse**. Closed Saturday and Sunday. ~ 76 North Main Street; 307-684-7272. The 1910 **Occidental Hotel** has been fully restored and the Occidental Museum is open during the summer. ~ 10 North Main Street; 307-684-0451. Walking-tour brochures can be obtained from the **Buffalo Chamber of Commerce**. ~ 55 North Main Street; 307-684-5544.

Of particular interest to visitors is the **Jim Gatchell Memorial Museum of the West**, at the corner of North Main Street beside the courthouse. Beginning as a local pharmacist's private collection, the museum was moved into its own two-story home in 1957; it subsequently expanded into the adjacent 1909 Carnegie Library. The collection includes dioramas of the Wagon Box Fight, the Johnson County Cattle War and early Buffalo. More than 10,000 artifacts of American Indians, soldiers, ranchers and other settlers are also on display. Closed December to mid-April. Admission. ~ 100 Fort Street, Buffalo; 307-684-9331.

A large, sparsely populated region, Johnson County stretches from the summit of the Big Horns to the badlands along the Powder River. Among several points of interest (outside of Buffalo and Fort Kearny) is **Lake De Smet** (Monument Road), a major rainbow trout fishery and waterfowl haven seven miles north of Buffalo off Route 90. Named for renowned Jesuit missionary Pierre De Smet, the lake is reputed to be the home of a Loch Ness–type sea monster: a topic for *Unsolved Mysteries*, perhaps.

There's no mystery as to where **Kaycee** got its name. This village, 45 miles south of Buffalo off Route 25, was christened after the KC Ranch, the nearby 19th-century ranch where two sheep "rustlers" were killed to set off the Johnson County War of 1892. On the town's false-fronted Main Street (looking like something straight out of a TV oater), next door to the old log-cabin jail, is the **Hoofprints of the Past Museum**, which preserves all manner of cowboy gear and other memorabilia from the history of southern Johnson County. Closed November through May. ~ Main Street, Kaycee; 307-738-2381.

Butch Cassidy and the Sundance Kid knew this territory well. Kaycee was the nearest community to their notorious **Hole-in-the-Wall** hideout, about 26 miles southwest. Despite its reputation, Hole-in-the-Wall was not a deep, dark cave nor a steep-sided canyon; it was (and is) a lush and spacious valley named after a London pub by two English brothers who established a cattle ranch at this remote location. Robert "Butch Cassidy" Parker may have chosen the hole as a place to train getaway horses for his "Wild Bunch" of outlaws, which also included Harry "Sundance Kid" Longabaugh and Harvey "Kid Curry" Logan. Other places may have been more secure, but few lawmen tried to penetrate the stronghold.

◄ HIDDEN

Modern travelers can visit the site by four-wheel-drive vehicle, horse or mountain bike. Take Route 190 west from Kaycee 17 miles to the townsite of Barnum, where the pavement ends. Turn left on dirt Arminto Road and follow a red-walled canyon four miles to the Bar C Ranch. Stay on the maintained road. The closer you get, the more rugged the road. ~ Kaycee; 307-738-2243.

The **Cloud Peak Inn** will have you feeling right at home in a wealthy rancher's former "town house." This 1906 bed-and-breakfast home has five bedrooms, three with private baths and all furnished with period antiques. Guests can enjoy a jacuzzi tub and a fireplace. A full gourmet breakfast is served each morning. Smokers beware: Cigarettes are allowed only on the porch. ~ 590 North Burritt Avenue, Buffalo; 307-684-5794, 800-715-5794, fax 307-684-7653; www.cpibandb.com. MODERATE.

LODGING

Parklike grounds accented by spruce and apple trees surround the **Z Bar Motel**, a half-dozen blocks west of Buffalo's historic downtown. The motel consists of 20 quaint individual log cabins with modern Western decor. Each unit has a refrigerator and private bath; some kitchen units and king-size beds are available. ~ 626 Fort Street, Buffalo; 307-684-5535, 800-341-8000, fax 307-684-5538; www.imalodging.com. BUDGET.

Want to get out of town and into the Big Horn Mountains? Then the **South Fork Inn**, 16 miles west of Buffalo in Bighorn National Forest, is for you. Twelve cabins—some one-room and rustic, some two-room and modern—surround an early-20th-century log lodge, which also contains a restaurant and lounge. Daily trail rides and pack trips into the nearby Cloud Peak Wilderness Area start at the inn's South Fork Corrals; a horseback riding or walking trail system also begins here. The inn rests at 7700 feet elevation on the South Fork of Clear Creek. Closed April. ~ P.O. Box 96, Buffalo, WY 82834; 307-684-9609; www.wilderwest.com/trailwest. BUDGET.

DINING

Hard by Buffalo's Route 25 interchange, you may catch the surprising sight of an antique (1925) carousel with 36 horses modeled after famous steeds of the American West. **Colonel Bozeman's Restaurant & Tavern** is an integral part of The Carousel Park. Situated on the Bozeman Trail crossing of Clear Creek, this Old West–style tavern is open for breakfast pancakes, lunch sandwiches, dinner steaks and bedtime desserts. The adjacent park also has a Ferris wheel, a miniature golf course, an ice-cream parlor, a gift shop and a motel. ~ 675 East Hart Street, Buffalo; 307-684-5555. MODERATE TO DELUXE.

Sagewood Gifts and Cafe has two faces: a shop in front proffering gifts and souvenirs and an eatery in back serving homemade soups, sandwiches and desserts. Try the "dillacado," dill bread

---

✔ CHECK THESE OUT—UNIQUE DINING

- *Budget to moderate:* Deliver yourself to **Bailey's Bar & Grill**, which serves up hearty fare in a turn-of-the-century post office. *page 281*
- *Moderate:* Head to the **Lodore Supper Club**, a 1919 dance hall, for an evening of dining and dancing. *page 274*
- *Moderate to deluxe:* Have dinner at the **Flying V Cambria Inn**, all that remains of a gold-mining ghost town near the Black Hills. *page 289*
- *Deluxe to ultra-deluxe:* Toast the memory of Buffalo Bill at the **Sheridan Inn**, where Cody once auditioned Wild West Show acts. *page 273*

Budget: under $7   Moderate: $7–$12   Deluxe: $12–$20   Ultra-deluxe: over $20

piled with smoked turkey, seasoned peppers and avocado. Lunch only. Closed Sunday. ~ 15 North Main Street, Buffalo; 307-684-7670. BUDGET.

Up in Bighorn National Forest, **The Pines Lodge Speak Easy & Supper Club**, 14 miles from Buffalo, is a popular stop for folks coming from, or going to, mountain recreational areas. Three meals a day are served, with steak and seafood highlighting the evening menu. Closed September through May. ~ Route 16 West; 307-351-1010. MODERATE TO DELUXE.

Locally raised beef—prime rib and steaks—are the meals that keep drawing travelers back to the **Hole-in-the-Wall Bar**, 45 minutes' drive south of Buffalo. Decor is as rough-hewn as could be, but that doesn't bother folks just in from the Powder River badlands. Breakfast, lunch and dinner. ~ 349 Nolan Street, Kaycee; 307-738-2520. BUDGET TO MODERATE.

Margo's Pottery & Fine Crafts makes pottery, sterling silver jewelry, glass vases and other gifts. Closed Sunday through Thursday from January through March; closed Sunday from April through December. ~ 26 North Main Street, Buffalo; 307-684-9406.   **SHOPPING**

Housed in a narrow brick building, **Art + Works Too & Cowboy Coffee Café** exhibits local, regional and American Indian art. Light eats and espresso drinks are served at the back of the gallery. Closed Sunday through Wednesday from January through May. ~ 94 South Main Street, Buffalo; 307-684-1299.

On Friday and Saturday evenings, you can catch a local musician performing folk or blues at **Art + Works Too & Cowboy Coffee Café**. ~ 94 South Main Street, Buffalo; 307-684-1299.   **NIGHTLIFE**

There's more to this region than first meets the eye. Gillette, Wyoming's fastest-growing city, is at the heart of one of the richest mineral deposits in North America, and the Thunder Basin National Grassland is an immense tract of wildlife-rich high plains.   ▼▼▼▼▼▼▼▼▼
Gillette Area

There's not a lot to look at during the one-hour (68-mile) drive east on Route 90 from Buffalo to Gillette. A roadside rest area sits about halfway between the two cities, at the crossing of the **Powder River**. This prairie river isn't quite the proverbial "mile wide and an inch deep" stream, but citizens of Kaycee like to say that the Powder is "too thick to drink, too thin to plow."   **SIGHTS**

Gillette is a modern-day boom town. Though established more than a century ago as a railroad depot, it grew only modestly (as a shipping center for livestock, grain and coal) until oil and uranium were discovered in the 1950s. Now a city of 21,000, Gillette calls itself "the energy capital of the nation."

The area's mineral wealth is staggering. Experts estimate that the low-sulfur coal reserves under Campbell County alone could answer the fuel needs of the United States for the next 200 years. The 16 open-pit mines surrounding Gillette produce 90 percent of Wyoming's coal, more than all the mines in either West Virginia or Kentucky.

About 25 million barrels of crude oil are pumped annually from 200 wells in Campbell County.

Tours can be scheduled at several Gillette-area coal mines. The Amax Coal West, Inc.'s **Eagle Butte Mine** is just eight miles north of Gillette. The Gillette Convention & Visitors Bureau conducts tours Memorial Day to labor Day that leave at 9 a.m. and 11 a.m. Reservations required. ~ Route 14/16. The **Cordero Mine**, 25 miles south of Gillette, has been honored as "the nation's safest surface coal mine." ~ T-7 Road, 25 miles south of Gillette; 307-682-8005. The **Wyodak Mine**, three miles east of Gillette, is the oldest operating mine in the Powder River Basin, established in 1922. ~ Route 51; 307-682-3410. The **Gillette Convention & Visitors Bureau** will also make tour arrangements. ~ 1810 South Douglas Highway (I-90 Exit 126); 307-686-0040, 800-544-6136.

For a survey of Campbell County's natural-resource base, drop by the **High Plains Energy Exhibit**. At this outdoor exhibit visitors are encouraged to develop a close personal relationship with heavy mining equipment, including coal drills, oil rigs, locomotives and bulldozers. This small science exhibit is only one of several elements of the Cam-plex, Wyoming's largest multipurpose events center. The 1000-acre complex hosts everything from conventions and cultural events to horse racing and rodeo. ~ 1635 Reata Drive, Gillette; 307-682-0552.

Near downtown, the **Campbell County Rockpile Museum** is a repository of artifacts and memorabilia that tell the history of the Gillette area. They include prehistoric arrowheads and grinding stones; 19th-century ranchers' saddles, guns and branding irons; a piece of the original railroad track built across the county; machines and appliances from early businesses and pioneer homes; and an impressive collection of photographs and pen-and-ink drawings. Closed Sunday from September through May. ~ 900 West 2nd Street, Gillette; 307-682-5723.

Until 1976, Gillette was the only incorporated town in Campbell County. That year, **Wright** was established 37 miles from Gillette to provide housing and services for mineworkers in the southern part of the county. Now with a population of about 1400, the town is prospering.

HIDDEN ▶   One of the largest private bison herds in existence makes its home about 30 miles south of Gillette at the **Durham Buffalo Ranch**. More than 3500 bison roam the ranch's 55,000 acres. Tours are available by appointment year-round. ~ Route 59, Wright; 307-939-1271.

Wright is also a gateway to **Thunder Basin National Grassland**, the nation's largest national grassland, a 572,000-acre tract of high plains and plateaus shared by five counties. Sheep and cattle share the acreage with one of the world's largest herds of pronghorn antelope. ~ Routes 59 and 450; Forest Service office, 2250 East Richards Street, Douglas; 307-358-4690.

LODGING

Gillette is a haven for national chain motels and motor inns that cluster around interstate highway exchanges. One of the best is the **Best Western Tower West Lodge**, at Exit 124 on the west side of the city. A heated swimming pool is the focal point of this two-story, 190-room inn. Children under 18 accompanied by a parent stay free. ~ 109 North Route 14-16, Gillette; 307-686-2210, 800-528-1234, fax 307-682-5105. MODERATE.

The city's other finest hotel is the three-story **Holiday Inn of Gillette**. Some of its 158 rooms have balconies that overlook the Holidome indoor recreation center, which has everything a traveling recreation addict could hope for: a swimming pool, sauna, whirlpool, exercise room, putting green, ping-pong, foosball and video games. All rooms have coffeemakers and refrigerators. The hotel has a full-service restaurant and live-music lounge, as well as a business center, coin laundry and gift shop. ~ 2009 South Douglas Highway, Gillette; 307-686-3000, 800-465-4329, fax 307-686-4018. MODERATE TO DELUXE.

The **Mustang Motel** has no swimming pool to cool you off on hot summer afternoons, but you will get a clean room (there are 30) with cable TV and kitchen facilities (if you need them). The coffee is free in the lobby, and a coin laundry is open to guests. What's more, they'll welcome your pet. ~ 922 East 3rd Street, Gillette; 307-682-4784, fax extension 114. MODERATE.

DINING

A Gillette favorite is **The Prime Rib Restaurant**, which serves up hefty helpings of pasta, steak, seafood and (of course) prime rib. The restaurant, which sits just north of the downtown freeway interchange, has been honored in recent years by both American Express and *Wine Spectator* magazine. The lounge lures diners for before- or after-dinner drinks; the restaurant menu is also available here. No lunch on Saturday or Sunday. ~ 1205 South Douglas Highway, Gillette; 307-682-2944. MODERATE TO ULTRA-DELUXE.

If you're in the mood for Italian, consider **Ole's Pizza & Spaghetti House**. Located in the Powder Basin Shopping Center, it serves up the town's best pasta and pizza in a very friendly atmosphere. You can also fill up here on barbecued beef ribs and luncheon sandwiches. ~ South Douglas Highway and Lakeway Road, Gillette; 307-682-8484. BUDGET TO MODERATE.

The turn-of-the-century atmosphere of **Bailey's Bar & Grill** perpetuates the mood of the old downtown post office building in which it's lodged. The menu here runs the gamut from hamburger lunches to gourmet chicken dinners. The restaurant features a fresh salad bar and delectable homemade pies. ~ 301 South Gillette Avenue, Gillette; 307-686-7678. BUDGET TO MODERATE.

The **Hong Kong Restaurant** serves passable Chinese food, from Hunan beef and lemon chicken to the more Americanized chop suey and egg foo yung. ~ 1612 West 2nd Street, Gillette; 307-682-5829. BUDGET TO MODERATE.

SHOPPING
The largest Western store in northeastern Wyoming is **Corral West Ranchwear**, which carries every sort of men's and women's clothing you might be seeking—and then some. It also offers a selection of American Indian jewelry and pottery, Navajo blankets, silver belt buckles and novelty gifts ranging from rattlesnake eggs to jackalopes. ~ 2610 South Douglas Highway, Gillette; 307-682-6200.

Numerous small malls and shopping centers are located around Gillette. The largest is the **Powder Basin Shopping Center**. Three department stores and several clothing stores are among the retail outlets. ~ South Douglas Highway and Lakeway Road, Gillette.

NIGHTLIFE
Gillette's main entertainment venue is the **Cam-plex**. Within the 1000-acre grounds of this multipurpose events center are the 960-seat **Heritage Center Theater** for concerts and live theater, two convention pavilions, a horseracing track and a rodeo arena. In adjacent Cam-plex Park, the **Gillette Community Theater** performs summer melodramas. ~ 1635 Reata Drive, Gillette; 307-682-0552.

Bands rock the crowd at **Mingles** on Wednesday, Friday and Saturday nights; deejays spin tunes the rest of the evenings. Otherwise, knock back a beer, rack up a game of pool or feed quarter-hungry video games. Cover for live music. ~ 2209 South Douglas Highway, Gillette; 307-686-1222.

PARKS
THUNDER BASIN NATIONAL GRASSLAND 🏃 🚲 🐎 🔥 The national grassland program was created under the aegis of the National Recovery Act to regenerate arable lands turned into "dust bowls" by overzealous homesteaders in the early part of the 20th century. With 572,000 scattered acres of high plains and plateaus, Thunder Basin is administered by the U.S.D.A. Forest Service. Sheep and cattle share the acreage with one of the world's largest herds of pronghorn antelope. The Black Thunder Mine, America's largest coal producer, and other companies also operate here under special permit. ~ Routes 59 (south from Gillette to Douglas, and north through Weston), 450 (east from Wright to

Newcastle) and 116 (south from Sundance to Upton and Route 450) pass through the Thunder Basin; 307-358-4690.

The famed Black Hills of South Dakota lap over into Wyoming's northeastern corner, providing the state with such sites of keen recreational interest as Black Hills National Forest, Keyhole State Park and the unmistakable Devils Tower National Monument.

Devils Tower and the Black Hills

SIGHTS

Traveling east on Route 90 from Gillette, the town you'll come to is **Moorcroft,** which in 1891 was the largest cattle-shipping depot in the United States. Today, located less than a half-hour's drive east of Gillette on the interstate, it serves the coal and oil industries as well.

Moorcroft is just 16 miles from **Keyhole State Park,** which surrounds manmade Keyhole Reservoir on the Belle Fourche River. Park facilities, including boat launches and campgrounds, are located along the lake's southeastern shore. The reservoir offers excellent fishing for warmwater species, and it attracts a wide variety of wildlife, from white-tailed deer and wild turkeys to resident and migrating waterfowl. Waterskiing and windsurfing are popular diversions. Admission. ~ Route 113, Pine Haven; 307-756-3596.

Northeastern Wyoming's No. 1 attraction is 33 miles northeast of Moorcroft. Although it was the site of *Close Encounters of the Third Kind,* visitors should *not* expect to see UFOs hovering over **Devils Tower National Monument**. America's first national monument (established by President Theodore Roosevelt in 1906) is, rather, a site of geological fascination and a place to enjoy wildlife and numerous outdoor activities, including swimming, fishing and camping. Rock climbers also come to test their skills on the tower's nearly vertical walls.

Visible for many miles around, Devils Tower looms above the Belle Fourche River, where the pine forests of the Black Hills meet the grasslands of the Powder River Basin. Its formation began about 60 million years ago, when molten magma surged near the earth's surface and cooled underground as igneous rock. Sedimentary rocks eroded away around it, exposing this harder plug. Today, the monolith—the tallest rock formation of its kind in the United States—rises 867 feet above its base, 1267 feet above the river and 5117 feet above sea level. It is 1000 feet around at its base, an acre and a half on its sagebrush-and-grass-topped summit.

Kiowa Indians, who called the monolith *Mateo Tipi* (Bear Lodge), had their own explanation for how the Tower came to be. In their legend, seven sisters at play were threatened by a great bear. Fleeing in terror, they came to the stump of a huge tree, which they climbed. As they did so, the stump began to grow toward the heavens. The bear couldn't reach them, although its claws made long gouges on all sides of the tree. The sisters were carried into the sky, where they became the stars of the constellation Ursa Major, the "Big Dipper," or "Great Bear."

The "gouges" are still the most striking feature of Devils Tower. At close range, the nearly vertical walls appear as a mass of fluted, polygonal columns. Where the columns have broken off, they lie as a talus of boulders at the Tower's foot. Adventurous visitors may scramble through the boulder field for a closer look at even more adventurous rock climbers, who bring all their technical skills to bear in scaling the Tower.

The first recorded ascent of the Tower took place on July 4, 1893. More than 1000 spectators cheered as William Rogers and Willard Ripley, using a handmade 350-foot wooden ladder for the steepest lower face, carried the 44-star flag (Wyoming was the 44th state) to the summit. Curiously, there already was a flagpole there to raise Old Glory on this Independence Day. Today, more than 5000 people climb the tower every year by some 80 specified routes. Climbers must register with a ranger before and after their ascents at either the **visitors center** (open April through October) at the foot of the Tower or at the administrative building when the center is closed. The rough-hewn log structure, three miles from the national monument's entrance station, was built during the 1930s by the Civilian Conservation Corps. It offers displays on the Tower's history, geology and wildlife.

The 1.25-miles-long **Tower Trail,** which circles the foot of Devils Tower, also begins at the visitors center. Interpretive signs explain the diverse ecosystem of the Tower area, which represents every step in the process of establishing a forest, from bare rock to grassland, scrub vegetation to pines. More than 90 species of birds have been recorded in the 1347-acre national monument, and whitetail deer are among the most commonly observed mammals.

◆◆

THE BLACK HILLS OF WYOMING

A significant portion of the pine-covered slopes of Black Hills National Forest are in northeastern Wyoming. The hiking and fishing are good here. Highlights include Inyan Kara Mountain (Schlup Road), an extinct volcano 15 miles south of Sundance, where General George Armstrong Custer carved his name in a granite wall near the summit in 1874; and Cook Lake (Bear Lodge Road), 18 miles north of Sundance, circumnavigated by a one-mile trail that offers access to the only trout fishing in this part of the state.

Most common of all, however, is the blacktail prairie dog. A **prairie-dog colony**, or "town," flourishes beside the Belle Fourche River about a half mile from the entrance station, not far from the campground and amphitheater. Though they're cute and appear docile, visitors should avoid getting too close to them—they can bite and their old burrows may be occupied by rattlesnakes. Don't even think about feeding them. But it is a delight to watch their clan behavior from a distance. Admission. ~ Route 110, Devils Tower; 307-467-5283.

Some folks think **Sundance**, 30 miles southeast of Devils Tower on Route 90, was named for the Sundance Kid. That may be true of a town of the same name in Utah, but here exactly the opposite was the case. In 1889, after serving 18 months in the Sundance jail for horse stealing, Harry Longabaugh simply began calling himself "The Sundance Kid."

The town, in fact, was named for nearby **Sundance Mountain**, the Temple of the Sioux *(Wi Wacippi Paha)*. At the base of this rocky mountain, warriors once undertook their mystical (and often self-torturing) sun dances to restore harmony to the world.

The **Vore Buffalo Jump**, 16 miles east of Sundance, is a work in progress. Discovered during the construction of Route 90 in the 1970s, the site revealed layer upon layer of bison bones . . . from perhaps as many as 20,000 animals that were stampeded over the rim of a ridge and into a deep natural sinkhole at various times between A.D. 1500 and 1800. Though there are other buffalo jumps, or *pishkun,* in the northern Rockies, this one is unique in the exceptional preservation of its bones and artifacts and the remarkably accurate dates that researchers have established for the site. The original land owners, Woodrow and Doris Vore, donated the "jump" in 1989 to the University of Wyoming, whose scientists and students continue to excavate. Interpretive trails and a visitors center are planned. ~ Route 14, Beulah; 307-283-1192.

◄ HIDDEN

At the eastern edge of Thunder Basin, 70 miles from Wright and 50 miles south of Sundance on the old Cheyenne-Deadwood Stage Road, is **Newcastle**. Named for the English coal port of Newcastle upon Tyne when it was founded in 1890, it has since developed into an oil-refining center astride Route 85, the principal route from Cheyenne to South Dakota's Black Hills. It is of interest to visitors mainly for its **Anna Miller Museum**, whose focal point is the Jenny Stockade: a combination fort, hotel, store, telegraph office, blacksmith shop and stagecoach way station for a U.S. government–sponsored gold camp in the 1870s. Closed weekends. Open Saturday from June through August. ~ 401 Delaware Avenue, Newcastle; 307-746-4188.

Text continued on page 288.

The Black Hills of South Dakota

Just across the Wyoming state line from Sundance is one of the most tourist-friendly regions of North America: South Dakota's Black Hills.

Centered around the Old West gambling center of Deadwood, and including Mount Rushmore National Memorial and some of the nation's most remarkable caves, the Black Hills can easily be made a full week's vacation destination in themselves. Traveling east from Sundance or Devils Tower, Route 90 skirts the northern edge of the Black Hills as it drops southeasterly past the towns of **Spearfish** (known for its outdoor passion play, held three nights weekly in summer), **Sturgis** (site of North America's biggest motorcycle rendezvous each August) and **Rapid City**. **Badlands National Park** is less than an hour's drive east of Rapid City; the savage beauty of this landscape, heavily eroded by wind, rain and extremes of temperature, is unforgettable.

Deadwood and its sister town of **Lead** are sheltered in a steep-sided canyon at the northern edge of the Black Hills. Revitalized in recent years after the legalization of casino gambling, Deadwood was founded during an 1876 gold rush, when 25,000 miners swarmed the Black Hills. The rowdy town could almost have furnished a Who's Who of the American West; Wild Bill Hickok, who was murdered here, and Calamity Jane Canary are buried side by side in its Mount Mariah Cemetery. Some of the faces can be seen today at the **Ghosts of Deadwood Gulch Wax Museum**. And tours of authentic gold mines will take you underground through the **Broken Boot Mine** and through the surface workings of Lead's **Homestake Mine**, the largest gold mine in the Western Hemisphere.

Mount Rushmore, 21 miles south of Rapid City, is sculptor Gutzon Borglum's unforgettable homage to U.S. presidents George Washington, Thomas Jefferson, Abraham Lincoln and Theodore Roosevelt. Sculpted from a granite mountainside between 1927 and 1941, it draws more than a million visitors annually from all over the world.

The 20 miles between Rapid City and Keystone, the nearest town to Mount Rushmore, are the sort of stretch that kids love and parents . . . well, parents love, too, because it keeps their kids happy. Here you'll find the likes of **Bear Country U.S.A.** (a drive through a captive wildlife park), **Cosmos of the Black Hills** (one of those "vortex" constructions where no one stands straight), **The Ranch Amusement Park** (go-karts, bumper boats, mini-golf and a midway), **Reptile Gardens** ("America's largest," with alligators and birds of prey), the **Rushmore Waterslide Park** (400-foot twister slides, inner tubes through rapids), **Story Book Island** (nursery rhymes come to life!), and more.

The town of **Custer**, to the south of Mount Rushmore, has its own **Flintstones' Bedrock City** where you can eat a brontoburger while strolling through the Stone Age. Yabba-dabba-doo. There are even a couple of dinner theaters with Branson-style country music.

But not all is devoted to blatant commercialism. One of America's largest buffalo herds roams the 114 square miles of **Custer State Park** between Mount Rushmore and Custer. This is a great place for overnight camping and fishing in its streams and lakes.

Immediately to its south is **Wind Cave National Park**, whose multi-level, labyrinthine limestone passages (10.5 miles of which have been explored) are inlaid with unique calcite boxwork. Discovered in 1903, the cave took its name from a reversible wind that flows into or out of the cavern, depending upon outside barometric pressure.

West of Custer is **Jewel Cave National Monument**, the nation's second-longest cavern with 76 miles of passageways. And throughout the Black Hills you'll find other, smaller caves inviting exploration (usually for a fee): Rushmore, Crystal, Sitting Bull, Stage Barn, Wonderland and so forth.

Clearly, there need never be a dull moment in the Black Hills. There are museums (mining, geology, pioneer, cavalry, woodcarving, air and space); trout farms and waterfalls, a petrified forest, an archeological dig, backcountry hiking and biking trails galore. If you have an interest in extending your Wyoming holiday into this portion of the Black Hills, contact the **South Dakota Department of Tourism** for more information. ~ 711 East Wells Avenue, Pierre, SD 57501; 605-773-3301, 800-732-5682; www.travelsd.com.

LODGING   If you need a place to rest your head in Moorcroft, the **Cozy Motel** will fill the bill. A "ma-and-pa" place since the 1940s, its 23 rooms have been updated with cable TVs and air conditioning; they're clean and comfortable. A restaurant is next door. Closed December through March. ~ 219 West Converse Street, Moorcroft; 307-756-3486, fax 307-756-9614. BUDGET.

A good base for exploring Devils Tower and the Black Hills is the **Bear Lodge Motel**. A big fireplace surrounded by trophy mounts welcomes visitors to the spacious lobby of this two-story, 32-room motel. There's a large spa for all guests. ~ 218 Cleveland Street, Sundance; 307-283-1611, 800-341-8000, fax 307-283-2537; www.dcomp.com/sundance/bearmotl.htm. MODERATE.

If your pockets are a little deeper, check out the **Best Western Inn at Sundance.** Here you get all the extras: an indoor swimming pool, a hot tub, free continental breakfast, free local calls and morning newspaper, and guest laundry. However, the 44 rooms are Best Western standard-issue. ~ 2719 East Cleveland Street, Sundance; 307-283-2800, 800-528-1234, fax 307-283-2727; www.sundancewyoming.com/bestwestern. MODERATE TO DELUXE.

Nearer to Devils Tower is the **Diamond L Guest Ranch**, located 18 miles north via Route 112. A seriously recreation-oriented resort, this 4000-square-foot cedar lodge offers horseback riding and backpacking, fishing and mountain biking in summer; snowmobiling and cross-country skiing in winter. The three rooms in the lodge are warm and comfortable; one has a private bath. In addition, a pine cabin features two quarters with wood-burning stoves and private baths. All ranch activities are included, as are use of the hot tub, mountain bikes and volleyball courts. Three home-cooked meals are served buffet-style. Three-night minimum from July through August. ~ P.O. Box 70, Hulett, WY 82720; 307-467-5236, 800-851-5909, fax 306-467-5486; www.diamond lranch.com. ULTRA-DELUXE.

In Newcastle, the **Sundowner Inn** has 30 units and provides king- or queen-size beds and kitchenettes to those who request them. A restaurant and lounge are next door. ~ 451 West Main Street, Newcastle; 307-746-2796, fax 307-746-9992. BUDGET.

Set in a historic stone building, **Flying V Cambria Inn** is located at the foot of the Black Hills. Some of the ten units are of the modern variety while others are decorated with antiques; some rooms share baths. Borrow a rod and reel and try your luck in the stream out back. Full breakfast included. Closed January to Mother's Day. ~ 23726 North Route 85, Newcastle; 307-746-2096; www.trib.com/~flyingv. MODERATE.

DINING   **Donna's Diner** has made its local fame as an ice-cream parlor, but this is also a decent restaurant with a full three-meal menu. Come for eggs in the morning, sandwiches at midday, all-American entrées in the evening. ~ 203 Converse Street, Moorcroft; 307-756-3422. BUDGET TO DELUXE.

The three-way intersection at Devils Tower Junction is the site of the **Crook County Saloon**, where you can get steak, seafood and Mexican food and enjoy them with your favorite beverage. No lunch from Labor Day to Memorial Day; closed Monday through Wednesday from Labor Day to Memorial Day. ~ Routes 14 and 24; 307-756-3201. BUDGET TO DELUXE.

For good homestyle cooking, look no further than the **ARO Family Restaurant** in Sundance. This local favorite serves three meals daily, including juicy burgers and chicken-fried steaks. ~ 203 Cleveland Street, Sundance; 307-283-2000. MODERATE TO DELUXE.

The ambience is more casual yet at **Flo's Place**, where burgers, pizza and fried chicken are the orders of the day. ~ 226 Route 585 South at Route 90, Sundance; 307-283-2205. BUDGET.

For family and fine dining, check out the **Old Mill Inn,** which indeed is lodged in a historic flour mill. Although breakfast and lunch are served here as well, the acclaim comes for its steak and prime-rib dinners, accompanied by the region's best salad bar. ~ 500 West Main Street, Newcastle; 307-746-2711. MODERATE TO DELUXE.

Worth a stop if you're in the neighborhood is the **Flying V Cambria Inn**. This historic stone building, eight miles north of Newcastle on the road to Sundance, is all that remains of the coal-mining ghost town of Cambria. Dinners—served every night between Mother's Day and New Year's Eve—feature steaks, prime rib, seafood and Italian cuisine. ~ 23726 North Route 85 near Salt Creek Road, Newcastle; 307-746-2096. MODERATE TO DELUXE.

◄ HIDDEN

Old-time general stores are always fun to visit, but in cities—even in the West—they've invariably been replaced by supermarkets and strip malls. Off the beaten track in the Black Hills of northeastern Wyoming are two good ones.

SHOPPING

The **Aladdin General Store** is probably the *only* reason to visit the village of Aladdin (population: 10) unless you're taking the back route from Devils Tower to the Black Hills. Located 20 miles northeast of Sundance (and eight miles north of Route 90), the store was built as a saloon in 1896 and has been in continuous operation since. It sells (alphabetically, to name but a few) antiques, art, books, clothing, fishing and hunting supplies, gasoline, groceries, liquor, outdoor equipment and souvenirs of all sorts. In addition, it operates as the local post office. Nearby there is a café and a motel. ~ Routes 111 and 24; 307-896-2226.

◄ HIDDEN

At **Four Corners Country Store**, 18 miles north of Newcastle and 28 miles southeast of Sundance, you'll find an amazingly wide variety of modern and not-so-modern goods beneath antique lighting fixtures. Four Corners also has a diner, a country inn and a church. ~ Route 85 and 585; 307-746-4776.

PARKS

BLACK HILLS NATIONAL FOREST 🚶 🚲 🐎 ⛺ 🎣 🛶

The Wyoming portion (175,000 acres) of this 1.25-million-acre forest is small compared to what's across the border in South Dakota. But there are nice stretches of pine-covered hills north and south of Sundance, featuring such attractions as Cook Lake, Inyan Kara Mountain and Cold Springs Creek canyon. The Lakota Sioux called the hills *Paha Sapa* (hills that are black) because the forests of ponderosa pine covering them appeared dark from the plains. Elk, turkey and white-tailed deer abound. Facilities include picnic areas and restrooms. Day-use fee (Memorial Day to Labor Day only), $2; a $10 annual pass is available at any district office. ~ To Cook Lake, take Forest Roads 838 (Warren Peak Road) and 830 (Bear Lodge Road) north from Sundance 18 miles. To Inyan Kara Mountain, take Route 585 south from Sundance 17 miles to Schlup Road; then turn west and continue for three and a half miles. To Cold Springs Creek, take Route 90 east from Sundance four miles to Exit 191, turn southeast on Moskee Road and continue for eight miles, and then turn north on Forest Road 863, which runs about 18 miles to Beulah; 307-283-1361; www.fs.fed.us/r2/blackhills.

> The lowest elevation in Wyoming is 3125 feet, in the valley of the Belle Fourche River where it enters South Dakota northeast of Sundance.

▲ There are 66 RV/tent sites at four Wyoming campgrounds (no hookups); $7 to $11 per night; 14-day maximum stay. Sites at two of the campgrounds (Cook Lake and Reuter Camp) can be reserved by calling 877-444-6777.

KEYHOLE STATE PARK 🎣 ⛺ 🛶 🏊 🚤 There aren't many places to engage in water sports in semiarid northeastern Wyoming. In fact, Keyhole Reservoir is just about it. Created by a Bureau of Reclamation dam on the Belle Fourche River, the lake is completely encircled by the 15,674-acre park. Most facilities—including a swimming beach and boat launches—are on the eastern shore. Board sailors appreciate the breezes that blow down the western flank of the Black Hills. Anglers fish for northern pike, walleye, catfish, perch and smallmouth bass. The park has excellent birdwatching, from resident flocks to migratory species. Facilities include picnic areas, restrooms, an amphitheater and a playground. The nearby hamlet of Pine Haven offers a marina, motel and café. Day-use fee, $3. ~ From Route 90 between Moorcroft and Sundance, take Exit 165 (Pine Ridge Road) north six miles to the main park complex. Or follow Route 14 north five miles from Moorcroft; turn right on Route 113 and continue another five miles; and turn north on Pine Haven Road and continue two and a half miles to Pine Haven; 307-756-3596.

▲ There are 140 RV/tent sites at three campgrounds (10 electrical hookups); $4 (no hookup) and $8 (hookup) per night; 14-day maximum stay.

DEVILS TOWER NATIONAL MONUMENT 🏃 🚣 🎣 Protruding like a sore thumb from pine forests on the fringe of the Black Hills and the Powder River plains, this ancient monolith—a volcanic plug known to the Sioux as *Mateo Tipi*—was the first U.S. national monument. Today it attracts campers and hikers as well as rock climbers who test their skills on the Tower's nearly vertical, sky-high walls. A prairie dog colony by the Belle Fourche River is another attraction. The visitors center is open April through October. Facilities include picnic areas, restrooms and an amphitheater. Day-use fee, $8 per vehicle for a seven-day pass. ~ Take Route 14 from Sundance (20 miles) or Moorcroft (26 miles) to Devils Tower Junction. From there, take Route 24 north six miles, then Route 110 west one mile to the park entrance; 307-467-5283; www.state.sd/tourism/devtower.

▲ There are 50 RV/tent sites in one campground (no hookups); $12 per night; 14-day maximum stay. Closed November through March.

▼▼▼▼▼▼▼▼▼▼▼▼▼▼
Outdoor Adventures

FISHING

On the east slope of the Big Horn Mountains you'll catch brown and rainbow trout in the Tongue River, Clear and Piney creeks and the Middle Fork of the Powder River. Higher-elevation lakes like Cloud Peak and Willow Park reservoirs, west of Buffalo, offer brook and cutthroat as well as rainbow trout. Lake De Smet, in the Powder River Basin north of Buffalo, has crappie, yellow perch and rock bass as well as rainbow and brown trout.

In the far northeast, try Keyhole Reservoir for walleye, northern pike, yellow perch, smallmouth bass and channel catfish. Brown trout populate Sand Creek in Black Hills National Forest, just inside the South Dakota border.

Worth a stop is the **Sheridan District Office and Visitors Center** of the Wyoming Game & Fish Division. The center has a very nice exhibit on wildlife management, with a lifelike diorama, and a licensing desk. ~ 700 Valley View Drive, Sheridan; 307-672-7418.

The full-service **Fly Shop of the Big Horns** rents equipment and offers guide service. Closed Sunday from Labor Day to Memorial Day. ~ 227 North Main Street, Sheridan; 307-672-5866. **The Sports Lure** offers equipment rentals and guided trips. ~ 66 South Main Street, Buffalo; 307-684-7682. Closed Sunday from mid-August through May. In Big Horn contact **Paul Wallop Mountain Fly Fishing**. ~ P.O. Box 11, Big Horn, WY 82833; 307-674-6239.

WATER SPORTS

There are several boat launches and a few rentals at **Keyhole State Park**. ~ Route 113, Pine Haven; 307-756-3596. Keyhole is also a popular location for windsurfing, waterskiing and fishing.

DOWNHILL SKIING

Two small ski areas are located just on the west side of the Big Horn crest in Bighorn National Forest. The **Antelope Butte Ski Area** is 64 miles from Sheridan on Route 14; the **Powder River Pass Ski Area** is 41 miles from Buffalo on Route 16. Their facilities are described in detail in Chapter Four.

Ski Rentals   Full rental packages are available for downhill and cross-country skiers, snowboarders and snowshoers at **The Sports Lure**. Closed Sunday from mid-August through May. ~ 66 South Main Street, Buffalo; 307-684-7682.

CROSS-COUNTRY SKIING

In the Big Horn Mountains, the **Willow Park Ski Touring Area**, 45 miles east of Worland near Meadowlark Lake, offers 37 kilometers of groomed trails. There is a trail charge here. ~ Route 16, Ten Sleep; 307-672-0751.

Bighorn National Forest also boasts the **Pole Creek Ski Touring Area** (Route 16, Buffalo), with 23 kilometers of groomed marked trails and a warming hut about 22 miles southwest of Buffalo, and the **Sibley Lake Ski Touring Area** (Route 14, Burgess Junction), with 13 kilometers of trails about 19 miles southwest of Dayton. Both are open to the public at no charge.

In Black Hills National Forest, there's a system of novice and intermediate trails emanating from the **Reuter campground**, six miles northwest of Sundance. ~ 307-283-1361.

For information on renting equipment, see the ski-rentals section in "Downhill Skiing" above.

OTHER WINTER SPORTS

A 375-mile chain of snowmobiling trails on the west side of the Big Horn Mountains extends from Freeze Out Point (on Forest Road 168 near Dayton) on the north to Munkres Pass (on Route 16 south of Buffalo) on the south. The trail system is 75 percent groomed. No snowmobiling is permitted within the Cloud Peak Wilderness Area, but branch trails north and south of the wilderness connect to Big Horn and the South Fork Inn. Get permits, rentals and, if you like, guides at **Big Horn Safari**. ~ 2110 North Main Street, Sheridan; 307-674-6842.

In far northeastern Wyoming, there are popular snowmobiling areas north and south of Sundance. The Bear Lodge trail system covers 73 miles between the Reuter campground of Black Hills National Forest and Cook Lake. The Black Hills system from Four Corners has just 45 miles of trail in Wyoming, but it connects with 290 additional miles across the South Dakota border. Consult the **Arrowhead Motel** for permits and information. ~ 214 Cleveland Street, Sundance; 307-283-3307.

Golf is highly seasonal in Wyoming. Courses may open by April 1 and remain playable through October.

Sheridan's 18-hole **Kendrick Golf Course** has been ranked as one of the top five in the state of Wyoming. It has a pro shop with rentals, a driving range and a restaurant. ~ Route 331, Sheridan; 307-674-8148.

A municipal 18-hole links with a driving range is the **Buffalo Golf Club**. ~ West Hart Street and De Smet Avenue, Buffalo; 307-684-5266. Another is the **Bell Knob Golf Club**. ~ 1316 Overdale Drive, Gillette; 307-686-7069.

A few communities have nine-hole courses. These links include **Horseshoe Mountain Golf Club** (Dayton; 307-655-9525); **Gillette Golf Club** (Gillette; 307-682-4774); **Keyhole Golf Club** (Pine Haven; 307-756-3775); **Sundance Golf Course** (Sundance; 307-283-1191) and **Newcastle Country Club** (Newcastle; 307-746-2639).

GOLF

In Sheridan there are four public courts at **Kendrick Park**. ~ Loucks Street at Big Goose Creek; 307-672-2485. There are six courts with lights at **Thorne-Rider Park**. ~ Spaulding and 11th Street; 307-674-6421.

In Gillette, there are public courts at **Bicentennial Park**. ~ 300 West Warlow Drive; 307-686-5187.

TENNIS

Riding the Big Horns is the realm of several outfitters based along the east flank of the range. Explore the Cloud Peak Wilderness Area of Bighorn National Forest with **Trails West Outfitters**. There are one- and two-hour guided trail rides; full-day trips trek to a high mountain lake where you can fish or just enjoy the surroundings. Closed December through May. Trips leave from the South Fork Inn. ~ P.O. Box 111, Buffalo, WY 82834; 307-684-5233; www.wilderwest.com/trailswest.

RIDING STABLES

✔ CHECK THESE OUT—UNIQUE OUTDOOR ADVENTURES

- Test your rock-climbing skill on the fluted columns of Devils Tower, which rises 867 vertical feet above surrounding pine forests. *page 291*
- Try out your swing at Sheridan's 18-hole Kendrick Golf Course, rated as one of the top five in the state of Wyoming. *page 293*
- Pedal down the Clear Creek Trail System for a lesson in both anthropology and natural history. *page 294*
- Let a llama carry your load into the Cloud Peak Wilderness Area, whose high alpine lakes offer anglers brook, cutthroat and golden trout. *page 294*

PACK TRIPS & LLAMA TREKS

Trails West Outfitters has a summer base camp (with a full-time cook!) in the Cloud Peak Wilderness for its guided backcountry pack trips. Drop trips use horses and mules. Closed December through May. ~ P.O. Box 111, Buffalo, WY 82834; 307-684-5233; www.wilderwest.com/trailswest.

Llama excursions into the Bighorn National Forest can be booked with **Cloud Peak Llama Treks**. ~ Story; 307-683-2548.

For a complete listing of licensed backcountry outfitters, contact the **Wyoming State Board of Outfitters and Professional Guides**. ~ 1750 Westland Road, Cheyenne; 307-777-5323.

BIKING

The roads and trails south and east of Burgess Junction are especially recommended, including **Forest Road 26** from Owen Creek campground (on Route 14) past the Sawmill Lakes to Red Grade Spring, near the town of Big Horn. The 32-mile-long road, which skirts the north edge of the Cloud Peak Wilderness, descends from 9400 feet to 5100 feet. Bighorn National Forest publishes a map of all roads and trails; obtain one from the head office for $4. ~ 1969 South Sheridan Avenue, Sheridan; 307-672-0751.

In Buffalo, the **Clear Creek Trail System** extends 8.5 miles through town, traversing areas rich in both human and natural history. The trail is alternately paved, graveled and unsurfaced.

In Gillette, a citywide system of bike paths extends through most parts of the community, including the Cam-plex.

Bike Rentals For rentals, repairs and touring information, consult **Back Country Bicycles**. Closed Sunday. ~ 334 North Main Street, Sheridan; 307-672-2453. **The Sports Lure** has full information on local trails as well as rentals. Closed Sunday from mid-August through May. ~ 66 South Main Street, Buffalo; 307-684-7682.

HIKING

All distances listed for hiking trails are one way unless otherwise noted.

SHERIDAN AREA Most of the best hikes are in Bighorn National Forest, whose ranger stations have maps and information on hikes in the Big Horns, including Cloud Peak Wilderness. ~ 1969 Sheridan Avenue, Sheridan; 307-672-0751.

Tongue River Canyon Trail (11 miles) climbs between towering 1000-foot walls west of Dayton, off Tongue Canyon Road, and to Forest Road 166. This was where Crazy Horse had hoped to make his final home. There's an elevation gain of about 4300 feet to 7300 feet on this moderate hike. Keep an eye out for wildlife and an old log flume.

The **Stull Lakes–Coney Lake Trail** (3 miles) leaves from near Twin Lakes picnic area on Red Grade Road (Forest Road 26), about 23 miles west of Big Horn. The moderate hike winds up-hill into the Cloud Peak Wilderness, through lodgepole and spruce forests to the three Stull Lakes and, a mile far-ther, to little Coney Lake, nestled between moun-tains at 9300 feet. There's an elevation gain of about 900 feet from the trailhead.

BUFFALO AREA Sherd Lake Trail (6.8 miles) climbs just 500 feet from its trailhead—the Circle Park campground, at 8100 feet off Route 16, 18 miles west of Buffalo—to Sherd Lake in the Cloud Peak Wilderness Area. Bring a fishing pole, and watch for deer and elk. Easy. Steeper trails continue to other lakes.

> In 1909, a cowboy named Harry Lewis entered and won a horse race in Sheridan. His prize: a bride, Hazel Foster.

DEVILS TOWER AND THE BLACK HILLS At Devils Tower National Monument, the **Tower Trail** (1.25 miles), which loops around the base of Devils Tower, is by far the most popular hike. Starting and ending at the visitors center, this easy paved trail with benches en route is accessible to the elderly and the moder-ately disabled. Interpretive markers describe various aspects of geology and natural history.

The **Joyner Ridge Trail** (1.5 miles) is a moderate-level loop trail that begins and ends in the northern section of Devils Tower National Monument, about a mile from the visitors center. Park officials consider it "the gem of the monument." The trail tra-verses several ecosystems, including a ridgetop forest, sandstone cliffs and secluded meadow and prairie. Interpretive plaques are placed en route.

In Black Hills National Forest, **Cook Lake Trail** (2-mile round-trip) circles the shoreline of a pretty, pine-shrouded lake that pro-vides the only trout fishing in this part of Wyoming. This easy hike begins and ends at the Cook Lake campground, 18 miles north of Sundance off Bear Lodge Road. Contact Black Hills National Forest for complete trail information and maps. ~ Route 14 East, Sundance; 307-283-1361.

Equipment Get maps and all the gear you'll need at **Big Horn Mountain Sports**. ~ 335 North Main Street, Sheridan; 307-672-6866. Another outdoor stop is **The Sports Lure**. ~ 66 South Main Street, Buffalo; 307-684-7682. Closed Sunday from mid-August through May. In Gillette, visit **Spoke & Edge Sports**. ~ 201 South Gillette Avenue, Gillette; 307-682-9343.

Interstate highways make access to northeastern Wyo-ming quite simple. East–west **Route 90** and north–south **Route 25** join at Buffalo, a half-hour's drive south of Sheridan. Route 90 continues north and west to Sheridan, Billings and Seattle; east to Gillette, Sundance and Boston. Route 25 con-nects south to Casper, Cheyenne, Denver and El Paso, Texas.

Transportation

CAR

The distance between Sheridan and Gillette is 103 miles. From Cheyenne, it's 325 miles to Sheridan, 242 miles to Gillette (via Route 59 north from Douglas).

For road reports, call 888-996-7623 (within Wyoming) or 307-772-0824 (outside Wyoming).

AIR

Two regional airports offer daily connections with Denver via United Express (800-241-6522). One is **Sheridan County Airport**. ~ 908 West Brundage Lane, Sheridan; 307-674-4222. The other is **Campbell County Airport**. ~ 2000 Airport Road, Suite 108, Gillette; 307-686-1042.

BUS

Powder River Transportation is the regional line, connecting with national Greyhound routes from Denver, Colorado, and serving Casper and Billings, Montana. ~ 580 East 5th Street, Sheridan; 307-674-6188.

Besides the central depot in Sheridan, bus stations are located in Gillette (1700 East Route 51; 307-682-1888) and most other sizable northern Wyoming towns.

CAR RENTALS

Avis Rent A Car is represented at the Sheridan County Airport. ~ 800-831-2847.

TAXIS

In the absence of public bus systems, **Sheridan Taxi** (Sheridan; 307-674-6814) and **Gillette Taxi** (Gillette; 307-686-4090) do yeoman's work.

Index

Lodging Index

LODGING SERVICES

Dining Index

HIDDEN GUIDES

Adventure travel or a relaxing vacation?—"Hidden" guidebooks are the only travel books in the business to provide detailed information on both. Aimed at environmentally aware travelers, our motto is "Adventure Travel Plus." These books combine details on unique hotels, restaurants and sightseeing with information on camping, sports and hiking for the outdoor enthusiast.

THE NEW KEY GUIDES

Based on the concept of ecotourism, The New Key Guides are dedicated to the preservation of Central America's rare and endangered species, architecture and archaeology. Filled with helpful tips, they give travelers everything they need to know about these exotic destinations.

ULTIMATE FAMILY GUIDES

These innovative guides present the best and most unique features of a family destination. Quality is the keynote. In addition to thoroughly covering each destination, they feature short articles and one-line "teasers" that are both fun and informative.

Ulysses Press books are available at bookstores everywhere. If any of the following titles are unavailable at your local bookstore, ask the bookseller to order them.

You can also order books directly from Ulysses Press
P.O. Box 3440, Berkeley, CA 94703
800-377-2542 or 510-601-8301
fax: 510-601-8307
e-mail: ulysses@ulyssespress.com

Order Form

HIDDEN GUIDEBOOKS

____ Hidden Arizona, $14.95
____ Hidden Bahamas, $12.95
____ Hidden Baja, $14.95
____ Hidden Boston and Cape Cod, $13.95
____ Hidden Cancún & the Yucatán, $16.95
____ Hidden Carolinas, $17.95
____ Hidden Coast of California, $17.95
____ Hidden Colorado, $13.95
____ Hidden Florida, $17.95
____ Hidden Florida Keys & Everglades, $11.95
____ Hidden Georgia, $14.95
____ Hidden Hawaii, $17.95
____ Hidden Idaho, $13.95
____ Hidden Maui, $12.95

____ Hidden Montana, $14.95
____ Hidden New England, $17.95
____ Hidden New Mexico, $14.95
____ Hidden Oahu, $12.95
____ Hidden Oregon, $14.95
____ Hidden Pacific Northwest, $17.95
____ Hidden Rockies, $16.95
____ Hidden San Francisco and Northern California, $17.95
____ Hidden Southern California, $17.95
____ Hidden Southwest, $17.95
____ Hidden Tahiti, $17.95
____ Hidden Tennessee, $15.95
____ Hidden Washington, $14.95
____ Hidden Wyoming, $14.95

THE NEW KEY GUIDEBOOKS

____ The New Key to Belize, $14.95
____ The New Key to Costa Rica, $17.95
____ The New Key to Guatemala, $14.95

____ The New Key to Ecuador and the Galápagos, $16.95

ULTIMATE FAMILY GUIDEBOOKS

____ Disneyland and Beyond, $12.95

____ Disney World and Beyond, $13.95

Mark the book(s) you're ordering and enter the total cost here ⇨ ⬜

California residents add 8% sales tax here ⇨ ⬜

Shipping, check box for your preferred method and enter cost here ⇨ ⬜

⬜ BOOK RATE   **FREE! FREE! FREE!**

⬜ PRIORITY MAIL $3.00 First book, $1.00/each additional book

⬜ UPS 2-DAY AIR $7.00 First book, $1.00/each additional book

Billing, enter total amount due here and check method of payment ⇨ ⬜

⬜ CHECK   ⬜ MONEY ORDER

⬜ VISA/MASTERCARD_____ EXP. DATE _____

NAME _____ PHONE _____

ADDRESS_____

CITY_____ STATE _____ ZIP_____

MONEY-BACK GUARANTEE ON DIRECT ORDERS PLACED THROUGH ULYSSES PRESS.

ABOUT THE AUTHOR

JOHN GOTTBERG is an author or a co-author of *Hidden Montana*, *Hidden Idaho* and *Hidden Pacific Northwest* for Ulysses Press. A graduate of the universities of Oregon and Washington, he has traveled and worked all over the world, including as chief editor of the Insight Guide series and as travel news editor for the *Los Angeles Times*. He has written or co-authored 19 books and edited two dozen more, and his credits in more than 55 magazines and newspapers include *National Geographic Traveler*, *Travel & Leisure* and *Islands*. Gottberg is now western U.S. editor for a major European travel publisher.

ABOUT THE ILLUSTRATOR

DOUG MCCARTHY, a native New Yorker, lives in the San Francisco Bay area with his family. His illustrations appear in a number of Ulysses Press guides, including *Hidden Tennessee*, *Hidden Bahamas* and *The New Key to Ecuador and the Galápagos*.